ANTI-PRIMITIVISM
AND THE DECLINE OF THE WEST

The Social Cost of Cultural Ignorance

Volume Two
The Failure of Christianity, Progress, and Democracy

ANTI-PRIMITIVISM
AND THE DECLINE OF THE WEST

The Social Cost of Cultural Ignorance

Volume Two
The Failure of Christianity, Progress, and Democracy

C. Stanley Urban
S. Thomas Urban

In Collaboration With
Jeff Urban

The Edwin Mellen Press
Lewiston/Queenston/Lampeter

Library of Congress Cataloging-in-Publication Data

Urban, C. Stanley.
    Anti-primitivism and the decline of the West : the social cost of
cultural ignorance / C. Stanley Urban, S. Thomas Urban in
collaboration with Jeff Urban.
        p.   cm.
    Includes bibliographical references and indexes.
    Contents: v. 1. The primitive and the supernatural -- v. 2. The
failure of Christianity, progress, and democracy.
    ISBN 0-7734-9855-9 (v. 1). -- ISBN 0-7734-9857-5 (v. 2)
    1. Progress--Religious aspects--Christianity. 2. Christianity-
-Controversial literature. 3. Christianity and other religions.
4. Religion, Primitive. 5. Ritual. I. Urban, S. Thomas.
II. Urban, Jeff. III. Title.
BR115.P77U73   1993
306--dc20   92-45203
                                                                CIP

A CIP catalog record for this book
is available from the British Library.

All rights reserved. For information contact

The Edwin Mellen Press   The Edwin Mellen Press
        Box 450   Box 67
Lewiston, New York   Queenston, Ontario
    USA 14092   CANADA L0S 1L0

                Edwin Mellen Press, Ltd.
                Lampeter, Dyfed, Wales
            UNITED KINGDOM SA48 7DY

        Printed in the United States of America

To Rebecca
my life-long love
who,
like a good primitive,
has inspired and sustained
from
beyond the grave.

TABLE OF CONTENTS

Foreword vii

Part I
The Spiritual Claims of The West

Chapter XI. Modern Art: Its Kinship with the Primitive 1

Chapter XII. Science and History Versus
Christian Cosmology 15

Chapter XIII. Secular versus Ritual Man.....................................35

Part II
The Secular Claims of the West

Chapter XIV. History versus Communist
Russia (Soviet Union) 79

Chapter XV. An Historical Introduction
to American Democracy 113

Chapter XVI. History versus the Democratic,
Peaceful, and Industrialized State:
Democratic? 123

Chapter XVII. History versus the Democratic,
Peaceful, and Industrialized State:
Peaceful? 165

Chapter XVIII. History versus the Democratic,
Peaceful, and Industrialized State:
Industrialization and Public Welfare?................203

Part III
Conclusion

Chapter XIX. Full Circle 247

Bibliography 295

Author Index 345

Subject Index 353

FOREWORD

One of the most important revolutions of the twentieth century, perhaps the least talked about and understood, has been what Crane Brinton called "the desertion of the intellectuals." Ironically, this originates from those few whom society liberated from the mundane chores of the rest of mankind. Because of their acquired learning and understanding, they eventually come to believe they can no longer continue to support the very establishment which gave them the requisite leisure to disassociate themselves. Without their expressed ideas, there would be no revolution. "This does not mean that ideas *cause* revolutions, or that the best way to prevent revolutions is to censor ideas." But, revolutions cannot intelligently be considered apart from this desertion of intellectuals. (*The Anatomy of Revolution*. New York, Prentice-Hall, 1952, 25, 49-50.)

Once we decided to look at our society precisely as if we were anthropologists examining an alien culture, we were following the lead of Thucydides and Polybius, historians of Classical Antiquity. While in theory this can easily be reconciled to the principles of an open and democratic society, in practice it is often deeply resented. One of the reasons, as Polybius understood, is this critical perspective lies beyond both the duty and the capacity of the average man. Understandably, therefore, he resents the new, unexpected, and critical approach.

The developing conflict between the scientific outlook of the intellectual and the religion of the man in the street can first be perceived in PART I., THE SPIRITUAL CLAIMS OF THE WEST. This was predicted by Max Weber. Survivors of the eighteenth century Enlightenment - heirs of the rational man school - think and act in terms of natural cause and effect. Others - whom we designate as ritual man - believe that behind the sensate level lies a spiritual being, or beings, who can and do respond to piety and prayer. This effects the miraculous, negating natural cause and effect. The ties binding ritual man together throughout the ages -the primitive, pre-Christian, Hebrew and Christian - are miracle, mystery and magic. The ideological differences between the rational man and ritual man are quite profound. The chasm between the two can never be surmounted. Nevertheless, a great deal of time is spent, mostly by the ritualist, pretending that there is no irreconcilable conflict between them.

Modern research shows primitive and pre-Christian religions anticipated virtually the entire cosmology of the Judeo-Christian tradition, thought by us to be unique. The range includes creation itself, the first man and woman, paradise, the fall and man's exile from the grace of the gods, the Virgin Birth, the miraculous life, suffering, death and resurrection of the savior-hero, the Second Coming, and Paradise Regained.

The only basic difference between Christianity and all other religions lay in its historical and factual claim that a God had actually become man and triumphed over death on the cross. His Resurrection meant the remainder of history should just be an interval between that event and His Second Coming to put an end to conflict, and usher in metahistory.

Perhaps nothing better illustrates this running strife in recent history than the transition of Jesus from an actual historical being - who lived, suffered, died on the cross, and was resurrected - to a mythological one whose story existed only in the mind of the believer. Of course, this did not immediately affect the thinking of Catholic theologians who were still mired in the thought processes of the Counter-Reformation of the sixteenth century. It did profoundly affect the thought and writing of a great many mainline Protestant theologians. Some, however, professed indifference to the fact that Christ may never have done what he was supposed to have done, or may even never have lived at the time, if at all. This dramatized the separation of the Christian religion from both history and science.

How is one to account for this, other than to conclude that, as concerns the Four Gospels, writers focused on the message of Jesus and not his person.

The crucial message would not have been heard and believed by the masses unless and until they were convinced of the miracles of Jesus, especially His Resurrection. In the entire history of the West, that is the only one - His - which obtained past credence. Every man longing for immortality might take comfort in the fact that He was resurrected and provided everlasting life for all who believed in Him. Thus, the message and the miraculous were hopelessly intertwined. Jesus, the historical figure, ever remained a shadowy one. It required an assertion of faith to make him come alive and live in an historical sense. Throughout the ages, however, ritual man was always capable of this, as the Catholic seven sacraments illustrate.

Today, however, the modern individual is greatly influenced by science and technology, the two forces most responsible for wiping out overnight primitive faith in their gods. What naturally follows is skepticism of the alleged miracles which fill the passages of both the Old and New Testaments. No twentieth century sleuth worth the attention of the modern detective writer would waste any time pursuing the theory that it was an angel who rolled away the stone of His grave by night so that Jesus' "dead" body might arise and leave the tomb. They would have no option but to operate with the assumption that it was a human agency at work.

Since intellectuals fail to respond to stories of the miraculous and disbelieve them - and the message and the miracles are intertwined - the result is predictable. The message itself is suspect: "I am the way, the truth and the life." Surely, there is more than one way of life for countless billions of separate and diverse peoples, or more ways of admittance to Heaven than through the monopoly of Christ. Further, there is no historical evidence that Jesus himself declared no one came to God other than through Him. Once again, it is quite possible that much later a zealous disciple far exceeded the claims of his master, or teacher.

Thus, as far as science and history are concerned, there is no verifiable evidence that Christianity is superior to other religions. Its old claim to Ultimate Truth is made in complete isolation and must always remain unconfirmed. Rather than Christianizing the whole world, our prediction is that it will ultimately be seen as but another major religion. Its spread in the first instance can never be divorced from military and technological conquest. And today, as far as it is vigorous in the Third World, we think this is due to the money and power of Christians in this country, and perhaps the West as well.

Likewise, we no longer accept at face value THE SECULAR CLAIMS OF THE WEST, PART II of this volume. Curiously enough, two bitter enemies, Soviet Russia and the United States, were both devoted to the secular idea of progress. Both appealed to the element of the miraculous to arrive at the supposed happy "end" of history. While the communists postulated final attainment of the withering away of the state, and the emergence of the free and enlightened individual, seventy years of harsh and arid rule dissipated that fairy tale. One recalls that Werner Heisenberg postulated the principle of uncertainty regarding the atom, i.e., if one knows the exact position of a particle inside the atom, one cannot know at exactly the same time its velocity; if one knows the precise velocity, he cannot know simultaneously its position. We assert that Mikhail Gorbachev did exactly the same thing with regard to the political and economic situation in Russia, Europe and the world itself. Events now promise to control us all. Only one thing is certain. One of our three twentieth century gods died while we were at the bedside.

Serious domestic conflict, however, is engendered as soon as one attempts an examination of Thorstein Veblen's hopes for a democratic, peaceful state with a benign and efficient industrial system. The following excerpt was taken from an unpublished paper written some twenty years ago: "In his *The Engineers and the Price System,* Veblen states his preference for a system which he hopes will replace that of the doomed free enterprise variety. It involves one in which the engineer, the economist, the technician and the laborer combine to produce to their full capacity the best product at the cheapest cost. It is one in which the machine is servant to man and one in which man has been inculcated with a natural cause and effect philosophy, itself derived from a long observation of the way in which the machine works. This new system necessarily disposes of the old anthropomorphic concept of the universe which is always twisted to mean that God intends for the Establishment to govern and for the governed to submit. It also eliminates the eighteenth century Natural Rights concept which argued that a man could do with his own what he willed, including shutting down a factory and locking out a labor force. It is essential for any modern revolutionary to pay particular attention to Veblen's insistence that any revolution aimed at the economic sector has to provide immediately a system which works better than that cast aside. Merely to destroy or paralyze an on-going economic system is to introduce irrationality and chaos." (C. Stanley Urban, "Veblen's Analysis of American Capitalism," 9 pp., Park College, 4 May 1970), 7. The above system is the polar opposite to the leisure-class state of eighteenth century England and the vested interests (businessman and banker) of the pre-New Deal era in the United States.

If we *were* all this - a democratic and peaceful state with an industrial system which was benign and efficient - we could all assent to the idea of progress itself. We could look forward to secular history with vast confidence and assurance. Even the masses would eventually share in both prosperity and enlightenment, devoid of the dictatorship of any class.

One would have the best possible moral and ethical justification for our suppression and obliteration of primitive peoples. In this instance, might and right coalesced. Perceived in such light, it is clear that all three - Christianity, communism and the so-called peaceful, democratic state - offer themselves as the Supreme Good, or Ultimate Truth. All appeal to the magical and the mystical to effect their ends. All offer themselves as the way, the truth and the life.

If one goes beyond the usual rhetoric, and sets up an operational definition of democracy, it is possible to see how far removed we are. It is like Camelot, an ideal to be pursued but never to be attained. In that sense, it reminds one of communist mythology. While the prerequisites for democracy call for an educated, informed and active electorate, the most recent national elections demonstrated the pervasive influence of money, the absence of basic issues and the substitution of character assassination, and, finally, a voter's boycott. Furthermore, our conception of democracy is intimately associated with the idea of progress and the American Dream.

This promises even more prosperity and happiness for an ever-increasing number of people *ad infinitum*. At the same time this philosophy distinguished itself by a disregard for the terrible waste of natural resources and the poisoning of the global environment. Lastly, its exponents have not hesitated to declare, with great fanfare, war on such sorry affairs as poverty, homelessness, crime and drugs. However, they are careful to disregard or disguise their inevitable failures. The persistence of these ills decry the philosophy of progress and the realization of the American Dream for the total society. Democracy supposedly benefits all.

An equally dubious proposition is that we are a peaceful folk. Save for the exception of the New Deal and the Good Neighbor policy of the Thirties, we had pronounced tendencies to bully our much smaller neighbors in this hemisphere before and after that era. Our military triumphs in World War II, combined with paranoia over communist aggression throughout the world, induced us to contest for the hegemony of the continent of Asia in both Korea and Vietnam. In 1950, we abandoned the Acheson defense perimeter policy, one which could have easily and cheaply defended Japan and our Pacific bases with only sea and air power. For this, we exchanged an Asian continental bloodbath for the next twenty-five years.

This overriding concern for markets and sources of raw supplies could only be sold to the public as a struggle for the freedom and democracy of Asians. Certainly, they had never had the latter. It existed only in the minds of the Washington political elite. Curiously, as the most materialistic minded people in the world, we refused to go to war for such reasons. We always preferred the impossible theme of Making the World Safe for Democracy.

Veblen's hopes that the people would effect an economic system both efficient and benign were forestalled by the pervasive influence of money and property. Big Business acted as Adam Smith predicted the business man would, preferring self-interest over that of a national one. However, even national interest was short-sighted in the post-war era. It made it possible for Japan, having lost the military struggle, to win a far greater victory in business and finance. Meanwhile, our post-war military protection of the island probably made that unhappy event possible. Thus, in a single generation, we squandered our world hegemony, wasting both precious manpower and resources.

The stupendous contrast became apparent in the last quarter of this century. When engaged in the terribly expensive war in Vietnam in the Sixties, President Johnson could also embark on a costly war against poverty at home and another in South Vietnam. It was his conception of the Great Society. Likewise, he could offer North Vietnam a large financial bribe to cease its aggression against the South, one that only a non-Western mentality could refuse. On the contrary, it is dubious there could have been a rescue for the oil-rich, theologically intolerant and undemocratic princes of Kuwait and Saudi Arabia unless and until we passed a tin cup around the international community. The process began with large pledges from the two Arab states, one conquered and the other threatened. The prince may become a pauper - sort of - but he continues for a time to act as if his former self. Eventually, however, the public itself becomes aware of his loss of status and power. For our age and time that has always been based upon industrial might.

One final caveat is necessitated by the spirit of the times as global communism seems about to be replaced by the so-called free market system. Americans pride themselves on this, if indeed they do not worship it. We tend to forget, however, that this impersonal system always subordinates and sacrifices the individual worker to its dictates. This is true even in good times. Decisions throwing thousands out of work in one city are made by a small coterie of men in another. It is, however, less apparent then. Those of us old enough to remember the Great Depression of 1929-1933 know that laissez faire capitalism collapsed. In the early months of 1933, big business and finance pleaded for government intervention in the market system. Thus was inaugurated the New Deal. If another such crunch comes, wage and salaried workers may not be so acquiescent and supine. They may seek to do for themselves by legislation what the private sector deprived them of, and a minority will call this socialism and class warfare.

As far as Eastern Europe is concerned, there is real danger we will disregard Veblen's warning, i.e., a new economic system has immediately to be more productive than the one discarded. What happens when the one-time welfare states of those regions quickly produce - under the free market system - a sharp increase in rents and prices of necessary commodities while unemployment rises dramatically due to the introduction of cost-efficient machines?

While the West [PART III. CONCLUSION: FULL CIRCLE] uniformly exulted in the conquest of paganism in the name of Christianity and progress, the last part of the twentieth century saw the perceptible decline of both from their monopolistic position. The net effect has been to expose the schizophrenic character of our society, or conflict between the ritualistic and the natural cause and effect school of the Enlightenment.

What most fascinates us is primitive belief systems that have either survived, or been revived in the West.

For example, scientists and environmentalists forsook the beguiling themes of progress for primitive attitudes of reverence towards nature. This meant the perception of the old idols of Western capitalism - an ever-increasing population or market, business growth, industrial progress and monetary profits for the next quarter - as mankind's real enemy. Instead, they substituted a radical solution of zero growth. Like the primitive behavior pattern, this was an accomodation to the demands of nature, thereby insuring man's survival as another animal in the highly complex food chain.

We think this new movement will prove a much more formidable foe to capitalism than did communism. The latter could easily be attacked as a foreign ideology whereas the environmentalist movement is of domestic origin. It is strengthened by every oil spill, and other technological disasters, whose capitalistic prophets assured us could never occur, certainly not in our lifetime.

Simultaneously, old and traditional forms of Christianity, like Catholicism and urban mainline Protestantism, declined in membership and vitality. Protestant fundamentalism and pentacostalism had a much greater democratic or mass appeal. This required the simplest of messages, combined with a sense of the theatrical and, of course, the miraculous. The rational Enlightenment also lost many American adherents to mystical cults of the Orient. Like the fundamentalist Christian, the demand here was to surrender the intellect to an unseen power. It would then assume the care and custody of that individual daring to abdicate decision-making to a supernatural being. We think it was all pitched on no higher intellectual level than the Ghost Dances of the American Indian in the 1890's. Some critics have called it the age of unreason, or the new age of enchantment. Willing or not, we are all being dragged into it.

Although our vision of the future is murky, one thing is clear. We not only believe in Gorbachev's glasnost (openness) and perestroika (restructuring) for Soviet Russia, but in their full application to this country as well. In so far as this work is noticed, however, this is the very thing apt to produce a domestic furor.

Chapter XI

MODERN ART:
ITS KINSHIP WITH THE PRIMITIVE

The great revolution in twentieth century art was not limited to a rejection of traditional or classical art which worshipped either the human figure or nature or both. When the former intentionally distorted, disfigured or obliterated man and his artifacts, as well as his environment, or nature, it was also an attack upon the world view of Newtonian physics and empiricism. It swept all externals aside as of no consequence and attempted instead to penetrate to the very essence of things in a Platonic sense. One intuited or perceived reality directly, rather than slowly coming to terms with it only through the five senses. Between the artistic revolutionaries and Renaissance man, it was an either-or proposition. Instead of conventional guides to human perception, they substituted the proposition that reality could be best revealed through their own words or paintings.

They would have immediately agreed with Raimundo Panikkar: "The symbol is the true appearance of reality.... It is in the symbol that the real appears to us."[1] However, the primitive everywhere had long since operated on the same principle, at least in the artistic areas where the gods were concerned.

When one addresses himself to art as part of the Trinity of cosmology, ritual and art of modern man, he is apt to discover three important facts. First, despite an obvious and wide divergence of art forms in the Christian West from that of primitive - none of which are pertinent to our theme - there are, however at least two significant instances in the spiritual realm where they appear to coincide. One lay at the center of the art of the historic Catholic Church. The other in the thought and experimentation of the giants of twentieth century art. Let Tom Urban add a disclaimer. We are not interested in an attempt to write a history of modern art. Our analysis is - as throughout the book - solely restricted to an investigation of these situations where Western man approximated the thought and behavior patterns of the primitive. Both Western instances are impregnated with elements of the magical and the mystical. An exploration of these facets enable us to understand both the primitive and ourselves better. Second, among the three elements, art appears unique because there were no outside intellectual forces attacking it - at least not successfully - as history and science did with the Christian cosmology, or as secular and industrial man did with ritual man. Third, and again in a unique sense, the tension within modern art was internalized in a struggle against the values of humanistic or Renaissance art. There, even with a spiritual message as an objective, the artist glorified the human body and even the idea of humanity itself. Just as the Impressionists of the late nineteenth century freed color from the restrictions laid on it by Renaissance art, so twentieth century art freed form and design. Every-day subject matter, including man himself, was at first distorted, then obscured and, finally, abandoned as subject matter. Each creative artist, therefore, was left with a state of mind, a mood or an inspiration he wished to express. This was aptly called an abstraction and its product abstract art. It constitutes the dynamic or revolutionary element explored because it was impregnated with Platonic idealism, as was primitive art. It conveys a simple message: while the senses but distort truth, the mind apprehends and perceives it perfectly.

One recalls that the highest art forms in the primitive world united in the contributions of sculpting, painting, music, dance and song to produce a stage setting by flickering fire-light. Emotions peeked at that precise moment when all concerned, mask dancer and audience, were convinced that god became man and man became god. If stimulants like tobacco and alcohol were used, it was for the sole purpose of enabling the audience to rise to the proper spiritual level so that they could experience the sought-for catharsis.[2]

For two thousand years the Catholic Church used art forms in the holy mass to accomplish the same end for its worshippers. The high vaulting and stained-glass windows of the Gothic cathedral, the Gregorian chant, the rich vestments of the clergy, the tapers, the incense, the bells, the icons, the sacred wafer and the wine, all of these were calculated to seduce the five senses. These allowed the worshippers to rise to the proper spiritual level so that they could experience the sought-for catharsis.[3]

For man supernatural creation is not enough. Neither Aristotle's prime mover[4] nor the god of the eighteenth century Deists satisfy the deep emotional needs of mass man.[5] He needs, as Freud insisted, to nurse and feel the Father image, of Him who not only created but loves and cares for His people and who is always near them.[6]

Likewise, it seems apparent that art rituals of this sort were especially effective, even indispensable, among non-literate audiences. Once, however, mass literacy occurred within a particular space-time frame, say Northern Europe in the sixteenth century, Calvinists were to discover that such things which seduced the senses also degraded them. They were, therefore, to be discarded, save as verified by the New Testament, in favor of rationalism, long sermons by the clergy and individual reading of the Bible itself.[7]

The best explanation for behavior of this sort was advanced by Max

Weber. The less magic and mysticism possessed by a religion, and the more doctrine, especially the written variety, the greater the need of rationalization.[8] Parenthetically, but logically, it would not be long before this led to serious disputations between lay and ecclesiastical authorities within Calvinist churches as to what the Bible itself meant.[9]

Here, however, the crucial point is that the de-emphasis of religious art forms in favor of the intellectual process eventually created a chasm between Protestant missionaries and primitive peoples. It no doubt helps explain why Catholic priests were so much more successful as proselytizers.[10]

The other Western area of congruence with primitive art is modern art, a fact which surprises only those who know little about it. The common denominator is the tendency toward abstraction, universally prevalent in primitive religious art. In effect this means an abandonment of what might be termed naturalism or realism, or conformity with sense data by the artist. It finds reality not on the empirical plane but on an inner or spiritual one.

Some authorities believe such art tends to arise in those societies which are ill at ease with the flux of nature. By virtue of this kind of art, they attempt to maintain an independence by discovering enduring and unchangeable elements. They are groping for a more meaningful world behind the externals of that nature.[11] Its mood was best caught by that primitive artist on the Pacific Northwest Coast who declared that he painted not the animal itself but its essence or spirit. That was what the animal really was.[12]

Perhaps this art can best be understood when considering primitive masks for the gods, say that of Thunder and Lightning. Now no one in the tribe, quite naturally, has actually seen those gods, yet the tribe itself has made a collective judgment of what they must *really* look and act like and the mask is that collective intelligence. It is, therefore, the very serious business of the dancer within the mask to bring those gods down to earth. Thus, they may communicate with their children, giving all a common spiritual experience of earth-shaking proportions.

Art, therefore, was the indispensable vehicle whereby, through ritual and prayer, the tribe was made perpetually aware of its cosmology and mythology. This explained the creation of the Universe, the First Man - its direct ancestor - and the original Social Contract between him and the gods. Cosmology, ritual and art combined to provide the navel of the universe, or that point where the tribe lived, moved and had its being.

While modern art obviously lacks such unity and purpose, its dedication to abstraction resulted in new art forms. Primacy was given not to the outer quality of things but to the artist's subjective reaction to his experience or to what he thought he experienced. This was the point where the modern artist found kinship with primitive art. Parenthetically, authorities seem to be in agreement that this was the most important facet of twentieth century art. Certainly, it is the one which has had the greatest psychological, if not artistic, impact upon me, if not my co-author.

While abstraction freed the artist from the tyranny of classical art, it left him not free to do as he chose. Rather he was under the compulsion to penetrate behind the facade of the empirical world to discover a new world of essence or being.

Suggested by the aesthetics of Henri Bergson, abstract art rested on the assumption that, at best, nature had surface meanings which were useful to man but not true in a metaphysical one. This metaphysical truth could be grasped only by artistic and philosophical intuition. Once understood, however, these inner meanings added up to cosmic order.[13] Like the old Oriental method of Lotze, there was only one way of imagining things from the inside. That was putting oneself inside of them.[14] To Braque, the senses deformed, but the mind corrected and formed properly.[15] Mondrian scorned to seek the illusion of a scientific perceptual reality such as Renaisssance painters sought. Instead, he was concerned with states of emotion, of feeling.[16] This enabled him to ignore physical objects and attempt by the use of horizontal and vertical lines and color to capture the sense of the infinity of nature.[17]

All of this reminds one of the presuppositions of primitive art, previously described as Platonic idealism, while aware the primitive anticipated the idea itself.[18]

Modern art has an affinity with the primitive variety, particularly that of a spiritual nature. This comes when it disreagrds or distorts those matters precious to historians and Western man himself: the human personality, subject matter, sensed space and historical time.

Rather dramatically, Lewis Mumford charged modern art with responsibility for the death of the human personality. Twentieth century art transformed modern man into a displaced person.[19] His dominion was taken over by the machine which, rendering him both servile and mechanical, severed man from his historical values and purposes. It left his nature progressively empty and meaningless. Here one instinctively thinks of Fernand Leger's *Three Women*. It has been aptly described as a work representing human beings reduced or transformed into crankshafts, cylinders, casings and instrument boards.[20] World War I gave support to this contention that man was confronted by a bleak world, devoid of meaning as well as of natural and plant life. In this theatre of operations, man, because of his *id* or aggressive impulses, found himself a prisoner of the very machines he erected to conquer his foes.[21] While not attempting to deny the contemporary influence of this school, it is obvious that its life interpretation or, more correctly, its death wish, give it nothing in common with life-giving primitive impulses.

A similar but yet somewhat different chord was struck by Ortega y Gasset: Searching for the generic or characteristic note in modern art, he found it in the tendency to de-humanize man himself. The trick seemed to be to paint a man who had the least resemblance to that species. Beyond this, there was an even more subtle attack upon the humanity of man and that was by ignoring him as subject matter.[22] The re-emergence of geometric (modern) art might well be the precursor of a corresponding attitude towards the world and the breakup of the Renaissance humanistic attitude.[23]

The death of the human personality occurred in large measure because accuracy in drawing the human anatomy no longer was a valid criterion for art. Contrast cubism, for example, with that of the champion of Renaissance art, Bernard Berenson. He declared that, without a mastery of the nude, no art of figure representation could be nurtured.[24] In his work on the Florentine painters, Berenson stressed the essential character of the life communicating qualities yielded by form and movement.[25] In this sense, and not a puritanical one, the celebrated painting, *Nude Descending a Staircase,* is indeed shocking. This is because, though preserving the illusion of movement,[26] it made an abrupt departure from tradition in its representation of form, or the female nude.

A defender of modern art, Roger Fry, thought that it was essentially a return to ideas of formal design. These had virtually been lost sight of in the fervid pursuit of naturalistic representation.[27] Critics almost uniformly think of Cézanne as the father of modern art. Rejecting the notion that painting was a process whereby the hand ought to paint what the eye saw, he painted like a blind man. He stressed tactile values or the feel of objects both inside houss, and in nature itself.[28] In both choice of form and color, mostmodern artists were influenced by Cézanne.[29]

Cubism was art without subject but not without meaning. Much of cubism, for example, was representational art, even thought the subject was not the important element in the painting itself. Its central postulate was the revolutionary one of painting an object not from a single perspective but from many, some from memory and others from anticipation. From this, one obtains Picasso's *Girl Before a Mirror* or *Portrait of a Lady*.[30]

Since cubism was the first modern school which proved indifferent or destructive of the human body, it is with considerable interest that one follows the evolution of Picasso's work. It began in 1907, with his *Les Demoiselles d'Avignon,* when he drew the central figure in full face with the nose sideways. By 1910, in *The Woman and the Chair,* the weight and solidity of the body have begun to slip away and, still later, in "Ma Jolie" only vestiges of the human anatomy remain.[31]

Picasso's versatility derived from the fact that, while he had a passionate attachment to the significance of form, he was also capable of mastering this impulse and substituting others.[32] His conquest of artist representation of naturalistic form and movement was displayed in a ram he drew for an edition of Buffon's *Historie naturalle.* It combined both a splendid technique and a remarkable capacity to seize upon the essential features of the animal, endowing it with life qualities.[33]

While John Dewey believed that space and time were integral parts of every art product,[34] abstract art appeared to have distorted both. Contrary to representational art which depicted figures with an inner vitality occupying a kind of dynamic relationship to each other and to the space which enfolded them, pictorial cubism resulted in what critics aptly called static rigidity. Any solids depicted appeared immovable and seemed to possess no visible relationship with any other solids or to the space which surrounded them.[35] In Gris' *Guitar and Flowers,* for example, instead of objects being experienced in the sense world, one is confronted by geometric order instead. This impression was obtained because the canvas was divided four ways: vertically, horizontally, and twice diagonally.[36] The canvas was divided intuitively into forms of ideal realilty to which external objects had no choice but to conform. It was a return to the ideals of the neolithic artist.[37] Using both cubism and flat patterns, Georges Braque spent twenty years experimenting how to dissolve a visible object beyond recognition. His *Guitar, Fruit and Pitcher* was typical of his ability to transform objects into small and related units bound together by basic compositional lines.[38]

Along with the human figure, subject matter was chipped away at until little remained other than pure design. This was meant, through the medium of mood, to convey not only a sense of aesthetic beauty but intuitive truth of the highest order. F.S.C. Northrop made precisely that point when discussing Georgia O'Keefe's celebrated *Abstraction No. 11. The Two Blue Lines*. The single blue line represented the female aesthetic component and the other the male scientific component. Since they both emanated from the same base, the author wished to convey the idea that, while separate and distinct from one another, they were still united.[39] When looking at Monet's *Haystacks,* Kandinsky suddenly realized that objects themselves were no longer indispensable. He was left stunned but ultimately was receptive to the idea. Like other artists, he first used objects as a point of departure for the making of an unconventional product.[40] The best example of this was *Composition I or Improvisation,* a water color painted in 1910. Within three years, using abstraction as a point of departure, he created what some critics called his most compelling pre-World War I abstraction, entitled *Black Lines*.[41] My own Kandinsky favorite is *Painting with Red Spot* (1914).

At any rate, as art departed from empirical reality it became more and more of an internalized process within the artist himself. Kandinsky explained the evolutionary process. Objects, as he saw them, gradually lost an optical reality and assumed one of absolute reality. This meant that an object in nature was replaced by a "spiritual" image whose laws depended upon an "inner necessity."[42] Mondrian had a similar explanation for his drive for intuitive truth of the highest order. Impressed by the vastness of nature, he wanted to express its expansion, its rest, its unity. First of all, he was aware of the fact that the visible expansion of the universe had sharp limitations. But deductively, however, he concluded that vertical and horizontal lines were the expression of two opposing forces found everywhere in nature and whose reciprocal action dominated life. Accordingly, he used no representational content at all but merely colored lines intersecting one another at right angles.[43]

Whether one considers the aims and motivations of O'Keefe, or Kandinsky, or Mondrian, the central truth is that the primitive artist would have known intuitively what they were talking about and would have been in complete agreement. He had instinctively and perennially used a quite identical art form for the purpose of stating religious or cosmic truth.

In their passionate desire to return to the sources of creation, the surrelists were led to a dependence upon supernatural powers, the mysteries of primitive magic and esoteric ritual of ancient times. One thinks of such artists as Breton, Tanguy, Dali and Miró.[44] The best of the surrealists, such as Miró, were the most abstract in their productions. Like Kandinsky he was uninterested in the portrayal of the visible world.[45]

In conclusion, the harmony which exists between much in modern art and the religious impulse is perhaps best shown in the fact that the clerical elite of France have not hesitated to have the most revolutionary artists commissioned to do church decoration through the country.[46]

In retrospect, when one virtually obliterates the natural appearance of the human figure, subject matter and spatial arrangements, and is left with a unfamiliar aesthetic forms in flat patterns, one distorts or destroys the sense of historical time. First of all, the externals of the human figure in its natural surroundings, meaning such things as artifacts, landscape, and spatial relationships, give the normal observer a clue as to both space and time in which the work of art originated. On the contrary, colors and lines in geometric relationships, or forms, have a universal rather than a particular aspect. That is to say, they have a rather timeless or non-historical quality about them.

However, just as the liberties indulged in by modern and abstract art would, if practiced, prove inimical to historical writing, so their principles could be utilized quite well in the formulation of a primitive spiritual art form.

Footnotes

1   *The Trinity and the Religious Experience of Man. Icon-Person-Mystery* (New York, Orbis Books, 1973), 9.

2   See Vol. I, Chapter VIII, "ART," footnotes 92, 93, 96, 97.

3   From my own experience in 1948 or 1949 at the Benedictine Abbey at Conception, Missouri,, I can verify this. The combination of all these, plus that of the monks in their robes amid the semi-darkened chapel, gave me a genuine religious impulse for a few moments. The illusion, however, was shattered when the Latin words of the song and service were flashed on a screen in English for the outsiders. Almost immediately, I said to myself: "I don't believe this."

4   For Aristotle, God is an intelligent force which moves everything else but which itself is unmoved. *Aristotle's Metaphysics*. Translated with Commentaries and Glossary by Hippocrates G. Apostle (Bloomington, Indiana, University of Indiana Press), 1966, 204-205. Although God does not invade or penetrate the world, it depends or hangs upon him; he represents the world's unity though he Himself is not a part of it. Werner Jaeger, *Aristotle. Fundamentals of the History of His Development*. Translated by Richard Robinson (London, Oxford University Press, 1948), 385.

5   As an integral part of eighteenth century liberalism, the Deists rejected Catholic notions of original sin, the immaculate conception, the miracles of Jesus and the doctrine of the Trinity, all "evidences" of God's immanent nature or his intervention in history. On the contrary, Deists believed in God, virtue and morality and in the sufficiency of nature and nature's God. Herbert M. Morais, *Deism in Eighteenth Century America* (New York, Columbia University Press, 1934), 13, 102, 129.

6   At root, God is little other than a glorified Father. *Totem and Taboo. Some Points of Agreement between the Mental Lives of Savages and Neurotics* (New York, W.W. Norton, 1950), 147.

7   Compared with Catholicism, Protestantism, especially Calvinism, represents a remarkable subtraction of the sacred in religious worship. As far as possible, Protestants removed themselves from its most precious elements - mystery, miracle and magic. Peter L. Berger, *The Sacred Canopy. Elements of a Sociological Theory of Religion* (Garden City, New York, Doubleday, 1967), 111-112.

8   *Essays in Sociology.* Translated, edited, and with an Introduction by H.H. Gerth and C. Wright Mills (New York, Oxford University Press, 1953). 351.

9   *Ibid.*, 350.

10   See Vol. I, CHAPTER IX, "THE CULTURE CLASH: IDEOLOGY V. TECHNOLOGY," footnotes 133-137.

11   T.E. Hulme, *Speculations. Essays on Humanism and the Philosophy of Art.* A Harvest Book (New York, Harcourt-Brace and Co., first published in 1942), 85-86.

12

12   See CHAPTER VIII. "ART," footnote 21.

13   Weitz, *Philosophy of the Arts* (Cambridge, University of Harvard Press, 1950), 84.

14   Maurice Souriao, French scholar, 1889 in I.A. Richards, *The Foundations of Aesthetics* (New York, Lear Publishers, 1925), 65-66.

15   Roy McMullen, *Art, Affluence and Alienation. The Fine Arts Today* (New York, Praeger, 1968), 140.

16   Herbert Read, *Icon and Idea. The Function of Art in Development of Human Consciousness* (Cambridge, University of Harvard Press, first published in 1955), 131.

17   See footnote 39 of this chapter.

18   See Vol. I, CHAPTER VIII,"ART," footnote 17-22.

19   *Art and Technics* (New York, Columbia University Press, 1952), 8-9.

20   *Art and Mankind. Larousse Encyclopedia of Modern Art from 1800 to the Present Day,* edited by Réne Huyghe (New York, Prometheus Press, 1961), 285; Alfred Barr, Jr., *Masters of Modern Art.* The Museum of Modern Art (Garden City, New York, Doubleday, 1958), 84-85.

21   Huyghe, *Art and Mankind. Larousse Encyclopedia of Modern Art,* 272.

22   "The Dehumanization of Art," 411-419 in *A Modern Book of Esthetics. An Anthology,* 3rd edition (New York, Holt, Rinehart and Winston, 1960), 417-418.

23   Hulme, *Speculations,* 78.

24   *Aesthetics and History* (Garden City, New York, Doubleday, 1948), 84, 94-95.

25   Hulme, *Speculations,* 168.

26   DeWitt H. Parker, *The Analysis of Art* (New Haven, Yale University Press, 1926), 165.

27   *Vision and Design* (New York, Brentano's, no date), 290.

28   H.G. Collingwood, *The Principles of Art* (Oxford, England, Clarendon Press, 1955), 144.

29   Clive Bell, *Art* (New York, Frederick A. Stokes, no date), 220.

30   Alfred Barr, Jr., and William S. Liberman, *Philosophy of the Arts* (Cambridge, Harvard University Press, 1950), 83, 85.

31   Barr, Jr., *Masters of Modern Art,* 68-70.

32   Clive Bell, *Since Cézanne* (Freeport, New York, Books for Libraries Press, reprinted

1969), 86.

33   Benjamin Rowland, Jr. likened Picasso's work to that of one of the most famous painters of the Yuan dynasty in fourteenth century A.D. China. *Art in East and West. An Introduction through Comparisons* (Cambridge, Harvard University Press, 1954), 119-122.

34   *Art as Experience* (New York, Minton, Balch, 1934), 183.

35   Read, *Icon and Idea*, 130-131.

36   Barr, Jr., *Masters of Modern Art*, 73.

37   *Icon and Idea*, 130-131.

38   *Treasury of Art. Masterpieces from the Renaissance to the Present Date*, edited by Thomas Craven (New York, Simon and Schuster, 1952), 296.

39   *Meeting of East and West*, 163-164.

40   Huyghe, *Art and Mankind. Larousse Encyclopedia of Modern Art*, 246, 297.

41   *McGraw-Hill Dictionary of Art*, edited by Bernard Myers (New York, McGraw-Hill, 1969), 290.

42   *Encyclopedia of World Art*, vol. VIII (New York, McGraw-Hill, 1963), 952.

43   John Hospers, *Meaning and Truth in the Arts* (Chapel Hill, University of North Carolina Press, 1946), 101.

44   Huyghe, *Art and Mankind. Larousse Encyclopedia of Modern Art*, 297.

45   Roy McMullen, *Art, Affluence and Alienation. The Fine Arts Today* (New York, Frederick Praeger, 1968), 144.

46   Huyghe, *Art and Mankind, Larousse Encyclopedia of Modern Art*, 303.

SCIENCE AND HISTORY VERSUS CHRISTIAN COSMOLOGY

Once we are no longer determined to maintain the parochial illusion that we alone possess Ultimate Truth, via the Trinity, we discover an amazing similarity between our Christian cosmology and that of the "lowly" primitive. Both start with the contention that, behind an apparently indifferent nature, is an intelligent spirit or spirits with whom man can communicate and influence. Because of this, natural cause and effect can be overcome by virtue of piety and prayer, and the magical and mystical substituted instead. Both terminate with the assumption that their cosmology gives the social group the most important knowledge in the universe.

In such a social context, man's knowledge of the universe, nature and self - science and history - were, as in Christian history and

tradition, welcomed only as long as both were
content to serve the needs of Theology, Queen of
the Sciences. However, the natural destiny of
each was and is to become independent of sacred
knowledge.

    Of course, the universe is unquestionably
draped in mystery, some of which is
unresolvable. However, while both primitive
and Christian cosmologies revered that mystery
and sought to perpetuate it intact, both science
and history sought to shrink or reduce it. The
outcome is clear enough. Man's sense of
"independence" from the supernatural tends to
grow in direct proportion to his increased
understanding of how the universe and nature
works and how he can rationally react to it, to
other men and to self.

    This chapter is primarily concerned with the breakaway of that scholarship - science and history - from the guardianship of Holy Mother Church and its sacred doctrine. It records the loss of the Church's monopoly on intellectual enterprise and the adverse consequence of that severance to Christian belief. The movement culminated in the nineteenth century and after when Protestant theologians took science and history seriously, or on their own terms. True, they first tried to reconcile them with Christology, but often ended up forced to accept a divorce between the Christ and the history of actuality. To Catholic theologians, who remained loyal to traditional doctrine and dogma, this was "heresy." Their psychological ordeal came later and is described in the following chapter.

    A secondary theme is the intense conflict which existed in Classical Roman history between intellectuals and Christian churches, saints and martyrs. The reason is clear. Then, as well as now, scientists and historians could not be trusted as disciples of the true and only faith. Both always raise far more questions than they answer. Even so, the answers themselves are not permanent, nor meant to be so. Thus, the sense of The True and The Eternal is lost and all is in flux. The conflict between the man of piety and prayer and that of the ever-questioning and skeptical intellect is not accidental and fortuitous. Rather, it appears to be built into the fabric of things.

As Thorstein Veblen explained, the roots of this conflict lay in the Hebraic heritage of Christianity: "...the pastoral peoples [such as the ancient Hebrews] tend strongly to take on a predatory cultural scheme. Such a people will adopt male deities ... and will impute to them a coercive, imperious, arbitrary animus, and a degree of princely dignity. They also tend strongly to a monotheistic, patriarchial scheme of divine government; to explain things in terms of creative fiat; and to a belief in the control of the natural universe by rules imposed by divine ordinance. The matters of prime consideration in this theology are matters of the servile relation of man to God .... The emphasis falls on the glory of God rather than on the good of man."[1]

However, the remarkable modern contrast with this arbitrary pastoral mythology is that the Christian myth of the Fall of Man, the Incarnation and the Resurrection, which gave a unique meaning to Western history for centuries is now "broken" myth. That is to say, it is no longer believed to be identical with history itself.[2]

The Christian myth concerning the Holy Family was fashioned in historical time to assuage man's anti-polar needs for a God who was both immanent and transcendent, in time and beyond it, corporeal and incorporeal. The conflicting demands which were satisfied, therefore, were those for fatherhood, motherhood and family while at the same time sexual immaculacy was maintained. Wifehood was now coupled with virginity and everything was liberally peppered with both magic and morality.[3] It is for that reason today scholars believe an adequate Christian philosophy of history must be, not philosophical, but mythological. It is impossible to make the doctrine that Jesus was both fully human and fully divine metaphysically plausible, or to satisfy the demand of reason.[4] Nineteenth century scholars, like Kierkegaard, noted the insufficiency of history, limited to probable knowledge, to support the rigorous demands of the Christian faith.[5] The historical break with Christology might be dated from the futile efforts of Albert Schweitzer to reconstruct a historically but emotionally satisfying picture of Jesus. Finally, he had to confess that, historically speaking, Jesus must remain a mystery to modern man. His significance to our times was thus independent of scholarship, but dependent upon man's emotional and spiritual life.[6]

As soon as one is immersed in the historical, and not the Biblical, Jesus, certain problems emerge which are not solvable on the basis of the data alone. First of all, it was the prominent British historical anthropologist, Lord Raglan, who pointed out that, far from having a unique concept of history, Christians must share the notion of a "savior-hero" with many other cultures over a long time span. A more important fact is that in all such cultures the "Savior-hero" conforms with twenty-two demand points, including his unique birth, ministry, passion, burial, resurrection and union with Divine.[7] While pointing out about eighteen such similarities between the lives of Socrates and Jesus, Arnold Toynbee concluded that a common source for stories about pagan heroes and Jesus, independently derived from folklore, may have been the legend of Hêraklês.[8] Although admitting that Christianity was a religion in which God revealed himself in history, Toynbee was forced in many instances to question the Gospels for their historical accuracy.[9] The concept of the Virgin Birth is exploded in the very sources, Matthew and Luke, which gave rise to the myth itself. They traced the genealogy of Jesus from King David through his father, Joseph.[10] It was for reasons such as this that one authority concluded the four Gospels were written as religious treatises rather than history.[11] Writing as a Christian, another believed the Gospels virtually self-validating. As an historian, however, he recognized the existence of such conflicting evidence about the person of Jesus as to compel one to remove the matter of his identity from the field of scholarship.[12]

More spectacularly, the theologian Paul Tillich concluded that, while there was an individual behind the picture we have of Jesus, his identity was open to debate. The exploits claimed for Jesus of Nazareth of the first century A.D., as they appear in the Gospels, may not have actually happened to him. Likewise, it is even possible he did not exist at that moment in space and time.[13] Other theologians of equal stature thought it unlikely Jesus proclaimed himself as a unique Son of God. Consequently, to place such a claim in the Gospels was not historically accurate, despite its being theologically acceptable.[14]

It was for such reasons that Jesus defied the tools of historiography. Without denying its method and viewpoint, history cannot grant the person of Jesus any special consideration and privileges not open to others.[15] Thus, history can only record another unique fact that the Church and Western culture have attached the greatest religious significance to him and his life. History, therefore, neither proves nor disproves the extravagent claims made on the behalf of the Messiah by his followers.[16]

However, the modern break of historians from the dogmas of Christianity in no way dismayed many influential Protestant theologians. As early as 1911, Paul Tillich dared raise the question as to the persistence of the Christian faith if the non-historical existence of Jesus became historically probable. For him there was no question. Faith would remain untouched. For him the foundation of Christian faith was not the historical Jesus, but the Gospels themselves, or the Biblical picture of Christ.[17] Others were equally indifferent to the separation of history and religion.[18] If God really became man, then this truth can only be accepted and understood as a consequence of revelation, or God's grace to us. It lies beyond our understanding because it makes the impossible possible. Mere knowledge cannot rise to this level. It can only derive from it.[19] Here we have the frankest recognition of the severance between faith and history and theological indifference to that fact. Protestant theologians not only countenanced the separation of Christian myth from history, but exulted in it as promoting the cause of Christianity.[20]

However, since Christian myth was no longer identical with history, certain adverse consequences could be postulated. The traditional Christian linear concept of time - such as the idea of progress itself - might give way to a revival of classical and Eastern notions centered around the basically static or cyclical view of history. This would perhaps be accompanied by the same indifference shown historical truth by Christians as habitually displayed by the followers of Hinduism or Buddhism. No one could successfully predict the outcome of the Western Church returning to its Eastern philosophical origins.[21] One radical difference, however, was at once apparent to perceptive observers like Peter Berger. The resurrection of Christ could no longer be regarded as an event which actually happened in the external world in historical time, but was somehow transferred to a life of its own in the consciousness of the believer.[22] This meant a sudden and dramatic break with the Church's past of almost two thousand years because its powerful and compelling message had been built upon the certainty of the historical birth, crucifixion and Resurrection of Jesus.[23] It was bound to introduce the principle of uncertainty.

That uncertainty about the Godhead invaded the highest levels of the Anglican Church in England. In 1984, just after his appointment as the Bishop of Durham, David Jenkins gave an interview on national television in which he confessed his belief the Virgin Birth story was formulated well after the event in order to stress Jesus' unique union with God. It was not "necessary for a Christian to believe that Jesus was God made flesh." "It doesn't seem to me that there was any one event which you could identify with the Resurrection." At the time, the same TV program polled England's thirty-one Anglican bishops for their views on the subject: "Nine of the bishops sided with Jenkins on the Resurrection, 10 on the Virgin Birth, and 15 on miracles. Nineteen agreed with him that Christians did not need to believe that Jesus was God made flesh."[24] In a diocesan newsletter in the following year, Jenkins attempted to clarify the situation. Although he believed in the Resurrection, it was in no way dependent upon the old story of the empty grave. He was "wholly uncertain about the empty tomb as literal historical fact." Later in the same article, Jenkins dropped the bombshell: "The alternative and plausible explanation that the disciples stole the body was around pretty early on."[25] Certainly, if one were going to argue, as the disciples did, that Jesus' body made a direct ascent into heaven, it would not do to have his body still in its grave. What was perhaps even more sensational, however, was the subversive question raised by Hugh Montefiore prior to his installation as the bishop of Birmingham. "As a Cambridge don he had inquired whether it was possible that Jesus had been a homosexual - a query that hit the headlines as few lectures do."[26] We expect more of these heresies at the highest theological levels despite a plaintive response from the archbishop of Canterbury, primate of all England: "It won't do for us as Christians simply to think of the stories about Jesus as beautiful or helpful or meaningful. It won't do for us to strain out of the stories all that we find difficult because it has an element of miracle or mystery about it."[27]

There is one aspect about the Second Coming of Christ which, in the hands of conservative Christian theologians, is certainly not beautiful. That involves the terrible threats to non-believers. A typical example came in a recent Christmas celebration by a professor at a Lutheran seminary in St. Louis, Missouri: "The second time he [Christ] comes as a conquering judge, he will bring all history to an end and determine who will live with him in the new heaven and earth and who will be banished from his sight forever in hell. The determining factor is not goodness or badness but whether we believe in him as our Savior and God. ... The second time, it will be a great day of joy for those who love him and terror for those who rejected him...."[28]

Once, however, some perceptive Protestant theologians were free from the age-old conviction that the Godhead had actually descended into the world, been crucified, and miraculously resurrected, it paved the way for the field of comparative religion. Here one must be prepared to dispense with Christianity's old postulates that all other religions were illusory and all other gods were but idols, while the Christian religion, on the other hand, had a monopoly of God's truth.[29] As a matter of fact, there is no generic Christian religion, but merely your faith, mine, and that of others.[30] God did not "give a fig for Christianity."[31] Jesus himself was uninterested in it, absorbed only in God and man.[32] The earliest Christians were not conscious that they were founding or beginning a new religion.[33] Raimundo Panikkar laid waste to the mythology that only the Christian world was "given" the truth of the Trinity.[34] Although no one can really approach the Father other than through the Son, as the Christ, he does not presume that Jesus of Nazareth is that figure.[35] Finally, a former colleague of mine, Woodbridge O. Johnson, has written a book based on the denial of a premise that an otherwise remote God invaded this universe once, and once only, by birthing His only Son in the body of a Jewish carpenter 2,000 years ago in Palestine. He believed this to be nothing more than a parochial concept. It not only scorned the legitimate religious aspirations of all other earthly peoples and faiths, but ignored the increasing probability that other creatures in other solar systems also needed spiritual salvation. The book itself was designed to show that there had been other incarnations of God in the flesh. Jesus as the Christ "is not the absolute center about which all truth and value revolve, but, rather, only a number of self-disclosures about God....[36]

Nevertheless, as my co-author reminded me, despite this soul-searching by Protestant thinkers, the great mass of believers were spared their doubts and agonies. Once again, ignorance had proved its sterling worth.

One must add, however, that Catholic theologians played no part in effecting the break between Christian mythology and history. This was, no doubt, due to their centuries-old understanding that the primary role of history was as a handmaiden of theology.[37] In 1883, Pope Leo XIII explained this when he affirmed an objective reading of history would itself provide a superb defense of the claims of the Catholic Church and its Holy Pontiff.[38] Save for the isolated position of Étienne Gilson, who thought the whole questions of God was outside the domain of science and therefore of scientific historical writing,[39] one perceives a consensus of Catholic opinion. It is through the application of the principles of philosophy or metaphysics that one may be certain of historical truth, provided it is pursued with the proper mixture of empirical method tempered by rationalism. Since eyewitness accounts may be trusted, it is possible for historical criticism, drawing upon auxilliary sciences, to establish with certainty what actually happened.[40] While faith in no ultimate sense depended upon historical verification, it is also true that there could be no conflict "between Catholic Truth and Historical Truth."[41] Conversely, history itself was basically spiritual[42] and a proper study of it revealed Christ in history.[43] The Apostles themselves anticipated this view for the Four Gospels were in reality "four little histories."[44]

Paul Tillich explained this comparatively static character of Catholic theology. It was the result of a presupposition that those doctrines validated by canon law - such as the historical work of the papacy and Church councils - were in basic agreement with the New Testament itself. This was why, although the Church would admit criticisms against any individuals within it, including popes, it was not prepared to tolerate it in church essentials, or those involving doctrine, ethics, and the church hierarchy. Thus, Church history becomes sacred history and one elevated above all other history.[45]

Catholic sources virtually agreed when they acknowledged the vast influence the thirteenth century theologian, St. Thomas Aquinas, had upon the church council of Trent in the mid-sixteenth century and that of the Vatican I council of 1870.[46] True history could only buttress and reinforce true faith.

The break of science with Christianity was even more dramatic and, in the opinion of my co-author, the most decisive factor in effecting the separation of secular from sacred spheres. The marriage of the two may be said to have culminated in the philosophy of St. Thomas Aquinas. He argued that Christian philosophy was an exercise of reason which abstracted from the data of experience, or the empirical realm, in a scientific manner. This is formulated into an intelligible system separated from theology and mysticism, but subordinated to a superior light of faith and grace. Such product of man's intelligence and ingenuity gave us a system which justified that already known by God's revelation to man.[47] However, the following century, the fourteenth, was so disruptive it may be said to have terminated the Middle Ages, or the Age of Faith. First of all, the Black Death carried such dread economic and social consequences as to split the fabric of European society.[48] Philosophically and scientifically, William of Occam accomplished much the same end when arguing that Christian mysteries were beyond the reach and understanding of reason itself. Thus, man's knowledge, based on history and science, were inexorably cut off from Christian knowledge and experience.[49] Within two hundred years science opened the breech with its publication of the heliocentric theory of astronomy. It upset the centuries-old notion that the earth was the center of the universe and that the sun revolved about it.[50] The Catholic Church compounded the error by making Galileo recant his correct theory.[51] Then in the mid-nineteenth century the break was completed when Charles Darwin published

The Origin of Species and *The Descent of Man*. Far from having been separately created from all other creatures, and given dominion over them, man, along with all the other animals, was perceived as being in a long and tortuous evolutionary process. It was a humble pedigree. Both the heliocentric theory, and the one involving evolution, threw man back upon his own devices and made it possible for the idea of progress to emerge.[52]

In a scholarly sense, therefore, history and science demolished the claims of Christianity to be separate and apart from all other religions - by virtue of having produced a living, historical God[53]- and thus superior to them. If, as a consequence of its severance from both history and science, Christianity must advertise itself as a product of faith, intuition, emotion and mysticism, then it occupies no higher ground than both primitive and oriental religions which openly admitted that fact from the outset. If one religion is indeed superior to all the others, then it is a matter for God - not the Christian God but the God of all -to make a judgment. Until He abandons His silence on the matter, we can only emulate Him. Meanwhile, it is sobering to note that while faith, intuition, emotion and mysticism invariably proved enough to satisfy the primitive's curiosity about the universe, and the way in which it is run, it has never been so with modern man.

Before abandoning the subject of the conflict between history and science on the one hand and Christian cosmology on the other, it must be said that it was a very old and bitter struggle. The early Church distinguished itself for its consistent and rigorous opposition to intellectualism in all its forms, particularly that of ancient and pagan philosophy, the legalistic scholarship of Judaism and off-shoots like the Gnostics.[54] The last named was a middle class phenomenon among Gentile intellectuals in the 2nd century A.D. Rejecting both Judaism and the Old Testament as a foundation for Christian faith, they were strongly influenced by the Platonic tradition of the dualism of the mind and body. They told the story of Jesus in purely symbolic terms. Like Jesus, a Gnostic was a man in the world, but not of it.[55] A natural philosophical outcome of this logic was that, as a Divine being who descended into an evil world and took on flesh, Jesus could not suffer.[56] Church authorities today are divided as to their importance. Some think, because of their contempt for objective science, they were guilty of the suicide of classical reason.[57] Others count them as the first Christian theologians.[58]

To the early Church fathers the way to Salvation was not through intellect and academic training, rather in simple piety and faith.[59] Anything else was heretical. Perhaps the main reason for the indifference of early Christians to history was the mythology of the imminent Second Coming of Christ. Why become absorbed in history and world affairs, of which the historian wrote, when it was all going to come to an early end?[60] Showing his contempt for history, Tertullian, a prominent Church father of the second century A.D., directly attacked the idealization of classical Rome, as exemplified in the works of Cicero and Vergil. There was, he affirmed, nothing unique about secular Rome for all empires rested upon the sword alone. It was, therefore, the temple of evil and not the goal and climax of noble human effort.[61]

On the contrary, one thing which distinguished the pagan and classical scholar and intellectual was his devotion to reason and to the City of Man. It is difficult, for example, to read Pericles' Funeral Oration,[62] or the orations and letters of Cicero,[63] without becoming aware of their absorption in what we would term civic-mindedness.

One of the first clues that this secular age was over came in 361 A.D. The Roman Emperor - apparently Constantine II - confessed that the Empire was sustained more by Christianity, and its Trinity of the magical and the mystical, than by government itself, or the labor of the common man.[64] Such an admission would have been unthinkable had pagan and classical Rome still been in the ascendancy.

With the obvious decline of Roman power and grandeur by the early fifth century A.D., the task for Christian theologians had changed, and St. Augustine was admirably suited to the challenge. In his *Social Change and History*, Robert A. Nisbet rightly gave much attention to the very considerable tension which St. Augustine believed existed perennially between the City of Man, Roman secular society and customs, and that of the City of God, the Heavenly City. It represented an eternal conflict between the impermanent and evil and the permanent and good. It would only be resolved with the eventual decay and demise of Rome. All outward signs pointed toward it and with it the terminal date of the world itself.[65] Augustine's work, *The City of God,* shaped and controlled Catholic historiography ever since.[66]

The noted historian, M. Rostovtzeff, dramatized this conflict when discussing the causes of the fall of Rome, or, more properly, the symptoms of the fall. Pagan and classical scholars had given allegiance to the City of Man, taking pride in secular prowess and progress. But, as the Roman Empire suffered political turbulence, economic deterioration and social demoralization in the third century A.D. and after, men turned greedily to Christianity. Scorning this vale of tears, it promised solace and eternal bliss in the next. Christianity, therefore, was not responsible for the decay and fall of Rome. It was rather the one option remaining to those who despaired of its secular power or, rather, to the decay of it. It only hastened the fall and made it seem less important.[67]

Our historical analysis of the conflict between the secular and the sacred in both Roman and modern times logically leads to a psychological explanation of the phenomenon itself. Whereas the scientist and the historian can live at peace within an imperfect universe where certain fundamental queries cannot be laid to rest before nightfall, and can only be answered by patience and sustained research, if then, not so with other men. They must construct churches and gods "which will presumably do this obviously impossible task of giving magic answers to every conceivable question that he may ever ask. His quest -or, rather, demand, - for certainty thereby inevitably leads him into irrational thinking and behaving."[68] I well recall my own experiences at a Jesuit college in the early Thirties in such classes as Epistemology (the science of the certitude of our own cognitions). During the question and answer sessions, I was invariably reminded of a tennis court because, as rapidly as queries concerning morality, ethics and truth bounced into the instructor's court, he returned the ball, or the answer, perfect, complete and final. There was never a moment's hesitation. Furthermore, it possessed the absolute clarity that the responses of the oracle of Delphi often lacked. Of course, one has to understand this was the era when on such a campus one constantly heard the phrase: "Rome has spoken. The matter is closed." Likewise, I recall the chaplain at Park College in the early and middle Fifties whose tolerance for the social sciences ceased when one questioned Biblical "truth."

There were, no doubt, many such similar experiences over the years which prompted Albert Ellis to peer past and beyond the apparent triumph of science and technology in modern times and grope for deeper truths: "The facts of modern psychology and neuropsychiatry increasingly show ... that man is, at bottom, a highly irrational, religiously-trended animal...."[69]

However, it was younger son Jeff who pointed out this generalization may not apply to the historical Chinese civilization. Compared to others of its class, it was remarkably deficient of mythology and, as a consequence, of cosmology itself. "Their mythology...boasts of no lengthy, episodic narratives. Instead, it consists of only a handful of broken and isolated anecdotes, abruptly told without any sense of organization or artistry, whose characters seem to have entered from nowhere and then exited into the same nothingness."[70] As for cosmology, they were dependent upon a Buddhist importation of such crucial concepts as heaven and hell, paradise and limbo.[71]

Finally, while a great many writers over the ages have written in praise of faith, we think it appropriate to observe that one of the most difficult things to do, apparently, is to get inside of and appreciate another man's faith, one remarkably different than one's own. One is tempted to say the greater one's faith, the greater the intolerance for the other's. Wilfred Cantwell Smith aptly acknowledged this unfortunate tendency for Christianity. The bigotry displayed toward primitive peoples everywhere was also manifested toward all other religions.[72] At the same time, as an accomplished scholar of ancient Egypt, he lamented the fact he was not able to understand its belief that the sky was a cow. However, he thought he might if he knew more and persisted.[73] Yet, we confess equal bewilderment when he asserted that, while the Jesus of history is shadowy, the Christ of faith is strong and real.[74] How often has one heard or read the charge or admonition: "Oh, ye men of little faith," and never waited for a reply by the accused? It is time to speak in the defense of those in the docket. We think faith too precious a commodity to be pledged to anything seen in a dim light!

As long as the primitive was independent, and did not suffer prolonged food and water shortages, he was spared the pain of knowing knowledge about the gods was separate and apart from the everyday world; this was because their reality was suspect. Instead of a fragmented world of secular and sacred things, he lived in one where the sacred gave assurance, security and an inner harmony.

Footnotes

1   *The Place of Science in Modern Civilization and Other Essays* (New York, Russell and Russell, 1961), 48. He also correctly pointed out that medieval Christendom preserved this Hebraic theology intact. *Ibid.*, 48-49.

2   Lynn White, Jr., "Christian Myth and Christian History," 145-158 in *Journal of the History of Ideas*, III, No. 2 (1942), 156.

3   Gerald Heard, *Is God in History? An Inquiry into Human and Prehuman History in Terms of the Doctrine of Creation, Fall and Redemption* (New York, Harper, 1950), 203.

4   Reinhold Niebuhr, *Reflections on the End of an Era* (New York, Scribner's, 1934), 122, 265, 288, 290, and *The Nature and Destiny of Man, a Christian Interpretation, II, Human Destiny*. Gifford Lectures (New York, Scribner's, 1953), 70.

5   Reidar Thomte, *Kierkegaard's Philosophy of Religion* (Princeton, New Jersey, Princeton University Press, 1949), 205. Friedrich Nietzsche noted a tendency of history to destroy the religious impulse by depriving it of its pious illusions. *The Use and Abuse of History*, translated by Adrian Collins (New York, Liberal Arts Press, 1949), 49-50.

6   *The Quest for the Historical Jesus. A Critical Study of Its Progress from Reimarus to Wrede* (New York, Macmillan, 1948), 398-399, 401.

7   Some of the more dramatic ones are as follows: 1) the hero's mother is a royal virgin 2) the circumstances surrounding his birth are unusual 3) he is reputed to be the son of a god 4) at birth an unsuccessful attempt is made to kill him 5) he is reared by foster parents 6) we are told nothing of his childhood 7) upon reaching manhood, he returns and for a time prescribes laws, but later loses favor with his subjects, or the gods 8) he meets with a mysterious death, often on top of a hill 9) although his body is not buried, he has one or more holy sepulchers. *The Hero. A Study in Tradition, Myth and Drama* (London, Methuen, first published in 1936), 179-180. See also Heard, *Is God in History?*, 214-215.

8   *A Study of History*, 10 vols., VI (London, Oxford University Press, 1939), 469-475.

9   *Ibid.*, VI 536-538.

10   White, "Christian Myth and Christian History," *loc. cit.*, 150.

11   James Westfall Thompson, *A History of Historical Writing*, 2 vols., I (New York, Macmillan, 1950), 122.

12   Herbert Butterfield, *Christianity and History* (New York, Scribner's, 1950), 124-126.

13   John Dillenberger, Harvard Divinity School, to the author, Arlington, Massachusetts, June 29, 1956. Contrast that with the following situation involving Dr. George Buttrick, prominent Presbyterian pastor in New York City and spiritual counsellor

for President J.L. Zwingle of Park. It was the latter who invited him to address the Park faculty circa 1950. Dr. Buttrick bragged how he had exposed and embarrassed a professor before the latter's own class because he had declared that the historical account of Jesus was virtually non-existent. Unfortunately, Buttrick failed to fill in that biography which now everybody eagerly awaited. No one, however, dared call attention to this omission - certainly not I -lest it be construed as hostility to the faith. Buttrick was telling Zwingle and a great bulk of the faculty what they wanted and needed to hear. Had such a loose and unsubstantiated statement involved a scientific matter, there would have been questions galore. No one would have feared the consequences. This illustrates in part the chasm between science and theology.

14   Aldolph Harnack, *What is Christianity?* Sixteen Lectures delivered in the University of Berlin during the Winter Term 1899-1900. Translated into English by Thomas B. Saunders (New York, G.P. Putnam's, 1901), 145-146; Rudolph Bultmann, *Theology of the New Testament,* I (New York, Scribner's, 1951), 3. Historical probability in all such matter seems, at present at least, to lie well beyond our competence, as well as that of New Testament scholars. In effect, they need not concern us for the moment. Rudolph Bultmann, *Jesus Christ and Mythology* (New York, Scribner's, 1958), 16.

15   H. Richard Niebuhr, *The Meaning of Revelation* (New York, Macmillan, 1941), 55-56.

16   Herbert Butterfield, *Christianity and History* (New York, Scribner's 1950), 18-19.

17   *The Interpretation of History,* translated by N.A. Rasetzki and Elsa L. Talney (New York, Scribner's, 1936), 33-34.

18   Karl Barth, *The Doctrine of the Word of God. Prolegomena to Church Dogmatics,* being vol. I, Part I, translated by G.T. Thomson (Edinburgh, Scotland, T. and T. Clark, 1936), 188; Rudolph Bultmann, *Form Criticism. A New Method of New Testament Research, Including a Study of the Synoptic Gospels and Primitive Christianity in the Light of Gospel Research,* by Karl Knudson, translated by Frederick C. Grant (Chicago and New York, Willett, Clark, 1934), 60-61. Although Rudolph Bultman does not doubt the historical evidence for the existence of Jesus, he is of the firm opinion we can know nothing about his life and character. Mircea Eliade, *Myth and Reality.* Planned and edited by Ruth Nanda Ansher (New York, Harper and Row, 1963), 162.

19   Karl Barth, *Credo, a Presentation of the Chief Problems of Dogmatics with Reference to the Apostles' Creed,* translated by J. Strathern McNab (New York, Scribner's, 1936), 45.

20   Lynn H. White, Jr., "Christian Myth and Christian History," *loc. cit.,* 156-157. The only effective Christian myth is one beyond and independent of history. See "As Deceivers Yet True," 3-24 in Reinhold Niebuhr, *Beyond Tragedy. Essays on the Christian Inter-pretation* (New York, Scribner's, 1937).

21   "Christian Myth and Christian History," *loc. cit.,* 148, 157-158. For the traditional and historical importance of the linear concept of time to the Christian Church - or progress through space and time to a definite goal, the Second Coming - see Oscar Cullmann, *Christ and Time. The Primitive Christian Conception of Time and History.*

Revised edition. Translated from the German by Floyd V. Filson (Philadelphia, Westminster Press, 1964), 53-54.

22   *The Sacred Canopy. Elements of a Sociological Theory of Religion* (Garden City, New York,, Doubleday, 1967), 166. A good example of this was afforded by Karl Barth when he said that without the resurrection of Christ, he would not be a Christian theologian. Without this event, Christianity would be but an illusion and "moral sentimentalism." The resurrection certainly has a life of its own in the consciousness of such a man. See *The Knowledge of God and the Service of God According to the Teaching of the Reformation*, translated by J.L.M. Haire and Ian Henderson (London, Hodder and Staughton, 1938), 88.

23   Lynn White, Jr., "Christian Myth and Christian History," *loc. cit.*, 147.

24   John Capon in London. "Liberal Bishop's Appointment Causes a Stir in England," in *Christianity Today*, September 7, 1984, 74.

25   London Letter. "Durham: The Saga Continues," in *The Christian Century*, May 1, 1985, 437.

26   He was a member of a distinguished Jewish family who converted to Christianity while still in school. "Choosing Anglican Bishops," in *The Christian Century*, May 13, 1987, 460.

27   John Capon, "Liberal Bishop's Appointment Causes a Stir in England," *loc. cit.*, 74.

28   The Biblical scholar was Louis Brighton, professor of New Testament theology at Concordia Seminary in St. Louis. See Helen T. Gray, Religion Editor, "Christ's first coming was joy, but his return is fulfillment," in the Kansas City *Times*, December 16, 1989, F 1, 3. This age-old Christian conviction of a horrible death for the unbeliever probably motivated fundamentalists who consigned to "the lake of fire" all who defied Jesus by signing a recent Planned Parenthood declaration in the Kansas City *Star*. I personally received such a threat in a postcard signed "Hanovers, 606 N. 1st, Burlington, Ks. 66839."

29   Wilfred Cantwell Smith, *Meaning and End of Religion. A New Approach to the Religious Traditions of Mankind* (New York, Macmillan, 1963), 139-140.

30   *Ibid.*, 188-189, 191.

31   *Ibid.*, 127.

32   *Ibid.*, 106.

33   *Ibid.*, 60.

34   *Trinity and the Religious Experience of Man*, 42, 111.

35   *Ibid.*, 53. "Christ refers time and time again to someone greater than he, to someone Else to come...." *Ibid.*, 42.

36   *Other Christs. The Coming Copernican Christology* (New York, Pageant Press, 1971), 8-9.

37   See "Elements of the Medieval View. Philosophy of History," 143-147 in *Ideas and Institutions in European History 800-1715*, I, edited by Thomas C. Mendenhall *et al* (New York, Holt, Rinehart and Winston, 1948). By the thirteenth century there were signs of the emanicipation of history from theology. There was less universal history written and, in the accounts which appeared, a more rational chronicle was evident. Artificial distinctions between "sacred" and "profane" history - one invented in the patristic age and adopted by medieval historians - were either blurred or obliterated. The new historiography, regarding history in a more realistic fashion, ignored the old and pious way of dividing history into the six ages of man. It was part of an educational revolution begun in the twelfth century, as a result of European contact with Byzantine and Saracen cultures, and heightened in the thirteenth with the rise of universities. Thompson, *A History of Historical Writing*, I, 268-269.

38   George B. Flahiff, "A Catholic Looks at History," 1-15 in *The Catholic Historical Review*, XXVII, No. 1 (1941), 10.

39   *God and Philosophy* (New Haven, Yale University Press, 1946), 119-120.

40   Rev. Albert J. Shanley,, "Catholicism and the Writing of History," in *Studies in Sacred Theology*, 61 vols. (Washington, D.C., The Catholic University of America, 1941), XII, 6; Francis J. Siegfried, "Historical Criticism and Philosophy," 75-83 in *The Catholic Historical Review*, V, New Series (1925), 78. See also Étienne Gilson, *Being and Some Philosophers* (Toronto, Canada, Pontifical Institute of Medieval Studies, 1949), 215. He has a somewhat less optimistic account.

41   Rev. W. H. Kent, "Catholic Truth and Historical Truth," 275-293 in *The Catholic Historical Review*, VI, Old Series (1920), 293.

42   Joseph Schrembs, "The Catholic Philosophy of History," in *The Catholic Philosophy of History*, III. Papers of the American Catholic Historical Association, edited by Peter Guilday (New York, 1936), 4; Ross J.S. Hoffman, "Catholicism and Historismus," 401-410 in *The Catholic Historical Review*, XXIV, New Series (1939), 409-410.

43   Herbert C.F. Bell, "The Place of History in Catholic Education," 413-426 in *The Catholic Historical Review*, XXIII, No. 4 (1938), 419; George Shuster, "History: A Barrier or a Blessing," 185-190 in *ibid.*, XXII, No. 2, New Series (1936), 185-186.

44   The Rt. Rev. Thomas J. Shanan, "The Study of Church History," 303-332, *Catholic Historical Review*, II, No. 3, New Series (1922), 306-307.

45   *Systematic Theology*, I (Chicago, University of Chicago Press, 1951), 37-38; III (Chicago, University of Chicago Press, 1961), 166-168.

46   See the *New Catholic Encyclopedia*, XIV (New York, McGraw-Hill, 1967), 110.

47   It was an attempt to systematize God's revealed truth in a human fashion with the intent to make revelation better understood and appreciated by those persons possessing an orderly, logical and scientific mind. *New Catholic Encyclopedia*, XIV, 127. Also see

C.W. Previté-Orton, *The Shorter Cambridge Medieval History* in 2 vols. *The Later Roman Empire to the Twelfth Century* (Cambridge, England, The University Press, 1952), 630-631; James J. Walsh, *The Thirteenth Greatest of Centuries* (New York, Catholic Summer School Press, 1913), 281, 285. For the original work, consult St. Thomas Aquinas, *Summa Theologie*. Latin text and English translation, Introduction, Notes, Appendices and Glossaries, vol. II. *Existence and Nature of God* (New York, Blackfriars and McGraw-Hill, 1964).

48   Egon Friedell, *A Cultural History of the Modern Age, 3 vols. The Crisis of the European Soul from the Black Death to the World War, I. Renaissance and Reformation, from the Black Death to the Thirty Year's War* (New York, Alfred A. Knopf, 1930), 54, 71, 81.

49   *Ibid.*, I, 88-89.

50   If the heliocentric theory were correct, there must be many suns and a great many worlds inhabited by creatures called men who have necessarily sinned and thus need redemption. The Christian doctrine called for but one redemption via death and resurrection. White, "Christian Myth and Christian History," *loc. cit.*, 153.

51   Stillman Drake, "Galileo. A Bibliographical Sketch," 52-66 in *Galileo. Man of Science,* edited by Ernam McMullin (New York, Basic Books, 1967), 57-64.

52   J.B. Bury, *The Idea of Progress. An Inquiry into Its Origin and Growth* (New York, Dover Publications, 1932), 335, 348.

53   While many informed persons believe in God, they doubt that he was in history. This is a grievous truth becaue Christianity has always rightly claimed that it was a unique religion because it has produced the living god. While it is good that God should make himself evident, it is better that he should have made himself historical in the person of Jesus. Heard, *Is God in History?*, 1.

54   Max Weber, *The Sociology of Religion,* translated by Ephraim Fischoff. Introduction by Talcott Parsons (Boston, Beacon Press, 1963), 131.

55   F.C. Burkitt, "Pagan Philosophy and the Christian Church," 450-475 in *The Cambridge Ancient History,* vol. XII; *The Imperial Crisis and Recovery, A.D.,* 193-324. Edited by S.A. Cook *et al* (Cambridge, England, University of Cambridge Press, 1961), 469-472; R.M. Grant, *Gnosticism and Early Christianity* (New York, Columbia University Press, 1959), 12.

56   Paul Tillich, *A History of Christian Thought* (New York and Evanston, Harper and Row, 1968), 35.

57   Charles Norris Cochran, *Christianity and Classical Culture. A Study of Thought and Action from Augustus to Augustine* (New York, Oxford Press, 1944), 159.

58   Adolph Harnack believed them to be the first Christian theologians. Grant, *Gnosticism and Early Christianity,* 182.

59   Weber, *The Sociology of Religion,* 131.

60   Thompson, *A History of Historical Writing*, I, 125.

61   Cochran, *Christianity and Classical Culture*, 227.

62   Thucydides, *History of the Peloponnesian War*, translated by Richard Crawley. Everyman's Library, edited by Ernest Rhys No. 455 (London, J.M. Dent, 1945), 91-98.

63   John Higginbotham, *Cicero on Moral Obligation*. A new translation of Cicero's 'De officis' with Introduction and Notes (Berkeley, University of California Press, 1967), 14-17, 127; *Roman Civilization. Selected Reading*. Edited and with an Introduction and Notes by Naphtali Lewis and Meyer Reinhold, vol. I. *The Republic* (New York, Columbia University Press, 1951), 254; F.R. Cowell, *Cicero and the Roman Republic* (Baltimore, Penguin Books, 1964), 284.

64   James Harvey Robinson, *Readings in European History. A Collection of Extracts from the Sources*, 2 vols., I (New York, Ginn and Company, 1904), 25.

65   *Social Change and History. Aspects of the Western Theory of Development* (New York, Oxford University Press, 1969), 88, 97.

66   Thompson, *A History of Historical Writing*, I, 137.

67   *Rome*, translated from the Russian by J.D. Duff, edited by E.J. Bickerman. Galaxy edition (New York, Oxford University Press, reprint 1967), 318, 322, 324; *The Social and Economic History of the Roman Empire*, 2 vols. I (Oxford, England, Clarendon University Press, 1963), 509, 523-524.

68   Albert Ellis, *The Origins and Development of the Incest Taboo* (New York, Lyle Stuart, Inc., 1963), 153-154.

69   *Ibid.*, 159.

70   See, for example, K.C. Wu, *The Chinese Heritage* (New York, Crown Publishers, Inc., 1982), 1-2.

71   *Ibid.*, 16.

72   *Belief and History* (Charlottsville, University Press of Virginia, 1977), 32. "From a sociological view and even a 'scientific' point of view one cannot any longer consider Christianity as the 'whole' of religion as if the rest were not religious or false religions." Panikkar, *Trinity and the Religious Experience of Man*, 4.

73   *Belief and History*, 11-13.

74   *Ibid.*, 89.

Chapter XIII

SECULAR VERSUS RITUAL MAN

Ritual man is one who developed a schema for approaching the supernatural for the purpose of asking favors or, at least, avoiding wrath. His aim is generally two-fold: security, or comfort, in this world and as much bliss as may be summoned up in the next. If his assumptions are correct and true, then natural cause and effect has never been the major force in the universe, but rather the will and caprice of the supernatural. In the West, Catholics are the ideal ritual man.

Early modern Protestantism accepted the same precepts as those of science and technology. Science could be left unhindered because it would reveal the order and harmony placed in the universe by God.

When, however, science pitted its concept of evolution against the literal interpretation of

Genesis, the old alliance dramatically fell apart in the mid-Twenties. Its devastating impact is still felt upon the public school system as fundamentalists seek to censor both books and curriculum.

Secular man today is apt to be dosed with the same pervasive spirit of fundamentalism when watching athletic contests on TV. Heroes are apt to give all of the credit "to the Lord." This, of course, restores the medieval Catholic idea of life in an enchanted forest, one which early modern Protestantism scorned.

Secular man, on the contrary, had to confront raw nature without any such assurances. He was, therefore, forced to substitute experience, intelligence and rationality for religious faith. For a time, however, he found the same sort of refuge in the idea of progress as ritual man did in the Rock of Ages. Rocks, of course, have a peculiar habit of wearing away and that of ritual man, being older, was the first to decay. The idea of progress followed.

This chapter was originally divided into two parts, one dealing with the dilemma of Catholic ritual man and the other with his secular counterpart; such a device failed to satisfy my co-author who rightfully argued that, by concentrating upon Catholicism to the exclusion of Protestantism, one made the mistake of equating Christianity with the former. Of course, I had merely taken the easy way out, or the art of pursuing the quarry along the lines of least resistence. As long as Catholics everywhere obeyed papal edicts, or at least did not engage in open disputation, it was possible to generalize about their theological postulates. And even when open conflict broke out, in the time of Pope John XXIII, the smoke of battle did not obscure the players. It was still possible to see what was going on in the field itself. On the contrary, Protestantism naturally bifurcates. The more and the longer the process persists, the more difficult it is to say what it all means. Nothing poses the problem with greater clarity than when the unwary scholar tries to explain the recent history and meaning of twentieth century American Protestantism.

One may say with some assurance, however, that the centuries-old alliance between Protestantism and science came apart at the seams. Whether one discoursed about the social consequences of this, or of the traditional doctrinal position of Catholicism, it was basically about ritual man, who, because of man's essential unworthiness, had of necessity to seek God's mercy and forgiveness.

Likewise, it is clear that the modern secular adversaries of religious or ritual man were not only communism, but liberalism, which gave rise to the so-called peaceful, democratic and industrialized state. Both systems rejected the Christian notion of the inherent sinfulness of man[1] and the idea of Divine intervention in human affairs.[2] Curiously, communism was allied with Christianity only in the assumption of the weight and force of the irrational factor in human history, one virtually ignored by liberalism. But, while communists perceived this as hastening the decay only of capitalism, Christian theologians interpreted it as being responsible for the necessary failure of all secular collectives within human history.[3]

Throughout the complexities of this chapter, therefore, the essential reader's guide is simply this: none of the several twentieth century emperors dealt with here had any clothes. That perception applies to both Catholics and Protestants, conservative and liberal, religious and secular. The merchants of Ultimate Truth no longer had a monopoly, as in thirteenth century Christian Europe. Competing of necessity among themselves, they had to settle for an ever smaller share in the market place of ideas.

Nevertheless, these are the principle and contending forces of the modern Western world; if we are unimpressed, it was on the basis of performances. They always fall far short of universal pretensions and ideologies. Where such failures were due primarily to internal contradictions of the system, its devotees were, as always, happily unaware of them.

The primitive was and is a ritualist. The reason is not difficult to detect: where man's livelihood is concerned, he appears both self-serving and cautious. As a consequence, ritual man makes his appearance when and wherever man feels helpless to control events in nature. Parenthetically, when that feeling evaporated, he tended to fade away with it. Rarely, however, was the primitive allowed that luxury. So it was no accident he supplemented religion with magic to cover all the bases. Religion was man's confession of inadequacy without the help of the gods, and he studied self-abasement in order to procure it. Magic represented the belief that man, or certain men as shaman or medicine men, might, through the use of sacred objects and incantations, control events in nature for the benefit of the tribe.

Although ritual man appeared in all forms of pre-industrial societies, his true spiritual home was in agricultural ones. This was probably because their savants realized they were at the mercy of the gods from day to day. While the introduction of agriculture tremendously stepped up population density, it also remarkably enhanced the likelihood of catastrophe if anything went wrong with crop production. Hard, diligent and intelligent efforts could prepare the way toward bountiful and nutritious crops. Excessive moisture, droughts, big winds, hail, insects and a host of other "Acts of God" could wipe out a year's endeavor virtually overnight. Compared with the happy-go-lucky hunter-gatherers, who believed they would bag tomorrow the game they failed to spot today, such societies appear anxiety-prone. It is not surprising, therefore, that agricultural societies left as little to chance as possible, employing the fruits of both magic and religion.

Indeed, one would be hard-pressed to name a single agricultural community anywhere - one, that is, uncontaminated by the industrial mentality - which was not either very religious or superstitious or both. Vilhelm Moberg captured the essence of this mood or attitude in *The Emigrants*. It focused upon a mid-nineteenth century Swedish couple who are eventually forced to emigrate because the poverty of the soil and the harshness of the climate negated the Protestant ethic. Altering their words slightly, but not the spirit or the truth of the episode, what happened was something like this. For the last time the man looked with despair at the stony soil where he had labored so long and hard. For every ten crop rows of such efforts, eight produced nothing. He had now reached the limits of his endurance and, like Job, cursed God. "How could a decent and compassionate God be so utterly callous toward proper returns for the hard, diligent and intelligently-directed labor of his good and faithful servants? God must either be impotent, a fool or a misanthrope, take your choice." "Hush, hush," begged his horrified wife. "If He hears you, He will take away the last two rows. Let us instead give Thanksgiving for them." Thus, back to ritual.[4]

The true spiritual successor of the primitive as ritual man was the Western Catholic whose very religion and magic were muchly indebted to it. Sir James George Frazer mentioned three basic points where early man anticipated essential Christian doctrine. The notion of a man-god, a Jesus, endowed with divine or super-natural powers, belonged essentially to that earlier period of religious history. Here gods and man were viewed basically as of the same stuff. Both could lay claim to magic. Unlike modern intellectuals, the idea of a god incarnate in human form did not seem strange and exotic to pre-Christians. Likewise, they conceived the idea of worshippers deriving inspiration from sucking the blood of a freshly sacrificed victim, or that of Christ's blood in the holy chalice. Finally, they believed there was something holy in women and sometimes worshipped particular women as true and living goddesses, or the Virgin Mary theme.[5] Mircea Eliade suggested the commonality of similar religious precepts. For the religious person everywhere, the essential precedes existence. That is to say his existence begins at that moment when his essential nature is revealed to him, or when his primordial history is given to him and he accepts it. This is always sacred history for its actors are always either mythical ancestors or supernatural beings. This is equally true of primitive and oriental religions as well as the Judaic, Christian and Moslem. More dramatically, a common thread is that of a murdered deity who cannot be forgotten. It is primarily after his death that he becomes indispensable to his followers. By them he is remembered through ritual and in many cases he is present in the worshipper's body, especially from what he has eaten.[6]

Around such religious concepts, Catholics developed the Seven Sacraments, devised to protect the believer from the clutches of Satan and evil from the cradle to the grave, i.e., baptism, confirmation, penance, the Eucharist, the holy orders, marriage and extreme unction. The sacred appartus and ritual of the Church was the vehicle which united the worshipper with God, Jesus, the Virgin Mary and a host of saints. The prayers of the believers, even for the dead, might be heard and answered. The natural event level could be immediately displaced and succeeded by the miracle, itself induced by belief and not intellect. It represented what Peter Berger called the three most powerful concomitants of the sacred -mystery, miracle and magic.[7] Like the primitive world, concluded Max Weber, this was an enchanted world where, by magic, one could implore or master those in the supernatural world.[8]

The typical Catholic ritual man, at least that of the late Middle Ages, proved just as self-serving and cautious as the primitive. According to Erasmus Desiderius, the ordinary worshipper used the ritual system in hopes of bringing long life, wealth and happiness and, afterwards, a seat in Heaven at the right hand of our dear Lord, only no hurry about that, if you please! Prayers to the Virgin Mary, thought by the common people to be more approachable than the Son, and a host of saints were seldom, if ever, for virtue but only for happiness. This was falsely assumed to be the product of self-seeking and folly.[9] This was a normal occurrence. Even in the most otherworldly religions, the normal situation for prayer was one where the worshipper prayed both to avoid the external evils of this world while at the same time he asked to acquire its advantages.[10]

It was, however, the Protestant revolution of the sixteenth century which resulted in the disenchantment of the world. The sacramental apparatus was reduced to a minimum. The miracle of the mass disappeared as did that vast network of intermediary souls who were the go-between of God and his worshippers. Protestants ceased praying for the dead, as Catholics did in order to speed their way through Purgatory.

Thus was born what Max Weber called the spirit of rationalization and intellectualization. Its basic principle was no mysterious and incalculable forces come into play and dominate this world. Instead, man could by calculation and technical means perform the kinds of services previously thought the result of religion and magic. This was the process of intellectualization. Man could not easily harbor this thought and at the same time conceive of life as that in some sort of enchanted forest. Thus, the idea of the disenchantment of the world.[11] Ultimately, however, there would be tension between religion (Protestantism) and intellectual knowledge wherever rational thought and empirical knowlege had accepted the disenchantment principle and progressed to the idea of conceiving the world as a causal mechanism.[12]

It is R.H. Tawney who helps us comprehend the social significance of the transition from Catholic domination before the Reformation to Puritan influence thereafter. Despite an initial reluctance to abandon the old Catholic social ethic, the mood which emerged triumphant in the English Protestant Reformation was one which worshipped mathematics and physics. With few exceptions, John Locke, for example, practitioners of economic science were businessmen. Knowledge became a kind of measurement whereby one could reduce the complex to simple, constant and measurable forces. Religion and morality became secondary considerations and the province of secondary men. Money-making was elevated into a religious calling and individualism ultimately became one's chief concern as a Christian. It was reflected in a new and uncharitable attitude toward the poor, i.e., their condition was solely their fault and, as long as they were coddled, they would remain as they were. Only the goads of hunger and positive deprivation would motivate them to become productive citizens. On the contrary, business virtues were elevated and equated with Christianity itself - diligence, moderation, sobriety, and thrift. As the church ceased to think, the doctrine laissez faire superseded it. Sharp business practices became the rule in the money markets. Society, like science and technology, had become impersonal.[13]

Another pertinent version of the same phenomenon was offered by Robert K. Merton. Operating upon the theory the more the scientist studied nature, the greater his respect would be for the power, the wisdom and majesty of God, the Protestant business civilization of the sixteenth and seventeenth centuries endorsed both science and technology.[14] Scientists like Robert Boyle and Francis Bacon responded.[15] Thus was the marriage consummated by both parties, filled as they were by the spirit of utilitarianism, empiricism and rationalism, and certain in the joint faith that science would reveal God's order in the universe.[16] So great it was that, save for some extreme Calvinists,[17] both Puritans and Pietists were willing to set no limits to scientific studies, including that of the lowliest of God's creatures.[18] They were even willing to allow individual questioning of authority, or liberty of conscience, which extended to free individual interpretation of the Bible. Experience and reason were relied upon as guides.[19] A second dominant tenet of Puritanism was one which designated social welfare, or the good of the many, as a social goal. Francis Bacon believed science held the power to better the material condition of mankind, something Christ fully approved.[20] Since that time, wherever Puritans and Pietists predominated, schools of science and technology thrived. By contrast, Catholic schools of the Higher Learning stressed classical and theological studies.[21] When, however, Merton claimed the alliance between science and Protestantism persisted to the present,[22] that was not without problems to this study.

The views of F.S.C. Northrop are closer to those of Tawney than of Merton. By the latter part of the seventeenth century, Protestantism settled on the Newtonian and Lockian principle that the smallest particle in the universe was the atom. In turn, this supported the Protestant idea of the primacy of the individual, as opposed to the older Catholic idea of community supremacy. This eventuated in the Protestant preachment of laissez faire economics. Bankers and big businessmen were the pillars of these churches.[23]

We have a Protestant faith science will freely give what it was obligated to do for the Catholic Church prior to the Renaissance. That was to support orthodoxy. Nevertheless, the alliance between the two held together rather well until the twentieth century.

By taking Southern Baptists as a nineteenth century American example of pietism, and the Catholic Church a ritualistic one, Paul Kleppner set up some essential contrasts. For the pietist the road to salvation lay not in rote learning of some credo, nor in regularized ritual practices, say the seven sacraments. Instead of through some human institution, salvation came by God laying his hands upon man himself, a creature who up to that point was wholly depraved and unable to save himself from sin and Hell.[24] This direct confrontation between God and man, excluding priest and minister, produced a profound change of heart, or the born-again Christian. It meant a miraculous spiritual regeneration. As a natural consequence right conduct followed and not as a result of thought patterns. On the other hand, ritualists believed salvation was imparted by the Church, or that divine institution which Christ originated and blessed. This was achieved by membership in good standing and by participation in ordained rituals. That institution expected its adherents to lead good moral lives and spoke of "good works" in a theological sense, but never of the born-again Christian.[25] As for the political affiliations of each, Puritans and Pietists gravitated to the Republican party whereas Catholics, particularly recent emigrants, chose the Democratic party. And yet this phenomenon defied easy explanation, particularly a purely economic one. Political parties at this time were "not an aggregation of individuals professing the same political doctrines but coalitions of social groups sharing similar ethnocultural values."[26] One immediately thinks here of Merton's stress upon utilitarianism, empiricism and rationalism as the cement for the nineteenth century ethnocultural values of Puritans and Pietists.

By the twentieth century, however, several cross-currents were at work which disrupted the three-centuries-old alliance between the Reformation movement and science. The first of these was that atomic science dispelled the specious Newtonian-Lockian theory that the atom was the smallest particle in the universe, an error to which Protestantism was firmly attached.[27] A kindred difficulty occurred when the Great Depression revealed the woeful inadequacy of laissez faire economics, so dear to the heart of Protestantism. Finally, tension will occur between Protestantism and holders of rational thought and empirical knowledge wherever the latter progressed to the point they conceive the world as a causal mechanism not interfered with by supernatural caprice as a result of the prayers of the pious. It would be hard to write a credible version of the intellectual history of the United States in this century without featuring such a conflict.

Since that time, the business civilization of Protestantism paid dearly for its indifference to theoretical problems in favor of life's real and practical ones. It lacks the necessary theoretical framework to solve them.[28]

Further, and perhaps more importantly, the preaching of Protestantism has become as empty and blank as that of Locke's *tabula rasa*.[29] It has become more verbal and devoid of meaning in terms of the modern science and philosophy it "purported to accept."[30]

Northrop's despair with regard to twentieth century American Protestantism was echoed by some prominent within the profession itself. In 1925, Reinhold Niebuhr understood why the institution was "so impotent ethically and why the achievements of the church so meager compared to its moral pretensions." Protestantism did not go beyond an emphasis upon personal loyalty to Jesus, assuming nothing more was needed for salvation. The terrible price for this was that it ignored pertinent social issues the church should have addressed. Furthermore, preachers never seemed to realize how many of the miseries of man were caused not by malice, or evil, but by misdirected zeal and unbalanced virtues.[31] Five years later, at the beginning of the depression, a highly successful Protestant cleric observed "no profession of men is so thoroughly empty of dignity and grace as that of the Protestant ministry today."[32]

Northrop's theory helps us explain, as Merton's does not, the tremendous aberration from scientific norms when fundamentalist Protestantism bet its life upon a literal interpretation of the Bible, or that hammered out in the reign of James I of England. Just as Catholic reaction to the Protestant break-away of the sixteenth century had produced the rigidities of doctrine and dogma in the Council of Trent, 1555, so was fundamentalism the same sort of instinctive reaction to the alliance between science and scholarship and that of the Social Gospel group of main-line northern and urban churches.[33] Men insist most fervently upon their certainties when their hold upon them has been shaken. Frantic orthodoxy is a method of obscuring doubt.[34] The famous Monkey, or Scopes, trial of the mid-Twenties dramatized not only the separation of the rural and plain man from science, but his professed scorn for it, if not fear. One might have thought Clarence Darrow's pitiless exposure at the trial of the ignorance of William Jennings Bryan - the champion of the common man - on matters of both science and religion might have laid this brand of folklore to rest.[35] But, no, sixty years later Protestant fundamentalists still reject the Darwinian concept of evolution for theirs of creationism, a doctrine once again based upon a literal interpretation of the Bible.

When the born-again Christian - like Ray Knight of the New York Mets - declared that his prayers to Jesus Christ from the bench in the seventh and last game of the 1986 World Series were answered, enabling him to discard the goat's role for that of hero, he revived the old Catholic idea of life in the enchanted forest. It is not talent, training, experience, fundamentals, persistence, courage, or even luck, but whose prayers the Lord chooses to answer. It is he who will emerge as the world's champions of baseball. Far from being unique, this scene is becoming a custom. One also sees, or hears about, the victorious team in devout prayer. Thus far, no one seems to have resorted to it following defeat. Little, it seems, has changed with ritual man since Constantine gave public credit and honor to Christ for his military triumph in 312 A.D. over his pagan rival, Maxentius, at Milvian bridge, near Rome.[36] The only perceptible difference between the medieval and modern version is that the born-again Christian has a direct pipeline to God, or Jesus. Thus, like a good merchant, he has successfully eliminated *his* middle man, the priest.

We believe the tie which binds fundamentalist Protestantism of the Twenties to that of today is the common desire to reduce to a simple formula a world which refuses to be simple. Then, as now, its appeal was to those most unaffected by the teachings of science and who, at the same time, are apt to occupy, educationally if not economically, lower levels of achievement.[37] In both instances, the message was carried by revivalism, whether under a tent or over radio and television.

There always seemed to be a close association of these people with first-generation capitalists. The latter found a message congenial enough to subsidize the mission. No wonder because they heard what they wanted to hear, i.e., the conspiracy theory of socialism and the affirmation that Christ endorsed capitalism.[38] Today, numerous evangelical enterpreneurs have made fortunes that may be worthy of the term "big business."[39] It was Oral Roberts who best dramatized the art of money-raising from the public pocket, displaying all the circus skills of P.T. Barnum. In January, 1987, he told a national television audience that God commanded him to raise $8 million dollars for his Tulsa empire by late March. Failure would be followed by a compulsory return to Heaven. It was fitting and proper that the goal was finally reached when a Florida dog race track owner contributed a check for $1.3 million dollars. Characteristically, ministry officials waited about a week to announce the happy outcome.[40]

To an outsider, it appears those branches of Christianity flourish best which deeply impregnate their followers with a sense of guilt and which equate sin in the sight of God with personal wrongdoing, like sexual aberrations from the norm. Evangelical Christians, whether of the Twenties or today, fall neatly into that category. The general area of their attack is sexual permissiveness which may account for their hostility to both homosexuals and abortions.

Is it not apparent what we attack most vigorously, consistently, and publicly is that which holds the greatest fascination? It may account for the recent scandal involving Jimmy and Tammy Bakker and their PTL (Praise the Lord) South Carolina television empire, one which involved both sex and drugs.[41] The consequent charges of blackmail and takeover by rival evangelicals educated as well as entertained. We understood the difference between pentecostals who speak in tongues, practice faith healing and other "gifts of the spirit," and religious fundamentalists, like Jerry Falwell, who do not.[42] Pentecostals, we think, would be quite at home in the era of ecstatic Old Testament prophets.[43]

Finally, in both eras - the Twenties and today - there was a clear repudiation by these individuals of the idea of progress, or belief in man's capacity, unaided, to improve the world. Conversely, there was an emphasis upon sin and tragedy which, as they saw it, the Social Gospel crowd negelected or deemphasized.[44] If, however, man *is* predisposed to sin, and only Jesus can forgive and redeem, then of necessity one is back to the ritual of psalm singing, Hell-fire sermons and fervent prayer. But ritual it is, even if far less elaborate than a High Anglican mass. The Reverend Jimmy Swaggart of Baton Rouge, Louisiana, is a good example of this form of Christian intolerance. Since Jesus is the only hope of mankind, all who choose a different religion must pay the consequences for this in the hereafter. Hell fire faces all sinners. Even Catholic Christians are not acceptable in his sight. His style epitomizes the hopes and aspirations of rural Southern Pentacostalism. It is "an emotional outpouring of faith that includes speaking in tongues and what he regards as other gifts of the Holy Spirit, and is relatively untempered by weighty theological discourse."[45]

Fortunately, this kind of Christian intolerance, manifested on broad fronts by both fundamentalists and pentacostals, is beginning to draw public censure from more responsible Christian sources. It is easy to fix upon our current plight as being in part a product of television. For a great many in America religion "has become a department of the entertainment and communications industry." The television pulpit "is the domain of showmanship, style, emotionalism designed to seduce and overwhelm the viewing audience." Its preachers "package a 'believer lifestyle,' and rail against everyone who doesn't fit it - homosexuals, communists, secular humanists, Jews and other non-Christians, sex educators, and so on." A prominent Episcopal priest at Los Angeles sounded this warning: "...no group, large or small - not even one associated with a particular president - has the right to determine and then impose a moral or religious standard on society... Religious intolerance must not be tolerated."[46] A church historian at a respectable southern seminary reminded us that one cannot compromise with fanatics. "By its very nature," he observed, "fundamentalism is possessed of an absolutist mentality that says: 'I am right. Therefore, only if you agree with me can you be right or Christian or saved or whatever it is we are talking about.'"[47] It is these kinds of religious excesses which have brought Protestantism to the very rim of anarchy itself.

Since the leftist revolution of the 1960s, conflicts between liberals and moderates occurred in almost every denomination. At the same time institutional loyalties evaporated. "Warfare has become endemic, with battles constantly breaking out over sexual issues, social programs, antiwar campaigns, abortion, church-state relations, ordination of women and, behind everything, different ways of understanding the authority of sacred texts and inherited teachings." Liberals among Methodists, Presbyterians and Catholics appear to be closer ideologically than with extreme conservatives of their own denomination. Judaism has long since institutionalized deep divisions within its ranks, i.e., Orthodox, Reform and

Conservative. For the most part, Orthodox rabbis contend the other two are illegitimate. The same ideological cleavage is apparent in the Catholic Church between Rev. Matthew Fox, Catholic leader of ecological "cosmic" Christianity and Cardinal John O'Connor of New York. The causal explanation lies in the same area we have repeatedly identified: "... the conflict has deep roots in the contrasting responses of believers to the challenges modern science, intellectual skepticism and political freedom pose for traditional sources of religious authority."[48]

In the last decade, the most dramatic and costly of civil wars occurred within the ranks of the fifteen-million Southern Baptists, America's largest Protestant denomination. During the 1960s and 1970s, its policy-making Christian Life Commission spearheaded liberal causes, such as civil rights, pro-choice on abortion, and against prayer in public schools. Likewise, it was critical of our involvement in Vietnam. However, about a decade ago, conservatives seized control of that influential body. Its new director, Richard Land, vowed support for anti-abortionists, for those who would reverse the long-standing opposition to the death penalty and for those young Baptists who thought it sinful to date non-Christians. The same group later banned the reading of the 28-page Surgeon General Koop report on AIDS because it did not advocate "total abstinence from sex outside marriage."[49] It was also responsible for the Home Mission Board's rejection of female pastors, and divorced persons, as missionaries. It assumed control of the Southeastern Baptist Theological Seminary in Wake Forest, N.C., forcing the resignation of its president, top administrators and some key faculty.[50] While denying their triumph, in the mid-June sessions of 1990 at New Orleans, would result in mass firings at Baptist seminaries, conservatives do not deny they want "to restaff them with people who have no question about the authority of the word of God."[51] An absolutist approach characterizes their behavior pattern. It is based "on a literal view of the Bible as 'inerrant' - free of error historically, scientifically and religiously."[52] At this point, it is difficult to distinguish between this rigid position and that assumed for two thousand years by the Catholic Church.

However, it was the firing of Michael Willett as a missionary by the Foreign Mission Board which revealed church dilemma over the alleged miracles of Jesus. Summoned before the board, Willett confessed doubt; "I am willing to allow the possibility that some of the miracle stories were expanded or perhaps created in the early church in order to glorify the risen Christ. ... The miracles I question are the nature miracles, such as Jesus feeding the 5,000, walking on water and changing water into wine." While accepting the resurrection, he questioned a "physical" one, resulting from a risen "dead" body. Christ rose in a spiritual body and it "was in this transformed existence, this spiritual body, that he appeared to the disciples."[53] Once again, as in the case of Bishop David Jenkins, we can dispense with the traditional miracle about the angel who rolled away the stone from the tomb of Jesus so his earthly body might directly ascend into heaven.[54]

Meanwhile, the plight of moderates within the ranks of Southern Baptists plunged them into a state of despondency, and the contemplation of a schism. They are bombarded with demands they accept and testify to the literal truth of the first eleven chapters of the Book of Genesis. This, of course, is the one with so many close parallels with primitive accounts from all over the world. Moderates also sense that not only individual consciences and interpretation of the Bible are threatened, but likewise the autonomy of local churches. These have been the historical and traditional positions of the Southern Baptist church. They were the kind of freedoms Bill Moyers knew as a youth growing up in Texas (PBS reports). As a direct consequence of the intransigence of conservatives, "seminary enrollment is down; there is a decline in missionaries, budgets are down; morale is low. We are a divided denomination."[55] Rev. Randall Lolley of Raleigh, N.C. gave an apt summary: "The denomination 'just may be mortally wounded.'"[56]

While Merton's thesis may apparently be salvaged by the admission that, in the twentieth century, well-to-do urban Protestants never abandoned the old alliance between themselves and science, the movement was characterized by a different spirit, one of social concern for the welfare of the mass. This new emphasis on the Social Gospel was American Protestantism's desire to soften or mitigate the harsh impact of laissez faire upon the working classes. It was no accident the movement had its initial impetus among those churches - Unitarian, Congregationalist and Episcopal

-which reflected the influence of the state Anglican Church in England, guardian of public morality and welfare. Later, the movement was swelled by support from others whose heritage was pietistic and separatist, such as the Baptist and Methodist.[57]

Born in the Progressive era - and inspired by both science in its concept of evolution and sociology in its emphasis on the value of social analysis and goals[58] - the movement was aborted by the patriotic fervor of World War I. It was not revived until the terrible depression, beginning in 1929, which cast serious doubts about not only the fairness but the very efficacy of laissez faire. Such was the revolution in thought toward a system long championed by American Protestantism, rooted as it was in the middle class.

What is clear, however, is the difficulty of saying much of importance about American Protestantism in this century, particularly as it relates to science and technology. To be asked to handle Protestantism is like being handed a greased plate which is bound to slip from one's grasp to break into a hundred pieces on the floor. Nor does it initially help to search for Protestant meaning from the works of any one thinker, say Reinhold Niebuhr. Like Pablo Picasso, he passed through many different phases in his art and thought.[59]

While churchmen like Niebuhr were strongly influenced by secular themes - witness his somewhat Marxian approach in *Moral Man and Immoral Society,* published in 1932 - his allegiance to the old concept of original sin forced him to pass beyond that stage. It quickly led to one where, along with the ritualist, he recognized the essential helplessness of man and the omnipotence of God. That, of course, was in stark contrast to one of social Christianity's most obvious beliefs, or progress.[60] That doctrine the Social Gospel exponents acquired from the intellectual climate of the era which, in turn, was under the influence of evolution.[61] While technology's ability to serve many different masters of vastly different political and social beliefs is unquestioned, science cannot long maintain a close alliance with anyone obsessed with the idea of original sin. This concept is exclusively the province of ritual man. Once again, Merton's assertion that the alliance between Protestantism and science has persisted to this day would appear to need some modification.

Instead, the faith Puritans and Pietists had in early modern times that science could remain unshackled because whatever it revealed would reflect God's order and majesty, was over-optimistic. Eventually, of course, science was bound to be loyal to its own tenets and precepts. Its nineteenth century doctrine of evolution directly challenged the poetic version of creation as found in Genesis. Conservatives, or those who felt the Bible was dictated by God to his scribes, saw in this a threat to their entire belief system. Instead of a buttress to the Christian religion, science must be considered as an enemy.

We dare not leave this subject without confessing an obligation to Peter Berger. He thought one of the consequences of Max Weber's "rationalization"[62] was a general breakdown in a whole society's ability to feel at home with a single religious explanation of the meaning of suffering and evil, such as Europe enjoyed until the Reformation. The general uncertainty it substituted "has brought religion into a serious crisis of plausibility. The age-old function of religion - to provide ultimate certainty amid the exigencies of the human condition - has been severely shaken. Because of the religious crisis in modern society, societal 'homelessness' has become metaphysical - that is, it has become the 'homelessness' in the cosmos." Single answers to the problems of suffering, sin, and death no longer satisfy entire societies in modern times. Yet the masses demand answers to those questions.[63] Religion itself, like property, has been "privatized." Its plausibility structure - unlike that of the primitive and Catholicism in the thirteenth century - has shifted from society as a whole "to much smaller groups of confirmatory individuals."[64] Twentieth century American Protestantism, then, is the essence of this phenomenon of privatization. If the theme of individual autonomy is the most important aspect of our modern world view in the West, it has also produced a feeling of alienation. This is the price to be paid for this individualization and privatization of religious impulses and answers.[65] In other words, Peter Berger has explained our dilemma in trying to reduce to meaning twentieth century American Protestantism.

It is equally true that Northrop's theory makes meaningful, as that of

Merton's does not, the appearance and philosophy of Thorstein Veblen, so influential in many intellectual and governmental quarters in this century. It is to this phenomenon that we now turn our attention. However, it was all a part of the modern secular state movement occurring in both Western Europe and the United States. Since in America there was no State Church to be disestablished, or severed from its national connection, it is easier to start our narrative in Western Europe. Likewise, because the conflict there between Catholic religion and science, liberalism and like secular doctrines were so openly displayed by the third quarter of the nineteenth century, we may concentrate on the conflict in Veblen's America between the sacred and the profane.

In Europe ritual man may have received a mortal blow as a partial result of the crushing of the Revolution of 1848, largely romantic and nationalistic, and the subsequent papal betrayal of that movement in Italy. This eventually gave rise to the secular state system, which in the case of both Italy and Germany could not occur without successful wars fought against outside foes. But, more uniformly, it was accompanied by a strong anti-clericalism within each society as the state tried to detach the educational system from the traditional control of ecclesiastical authorities. In France the new secular state endured a like struggle with Catholic clergy for the right to educate children, the legitimacy of civil marriages, divorce and like innovations and liberties. It was in the midst of this continental struggle that the papacy under Pius IX in 1864 issued its rather remarkable Syllabus of Errors. Chief among these were human reason, science, free religious thought, freedom of the press, separation of Church and State and the idea that the Church had no right to use force to ensure the perpetuation of its own correct doctrine. In brief, liberalism and nationalism were Satan's henchmen.[66]

In America the appearance of a secular and humanistic state, and one which sponsored an industrial and technological mentality, was an heir to Hippocrates. This was the natural cause and effect school, excluding supernatural events from consideration.[67] Curiously, superseding religion, it became one in its own right. One of its early and most dedicated of worshippers was Thorstein Veblen as he expounded in his *The Theory of the*

Leisure Class at the beginning of the twentieth century. The habit of mind best adjusted to his concept of the peaceful, democratic and industrial community was, above all, one which neither imputed an animistic propensity to things, nor resorted to supernatural intervention to explain puzzling affairs. Neither was it one which depended upon an unseen hand to guide our economic activities in the right direction. For the highest efficiency in such a splendid environment, the world process must habitually be perceived and comprehended in terms of quantitative, dispassionate energy or force and sequence. An understanding of mechanical sequence or cause-effect relationship of phenomena was imperative.[68] At this point it is irresistible for the historian to point out similarities between Veblen and his contemporaries, Henry and Brooks Adams. Like Henry, he thought of religion as an occult form of energy,[69] but worshipped the forty-foot dynamo as a moral force.[70] Like Brooks, he was suspicious of the modern banker who produced little other than a new spirit of usury to the disadvantage of those whose labor created wealth.[71]

Veblen perceived ritual as an archaic persistence of a warlike and barbaric culture. Here the fealty of the warrior-mass was pledged to one's superior or protector-chieftain.[72] Above all, what invariably emerged from ritual was the conscious stress upon the non-economic or the non-useful. Sacred holidays merely meant the absence of useful labor. Church edifices were monuments to non-economic utility. In the Lord's name, they were meant to celebrate conspicuous consumption. The priests themselves were non-producers and heavy consumers. Their ritual garments, long dresses or robes, were obviously fashioned to convey the idea that their wearers planned no productive labors.[73]

Judged by the much more efficient industrial mentality, ritual man was perceived as an atavistic trait or as a product of arrested spiritual development.[74]

Here one may identify a philosophy which had more in common with magic than it did with religion. Both the magician and industrial man refused to admit their helplessness before the gods. Both addressed themselves to an attempted mastery of the external world more pleasing to themselves and their fellow man. The one profound difference was over method. Whereas the magician invariably used ritual, the industrial man as often resorted to science and technology.

Veblen's unattractive prose was inevitably translated for the common man. The poor man's Veblen, Jake Holman in Richard McKenna's *The Sand Pebble,* expressed this philosophy soberly and well. There was no mystery about a machine. Just get yourself a clean rag and an oil can and listen for the engine's complaints. Take care of them, just as you would were it a baby. If you knew how to take care of the machine, and executed properly, you were safer than if you were in the House of God. But let a pious man neglect a machine for his theological exercises and sooner or later it would kill or maim him.[75]

Veblen's optimism for what might be termed the almost infinite possibilities for good and the efficient under the peaceful, democratic and industrial state - boundless human progress - was reflected in the literature of later scholars. Herbert Croly made the point neatly when writing *The Promise of American Life* in 1909. Democracy was inextricably tied up with the idea of human perfectability and thus toward the adoption of measures most apt to forward the search.[76] Walter Lippman had equally ambitious goals for the democratic state in his *Drift and Mastery* of 1914. Our business was to make a utopia plausible. The statesman was that genius among politicians who could, in his own time, deal with social forces which led to a better world. The new and reformed organization of society would substitute "design for accident, human purpose for brute destiny."[77]

Nor did the holocaust of World War I, and the subsequent coming to power of the authoritarian state in Russia and Italy, dim the enthusiasm of some American scholars for the idea of progress under the peaceful and democratic state. In his presidential address to the American Historical Society in December, 1923, Edward P. Cheyney tentatively formulated six laws of history, the last three of which were democracy, freedom and moral progress.[78] Repudiating the theory of an American economic elite which felt it had both the power and the right to shape the destiny of a nation, Cheyney believed that the entire collective, using the machinery of the regulatory state, could be depended upon to produce both wise legislation and administration for the common good. He gave clarity to the meaning of the terms peaceful and democratic when repudiating the notion of some industrialists who argued force would be justifiable if necessary to obtain access to critical materials in far corners of the world.[79] It is obvious he believed in the Wilsonian concept of open diplomacy, openly arrived at. It is almost impossible to read this address today without coming to the realization its superstructure rested upon a simple truth, that of a fervent belief in the inevitability of the perfection of man.

Writing after the easy optimism of scholars and others had been dispelled by the severe and prolonged depression of the Thirties, John Maynard Keynes could still summon up a message of hope. It came in his *The General Theory of Employment Interest and Money,* written in 1935. True, he faulted contemporary Western governments for their inability to provide for full employment and their indifference to the inequitable distribution of wealth and incomes. Were a state to solve both problems, it would have a better opportunity to maintain peace. Under the old system of laissez faire, the only means open to a government striving to improve economic conditions at home was to intensify competition abroad for new markets and new investment opportunities. World War I was in large measure a product of such a system. What was implicit in Keynes' approach was the idea that democracy meant an entire people using the machinery of state in an active and positive way. It was one designed to bring about a better life, not for a new or an old elite, but for the masses or the people themselves.[80]

Finally, Veblen's vision of the supreme good of the democratic and industrialized state was shared by the nation's strongest and ablest executives. In 1912, one could choose between Teddy Roosevelt's "New Nationalism" or Woodrow Wilson's "New Freedom." Following World War I, and the revival of the individualism of laissez faire as a counter to the collective demands of the war itself, the nation, as a consequence, blundered into the Great Depression. Its mass suffering demanded a revival of social reform through state action. No one could have undertaken this task with more enthusiasm and energy than did Franklin D. Roosevelt. The pre-war American impetus on purposely making a better social order was carried on in the post-war world by such veteran activists as Harry Truman and Lyndon B.

Johnson. The latter's Great Society, unfortunately, became entangled in the Vietnam adventure. At Honolulu in February, 1966, L.B.J. over-ambitiously proposed a Great Society for South Vietnam while at the same time entirely subsidizing the military conflict. Not even the bitter and prolonged war itself was going to be allowed to interfere with the struggle for human perfectability, neither at home nor abroad.[81]

As my co-author stressed, Veblen and his subsequent admirers were doomed to failure because their concept of a peaceful, democratic state with a benign industrialized system was a contradiction in terms. In its early stages of development industry always operated under terms of laissez faire. This meant low wages, long hours, and ever-increasing machine productivity which naturally outstripped the demands of a domestic market. To keep the economy going, governments had to find foreign markets for the purpose of siphoning off excess manufactured goods as well as obtaining supplies of raw materials to keep domestic factories operating. Markets which were open only in peace time were too unreliable. The navy's job, or the government's job if you like, was to see that these markets remained open in time of war. This meant establishing large navies, coaling stations, spheres of influence, colonies and the like, and soldiers stationed abroad to keep the status quo. From 1870 and after, competition for these foreign markets was very keen among industrialized nations. Actually, to have been a peaceful, democratic and industrialized state would have meant to be crowded out of this competition. In addition to the international loss of prestige and power, it would have suffered tremendous domestic economic dislocations as well. This was a price that no proud nation would voluntarily pay. Its spectre probably appeared more appalling than the prospect of World War I during the summer of 1914. That appears to us to be as good an explanation as any to account for the apparently senseless drift into the vortex which was to destroy the base of European world hegemony, one which had endured for hundreds of years.

Nevertheless, even the terrible experience of two world wars did not dim the faith of the capitalistic world, especially at its center in Washington, in this market-military solution. It was fueled by an overriding fear of communist Russia as competitor for world markets, one which made the bitter British-German rivalry of 1898-1914 seem the refined competition of gentlemen. This of course, is our subject in chapter XVII.

Meanwhile this entire movement culminated in a belief in man's omnipotence, and not that of God, and in the power of reason to master all challenges, regardless of kind, i.e., philosophical, practical or scientific. At the same time that it glorified the scientific attitude of mind, this remarkable energy system gave inspiration to a plethora of masterpieces in art and literature.[82] For all of its easy presuppositions, and almost incredible naivete toward the darker side of human nature, it may well have been Western man's finest hour, brief though it was.

Meanwhile, the dramatic success of the secular, democratic and industrial mentality in dissipating belief in miracle, mystery and magic all bound up in ritual, can best be summarized by the agonies of the Sixties and after suffered world-wide by Catholic theologians, priests, nuns and laymen. All were believers in a Church impervious to sharp doctrinal and liturgical change since the Council of Trent in the mid-sixteenth century.

While John XXIII may be said to have triggered the change by his call for Vatican II from 1962-1965, the ironical element was that when the Council met, its members still fervently believed that Jesus, as the Christ, was the Lord of History.[83] Furthermore, one of their major decisions later was to intensify the study of the Scholastics, particularly Saint Thomas Aquinas. His work was pervaded by the quaint idea that it was possible to make Christian miracles appear plausible to the logical and scientific mind.[84]

When one reads a summary of the work of the Council from *The New Catholic Encyclopedia,* one gets little or no hint of the forth-coming storm within the Church world-wide. Perhaps this was because only guidelines were laid down and the real work delegated to various priestly senates.[85] But the mere suggestion from the apex that the Church was open to change and reform set up whirlwinds at the base of the authoritarian system.

The initial reforms or changes in ritual conveyed little hint to the outsider that the floodwaters had risen higher than the dam itself. The mass was now to be said in the vernacular, instead of in Latin. The altar was changed so that, while saying mass, the priest could face his congregation.

Other instruments than the organ were, theoretically, deemed appropriate vessels for sacred music. Individuals could, for minor sins, choose between the traditional solace of the private confessional or resort to the public confession read by the congregation. Finally, women were no longer required to cover their heads at religious services.[86]

An almost immediate outcry, however, developed over experiments in the mass. It was bad enough when priests went beyond the rubric and laws to eliminate traditional vestments and gestures.[87] But when they joined underground Catholics in celebrating the mass with regular, instead of unleavened, bread and drank the consecrated wine from the sacred chalice in unorthodox ways, this was subversion itself.[88] After listening to the celebration of a mini-mass by Leonard Bernstein at the Mark Taper Forum in Los Angeles, one Catholic observer dismissed it as a hodgepodge of sound and fury. It signified little other than to make the deeply religious man blush. This was but a part of the furor over the so-called jazz mass.[89]

The continued controversy piqued the curiosity of the managing editor of the Oklahoma Courier, Catholic diocesan newspaper. His national survey appeared in large measure to explain the deviations from the norm. Catholics universally reported an emotional dilemma between their own tight and authoritarian world, where the stress was on piety and obedience, and freedom in a secular world where change and progress seemed to occur with regularity. Most members did not believe in papal infallibility. Consequently, they cared nothing about papal pronouncements. Furthermore, most Catholics no longer believed in the Virgin Birth, ignored diatribes against birth control devices, and were not sure where they stood on abortion.[90]

A panel of half-dozen young and educated Catholics, male and female, sponsored by the respectable Catholic magazine, the Commonweal, came to equally shocking conclusions. There was, first of all, general agreement as to the mediocrity of Catholic colleges and universities, their provincialism and Chinese brain-washing methodologies and tactics. It left students cold. Like their cohorts in secular institutions, they were primarily concerned, not with the supernatural, but with this world, their own lives and careers. Consequently, they all dismissed Catholic theology as marked by little other than sterility. There was little interest in papal opinion on the liturgy of the mass. There was, however, some indignation that the pope could claim Catholics were of a single mind on birth control.[91]

The demands for individual freedom and the dictates of conscience seemed to be making operational-Protestants of Catholics,[92] even at the highest levels. Dominated from Rome since its inception in 1889, Catholic University in Washington, D.C. witnessed a persistent cry from the lay faculty that a layman be its rector. Only he, and not an ecclesiastic, could present a true picture of the predominantly secular education dispensed at that institution.[93] Sister Annette Waters exposed the very high incidence of emotional breakdowns among nuns who had taken their final vows ten, fifteen and twenty years ago. Traditionally treated as minors in canon law, they sought relief from the petty tyrannies of priestly senates and their own mother superiors.[94] Educated females also chafed at the traditionally subordinate role of women in the church. As Mary Daly pointed out, French sociologists concluded wherever the Catholic Church was dominant, women were kept in a traditional position of inferiority.[95] When the masculine hierarchy proved obdurate to change, or the break-down of the authority of the bishops and archbishops, it resulted in what was almost a mass exit of nuns. Resignations more than doubled in five years in the mid-Sixties and, even more telling was the fact that the exodus largely consisted of nuns with long years of service.[96] This was from among the same age group that had a high percentage of emotional break-downs. Meanwhile, among the restive priests, it appeared to be celibacy which was the most galling, as well as the least defensible, requirement. When the hierarchy proved intractable to all appeals, a great many priests left the church, later to marry.[97]

Even that final product of secularism and science, the "God is dead" theme, penetrated the corridors of Catholic theology. Some felt that, since science could not prove the existence of God, it was better to eliminate the very word itself. Others believed man was sufficient by himself, or "man makes himself." Still others concluded it was the progress of science, and its ability to explain reality, which rendered superfluous the notion of transcendent divine reality.[98]

Even for those less radical, changes in religious attitudes and beliefs were still profound and to the disadvantage of the Church. The eminent Catholic theologian, Charles Davis, reluctantly left a Church he felt had become both unfree and obsolete and whose teaching authority, consequently, was increasingly irrelevant. His doubts about papal infallibility had been virtually ignored at Vatican II. He no longer believed in the Virgin Birth, or, as he put it, in Mariology,[99] an idea he thought closely associated with papal infallibility. Only Christ, he believed, was fundamental, as the Seven Sacraments, including the Eucharist, were not.[100]

The nature of Davis' charge was broadened by Peter Berger who declared there had not only been a decline in Catholic belief, but a Christian one as well. This was a product of increasing secularity or religious skepticism. It was more apt to occur among Protestants and Jews than Catholics, among those who lived in cities rather than rural areas, those engaged in industrial production, particularly the working class, as opposed to artisans and small shopkeepers, the middle aged as opposed to the very young and old and, finally, to men rather than women. It was this movement which shattered the plausibility of Church authority. Its monopoly on reality-definition had been broken by the stubborn fact of pluralism and a multitude of authorities in a free society. The contents of Christianity, like that of any other religious tradition, would sooner or later have to face analysis as human projections. Christianity would have to come under historical judgment.[101] This was something many Protestants had already experienced, but one the Catholic Church bitterly resisted. Nothing prepared that Church for an alternative life-style.

Finally, while deploring it, Arnold Toynbee was forced to conclude that we are and have been living in a post-Christian era. No longer having belief, we still futilely attempt to practice Christian virtues. At best he perceived this as a re-run of Greco-Roman classical and pagan civilization and, at worst, a lamentable regression of spiritual progress.[102]

Two decades following the turbulent Sixties have not mended the schism within the soul of the Catholic Church. On the contrary, they have deepened and accentuated the anguish and the wounds.

Perhaps the two most newsworthy cases of recent times - those dealing with Raymond Hunthausen, liberal archbishop of Seattle, and the

Rev. Charles Curran, theologian at Catholic University of America - best expressed the controversy between the Vatican and a vast number of American Catholics opting for more openness and freedom of inquiry. Hunthausen was criticized and stripped of authority in five key areas because he did not follow traditional positions in matters of marriage annulment, contraception, homosexuality and the liturgy itself. Also objected to, perhaps, was his open participation in anti-nuclear demonstrations.[103] The Rev. Curran was relieved of his teaching duties because of similar offenses. He himself declared that his papal judge Cardinal Ratzinger in September, 1985, demanded he rescind his thinking and teaching in the following areas: masturbation, premarital intercourse, homosexuality, contraception and sterilization, abortion and euthanasia, and the indissolubility of marriage.[104] One would find it difficult to summarize the religious furor over these incidents better than to quote *Commonweal:* "For all the Catholics distressed and confused by the coexistence of contending views in the church, there are as many or more who are dismayed and repelled by a church that would appear fearful of truth, hostile to inquiry, guarded against experience, suspicious of imagination."[105] A similar conclusion was arrived at by a writer in *America,* a weekly magazine published by Jesuits: "...the suppression of dissent leads to the comfort - and vitality - of the tomb. Roman intervention at the beginning of this century led to 50 years of theological ossification in the United States. Is that what we want when the world is being challenged as never before by scientific, technological and cultural sea-changes?"[106]

Meanwhile, the decay in the vitality of the Church can be seen at much lower levels of operation. Twenty years ago, of the more than 50 million Catholics, over 70% went to Mass regularly, but, in 1979, only about 40% did. In large cities, like New York, attendance is now less than 30%. About 10% of the Catholic population, or five million persons, are probably living in marriages which the Church considers invalid. Of every 1,000 marriages solemnized in the Church itself, 445 end in divorce. As many as 75% of American Catholic women are believed to use contraceptives.[107]

Meanwhile, nothing appears to stifle dissent within the ranks of both priests and nuns. Earlier in 1987, the Rev. John McNeil of New York was expelled from the Jesuits because he openly opposed papal policies with regard to homosexuals. More recently, the pastor of Sacred Heart parish in Norfolk, Virginia, resigned over the exclusion of the Dignity organization of homosexuals.[108] Meanwhile, Sisters Patricia Hussey and Barbara Ferrano of Charleston, West Virginia, members of the order of Notre Dame de Namur, were among 97 of those persons who signed a newspaper advertisement declaring it permissible for Catholics to hold more than one view on abortion.[109] It was probably disputations of this sort which induced Daniel Maguire, theologian of Marquette University, to observe: "In the time of Galileo, it was physics and astronomy. Today, it's pelvic theology. But the issue is the same. The issue is power, and the issue is control."[110]

To compound the problem, the Church has never ceased to be criticized for its innovations under Pope John XXIII in the Sixties. Those who assume this position are the same ones who feel they can no longer worship in churches where the services include guitar playing, sermons on social justice and parishioners shaking hands with one another. They argue that reverence and mystery have been taken out of the mass. They worship in their own little groups of secessionists.[111]

Today "the U.S. church finds itself caught up in a storm of internal debate ... from abortion to 'social justice' for the poor to nuclear weapons to the proposed ordination of women to the priesthood. ... the Catholic Church is now engaged in ... a full-blown 'crisis' - as religious vocations fall off everywhere, and urban parishes in major Eastern and Midwestern cities continue to close their doors, and stern-voiced critics continue to decry ... the 'racism' and 'sexism' and 'authoritarianism' of a church which has not changed fast enough to meet the demands increasingly placed upon it." As a consequence, the last two decades saw the ranks of new priests and nuns cut in half. Some female religious orders reported a drop-off of 75 percent.[112] The parish priests who are left have a very low morale. They feel overworked and undervalued. The pastor of St. John the Baptist in Kansas City feared another exodus of priests was in the offing, "because we're questioning what our identity is. What is a pastor today?"[113] What an unexpected question for the Catholic clergy to raise? It ties in, however, with gloomy reports that by the year 2,000, the Church is expected to have less than half the priests it does today. To increase their institutional difficulty, their average age will have jumped from 56 to 73.[114] In the opinion of many critics, the only solution is to ordain women as priests and allow ex-priests who married to return and dispense the sacraments.[115] While the Vatican remains adamant to all such proposals, the U.S. bishops no longer deserve the scornful title of "the church of silence," given them by their European counterparts at the Second Vatican Council of the 60s. In 1986, the nation's Roman Catholic bishops told the Vatican "that its draft document defining relations between Rome and bishops conferences was unacceptable."[116] Rome can speak as it wishes, but the matter remains open.

Nor is the plight of the Catholic clergy restricted to the United States. The same anguish is reported in the British isles. "A rapidly aging clergy and dearth of young men prepared to commit themselves to a life of celibacy and Christian service are threatening Britain's Roman Catholic Church with an unprecedented staff shortage." Glasgow, Scotland is a case in point. While more than half its priests are over fifty, and one-third over sixty, only one new parish priest is slated to be ordained this year. A prominent member of the hierarchy confessed: "... one of the problems of having a clergy so long in the tooth is that it presents the image to the young of something that is done by elderly gentlemen."[117]

I know from personal experience that the papal or conservative position on these ecclesiastical matters today is the same as was voiced by the Jesuit instructors I had in college in the early Thirties. But, this was in the middle of the period when there "was almost no intellectual life in the Catholic Church." This was due to Leo XIII and his edict of 1899 against those priests who favored the separation of church and state in America. His successor, Pius X, insured the papal victory by the appointment of a number of conservative priests as American bishops.[118]

The attempted rigid maintenance of doctrine and dogma by the Church for the last sixty years has been little, if any, more successful than like efforts by the Politbureau in the Soviet Union. Although causal factors are complex, it is clear the increasing insistence upon the freedom of inquiry has divided both houses. While public attention has focused upon the plight of communist Russia, and virtually ignored that of the Church, neither can continue to play the international role they once did. The continual refusal by the Vatican to initiate far-reaching reforms will merely accelerate problems within the organization itself. The price, however, that the Church must pay for the freedom to think is, no doubt, the kind of chaos which makes it so difficult to say what twentieth century Protestantism means. To say there is no easy solution is to be guilty of an understatement. Candor requires an admission there may be none at all.

While we always understood the inevitable and historical conflict between the free intellectual and the hierarchial Catholic Church, it is less easy to comprehend recent inroads on the latter by right-wing and fundamentalist churches. Thirty or forty years ago "it was not just traumatic for people brought up as Catholics to start attending a Baptist church, it was almost unheard of." But the rootlessness in America after World War II changed that. Yuppies, or socially mobile young people, moved far away from home. Denomination loyalities faded. Individual and family needs dictated psychological change. Now, for example, about half the 12,000 worshippers of Willow Creek Community Church in South Barrington, Illinois, are former Catholics. Part of church strategy, like that of the Community Church in Lancaster, California, is to eliminate the Southern Baptist label in their name and advertising. In a larger sense, they provide a kind of religious mall, i.e., one can buy there everything one needs in a religious and social sense. The California church offers an Olympic-sized swimming pool, a fully equipped Nautilus gym and racketball courts. Their associate pastor "envisions parishioners arriving for a workout in the gym and popping in a videocasette to watch ... how to rear Christian children or how to maintain a lifelong marriage, while pumping iron. Time is very valuable to the kind of people we want to attract [those with money and ambition] and this is a kind of time compression, so that they can exercise and learn how to strengthen themselves and their family mentally and spiritually at the same time." Sermons are geared to hopes and aspirations for personal happiness. Instead of potluck suppers their parents knew, church suppers are either catered or held at fashionable restaurants. One church in Indianapolis doubled its membership by specializing in the emotional needs of single persons and those recently divorced. It also set up classes for parents and Alzheimer support groups. Further, they recognized the yuppies' desire to blend in quietly with the new group, rather than have to stand up and introduce themselves, as traditional churches made them do. Recent converts were uninterested in history lessons and biblical stories. Personal needs preoccupied them. Perceptive pastors gave them what they wanted and could pay for. It was almost as if these churches turned over their membership problems to market research men and advertising copy writers. It could only happen in America.[119]

For those fundamentalists churches which stress both the Bible and its inerrancy, it is probably fair to say that, rejecting the imperfect society they live in, they embarked on a futile search for a perfect society, allegedly one existing somewhere in the past. Obviously, no system - whether capitalism, democracy, nationalism or socialism - has been able to duplicate it in present-day culture. "So people who ache from confusion and yearn for certitudes turn to old prescriptions, hallowed by custom but no more divinely assured than a new spark.... Fearful of the future, confounded by the present, they seek refuge in the past."[120]

Finally, we turn to Catherine L. Albanese for her explanation of the American religious dilemma, as expressed by the tension existing between the many and varied Christian faiths in an even more diverse cultural and moral environment. "What does all this mean, and to what does it all add up? The United States of America is probably the most pluralistic religious and social experiment in history. Its people live in a social situation complicated by a diversity unknown even in the most cosmopolitan societies elsewhere. Religions abound, and so do peoples, their beliefs, styles of worship, and moral codes. Community is fragile and temporary, and estrangement probably the one thing many have in common....

Thus living ... has proved a difficult task for the American people. There is, indeed, a tremendous gap between the millennial dream of community and the realities of estrangement only thinly veiled."[121]

Therefore, what religion does habitually for very small and homogeneous primitive societies, to provide cohesion, direction and purpose, it is incapable of doing in a society as large and diverse as ours. The same point was put by Ralph Linton in a slightly different way. Because of the element of free choice in our society - something not evident in isolated, primitive cultures - the core of our culture is rapidly shrinking. As a consequence, we are fast approaching the point where there are no longer enough items all agree upon to give our culture form and pattern.[122] And, if a culture does not hang together, it, to paraphrase Ben Franklin, hangs apart.

Here again, one is confronted by the price of hubris. Armed with the spirit of righteousness, and marching as to war, Western Christendom searched out the whole pagan world in order to induce it, to entice it, to force it to accept the Christ, our Christ. And at the time, the entire nineteenth century and up to the onset of World War I at least, all decent and honorable men had a common faith in that mission. Today, altogether successful, in an outward sense at least, the price to be paid for that arrogance, that hubris, is a progressive disintegration of that belief at home, as well as abroad. Where Christianity still exists, there appears a lot more agony than ecstasy.

While Christianity will never fail those determined to believe in it - because it assures them of a future immortality, as well as offering the immediate prospect of supernatural assistance in this world - it has failed if we judge it by its own universal pretensions. First, its doctrine of a Savior-hero was not unique, as advertised, but quite similar to that of many other religions. Second, the universality of man's approach to God through ritual was fragmented with the Protestant Revolution or Reformation. Once begun, it progressed to a kind of chaos where individual conscience emerged as the true rival of ritual man. This meant dispensing not only with the Seven Sacraments, but in some instances with the minister and perhaps even the Church itself. Henry David Thoreau was far from uncomfortable celebrating the Sabbath by himself in the midst of nature at Walden.[123] Despite the fact that we rebels may find this fact exhilerating, we confess there is more than a hint of anarchy about it. Third, and contrary to what we were taught as Christians, the message of Christ did not characteristically make converts among the heathen. They had either to be reduced by force, or seduced both by medicine, as magic, and material comforts before Christianity was accepted. When force was withdrawn, the native religions revived. At best, Christianity was absorbed into the native culture with the result that it bore little resemblance to that on a global level. This process can adequately be explained by anthropologists as a typical act of culture borrowing. One would have to conclude, therefore, that Christ is not the hope of the world, as we all once assumed. Fourth, the historic Christian Church based its chief claim to uniqueness and superiority on the historical fact that Jesus, as the living Son of God, had actually been crucified, died but was Resurrected. For centuries the Catholic Church employed embryonic history and science to buttress that claim. But one of the main features of the modern world has been the rejection of that assertion, whether explicitly or implicitly, by both history and science. Neither postulates supernatural intervention in world affairs. This produces a dilemma for the educated Christian. He can continue to assert the truth of the historic claim and thus fly in the face of both science and history, a somewhat distasteful prospect. Or, he can drop the assertion that this event actually happened within historical space and time while still believing in it as a religious "truth." Either decision carries its own traumatic reaction.

For the educated observer, and one who has avowedly taken the position of an outsider to his own "tribe," it is impossible to avoid the conclusion that Christianity has been divested of any pretensions to uniqueness and superiority. It is rather a matter of individual preference on academic grounds no firmer than that of emotion and intuition or of early rearing. However, we have simply gone a little beyond those Christian theologians who postulated the inevitable corruption and decay in human history of any other institution than Christianity. We merely included it in an act of moral pessimism.

One dare not leave this topic, however, without a final concession to Christian ritual man. As was previously demonstrated, with the decline of worldly fortunes within the Roman Empire, when men began to look to the Hereafter to fulfill their days of longing, both religion and ritual took a dramatic leap forward. As faith in history, science, and technology diminish today and tomorrow, we can expect a like revival in a resort to miracle, mystery and magic. Ritual man makes an appearance when and wherever he feels helpless to control events in nature.

Now we turn our attention to the plight of the secular state systems, or to those who are the heirs to the thinking of Thorstein Veblen.

Footnotes

1   Reinhold Niebuhr, *The Nature and Destiny of Man. A Christian Interpretation, I. Human Nature.* Gifford Lectures (New York, Scribner's, 1949), 23.

2   Rudolph Bultmann, *Jesus Christ and Mythology* (New York, Scribner's, 1958), 16.

3   Reinhold Niebuhr, *Reflections on the End of an Era* (New York, Scribner's, 1934), 112-113, 126-127.

4   (New York, Fawcett Popular Library, 1951), 69-74.

5   *The Magic Art and the Evolution of Kings* in two vols., I (New York, Macmillan, 1935), 374-375, 381, 391.

6   *Myth and Reality.* Planned and edited by Ruth Nanda Anshen (New York, Harper and Row, 1963), 92, 99.

7   *The Sacred Canopy. Elements of a Sociological Theory of Religion* (Garden City, New York, Doubleday, 1967), 111.

8   *Essays in Sociology.* Translated, edited and with an Introduction by H. H. Gerth and C. Wright Mills (New York, Oxford Press, 1953), 139, 155.

9   *The Praise of Folly.* With a Short Life of the Author by Hendrik van Loon.... Published for the Classics Club (New York, Walter J. Black, 1942), 162-163.

10   Max Weber, *The Sociology of Religion.* Translated by Ephraim Fischoff. Introduction by Talcott Parsons (Boston, Beacon Press, 1963), 26-27.

11   Weber, *Essays in Sociology,* 139, 155. At the same time one must be aware of the assertion by Richard Bendix that Weber assumed "the existence of a positive relation ... between Protestant piety and the 'capitalist spirit.'" "The Protestant Ethic Revisited," 299-310 in Reinhard Bendix and Gutenther Roth, *Scholarship and Partisanship: Essays on Max Weber* (Berkeley, University of California Press, 1971), 306. He accepted the fact that "the concept of historical certainty is simply relative, and (that) historical research must make do with the sources at its disposal." *Ibid.,* 310.

12   *Essays in Sociology,* 350.

13   *Religion and the Rise of Capitalism, A Historical Study* (New York, Harcourt, Brace, 1926), 189-273 passim.

14   "Puritanism, Pietism, and Science," 574-606 in *Social Theory and Social Structure.* Revised and enlarged (Glencoe, Illinois, Free Press, 1961), 574-575. See also pg. 380 of the same volume.

15   *Ibid.,* 576.

16   *Ibid.*, 581-582, 589.

17   *Ibid.*, 600.

18   *Ibid.*, 581.

19   *Ibid.*, 578-579, 582, 595.

20   *Ibid.*, 577.

21   *Ibid.*, 590-591.

22   *Ibid.*, 605.

23   *Meeting of East and West*, 142.

24   *The Third Electoral System, 1853-1892. Parties, Voters and Political Cultures* (Chapel Hill, University of North Carolina Press, 1979), 186-187.

25   *Ibid.*, 181, 185, 194.

26   *Ibid.*, 144.

27   Northrop, *Meeting of East and West*, 289.

28   *Ibid.*, 151.

29   In turn, this has given "expression to as many and varied specific moral and religious precepts in the concrete as there are diverse, contradictory, ill-considered impressions and opinions in the introspectively given consciousness of modern man." *Ibid.*, 93. This is why it is almost impossible to generalize about Protestantism in the twentieth century.

30   *Ibid.*, 289.

31   *Leaves from the Notebook of a Tamed Cynic* (Hamden, Connecticut, The Shoe String Press, 1956), 74.

32   Paul A. Carter, *The Decline and Revival of the Social Gospel. Social and Political Liberalism in American Protestant Churches, 1920-1940* (Ithaca, New York, Cornell University Press, 1954), 70.

33   *Ibid.*, 48.

34   Here the author quotes Reinhold Niebuhr. *Ibid.*, 56.

35   In 1925, the state of Tennessee passed a law forbidding the teaching of evolution in public schools. The American Civil Liberties was anxious to test the law and John Thomas Scopes, graduate of the University of Chicago and teacher of Dayton High, was an obvious candidate because he was young and unmarried. At the trial, Scopes ultimately faded from the scene and a new drama unfolded. The defense attorney, the celebrated

Clarence Darrow, invited or challenged the prosecuting attorney, William Jennings Bryan, to take the witness stand and demonstrate his theological expertise. It was a terrible error of vanity. Not only did he display a child's innocence on scientific and philosophical matters, but his "notions of biblical scholarship were grotesque; they might be summed up as 'ignorance plus credulity equals wisdom.'" L. Sprague de Camp, *The Great Monkey Trial* (Garden City, New York, Doubleday, 1968), 2, 8-11, 328. See also the chapter entitled, "Single Combat," 369-414 in ibid.

36   *Encyclopaedia Britannica* in 30 vols. (Chicago, Encyclopaedia Britannica, University of Chicago Press, 1975), V, 71-72.

37   Carter, *Decline and Revival of the Social Gospel*, 48-49. Families with the lowest income and education levels in the United States (below $15,000 a year), believe in God more strongly than prosperous and educated groups. They "are more likely to describe themselves as born-again Christians" and to believe in faith healing and speaking in tongues (charismatic Christians). They are also more likely to pray for material things. "Those with higher incomes and education levels are used to having more choices in their lives, and that extends into the area of religion. ... Those with incomes above $40,000 are almost twice as likely ... as those with incomes below $15,000 ... to say they never received an answer to prayer." George Gallup, Jr. and Jim Castelli, The Gallop Organization in the Kansas City *Star*, June 9, 1990, F-11. A recent New York Times-CBS News Poll indicates that slightly more than a third of 1,384 persons interviewed declared they were regular watchers of evangelical programs. This group was older, less educated, more likely to be rural than city dwellers or suburbanites, and to be women rather than men. New York *Times*, "Polls finds distrust of TV evangelicals," Kansas City *Times*, March 31, 1987, A-6. This was also the opinion of Rev. William F. Fore, author of a new book *Television and Religion*, Barry Garron, "Television in the Role of Religion," Kansas City *Star*, May 14, 1987, C-1.

38   Carter, *Decline and Revival of the Social Gospel*, 53. Even at the beginning of 1929, Baptists not only approved of free enterprise but of business dominance of the social order itself. This stand was characteristic of that of American Protestant churches. *Ibid.*, 102, 144.

39   The Oral Roberts complex at Tulsa, Oklahoma is valued at $500 million dollars. Katherine Foran, "Few are neutral on Oral Roberts," Kansas City *Times*, 28 March 1987, A-1, A-14. Before their downfall, Jim and Tammy Bakker had a net worth of $129 million and reached an estimated 13.5 million homes on PTL cable-television network over 178 stations. Haynes Johnson, "Televangelical drama more like 'Dynasty' or 'Dallas' than any biblical tale." Kansas City *Star*, March 27, 1987, A-15. Based in Baton Rouge, Louisiana, the Rev. Jimmy Swaggart runs a $140 million-a-year television ministry that attracts 8 million weekly viewers, according to the A.C. Nielson television rating service. He has 600 employees. From the Star's Wire Service, "A camp-meeting preacher in the big time," Kansas City *Star*, March 27, 1987, A-6; From the Times News Services, "Turmoil dividing ministers," Kansas City *Times*, March 26, 1987, A-1. Jerry Falwell, whose headquarters are at the Old Time Gospel House and Liberty University in Lynchburg, Virginia, drew an estimated $73 million dollars in contributions last year. The larger religious broadcasting industry itself draws an estimated $2 billion dollars a year income. Bruce Buursma, Chicago Tribune, "TV evangelists avidly espouse prosperity gospel," in Kansas City *Times*, April 17, 1987, A-12.

40   Paul Wenske, "PTL backers not at ease with Falwell," Kansas City *Times*, March 28, 1987, A-1, A-16; Forman, "Few are neutral on Oral Roberts," *loc. cit.*; By the Associated Press, "Roberts' vigil reaching conclusion," Kansas City *Star*, March 31, 1987, A-2; The Associated Press, "Roberts asks for 'overflow'", Kansas City *Times*, April 1, 1987, A-4.

41   Donald Kaul, "Whole evangelical nightmare is a secular humanist's dream come true," Kansas City *Times*, March 28, 1987, A-19. Later evidence indicated that a financial scandal occurred. The Washington Post, "92 million in PTL funds is missing," Kansas City *Times*, May 16, 1987, A-1. Still later, Falwell heard several accusations that Bakker was a homosexual, not a tolerable offense to him. While not confronting his accusers, Bakker and his wife seek to return to the PTL post he formerly held. Observers say the correct forecast is for a long and arduous struggle. "PTL success led to excess and disgrace," Kansas City *Times*, May 30, 1987, A-1, 14.

42   Wenske, "PTL backers not at ease with Falwell," *loc. cit.*

43   See Volume I, Chapter IV. RITUAL: SHAMAN, SORCERER AND PRIEST, footnotes 1-16.

44   Carter, *Decline and Revival of the Social Gospel*, 56-57.

45   From the Star's Wire Services, "A Camp-meeting preacher in the big time," Kansas City *Star*, March 27, 1987, A-6.

46   Peter G. Kreitler, priest at St. Matthews Episcopal Church, Los Angeles Times News Service, "Religious intolerance of powerful TV preachers cannot be tolerated," in Kansas City *Times*, March 20, 1987, A-17.

47   Such was the conclusion of E. Glenn Hinson, church history professor at the Southern Baptist Theological Seminary in Louisville, Kentucky and visiting professor in ecumenics at Catholic University in Washington, D.C., for the academic year of 1986-1987. The Washington Post, "Baptist schism may be the answer to internal fight, scholar says," in Kansas City *Times*, April 4, 1987, C-17.

48   Peter Steinfels, The New York Times, "Big religious battles of today are waged inside denominations," in the Kansas City *Times*, February 24, 1990, E-8.

49   Marjorie Hyer, The Washington Post, "Baptist group blocking U.S. pamphlet on AIDS," in the Kansas City *Times*, October 1, 1988, E-9.

50   New York, The Associated Press, "Modern Baptists set separate agenda," in the Kansas City *Times*, September 17, 1988, E-8.

51   Helen T. Gray, Religion Editor, "Southern Baptists prepare for faceoff," in the Kansas City *Star*, May 19, 1990, E-11. At these sessions, a conservative from Wichita Falls, Texas, defeated a moderate from the Atlanta suburbs by a vote of 58 percent to 42. It was the twelfth straight year conservatives won the presidency. The retiring president, one from Jacksonville, Florida, "told the convention that some want to leave 'room for all' in the denomiation, but 'that's too much room. ...denominations that haven't insisted on an 'infallible inerrant' Bible were bound for 'the garbage dump.'" The Associated Press,

New Orleans, "Southern Baptists choose fundamentalist president," in the Kansas City *Star*, June 13, 1990, A-4.

52   "Modern Baptists set separate agenda," *loc. cit.*, E-8. See also "Southern Baptists prepare for faceoff," *loc. cit.*, E-11. "Although some moderates, including candidate [Rev. Daniel] Vestal [the loser], are fundamentalist, or literalist, about the Bible, they leave room for other understandings under the Baptist view of 'soul competence' of the individual." "Southern Baptists choose fundamentalist president," *loc. cit.*

53   Helen T. Gray, Religion Editor, "Questions of theology costs Baptist missionary his job," in the Kansas City *Times*, September 5, 1988, B-3.

54   "Read his [Bishop Jenkin's] reply to the inquiry 'Who was Jesus?' in a newspaper last Christmas, and you will find no hint of belief that the man Jesus ('impossible to classify') was also, as that [Anglican] creed claims, 'very God of very God' or indeed God in any sense whatever. ... His doubts attack the very heart of Christianity." ... One (friendly) bishop says believers must reckon with the fact ... that it was faith that produced the resurrection stories, not the other way about." "Church unmilitant," in London, *The Economist*, April 1, 1990, 17-18.

55   "Southern Baptists prepare for faceoff," *loc. cit.*, E-11.

56   "Moderate Baptists set separate agenda," *loc. cit.*, E-8.

57   Charles Howard Hopkins, *The Rise of the Social Gospel in American Protestantism, 1865-1915* (New Haven, Yale University Press, 1940), 318.

58   *Ibid.*, 257, 320.

59   It might be argued that, at a minimum, Niebuhr went through a predominantly pastoral phase, a Social Gospel phase, a Marxian one, and a post-Marxian position, marked by an emphasis upon original sin. Carter, *Decline and Revival of the Social Gospel*, 153, 158-159.

60   *Ibid.*, 158-159.

61   Hopkins, *The Rise of the Social Gospel in American Protestantism*, 322.

62   Peter Berger, Brigitte Berger and Hansfried Kellner, *The Homeless Mind. Modernization and Consciousness* (New York, Vintage Books, A Division of Random House, 1974), 181.

63   *Ibid.*, 184-185.

64   *Ibid.*, 186.

65   *Ibid.*, 196.

66   Raymond P. Stearns, *Pageant of Europe. Sources and Selections from the Renaissance to the Present Day* (New York, Harcourt, Brace, 1947), 526-528. The official Catholic view clarifies what Otto von Bismarck called the *Kulturkampf*, or the struggle

74

between Church and State, which raged throughout Europe in the last half of the nineteenth century. The pope specifically protested against the anticlericalism of the Italian state of Piedmont and its attempt to take away from the clergy its traditional rights to educate the young. Likewise, the papacy rejected the assertion by the state of its unlimited civil powers, including the rights of marriage. This was an encroachment upon the sacred sacramental system. *New Catholic Encyclopedia*, XIII, 854-855.

67   *Hippocrates* with an English translation by W.H.S. Jones in 4 vols., (Cambridge, Massachusetts, Harvard University Press, 1948), I, "General Introduction," x, xiv.

68   *The Theory of the Leisure Class. An Economic Study of Institutions* (New York, Modern Library, Random House, 1934), 304-305, 319.

69   *The Education of Henry Adams. An Autobiography,* edited by Henry Cabot Lodge (New York, Houghton-Mifflin, 1924), 476.

70   *Ibid.,* 380.

71   *The Law of Civilization and Decay. An Essay on History* (New York, Macmillan, 1896), 321.

72   *Theory of the Leisure Class,* 302-303.

73   *Ibid.,* 307-309.

74   *Ibid.,* 305.

75   (New York, Harper and Row, 1962), 47, 114.

76   (New York, Macmillan, 1909), 454.

77   *Drift and Mastery. An Attempt to Diagnose the Current Unrest* (New York, Mitchell Kennerley, 1914), 322, 326, 330.

78   "Law in History," 231-248 in *The American Historical Review.* Vol. XXIX, No. 2, January, 1924, 245.

79   *Ibid.,* 244-245.

80   (New York, Harcourt, Brace, 1936), 372.

81   *The Pentagon Papers* as published by the New York *Times.* Based on investigative reporting by Neil Sheehan (New York, Bantam Books, 1971), 495-497.

82   M. Rostovtzeff, *Rome.* Translated from the Russian by J.D. Duff. Elias J. Bickerman, editor. Galaxy Book edition (New York, Oxford University Press, 1967), 319.

83   Kevin O'Shea, "Is Resurrection Theology Outdated," 7-11 in *The Catholic World,* vol. 209, No. 1, April, 1969, 7-9.

84   *New Catholic Encyclopedia,* (New York, McGraw-Hill, 1967), XIV 570.

85   "Pronouncements of the Council," 569-573 in *ibid.*, XIV. For example, the New Constitution on Liturgy stated that it should be the task of the post-conciliar commission to review and pass judgment on the rite and the language of the sacrament of Penance. W.M. Bekkers, "Mercy and the Sacrament of Penance," 228-232 in *The Catholic World*, vol. 203, July, 1966.

86   *Ibid.*, 230-232; *America*, vol. 116, January 21, 1967, 79; *U.S. News and World Report*, vol. 66, May 12, 1969, 16.

87   J.B. Mannion, "The Pope and Mr Dooley on Jazz Masses," 416-417 in *Commonweal*, vol. 85, January 20, 1967.

88   Douglas J. Roche, "The Catholic Revolution," 33-36 in *The Catholic World*, vol. 280, No. 1, October, 1968, 35.

89   W.I. Scobie, "Mini-Mass," 317-318 in *National Review*, vol. 25, March 16, 1973, 317-318. The joint singing and prayers were a fiasco, all of which were a part of the vulgarization of the church. William Buckley, "The Non-Latin Mass," 167-169 in *Commonweal*, vol. 87, No. 6, November 10, 1967, 167. Since we allowed democratic liturgical participation, the "most atrocious sounds" have resulted. Ralph Thibodeau, "Fiasco in Church Music," 73-78 in *Commonweal*, vol. 84, No. 3, April 8, 1966, 78. Perhaps the most devastating commentary on what might be called the humanizing of the mass came from one of the police characters in Joseph Wambaugh's *The Glitter Dome*: "How dare they intrude between him and his God? How dare these benighted priests fail to see that by emasculating the ritual and the mystery and guilt, they castrated The Faith. All the Catholic Church ever had been was ritual and mystery and guilt. And that was Everything. That was Order. Who could wish for more from God or man? Perfect order." (New York, William Morrow, 1981), 103.

90   Roche, "The Catholic Revolution," *loc. cit.*, 34-35.

91   "The Cool Generation and the Church. A Commonweal Symposium," 11-23 in *Commonweal*, vol. 87, No. 1, October 6, 1967, 11, 13-14, 18, 20.

92   An increasing number of committed Catholics now think it fitting and proper to consult their own consciences, rather than ecclesiastical authorities, in matters involving faith and morals. This is accompanied by a pronounced indifference to doctrine and dogman, something that the Catholic Church had always lived by. "Conscience and Orthodoxy," 53-55 in *Commonweal*, vol. 84, No. 1, March 25, 1966, 53.

93   "Out of the Backwaters? The Problem of Catholic University," 39-41 in *Commonweal*, vol. 86, No. 1, March 24, 1967, 41.

94   Sister Annette Waters, "The 'Double Bind' in Religious Life Today," 22-26 in *The Catholic World*, vol. 210, No. 1, 255, October, 1969, 25. As an example of the second class status of nuns, Vatical II started without them. Later, a few were admitted as auditors only. "All Things Considered. The Emerging Nun," 104 in *Commonweal*, vol. 82, No. 4, April 16, 1965.

95   "The Woman Intellectual and the Church. A Commonweal Symposium," 446-458 in *Commonweal*, vol. 85, No. 16, January 26, 1967, 448.

96   "Restive Nuns: Steady Loss Among Sisters," 66-68 in *Time*, vol. 89, January 13, 1967, 66.

97   The noted Jesuit sociologist, Eugene Schallert, recently estimated that fifteen percent - or about 75,000 priests - would have left the ministry by 1975. John C. Schwarz, "Celibacy: the foundations have shifted," 254-257 in *Catholic World Journal*, vol. 212, Fall, 1971, 254. An estimated 2,500 Roman Catholic priests in the United States left the ministry in 1968 and forty percent were married within a year. "Why Priests Marry?" 105-110 in *Reader's Digest*, vol. 95, December, 1969, 105. (Condensed from the *Christian Herald*). The National Association for Pastoral Renewal, an organization of nine hundred priests, met at a three-day conference at Notre Dame in 1967. It passed a virtually unanimous resolution asking the American hierarchy for individual choice rather than required celibacy. John A. O'Brien, "Crisis in the Catholic Church," 1233-1234 in *Christian Century*, vol. 88, October 20, 1971, 1233. Later, the Dutch Pastoral Council, a Church body consisting of bishops, priests, nuns, seminarians and lay men and women, voted 93 to 2 in favor of abrogating required celibacy. *Time*, vol. 95, January 19, 1970, 49.

98   Boniface A. Willems, "The Death of God Phenomenon," 17-19 in *The Catholic World*, vol. 204, No. 1, October, 1966, 17.

99   *A Question of Conscience* (New York, Harper and Row, 1967), 138, 178, 217-218, 242, 257. The essence of the Marian doctrine or Mariology, involved belief in the following: the Immaculate Conception, virginity, divine motherhood and Assumption or bodily ascent into Heaven.

100   Davis, *A Question of Conscience*, 257. Thus, a Catholic theologian said what Protestants have been claiming for centuries. Daniel Callahan, "Pie in the Sky Theology," 40-44 in *Commonweal*, vol. 88, No. 1, March 22, 1968, 40.

101   *The Sacred Canopy*, 108, 155, 166-168, 186.

102   *Civilization on Trial* (New York, Oxford University Press, 1948), 236-237.

103   "The Pope Gets Tough," *U. S. News and World Report*, vol. 101, No. 20, November 17, 1986, 67-68.

104   Charles E. Curran, "On dissent in the church," *Commonweal*, vol. 113, No. 15, September 12, 1986, 462.

105   "The Curran Effect," in *ibid.*, 452.

106   Richard A. McCormick, "The Search for Truth in the Catholic Context," *America*, Vol. 155, No. 13, 281.

107   From the Economist (London), "Can the pope command his flock in America?," in The Kansas City *Star*, April 29, 1984, D-1, 4. Reaction has been the same in both Western Europe and Australia. "Pope urges Catholics to return to church," The Kansas City *Times*, November 27, 1986, C-15.

108   George W. Cornell, AP Religion Writer, "Homosexuals see 'domino effect' after tougher Catholic stance," in The Kansas City *Times*, May 2, 1987, E-8.

109   "The Pope Gets Tough," *loc. cit.*, 66.

110   *Ibid.*, 64.

111   Rick Montgomery, Michelle Ruess and Terry Hughes, "Opinions differ in K. C. on Vatican moves against U. S. clerics, liberal stance," in The Kansas City *Star*, November 16, 1986, A-10.

112   Tom Nugent, "A birthday, but not a quiet one," in The Kansas City *Star*, November 5, 1989, E-1. For example, in downtown Detroit, Our Lady of Rosary Church "was among 24 inner-city churches whose futures were labeled questionable in the second stage of the largest Catholic church retrenchment in U. S. history. Thirty other parishes had been closed during phase one in early 1989." Gretel Wikle, The Associate Press, "Church survives budget cutting," in The Kansas City *Star*, March 17, 1990, E-11.

113   Elaine Adams, Metropolitan Star, "Overworked, taken for granted, priests near point of exhaustion," in The Kansas City *Times*, February 17, 1990, E-8.

114   From the Economist (London), "Can the Pope command his flock in America?," in The Kansas City *Star*, April 29, 1984, 4.

115   Helen Gray, Religion Editor, "Married priests await call from their church," in The Kansas City *Star*, March 17, 1990, E-10. A Roman Catholic petition, emanating from Chicago and appearing as an advertisement in The New York *Times*, asserted "that Catholics may be deprived of the sacraments unless the decline in the number of priests ... is reversed with the opening ... to women and married priests." A half-dozen prominent Catholics spearheaded the movement. The New York Times, Chicago, "Catholics appealing for reforms," in The Kansas City *Times*, February 28, 1990. A-3.

116   Marjorie Hyer, "U. S. bishops reject Vatican paper defining their ties to Rome," in The Kansas City *Times*, November 17, 1988, A-15.

117   Peter Beaumont, London Observer Service, "Fewer priests serving Britain's Catholics," in The Kansas City *Times*, March 3, 1990, E-11.

118   The quote was by Martin E. Marty, church historian at the University of Chicago. See "The Pope gets tough," *loc. cit.*, 65-66.

119   Kathleen Neumeyer, "Finding God in the 90s," in The Kansas City *Star*, October 1, 1989, H-1.

120   Flora Lewis, Cairo. New York Times News Service, "Fundamentalism thrives in three religions; fills vacuum in world of ideas," The Kansas City *Star*, December 29, 1986, A-9.

121   *America. Religions and Religion*, 370.

122   Redfield, *Folk Culture*, 349.

123   Actually he reversed the so-called natural order of events. He worked on Sundays and made the other six his Sabbath in which to absorb the sublime revelations of nature.

78

"Introduction," by Sherman Paul, xv in Henry David Thoreau, *Walden*. Edited with an Introduction and Notes by Sherman Paul (Boston, Houghton-Mifflin, 1957).

Chapter XIV

HISTORY
VERSUS
COMMUNIST RUSSIA (SOVIET UNION)

... society cannot exist without a 'dominant' or 'political' class.... ... the state, cannot be anything other than the organization of the minority. It is the aim of this minority to impose upon the rest of society a 'legal' order which ... can never be truly representative of the majority. The majority is thus permanently incapable of self-government. Even when the discontent of the masses culminates in a successful attempt to deprive the bourgeoisie of power there springs from the masses a new organized minority which raises itself to the rank of a governing class.

... There is no essential contradiction between the doctrine that history is a record of continued series of class struggles and the doctrine that class struggles invariably culminate in the creation of new oligarchies

which undergo fusion with the old. ...

Thus the social revolution would not effect any real modification of the internal structure of the mass. The socialists might conquer, but not socialism, which would perish in the moment of its adherents' triumph.

"*Democracy and the Iron Law of Oligarchy,*" 342-356 in Robert Michels, *Political Parties. A Sociological Study of the Oligarchial Tendencies of Modern Democracy.* Translated by Eden and Cedar Paul. Introduction by Seymour Martin Lipset (New York, Colier-Macmillan, 1962), 353-355. Author's Preface, Basle, 1915.

It has been over seventy years since the Bolshevik Revolution of 1917; thus, it is necessary to list one's priorities, else risk getting lost in the subject matter itself. The following, therefore, is an approximate statement of our mission. While it may be a bit more, it should not be less:

1) A brief explanation of how and why the predecessor governments, the Romanoffs and that of Alexander Kerensky, fell from grace.

2) Explore the old principle of Edmund Burke - and reaffirmed by Robert Michels - when a people overthrow their old masters by violence, they are apt to end up with a new set.

3) How and why the bright and easy promises of peace, bread, liberty and land were all quickly circumvented by the Machiavellian policies of Lenin and Trotsky.

4) How and why Russian communism appears compatible with religious systems which proclaim a monopoly on Ultimate Truth.

5) How management's efficiency and speed-up system of production proved irresistible to a state which was itself managing production, thereby betraying the workers.

6) The prevalence of the Freudian theme - God the Father - in Stalin's

erratic and brutal social order.

  7) How account for the prolonged economic failure of the communist regime to rival the productive apparatus of the West?

  8) Why is the most dangerous period for a repressive government when it tries to reform itself?

  A new god in the form of a secular state appeared on the European scene with the French Revolution of the late eighteenth century. Man, not God, now occupied the center stage of history as producer, director and leading actor in the drama. It was this state which in nineteenth century Europe wrested the education of the young from the tutelage of the Catholic clergy. Since, prior to our Revolution, there had been a separation of Church and State in America, the latter enjoyed uncontested control of a vast majority in its public school system. This obviated the need for open conflict. The second secular spin-off, as a result of the decline of ritual man in the West, was communism, an avowed foe of the traditional religious impulse. It is here that we begin our inquiry and analysis. While the worship of this entity of the secular state by the common man has persisted to the present day, events in our life time caused us to question the morality of that god, if not its immortality.

  Despite the dangerous risk of over-simplification, time does not permit more than a brief summation of how and why the Bolsheviks came to power in Russia in November, 1917. As to the fall of the Romanoff dynasty, no one has explained it any simpler than Sir Bernard Pares: "The reign of Nicholas II had gone bankrupt of itself."[1] His tragic mistake had been to attempt to combine autocracy and domestic repression with the equally unrelenting pursuit of an unpopular World War I, one studded with humiliating military defeats and frightful losses of manpower. In the public eye, both were attributed to fraud, corruption and incompetence in high places.[2] The error of his immediate successor, Alexander Kerensky, had been to continue and intensify the imperialist war by the fiasco of a July offensive. At the same time, he insisted that all domestic reforms be postponed until the termination of that hated war.[3] Meanwhile, the

Provisional Government proved no more competent than that of the Tsar in coping with the very social, political and economic unrest produced by that bourgeois authority.[4] Further, Kerensky's absence at the front allowed the Bolsheviks to gather strength and resolve. As one observer wrote: "...there was little to be done to help a government which did so little to help itself."[5] Only the Right was capable of checkmating the Bolsheviks. However, it was discredited following General Kornilov's break with Kerensky in August and his aborted attempt to establish a dictatorship. The failure of this reactionary scheme, one backed by the financier, Zayoyko, created a political vacuum into which the Left was willingly drawn.[6]

Accurately sensing that the great majority, made up of workers, peasants and soldiers, was both war-weary and anxious for immediate and drastic reforms,[7] the Bolsheviks came to power by means of unrealistic and deceptive promises of immediate peace, land, bread and freedom. Lenin was the architect of this master plan.[8] His "April Theses" called for "the abolition of police, army, the confiscation of all landlord estates, and the transfer of control over the production and distribution of goods into the hands of the Soviet."[9] At the time, the local Soviets appeared to run on democratic principles and procedures.[10] This proclamation had an irresistible appeal to the peasant army conscript.[11] It largely displaced the old professional army, one badly decimated by three years of brutal warfare.[12] Lenin recalled the original revolution against the Tsar had been launched in Petrograd by an army of recruits when the real army was still in the field against the German foe.[13] As a master strategist, Lenin was well-prepared to take advantage of those class and occupational interests which were willing to engage in self-deception for Bolshevik ends.

However, self-deception was not confined to foes, but penetrated upper levels of the revolutionary party. Take Raphael R. Abramovitch, for example. A man of high principle, he never sought to restore the Tsar to power, nor supported foreign intervention in behalf of the Whites. He believed instead in the principle of the self-determination of peoples. He was sympathetic to the idea of an early peace with Germany, one which Lenin and Trotsky exploited for party purposes. Finally, he believed in the ultimate ideas of socialism, to which Bolsheviks first gave lip service and later obviously betrayed.[14]

As my co-author observed, there are obvious parallels between Christianity and communism. The similarity of the two accounts for much of the hostility. They are natural competitors. Both are playing for the highest stakes - the Salvation of humanity - and there can only be one custodian. Both begin with their god, the Christians with the god of the Hebrews and the communists with theirs, history. Both have their messiah or prophet, the Christians, Jesus, and the communists, Marx; both of these were utopians, promising bliss, peace and joy, following a passage of time. Their word was carried most effectively by those who never saw the prophet, Paul for Jesus and Lenin for Marx. Both prophets would probably be confounded at what history and an institutionalized bureaucracy did to their pure ideology, substituting both materialism and power politics. Happily, both belief systems are able perpetually to shrug off failure. Actually, each has no empirical accountability because their miracles are not scheduled until the end of history, and history never ends. Time, therefore, never dims the appeal of the Second Coming, or the Day of Judgment, to the professing Christian, or the withering away of the state to the communist, followed by the emergence of individual freedom and real happiness for the first time anywhere on earth. To each, therefore, his own Heaven. The job of each is to peddle it abroad, throughout the globe itself. Thus there can be no compromise between the two, Christianity and communism.

However, as younger son Jeff argued, there are times when, precisely because of the similarity between Christianity and communism, individual priests, without compromising beliefs in their Lord and Savior, attempt to utilize communism in efforts to aleviate the plight of the very poor and homeless. True, these are, in the eyes of the Vatican at least, misguided, if not "renegade," priests. These aberrations from the norm occur all over Latin America and, today at least, notably in Nicaragua and El Salvador. Tom and I were thinking primarily of the perpetual duel between the two hierarchies, the two bureaucracies. We concede, for example, that it is at least theoretically possible for a "good" Italian communist also to be a committed Christian.

Although communism also accepted the peculiarly Western notion of the perfectability of man,[15] it early and conspicuously failed to attain its goal in Soviet Russia. Here one has to take note of Arthur Koestler who, condemning Soviet Russia for its corruption of the idea itself,[16] nevertheless pointed out the successes of communism in the Twenties in small frontier settlements in Israel. Yet he was quick to conclude that an idea which worked for a time in very small and elite societies might be totally unacceptable in vastly larger social orders.[17] Therefore, the failure of communism in the first real socialist state is impossible to gloss over. One here ignores the fact that time after time it callously, even ruthlessly, exploited workers in Slavic lands who were supposedly ideological, class and blood brothers. However, all idea systems are failures if judged solely by the way they treat outsiders. Rather, we are concerned with the way in which the great and luminous prospects of personal freedom amidst economic plenty quickly went down the drain under both Lenin and his successors.

The early and dramatic failure of Soviet Russia to redeem its promises to the masses inspired several scholarly explanations. The traditional, and perhaps liberal, view was the civil war, foreign interventions, the war with Poland, the disorganization of modes of production and transportation, shortage of technicians and the like. With the passage of time, however, it was more apt to be attributed to the flinty character of the leaders themselves, to their authoritarian ideas and, finally, to the inherent weakness of an overcentralized state and excessively bureaucratic authority. One, therefore, should not be surprised to discover that students of anarchism arrived at the same conclusion.[18] The insistence the characteristics of Soviet ideology and practice belong wholly to a bourgeois past, which was bound to betray the free circulation of revolutionary ideas,[19] reminds us of the admonition by Edmund Burke. When a people seek to destroy their old masters, they emerge with a set of new ones.[20] Milovan Djilas also opted for an internal explanation. There is always latent civil war between a communist government and its people. The state is not merely the instrument of tyranny; society itself is in almost continual opposition to the oligarchy. It forces the latter to reduce the opposition by force.[21] Even more spectacularly, however, the frenzy of the state machine, or its paranoid ruler, at times causes it suddenly and irrationally to destroy a substantial portion of its own ruling oligarchy. In such a secular state, armed with its own Index and Inquisition, the only constant factors appear to be a shortage of ideas, information, and news,[22] and a like one in consumer goods. The latter, apparently, is due to the almost necessary inefficiency of the vast bureaucratic structure, certainly as compared with the magnitude of its task of manipulating an entire economy.[23]

Almost from the outset of the Revolution the chief victim was the right of free thought and dissent. The tremendous free flow of information or news, and the tolerance for all sorts of differences of opinion in the first days and months of the March Revolution,[24] soon evaporated. It persisted for as long as the Provisional Government under Kerensky lasted, or until November, 1917. It was the first time in history that Russia had enjoyed such freedom and perhaps the last as well. During this period the radical and liberal intelligentia, principally the middle class, played the leading role. These thinkers impartially rejected autocracy, whether that of the Tsars or of the Bolsheviks.[25] In July, 1917, the masses were not only free from Kerensky's influence, but that of the Bolsheviks as well.[26] Yet the fact that they had never experienced freedom, that it had never travelled in the historical bloodstream of Russia, boded ill for the new experiment.[27] Even the day after the Bolsheviks seized power on November 7, the political forces of the opposition, despite the suppression of some newspapers, enjoyed a considerable measure of free play.[28] The last hurrah for political and social freedom occurred in late November when, in the last free election with universal suffrage, the Bolsheviks received a minority of the vote.[29]

Continuing economic and social dislocations soon produced a feeling that bread was more valuable than freedom. This was accompanied by a rising spirit of frustration, intolerance and a mood for action. Even before the November Revolution was consummated, the Second Congress of Soviets of Workers' and Soldiers' Deputies was the scene of mutual suspicion and hostility. It was difficult for speakers to obtain a hearing without being interrupted by shouts, "Lie, you lie." When fifty delegates from the Duma, the Mensheviki and Socialist Revolutionaries and the Executive Committee of the Peasants, seceded and withdrew from the hall, the remaining ones hooted, jeered, and cursed them.[30] Only Trotsky, in a celebrated speech, coolly dismissed them as bound for the "garbage-can of history."[31] Later, when a delegate from the Union of Railway Workers took the podium and declared the assembly was illegal following the departure of the fifty, he could scarcely be heard because of the verbal abuse he took from the enraged congress.[32]

Authorities generally agreed the last vestiges of such freedom had completely disappeared by sometime in the following year, 1918. Until July, 1918, the Soviets which existed were not dependent upon ideology and, instead, envisioned the widest possible consultation with the people, all working people that is.[33] However, Soviet elections became a farce in January, 1918, when the Constitutent Assembly, elected on the basis of universal suffrage, was promptly dispersed by Communist armed force. This episode occurred because the Bolsheviks had lost and were a minority.[34] The Bolsheviks were always determined either to dominate the Constitutent Assembly or to disperse it.[35] Even as early as October, 1917, Leon Trotsky piously noted the disappearance of the free-thinking intellectual in elected public assemblies.[36] The most caustic critic of the communists, Alexander Podrabinek, restricted the area of freedom in Russia to only four months, or March to June of 1917. That was the only time during which there were no political prisoners.[37]

With regard to the disappearance of free speech and press, Lenin bore as much or more responsibility than any other individual. Only Trotsky rivaled him in that regard.[38] Lenin manifested a spirit of intransigence in the first speech delivered after his arrival. He never relaxed that mood. His unbounded faith, his extreme views, his dogmatism, all of these prevented granting any tolerance to those disagreeing with him, no matter how close philosophically.[39] Even loyal and competent communists like Nikolai Bukharin lamented that Lenin did not give a tinker's damn for the opinions of others, but sought rather to impose his will upon everyone.[40] In September, 1917, Lenin despaired of waiting for a Congress of Soviets to assume power legally. Because of this, he proposed to arrest the Democratic Congress at the Alexandrine Theatre in Petrograd. The dirty job would be done, not by the Soviets, but by factory workers.[41] The fact that the event did not take place is relatively unimportant. Politically, his doctrine of intolerance toward those of little faith was based on his conception of the state as an adversary of freedom.[42] Its corollary was Lenin's instinctive distrust of the intellectual who tended to remain an individualist, and thus a potential deviant, even though nominally a loyal party member in good standing.[43] Thus, Lenin believed that the new Russian state, in order to succeed, would have to emulate the Prussian war model.[44] Of course its rigor, its violence - supposedly at least - would be temporary and terminal with the suppression of the counter-revolution,[45] and the consequent inauguration of the Golden Age. This was for Marxism the equivalent of the Second Coming of Christ for the Christians and the end of history, as far as it meant conflict and strife. The mythology called for it to be a Heaven on Earth.[46] Nevertheless, in his book *State and Revolution,* Lenin appeared to confess with some relief that the process of the state withering away would be a slow one of long duration.[47]

Worthy of special mention was Lenin's betrayal of the freedom and well-being of the Russian laborer for whom he supposedly bled. Before the Revolution, Lenin labelled as wage slavery the machine speed-up, piece and work, and incentive system.[48] All of these were featured in the efficiency system of Frederick Winslow Taylor,[49] one much admired by the industrialist, Henry Ford.[50] However, by the spring of 1918, Lenin discovered the virtues of that American system. He then confessed his belief that production output for each worker should be set by management - a grand piece work scheme - and bonuses ought to be offered for outstanding productivity. Large-scale industry demanded absolute submission to the single will of management, now in the hands of the state. While production was always necessary, so the argument ran, democracy was not. The pernicious aspect of a democracy of production fostered a whole series of radically fallacious ideas.[51] Because of a heightened concern for economic efficiency and the need for increased productivity, Trotsky agreed. He was thus able to rationalize in a workers' state - as opposed to management - the state normally had a right to coerce a citizen into laboring at any activity and at a time and place of its own choosing.[52]

The novel aspect of this sort of logic, by the standards of anarchists, presented the worker with a bourgeois state without the bourgeoisie themselves. It was not surprising, therefore, that by the spring of 1918, the authority of workers' soviets was terminated.[53] For a time industries were regulated by a Troika, consisting of workers' committees, the Party cell and the manager. This ploy was actually dispensed with in 1924, although not officially buried until 1937. Meanwhile, in 1929, the Party's Central Committee showed their contempt for the system by a resolution denying workers' committees any authority to interfere with a management function.[54] While the communist bureaucracy professed itself very satisfied with the administration of the piece-work system in its hands, the informed worker saw it in precisely the same terms as did his American counterpart. It was an excellent managment device to divide and conquer the masses, by pitting one man against another.[55]

No analysis of Lenin, however, seems complete without a resort to religious terminology. What was important, even crucial, was his fantastic faith in the cause, his inflexible determination to see it become actualized and, finally, the audacity of his vision and design.[56] The marriage between Lenin and communism seemed ideal. First consider the apocalyptic character of the message he both inherited and carried. Marx subscribed to one of the great eschatalogical myths of the Eastern Mediterranean world, that of the just man whose woes were destined to shape the future. He seasoned this myth with a Judeo-Christian one, obtaining a prophetic vision of the role of the proletariat as Messiah and of the final struggle between good and evil, ending, naturally enough, with the triumph of the former.[57] William Henry Chamberlin sensed this when he described Lenin in terms most often reserved for Old Testament prophets, Mohammed and even Jesus himself. Apparently indifferent to his own fame and fate,[58] Lenin was "the incarnate doctrine of militant Marxism, the revolutionary word become flesh."[59] While it clearly falls outside our scope, one would have to say this about the political events occurring in Russia throughout the year 1917: to write of them without reference to their magical and mystical elements would be to fail to grasp the spiritual aspect and thus a more complete meaning.

In a broader sense, the prompt disappearance of the right to critical thought and dissent came as a natural consequence of the triumph of the Bolsheviks. First, the communist machine stifled dissent from all its foes.

When this was accomplished, it pursued the same ends with regard to the minority party within the party itself. Finally, members of the majority party inevitably lost their freedom.[60] When weaker than a liberal adversary, the communist always asks for freedom because it is the liberal's principle. When stronger, he always deprives the liberals of it because it is not a communist principle.[61]

Without general elections, a free press and assembly, a Jeffersonian conflict of ideas in the market place and public forums, the verve is sapped and dies out in every instituion. All that remains is a mere semblance of life with bureaucracy providng the overt activity. As public life vanished, its successor was a few dozen party leaders who direct and rule by their inexhaustible energy and boundless confidence. The general reader will be surprised, one suspects, to discover the author of that observation was Rosa Luxemburg.[62]

The situation only worsened after the death of Lenin and the rise of Stalin. To buttress this generalization one needs only a few examples of almost incredible character. From 1929-1933 millions of kulaks in the Ukraine were either seized and shot, forced to emigrate, or allowed to starve because they dared oppose the imposition of the huge and impersonal state farm system.[63] Stalin was the architect of that vast and effective killing machine. Nikita S. Khrushchev merely confirmed in 1956 what historians had already concluded. The Moscow Trials of 1937-1938, which liquidated between a quarter to a half of the Communist leadership,[64] were due primarily to the paranoia of Stalin.[65] After the war, Khrushchev observed, he was even more hostile, brutal and suspicious.[66]

Meanwhile, under Stalin the party executed three complete and sudden reversals in attitudes toward the outside world. Nothing remained intact save the old leadership which repudiated previous policy after previous policy. Upon the imposition of the Popular Front of 1935, aimed at Hitler Germany, the party suddenly ceased to castigate capitalists, now calling them friends and allies. But after the Soviet-Nazi pact of August, 1939, and the beginning of World War II, Britain and France were suddenly imperialistic powers once more. Only after Hitler's invasion of Soviet Russia in July, 1941, and military supplies arrived from Britain and America, did the communist oligarchy regard the West as decent again.[67] The fact that Stalin could make a series of dreadful errors, including ignoring Britain's warning of an impending attack on the Soviet Union in 1941,[68] and pay no penalty for his stubborness and stupidity, could only occur in a system utterly without the freedom of inquiry. Finally, it is noteworthy to observe that Krushchev's revelations about Stalin were confined to the communist elite. They were not disseminated to the masses where the impact would have been unpredictable.[69]

At this point that Margaret Mead comes to our rescue, explaining why and how the Russians can tolerate sudden shifts either in domestic policy, or those with regard to the outside world. She does it by virtue of the use of the magical and the mystical. One recalls reading about thirty-five years ago a little book she wrote on *Soviet Attitudes Toward Authority*. One episode was used to illustrate how the power elite employed folklore to control the masses. During the era of Stalin, the mythology was, while Russians were safely tucked into bed, Stalin himself stood on the Kremlin walls, seeing everything and understanding everything. He was at the same time the Loving Father and the Great Protector. No fiber of his being reflected fatigue.[70] The seedbed for these nursery tales for adults had been laid down by Lenin. Because the leader had a perfect ability to diagnose reality, he could predict the future and develop a plan which would maximize the benefits from its flow.[71] Stalin's heart not only beat for the nation but, miraculously, there was in every Soviet citizen a particle of the great man.[72]

Meanwhile, the party itself was the fortunate repository for truth, integrity, and justice. Good party members, therefore, must regard themselves as mere tools to carry out the party line. They must never relax, nor look to enjoy the so-called good things of this life. The present generation was not born to rest, although it might bequeath that to its successors who would bless its memory. The function of the good party member with relation to his fellows, then, was first to instruct and then check for deviation. Everyone was a potential doubter, a sinner, a heretic. The smallest doubt could lead to the most monumental heresy and treason against the Worker's Paradise. Not only was the heretic himself corrupt but his mere presence in society spread the poison. Logic demanded his immediate elimination, even though he might be one's best friend or lover.[73] Since everybody was a sinner, and no one was innocent, it was unnecessary to prove a suspect guilty of a specific crime as in Western law. It was enough to know that he made errors, that he was guilty of either omissions or commissions and thereby was undeserving. Further, there was little distinction in sinful matters between thought and deed. Finally, it was necessary that the accused come to bear the same opinion of himself as entertained by the state prosecution.[74]

In short, the purity of the state demanded there be no true compromise with evil, whether when dealing with the wretched traitor at home or in matters of foreign policy with the unsaved or non-communists.[75] Finally, it was never necessary that the average Russian comprehend Truth, just where his party stood today. He had to be prepared to trample upon yesterday's Truth unless it was in accord with that prevailing today. Yesterday's hero might be today's villain.[76] In short, everything had to be up-to-date in the Soviet Union.

Mead's conclusion, therefore, should surprise few when she observed the behavior of the Soviet Union today had much more in common with a religious movement in its early days than it had with those of current Western democracies.[77]

Our own preference - without regard to time - is to compare behavior of the elite in the Soviet Union with dominant religious societies which know the Truth and, consequently, fears its deviation by a minority of dissenters, or subversives. In such instances, it is obvious that the moral, as well as the political, duty of law enforcement officials is to quiet the clamor, no matter the method of interrogation and punishment of the individuals involved. Such a philosophy of community self-preservation served equally well for the Catholic Index and Inquisition following the Albigensian Crusade of the 13th century,[78] and that of Calvin's sixteenth century Geneva when silencing theological differences of preachers like Jerome Bolsec and Michael Servetus.[79] In all such instances, historical truth is less important than the affirmation of the principle: my doxy is orthodoxy and yours is heterodoxy.[80]

Unlike Mead, we do not think such behavior was necessarily confined to early days. For example, take the doctrine of papal infallibility which was laid down in 1870.[81] If a dictator were assumed to be infallible in matters of faith and morals, he would need no other powers. No deed, certainly of a political nature, could safely be affirmed to be outside that jurisdiction. As for sudden revolutions in internal policy, few could be more dramatic than the decision to outlaw the traditional Roman mass as a result of Vatican II in the Sixties. Those who then clung steadfastly to the customs of yesterday certainly embarrassed the authorities. They had already moved ahead, but now lacked the necessary coercive force to impose the absolute conformity which the Papal Syllabus of Errors in 1864 allowed for and justified.[82]

Unfortunately, political freedom did not follow Stalin's demise in 1953 and the imposition of rule by a Central Committee headed by Khrushchev. There are at least two explanations for this. One is if, as it did temporarily, the state relaxed its discipline,[83] intellectuals and artists were soon thereafter accused of taking advantage. The inevitable crackdown occurred.[84] One astute observer of the contemporary international scene concluded that the most dangerous period for a bad government occurs when it tries to reform itself.[85] This situation is easy to envisage within a state system where intellectuals were always suspect, and why not? Who more than they were apt to originate and nurture an individual idea which threatened to topple the whole questionable edifice of thought control?[86] It appears that communist suspicion of intellectuals goes back to the very origin of the revolution.[87] According to Leon Trotsky, the first result of the October-November Revolution was that the local Soviets happily divested themselves of both the officer class and intellectuals. When the Congress met at Smoly on October 25, working-class gray prevailed in all the faces and clothes. Gone were the eye-glasses of officers and the neckties of intellectuals. It was a plebian congress of workers and soldiers from the local Soviets.[88]

The other hypothesis was advanced by Djilas who felt the party, knowingly or not, relinquished all opportunities for substantial change when it unveiled Stalin, the ex-God, as monster. Destroying the cult of creator, it simultaneously gave a death blow to its own ideological basis. Having renounced Stalin's methods, the ruling class was unable to preserve its dogma, because its methods were only an expression of it. Since the ideology of communism could no longer be relied on to keep the people in line, power must remain as the main means by which the oligarchy controlled the masses.[89]

In the post-Stalin era there was no relaxation by the state of its intent to use the Gulag Archipelago principle in order to cripple and destroy its foes, particularly intellectuals. Worse than mere prisons, these so-called corrective labor camps annihilated the intellectuals. They were denied books, paper and the solitude necessary for thought and spiritual comfort. They were forced to participate both in exhausting physical labor and in the "humiliating, buzzing ant heap" where no serious thought could be entertained and explored. Insidiously like Nazi concentration camps in World War II, the inmates were pitted against one another, and forced to compete for a very limited amount of bread and potatoes. No wonder gentle souls quickly perished. The institution, however, merely lived up to the expectations of its founders.[90] Despite the psychiatric violence, the secret trials, forged testimony and extremely harsh "legal" judgments, not a single person had been released since 1958 from these living hells as a result of a humane impulse by state authorities. Political motivations invariably accounted for any such release.[91]

Recently the state added a new and even more terrible weapon to its arsenal against its intellectual dissenters. A mailed summons is dispatched to a particular individual to report to hospital X. Failure to show up, or a reluctance to accept "treatment" is considered a sure sign the particular party is urgently in need of help. Once entered on hospital rolls, however, no remedy is available. One cannot defend himself because he has been pronounced insane. He cannot lodge a formal protest with authorities because he has not been arrested. He cannot appeal because he has not been sentenced. Meanwhile, drug injections have already begun. They continue until the patient is docile and easily manipulated by the hospital staff. Serious physical damage to the individual frequently occurs.[92]

Finally, one prerequisite for any successful revolution is, far from destroying the existing economic structure, it must institute one which fed, housed and clothed its citizens better than did the preceding system.[93] However, for seventy years following their seizure of power, the communists have been unable to compete with the "free" enterprise system of the West. André Gide was only one of a host of travellers to Soviet Russia who were perennially distressed and dismayed by the drabness and ugliness of clothes worn, by the poor quality of goods displayed in shops and the long hours spent in a queue for bread and consumer goods.[94] Others quite properly blamed the forced imposition of the state farm system for the breakdown in agricultural production. Forty years after its inception, the state itself was forced to import twenty million tons of grain.[95] Finally, we think the most convincing explanation for such dramatic failures was the entire economy of the Soviet Union resembled a large company town in Pennsylvania in the late nineteenth century. Order and discipline were obtained only at the expense of freedom and initiative.[96]

In 1985, two authors in *Foreign Affairs* spoke bluntly: Soviet propaganda customarily declared the final victory between capitalism and communism would rest with the system which produced the finest technology and achieved the highest production. Two-thirds of a century after coming to power, and forty years after World War II, there is no evidence that the Communist productive apparatus is superior. On the contrary, everything points to a virtual capitalistic victory. Indeed, the immediate problem for a perceptive elite in the Kremlin might be not how immediately to catch up with the West, but, rather, how to deter falling further behind.[97]

In retrospect, two opinions by historians tend to remain fixed in mind. Edward Hallett Carr, at the end of World War II, reminds us of the hope of many intellectuals. He postulated the measures of collective organization by the Soviets might mitigate some of the hardships and failures imposed by the rugged individualism of capitalism, and the future might see an ultimate synthesis of the two opposing ways of life.[98] One now perceives that this was the last opportunity for Soviet Russia peacefully to influence the West. Under Stalin, it was fated to flub the opportunity. The reflection of the other thinker was by Arnold Toynbee. While seeing the birth of communism as a protest against Western failure to live up to its Christian commitments in economic and social life, he preceives it as a remedy far worse than the disease itself. As both a doctrine and a way of life he finds it repugnant and unacceptable.[99]

We feel compelled to make one final, however tentative, observation. This deals with Mikhail Gorbachev, and his recent attempted reforms of the social order in the Soviet Union. Dissidents have been released from prison and others, including many Jews, have been allowed to emigrate. Writers like Boris Pasternak have been restored to honor. The media has been allowed to report on some, if not all, the domestic horrors under Stalin. Gorbachev has publicly attacked drug and alcohol abuse, absenteeism, corruption, inertia and other deterrents to a greater production and a higher standard of living. He envisioned not only the decentralization of economic controls and a general dismantling of the old bureaucracies, but the democratization of political life.

Let us start with one American expert on Soviet affairs who believes Gorbachev's politics and economic program is aimed at undoing the heavy hand of Joe Stalin, and the restoration of something like Lenin's New Economic Policy of the early Twenties. Then a private market economy existed along-side state enterprises, censorship was relatively mild, and open debate was the rule in government councils. It is a mistake to argue that these reforms are more apparent than real, or that nothing has changed, or that it is all a plot to soften Western European resistance to new Soviet aggressions. These traditional arguments not only obscure "one of the most fateful political dramas of our time," but block out the possibility of a new and significant relationship with Soviet Russia.[100]

Those more cautious argue that, while it is too soon to speak with authority, it is not premature to postulate three possible outcomes. The first: Gorbachev is still persuaded of the system's potential and does not regard radical reform as necessary. He will be content to streamline the system, fight corruption and improve performances in general. He will be to the Soviet economy what Franklin D. Roosevelt was to capitalism in the depression. The second theory postulates Gorbachev will begin with the process above, but will soon be convinced that radical reforms are necessary to check the general economic and social decline, and proceed to carry them out. The third option of observers is a bit more complicated. It assumes that Gorbachev wants to achieve radical reforms, but senses, given the strength of opposition to fundamental reforms at all levels, he cannot openly advocate them at present. Nevertheless, should he ultimately be in such a position, he and his associates might be caught up in the partial reforms they had already instituted, and thus committed to the vested interest of their constituencies. This is known in the United States as the art of settling for half a loaf.[101]

We think Gorbachev came close to summarizing the problem when, in June of 1986, he had a private meeting with about thirty leading Soviet writers: "Between the people who want and long for changes and the leadership that encourages them, there is an administrative staff of the party apparatus and the authorities who do not want changes...." The result thus far has been much anguish. To the list of his natural political opponents, however, one would have to add those managers and workers who feel threatened by his attacks on slovenly production attitudes and standards; others were alienated by his opposition to drugs, alcohol, prostitution and his advocacy of sex education.[102]

When and if, therefore, one assumes the present or imminent possibility of genuine reforms and the relaxation of the powers of state, special attention must be paid to the postulate: the most dangerous time for a bad government is when it attempts to reform itself.[103] Specifically, will the Soviet bureaucracy, which has suffered from his public prodding, even attack, allow him to proceed to the point where real and abiding reforms are instituted or, on the other hand, stymie or overthrow him as they did to Nikita Khrushchev? Further, if genuine reforms were instituted, will they satisfy a long-suffering public or, given a little freedom, will it reach for a lot and thereby imperil the very government which gave the freedoms in the first place? Two possibilities then ensue. The first is that the government saves itself by withdrawing the liberties extended, thereby entering another dreary period of repression and stagnation. Or another serious revolution begins with unpredictable consequences. To be truthful, another 1917 does not appear to be in the cards. One astute observer thinks it less likely he will be overthrown than he will be transformed by an intractable opposition into a status quo leader.[104] Others speculate, because he is making so many enemies, it was unlikely he would last another four years.[105]

Finally, there is an intriguing report from a long-time Soviet dissident of socio-democratic views, but one who is, curiously, closely associated with the elite within the Soviet Union. His rather gloomy analysis is only the beleaguered conservatives know what they want. The so-called Gorbachev reformers are so busy fighting for survival that they have no long-range plans, but mere day-to-day operations. Much democratization has come on many levels but, instead of following after economic reform, it exists only by itself. "Achieving cultural liberalization and expanding the rights of citizens turned out to be far easier than changing the system of administering production." Most impervious of all has been the propaganda apparatus. Meanwhile, conservatives are girding their loins for a counter-offensive following the first serious failure on the economic front. Due, therefore, to the lack of a radical economic plan, and the courage and persistence to implement it, the sands of time are running out on the authors of the attempted reforms.[106]

What does all this have to do with the primitive? It is obvious that the primitive feels more compatible, ideologically speaking, with the "fellowship" of communism than with the "individualism" of capitalism. And, contrary to expectations, communism could not arrive and prosper without elements of the magical and the mystical, those which the primitive had exploited so well and habitually. Like primitive man, communism was inflexible when a matter pertained to the "sacred," a concept always defined by its governors. However, there is no connection between totalitarianism in the Soviet Union and that which E. E. Evans-Pritchard called the "ordered anarchy" of a typical primitive people, the Nuer of the Sudan.[107] A.B. Guthrie, Jr. captured the spirit of hunting and gathering societies when he featured the lament of a Great Plains chieftain: "But what to do with my young braves: A chief is not a general. He can speak but not order, and his words fly away."[108] Further, there is a kind of hubris apparently at work. Small, decentralized and relatively defenseless primitive societies suffered repeated conquests from extremely large and disciplined state forces like the United States and Soviet Russia. Now, however, each of the conquerers appears to be suffering from the "curse of bigness" and the rigidities of the system it instituted.

Postscript:

The above account was last revised in 1987. We decided to leave everything as written in order to observe historical progression. What additional light, if any, could three years shed on the subject (June to mid-July, 1990)?

1) Things obviously worsened in the interval for Mikhail Gorbachev. The superstate threatens to break apart at its fringes, i.e., the Baltic states, Armenia, Azerbaijan and Soviet Central Asia where about fifty million Moslems live. According to a PBS report on May 21, 1990, even the Russians feel neglected and their culture threatened by the mission of the communist superstate. Comrade Boris Yeltsin's recent election as President of the Russian republic - despite Gorbachev's opposition - merely dramatizes the response of ethnic, cultural and religious minorities to both nationalism and communism. This republic includes 52 percent of the Soviet Union's population and three-quarters of its land mass.[109] Today, Soviet Russia is a classic example of a House divided.[110]

2) Regardless of the fate of Gorbachev - upon whom we spent so much time in 1987 - Russian communism can't go home again.[111] Stalinism has been repudiated, as the big and sustained lie has been exposed for all to see. Only conservatives like Yegor Ligachev, member of the Politburo, appear to see no cause for change in the old edifice of state and government.[112] However, the 28th party congress indicated conservatives were considerably stronger than previously suspected.[113] What the upper echelons of the armed services will do if demobilization threatens their jobs and careers is another matter. This has nothing to do with communism *per se*.[114]

3) While the entire countryside was ravaged in the name of industrial "progress" (Chernobyl for example) and agricultural as well (cotton in the Moslem south and east), production was always well below that of the West, both in quality and quantity. In large measure this was caused by a voluntary isolation from world consumer markets and manufacturing centers, as well as by bureaucratic inefficiency and corruption. (Just a few years ago on PBS we could see Western visitors to Soviet manufacturing plants telling local

management their product was inferior. The latter always vigorously denied it). One also has to mention worker indifference, absenteeism and alcoholism. This may have been due to the fact that working harder and more productively did not mean more creature comforts for the individuals involved. More rubles earned did not buy more consumer goods. Why? The goods were just not there. Why then work harder and more often?

4) In retrospect, far too much of a strained national budget was devoted to the military race and possibly to that in outer space as well. The needs of the consumer for basic products - as diverse as soap, meat and fruit - were neglected. How to explain such stupidity without stress upon Stalin's paranoia of the foreigner, and the perpetuation of a virtual war economy from 1941 to the present? Indeed, one old Moscow resident recently observed it was easier to obtain basic necessities during World War II than at present. Such irrationality culminated in an adverse labor reaction to Gorbachev's attempted economic reforms.[115]

5) Instead of accepting the challenge of the West in the areas of military domination and space, extended first by the Kennedy administration, the Soviets should have devoted their energies to satisfying the needs of the consumer. If one is correct in the assumption that the average man is largely interested in bread and circuses (creature comforts and entertainment), it is clear seventy years of communist ideology fell upon barren soil. If Nikolai Lenin was right that imperialism is the last stage of capitalism, then it was clear the West would in effect welcome the Soviet challenge. It gave us a demonstrable and reliable monster to hate and attack. By draining off young and able manpower for military and related industrial purposes, our unemployment could be kept at acceptable levels. Public subsidies for technological advances in weapons systems, bombs, missiles, aircraft and naval vessels, kept our economy humming. Superficial prosperity enabled the government to disguise the fact Japanese were financing much of this when buying our Treasury notes. In short, capitalists had always been the masters of waste and, like the North in our Civil War, they could afford to waste much more than the newly-industrialized Soviets and still win the war on production and consumption. Who can forget the showy, costly and scientifically implausible Star Wars of the Reagan era?

6) The movement for the re-unification of postwar Germany caught both Soviet Russia and the United States by surprise. Neither could have prevented it. Several hundred thousand Soviet troops continue to remain in East Germany for lack of a comprehensive peace treaty as well as the shortage of housing or jobs for them back home.[116] Although the recent arms talks in Washington left the Soviet with superior military strength in Germany, this is unimportant. We agree with A.M. Rosenthal who concluded: " ... the country [Soviet Union] is falling apart so fast that to use it [military force] against the West would demand an overwhelming national desire to commit suicide."[117] No informed observer we know about has ever charged Soviet leaders with this destructive impulse.

7) The one political and military question which must be resolved to the satisfaction and security of all - else it jeopardize the European movement toward democracy and the free market - is the future of Germany. That nation played a large part in bringing about World War I and was solely responsible for World War II. In the future, it could theoretically be free and isolated from all alliances, or solely allied with NATO, or effectively "demilitarized" by international agreement and German consent. Realistically, we must anticipate that neither of the first two propositions could reassure either the Russian government or people. Twice in this century they were attacked by Germany and barely survived each time. Ever since the repulse of the Persian invasions by the Greek city states in the fifth century B.C., history shows the tendency of defensive alliances to become aggressive, instead of disintegrating, once their avowed danger was removed. Recent history reveals when one side or alliance system feels quite secure, the other displays an equal amount of insecurity. Only when everyone feels militarily secure from aggression can there be economic progress. Only some variation of the third and last possibility can produce this desired end.[118]

However, any agreement which detaches Germany from NATO is apt to find bitter resistance from American conservatives. An article by Wm. F. Buckley, Jr. in late June lamented the fact a West German poll of March showed 49 percent of the populace preferred Germany to be neutral rather than in NATO. Since then, this figure has risen considerably. Why, he concludes, give the Soviet Union "what it couldn't get in the hottest days of the Cold War: the neutralization and denuclearization of Germany, and the withdrawal of U.S. troops? That would make detente worth more than a thousand nuclear warheads and a hundred divisions to the Soviet Union."[119]

8) Gorbachev's recent open solicitation of capital investment from the West is merely an official acknowledgment of an old argument, i.e., communist Russia lost the battle of production on virtually all fronts, and certainly all civilian fronts. America's Chevron (oil) and IBM (computers) negotiated joint venture agreements with the Soviet Union for the possibility of substantial profits. Such an influx - if allowed to run its course - should not only increase productivity there, but promises to integrate Soviet economy with that of the West. Both are desirable goals, not only for Gorbachev and Russia, but for us as well. The chief obstacle to this scenario is a general lack of foreign confidence in the value of the ruble. Much of the business of foreign nationals in the Soviet Union is rewarded by an exchange of goods rather than money. It is still a barter economy.

9) At any rate, the price to be paid for this Western influence is probably individual alienation. It already worked that way among the Moscow colony of underground artists, the one prior to glasnost and perestroika. Since these artists could not exhibit before the public, they were restricted to private showings in attics and small living rooms. Not legally capable of seeking individual fame and fortune, they settled for one another's fellowship and professional opinion. Art for art's sake was all that mattered. However, since the West swooped down on the Soviet market, a few of the locals found immediate acceptance. Their paintings sold for fantastic sums. They were then asked to do one-man shows in Paris, London, and New York. Meanwhile, the work of other artists - equally good perhaps - proved much less popular in Western eyes. They sold for much less, if at all. Immediately, the artistic fellowship dissolved. It was replaced by jealousy, envy and even greed. Instead of art itself being perpetually elevated and even worshipped, money and fame took its place. What happened was as inevitable as the laws of physics.[120]

10) Finally, one comes to the most perplexing problem of all because there is no historical experience to predicate one's answers upon. Until

recently, no nation state under communism switched to the so-called free market solution. Several in Central and Eastern Europe have now launched such programs. Even Soviet Russia is experimenting with one variety. Yet, there is no evidence that such was inspired by right-wing Reaganomics.[121] In the short run, certainly, optimism scarcely seems justified. Too many industrial plants are obsolete. Free outside competition will close them. Unemployment will sharply increase. One American businessman with experience in Eastern Europe thought Solidarity labor leaders in Poland were naive about the transition period. Apparently, they dreamed of life in the best of all possible worlds, one combining the old social welfare goals with capitalism's consumer paradise. The program they think plausible and possible does not even exist in the United States.[122]

To summarize, our ten points say nothing about solutions to problems. Rather, they merely point to them. All indicate the Soviet Union is in a new era. Three years from now the situation may be just as fluid.[123]

One last fact needs to be noted; this entire chapter records the failure of a totalitarian state to realize the idea of progress and the perfectability of man through state planning and coercion. We now turn to a study of the recent history of the United States to see if a freer society could achieve these same ends.

Footnotes

1   *The Fall of the Russian Monarchy. A Study of the Evidence* (New York, Vintage Books, Random House, 1939), 472.

2   Raphael R. Abramovitch, *The Soviet Revolution, 1917-1919.* Introduction by Sidney Hook (New York, International University Press, 1962), 21; Harry Best, *The Soviet Experiment* (New York, Richard R. Smith, 1941), 18.

3   Pares, *The Fall of the Russian Monarchy*, 478. War Minister Kerensky viewed the offensive as a means of restoring the morale of soldiers and the prestige of the govermment. Its purpose was to relieve the military pressure on France, getting a stalemate until American troops could arrive. Alexander Rabinowitch, *Prelude to Revolution. The Petrograd Bolsheviks and the July 1917 Uprising* (Bloomington, University of Indiana Press, 1968), 108-109.

4   Rabinowitch, *Prelude to Revolution*, 222.

5   Pares, *Fall of the Russian Monarchy*, 478, 482.

6   *Ibid.*, 482.

7   See "The Demands of the Workers, Peasants, and Soldiers in the Russian Revolution," 112-136 in Marc Ferro, *The Russian Revolution of February 1917.* Translated by J.L. Richards (Englewood Cliffs, New Jersey, Prentice-Hall, 1972).

8   Roger Portal, "Preface," in Ferro, *Russian Revolution*, iv-v.

9   Rabinowitch, *Prelude to Revolution*, 39.

10   This was the conclusion of Aleksandr Solzhenitsyn. See footnote 33 of this chapter.

11   Four words - peace, liberty, food and land - dazzled the peasant conscript and the city worker in the army. Best, *Soviet Experiment*, 19.

12   After the disasters of 1915, "the bulk of the Russian army was overwhelmingly tired of war, critical of its leadership, distrustful of its government, and generally ripe for rebellion." Rabinowitch, *Prelude to Revolution*, 19.

13   Pares, *Fall of the Russian Monarchy*, 462.

14   Sidney Hook made that point. "Introduction," Abramowitch, *The Soviet Revolution*, vii-viii.

15   There was nothing in the Russian past which allowed one to think of communism. Therefore, they had to borrow it from the West. Arnold J. Toynbee, "Russia and Western Civilization," 643-648 in *Soviet Society. A Book of Readings*, edited by Alex Inkeles and

Kent Geiger (Boston, Houghton-Mifflin, 1961), 646.

16   *Arrow in the Blue, An Autobiography* (New York, Macmillan, 1952), 260.

17   *Ibid.,* 137, 145.

18   Daniel Guérin, *Anarchism. From Theory to Practice.* Introduction by Noam Chomsky. Translated by Mary Klopper (New York, Monthly Review Press, 1970), 88-89.

19   Voline, *The Unknown Revolution, 1917-1921.* Foreword by Rudolf Rocker (New York, Free Life Editions, 1975), 247-249.

20   Burke, *Reflections on the French Revolution,* 61.

21   *The New Class. An Analysis of the Communist System* (New York, Frederick A. Praeger, 1957), 87.

22   An excellent example of this occurred in September, 1983, just after the Soviets destroyed the Korean Air Lines plane, flight 007, at a cost of 269 lives because it "invaded" their air space in the Far East. Five days followed before the Soviets admitted they had "stopped" the plane and eight days before a Soviet general acknowledged they had shot down a civilian plan. Jim Hampton, Knight-Ridder Newspapers, in the Kansas City *Times,* 15 September, 1983, A-15. The Soviets "are defensive to an irrational degree. It is a closed society, not only in the sense of shutting itself off from external influence but in the sense of excluding unauthorized ideas and independent thinking." Robert Wesson in The Kansas City *Star,* September 25, 1983, E-4.

23   The Soviets cannot make a better world because they have reposed too much power in the hands of too few. Stephen Spender, 229-273 in *The God That Failed,* edited by Arthur Koestler *et al* (New York, Harper, 1949), 269. See also footnote 69.

24   John Reed, *Ten Days That Shook the World* (New York, Penguin Books, 1977), 39-40. Fittingly, the first government after the March Revolution contained the principal of recall of officials in whom the people no longer had any confidence. This was a key principle in twentieth century democracy. William Henry Chamberlin, *The Russian Enigma. An Interpretation* (New York, Charles Scribner's, 1943), 84.

25   William Henry Chamberlin, *The Russian Revolution, 1917-1921* in 2 vols., (New York, Macmillan, 1935), I, 100, 281.

26   Daniel and Gabriel Cohn-Bendit, *Obsolete Communism. The Left-Wing Alternative.* Translated by Arnold Pomerans (New York, McGraw-Hill, 1968), 204.

27   Chamberlin, *The Russian Revolution,* I, 100.

28   *Ibid.,* I, 323.

29   *Ibid.,* I, 365.

30   Reed, *Ten Days That Shook the World,* 101.

31   Chamberlin, *Russian Revolution*, I, 321.

32   Reed, *Ten Days That Shook the World*, 143.

33   Alexsandr I. Solzhenitsyn, *Letter to the Soviet Leaders*. Translated from the Russian by Hilary Sternburg (New York, Harper and Row, 1974), 53-54.

34   The excuse, of course, was that the Constitutent Assembly merely provided a cover for bourgeois efforts to overthrow the government. But, as Chamberlin also pointed out, constitutional government was doomed in any instance. Had the Bolsheviks lost, the alternative would not have been constitutional government but a right-wing dictator, a man on horseback. Chamberlin, *Russian Revolution*, I, 370-371.

35   Voline, *The Unknown Revolution, 1917-1921*, 237-239.

36   *The History of the Russian Revolution*, 3 vols., translated from the Russian by Max Eastman (Ann Arbor, University of Michigan Press, 1932), III, 302.

37   *Punitive Medicine*. Foreword by Alexander Ginzburg (Ann Arbor, Michigan, Karoma Publishing, 1980), 3.

38   Both Lenin and Trotsky were willing to accept the isolation of their party. Reed, *Ten Days That Shook the World*, 126. See also G.F. Hudson, *Fifty Years of Communism, Theory and Practice, 1917-1967* (New York, Basic Books, 1968), 94, 101.

39   Chamberlin, *The Russian Revolution*, I, 118-119.

40   Voline, *Unknown Revolution*, 244.

41   Trotsky, *History of the Russian Revolution*, III, 286.

42   Lenin's theory was as follows: "Where there is a state there is no freedom and where there is freedom there is no state." Chamberlin, *The Russian Enigma*, 82.

43   Rosa Luxemburg, *The Russian Revolution and Leninism or Marxism?* (Ann Arbor, University of Michigan Press, 1976), 96.

44   Guérin, *Anarchism*, 87.

45   Lenin believed that terror should have a legal basis of authority under the Soviet system of government. Bertram D. Wolfe, "The Durability of Soviet Totalitarianism," 648-659 in *Soviet Society. A Book of Readings*, edited by Inkeles and Geiger, 656. Trotsky admitted that Lenin spoke out for terror before organized terror had gone into effect. Chamberlin, *The Russian Revolution*, I, 138.

46   Eliade, *Myth and Reality*, 183-184. Communism contains aspirations towards a beautiful and ideal society which attracts and inspires men possessing high moral standards. Djilas, *The New Class*, 152.

47   Guérin, *Anarchism*, 86-87.

48   Maurice Brinton, *The Bolsheviks & Worker's Control, 1917 to 1921. The State and Counter-Revolution* (London, Solidarity Press, 1970), 40-41.

49   The single most prominent feature of Taylorism was the task idea, planned by management on the preceding day. It not only specified what the laborer was to work at but how and the time allowed for the job. If the laborer succeeded he received a bonus as an incentive. Frederick Winslow Taylor, *The Principles of Scientific Management* (New York, Harper & Brothers, 1915), 39, 121.

50   Henry Ford was wedded to the written task idea. At both his main plant, as well as assembly plants, all work was standardized and inspectors could suddenly descend upon a plant anywhere and take an assembled product to Detroit for testing. He recognized that the human tendency was to depart from instructions. Henry Ford, *Moving Forward* (Garden City, New York, Doubleday, Doran, 1930), 149, 153.

51   Daniel and Gabriel Cohn-Bendit, *Obsolete Communism*, 115, 225, 232-233.

52   *Ibid.*, 230.

53   Worker self-management, the bureaucratic excuse ran, did not take into account one vital factor, that of the "rational" needs of the national economy. Guérin, *Anarchism*, 89.

54   Andy Anderson, *Hungary '56* (London, Solidarity Press, 1976), 32.

55   *Ibid.*, 33.

56   Reed, *Ten Days That Shook the World*, 128.

57   Eliade, *Myth and Reality*, 183-184. From Marx the communist party inherited "almost unimaginably high ideals: the abolition of inequality, the creation of a New Man, the paradox of freedom through collective effort." From The Economist of London in the Kansas City *Times*, February 28, 1984, A-9.

58   No politician seemed more indifferent to his own fame and fortune nor more dedicated to the selfless struggle for humanity. *The Russian Revolution*, I, 138; *The Russian Enigma*, 81.

59   *The Russian Revolution*, I, 140. By 1920, Bertrand Russell accurately noted of Leninism that it was not merely a political doctrine but also a religion with elaborate dogmas and inspired scriptures. However, despite the fact that it contained elements of both, Leninism was neither a religion nor a church. Djilas, *The New Class*, 127, 165.

60   Isaac Deutscher, *Ironies of History. Essays on Contemporary Communism* (New York, Oxford University Press, 1966), 8-9.

61   Harold H. Fischer, *The Communist Revolution. An Outline of Strategy and Tactics*. The Hoover Institute and Library on War, Revolution, and Peace (Stanford, California, Stanford University Press, 1955), 8.

62   *The Russian Revolution and Leninism or Marxism?*, 71.

63   Dagobert D. Runes, *The Soviet Impact on Society. A Recollection*. With a Foreword by Harry Elmer Barnes (New York, Philosophical Library, 1953), 99; Hudson, *Fifty Years of Communism*, 108; Alvin W. Gouldner, "Stalinism: a Study of Internal Colonialism," 209-259 in *Political Power and Social Theory. A Research Annual* in 3 vols., edited by Maurice Zeitlin (Greenwich, Connecticut, Jai Press, 1981), I, 229.

64   One of the weirdest episodes occurred last in March, 1938, and involved three physicians accused of poisoning their patients. As always, there was a complete absence of independent and corroborative testimony. Only the incredible confession remained to baffle the mind. Chamberlin, *The Russian Enigma*, 216, 218. Leaving the personal elements of paranoia and revenge to one side, the Moscow purges served many party purposes: they established the infallibility of the party, the purity of its doctrine and dogma, eliminated deadwood and promoted younger talent and, finally, supplied scapegoats for error. Wolfe, "The Durability of Soviet Totalitarianism," *loc. cit.*, 654. The bogus confessions were a form of bureaucratic ritualism designed to placate believers throughout the world. Gouldner, "Stalinism, a Study of Internal Colonialism," *loc. cit.*, 234-235.

65   When a man accepted an invitation from Stalin, he did not know whether he would end up at home or in jail. *The Anti-Stalin Campaign and International Communism. A Selection of Documents*. Edited by the Russian Institute, Columbia University (New York, Columbia University Press, 1956), 82.

66   *Ibid.*, 17-18, 59.

67   Koestler, *The God That Failed*, 62-63.

68   *The Anti-Stalin Campaign and International Communism*, 44.

69   Alvin W. Gouldner, "Stalinism: a Study of Internal Colonialism," *loc. cit.*, 210.

70   *Soviet Attitudes Toward Authority. An Interdisciplinary Approach to Problems of Soviet Character*. The Rand Series (New York, McGraw-Hill, 1951), 61-62.

71   *Ibid.*, 53.

72   *Ibid.*, 61.

73   *Ibid.*, 64-67.

74   *Ibid.*, 27, 32, 35.

75   *Ibid.*, 15.

76   *Ibid.*, 33-34.

77   *Ibid.*, 60

78   The Inquisition was first recognized by Innocent IV in 1252. It used the rack, fire and water torture to induce or force confessions in cases where the evidence was not conclusive. Since one principal object was to identify other heretics through confession, that heretic who denounced others became a witness to their guilt and might be tortured

as much as necessary or desired. *The Inquisition. A Political and Military Study of Its Establishment.* 2nd edition. With a Preface by Hilaire Belloc (Port Washington, New York, Kennikat Press, 1968), 211-214.

79   Servetus was burned at the stake ten weeks after his arrest because he proclaimed that the Trinity was used only after the Council of Nicaea, about 325 A.D., and that none of the early martyrs knew what it was. E. William Monter, *Calvin's Geneva* in New Dimensions in History. Historical Cities. Edited by Norman F. Cantor (New York, John Wiley and Sons, 1967), 129-131.

80   By modern terms, Servetus should not have been convicted. While from the beginning it was generally believed among Gentile Christians that Christ was a divine being and their Lord and Savior, this is not the same thing as a definite credo of the Trinity. Even by the end of the third century, the deity of Christ was not everywhere recognized. Many denied it. Two prominent Christian clerics who did so were Lucian of Antioch - martyred in 311 - and Arius, presbyter of the church at Alexandria. Arthur Cushman McGiffert, *A History of Christian Thought,* vol. I *From Jesus to John of Damascus* (New York, Charles Scribner's Sons, 1932), 246, 250.

81   *New Catholic Encyclopedia,* vol. 7, 497.

82   The Syllabus denied that men may choose whatever religion they please to bring them eternal salvation, that the Church must not use its powers without the consent of civil authorities, and that the Church has no right to employ force at its discretion. Stearns, *Pageant of Europe,* 526-527. "Many theologians attribute infallibility to the Syllabus, while others deny this. Nevertheless, the Syllabus must be accepted by all Catholics, since it comes from the Pope.... Its contents cannot be challenged by Catholics, and they are to give assent to it." *New Catholic Encyclopedia,* vol. 13, 855.

83   Stalin had apparently planned another purge just before he sickened and died. This was called off following his death because his successors felt it served no rational purpose. Social terror diminished perceptibly and artists and writers felt much more relaxed. Wolfe, "The Durability of Soviet Totalitarianism," *loc. cit.*, 654-655. Isaac Deutscher and other scholars temporarily believed it was then possible to make the transformation to a form of social democracy. Marshall D. Shulman, "Beyond the Containment Policy," 665-673 in *Soviet Society,* edited by Inkeles and Geiger, 667-669.

84   Forty years of corruption and terror have not deprived the artist of his conviction that his true allegiance is to individual creativity rather than to collective conformity. Wolfe, "The Durability of Soviet Totalitarianism," *loc. cit.,* 657. See also Deutscher, *Ironies of History,* 245. Krushchev never intended to institute democracy, but rather to return to the principles of Lenin. Hudson, *Fifty Years of Communism,* 170.

85   Verne W. Newton, "The Real Cause of Revolution," in the Kansas City *Star,* 9 October, 1983, H-4. See also Wolfe, "The Durability of Soviet Totalitarianism," *loc. cit.,* 658.

86   Let communism stand unsupported by coercion. Let those who propagandize for it do so on their own time and at their own expense. Let it take its chance in the Jeffersonian market place of free ideas. Solzhenitsyn, *Letter to the Soviet Leaders,* 48.

87   From the outset of the communist Revolution, intellectuals were subjected to verbal abuse. While they could never be genuine proletarians, it was their duty to try. Koestler, *The God That Failed*, 48-49. The hatred that was always felt by communists toward intellectuals was attributed to the fact that, prior to the Revolution, peasants could not read. Accordingly, they were suspicious of anyone who could. *Ibid.*, 154.

88   *The History of the Russian Revolution*, III, 302.

89   *The New Class*, 161, 169.

90   In prison one had the possibility of not only avoiding conflict with his neighbor but rather exchanging support and enrichment. In prison an intellectual did not mind solitary, especially if he had good books to read. Therefore, prison ennobled when contrasted with the corruption and hatred manifested everywhere in labor camps. One came to hate both the labor and one's companions. If weaker than the rest, you got beaten. If stronger, you got your neighbor's bread. Meanwhile, privacy was non-existent. Aleksandr I. Solzhenitsyn, *The Gulag Archipelago, 1918-1956. An Experiment in Literary Investigation*. Parts III-IV. Translated from the Russian by Thomas P. Whitney (New York, Harper and Row, 1975), 618-620.

91   Solzhenitsyn, *Letter to the Soviet Leaders*, 56.

92   Podrabinek, *Punitive Medicine*, 5, 19-20.

93   Thorstein Veblen, *The Engineers and the Price System* (New York, Viking Press, 1940), 86-87.

94   André Gide, 175-195 in *The God That Failed*, 174, 181. Janet G. Adams had a much more detailed and balanced assessment of consumer goods in the Soviet Union in the mid-Sixties. The most glaring weaknesses, vis-à-vis the West, came in durable goods, such as autos and household appliances. Though much progress had been made in housing recently, the Soviet Union was still perceptibly behind as far as space, quality and equipment was concerned. While clothing supplies were adequate, quality and styles were notably deficient. Worse, prices were high relative to the wage rate. Finally, although adequate in caloric content, the Soviet diet was deficient with regard to essentials like meat and dairy products, fruit and vegetables. "Consumption in the Soviet Union," 323-334 in *The Soviet Economy. A Book of Readings*, edited by Morris Burnstein and Daniel R. Fusfeld (Homewood, Illinois, Richard D. Irwin, Inc., 1970), 323. A decade later, Solzhenitzyn still deplored the fact the Soviet Union could not rival the West with regard either to consumer goods or leisure. Imperialistic ventures cost so much that the squeeze was passed on to the point of least resistence, the civilian consumer. Once divested of this burden, the system might rival the West in that crucial area. *Letter to the Soviet Leaders*, 42.

95   Solzhenitsyn, *Letter to the Soviet Leaders*, 33. In addition to this factor as a causal one for the low agricultural production, Janet G. Chapman also blamed an inadequate state investment in agriculture. "Consumption in the Soviet Union," *loc. cit.*, 329.

96   Louis Fischer, 196-228 in *The God That Failed*, 226.

97   Seweryn Bialer and Joan Afferica, "The Genesis of Gorbachev's World," 605-644

in *Foreign Affairs*, vol. 64, No. 3, 1985, 607. However, the most recent assessment of Soviet productivity, and this gathered by U.S. intelligence sources, is that in 1986 production grew slightly over four percent. It was twice the average growth in that country and considerably greater than the 2.5 percent in the United States. Such significant growth was achieved not only because of an excellent farm harvest but to less absenteeism in factories and assembly lines. "Report Cites Growth in Soviet Economy," from the Los Angeles Times in the Kansas City *Times*, March 28, 1987, A-1, 18.

98   *The Soviet Impact on the Western World* (New York, Macmillan, 1947), 109-113.

99   "Russia and Western Civilization," 643-648 in *Soviet Society: A Book of Readings*, edited by Inkeles and Geiger, 647.

100   Stephen F. Cohen, "Gorbachev's reforms would alter the very shape of Stalin's system," in the Kansas City *Star*, March 28, 1987, K-3.

101   Bialer and Afferica, "Genesis of Gorbachev's World," *loc. cit.*, 618-619. A similar analysis, although one less optimistic, is contained in an article by Ernest Conine. Los Angeles Times News Service, "Gorbachev's reform efforts face some very tough tests," the Kansas City *Times*, April 3, 1987, A-12.

102   Stephen F. Cohen, "Sovieticus," 511 in *The Nation*, vol. 234, No. 16, November 15, 1986.

103   See footnote 85 of this chapter.

104   Cohen, "Sovieticus," *loc. cit.*, 511.

105   These were the predictions of Marshall Goldman of Harvard's Russian Research Center and Peter Reddaway, director of Smithsonian's Kennan Institute. "Report Cites Growth in Soviet Economy," *loc. cit.*, A-1, 18.

106   N. Beregov, The Washington Post, "Soviets may be trying to reform, but they have no plan to follow," in the Kansas City *Star*, April 26, 1987, K-2.

107 *Nuer*, 6.

108   *Fair Land, Fair Land* (Boston, Houghton-Mifflin, 1982), 233.

109   The Associated Press, Moscow, "Gorbachev suggests reforming the union," in the Kansas City *Star*, June 13, 1990, A-1.

110   "... Boris Yeltsin, the country's most popular communist leader, suddenly chilled the [28th party] congress with the terse announcement that he was leaving the party so that it would not interfere with his work as president of the Russian republic. Implicit in his statement was an intimation that Gorbachev had mastered a party without much of a future." Bill Keller, The New York Times, Moscow, "Walkout may undo the gains Gorbachev won at congress," in *ibid.*, July 13, 1990, A-1. "The walkout by Yeltsin and other radicals is likely to reshape the Soviet political scene for the first time in Soviet history." Michael Dobbs, The Washington Post, Moscow, "Yeltsin leads defectors who demand share of assets," in *ibid.*, July 13, 1990, A-1. "The mayors of Moscow and

Leningrad ... were leaving the Communist party ... in a growing exodus that could ultimately transform Soviet politics." Gary Lee, The Washington Post, Moscow, "Others follow Yeltsin out of party," in *ibid.*, July 14, 1990, A-20.

111   "'No one is for him any more' a leading Moscow intellectual and beneficiary of glasnost told me recently.' He will probably stay in place as leader because there is no clear alternative. But nobody is following where he is leading.'" Jim Hoagland, Washington Post Writers Group, Washington, "Nobody is following," in *ibid.*, May 28, 1990, B-5.

112   "... Ligachev has become more open about his opposition to Gorbachev's endorsement of a market economy and his decision to give tacit encouragement to the democratic revolts in Eastern Europe," The Washington Post, Moscow, "Gorbachev hints he may quit party post," in *ibid.*, June 21, 1990, A-6.

113   Evidence came during a debate between Ligachev and a defender of Gorbachev. Of the almost five thousand delegates, "roughly two-thirds joined in prolonged applause for Ligachev, about one-third demonstratively applauded (Foreign Minister) Shevardnadze." Michael Dobbs, The Washington Post, Moscow, "Strained Soviet party wrenched anew," in *ibid.*, July 4, 1990, A-1, 17. Nevertheless, Gorbachev's picked candidate for the post of deputy general secretary, Vladimir Ivashko, defeated Ligachev. The vote was 776 for Ligachev and 3,642 against him. "The deputy general secretary will be responsible for the day-to-day running of the party, allowing Gorbachev to concentrate on affairs of state. ... The decision by Ligachev to stand against Gorbachev's candidate for a high party post was highly unusual." The Washington Post, Moscow, "Party picks Gorbachev ally," in *ibid.*, July 12, 1990, A-3.

114   At the communist Congress of early July, one foreign correspondent observed: "But it is striking that top military officials have not taken the podium to defend Gorbachev and his policies." Bill Keller, The New York Times "Soviet calls proposal 'the way to safe future'," in *ibid.*, July 7, 1990, A-14.

115   "The most serious resistance to his [Gorbachev's] economic reform has come from the ordinary Soviet workers alarmed by the prospect of further cuts in their already low living standards." Michael Dobbs, The Washington Post, Moscow, "Gorbachev prevailing in party, failing in economic crisis," in *ibid.*, July 15, 1990, A-14.

116   R.W. Apple, Jr., The New York Times, Washington, "Germany-NATO issue to steal summit spotlight," in *ibid.*, May 28, 1990, A-8. "His [Gorbachev's] strained economy cannot easily house and employ the thousands of troops scheduled for demobilization, creating a restive mood among career officers." Bill Keller, The New York Times, Washington, "Soviet Union today likened to Germany after WW I, " in *ibid.*, May 31, 1990, A-14.

117   New York Times News Service, "Warm moment in history chilled by Gorbachev's threat on immigration," in *ibid.*, June 8, 1990, C-9.

118   The Soviet Union does not object to the continued military presence of the United States on continental Europe. Valentin Falin, chief of the internal affairs of the communist party central committee, New Perspectives Quarterly, Washington, "New treaty, not NATO, needed to end German impasse," in the Kansas City *Star*, June 11, 1990, B-5.

119   Universal Press, Berlin, "Disheartening news of German unification front," in *ibid.*, June 27, 1990, C-11.

120   "USSR Art," PBS program, June 4, 1990.

121   "Not one of the grass-roots organizations now rearranging Soviet life claims any particular inspiration from any form of Americanism, particularly not from right-wing Republicanism, since many of the innovators want not capitalism but a purer socialism. In fact, there are in the Soviet Union more monarchists than Reaganites." Harry Eagar, Contributing Reviewer, "Seeds of change were planted long ago, historian contends," in *ibid.*, May 6, 1990, I-9.

122   Ted Koppel, "New Global Marketplace," PBS program, June 11, 1990.

123   At a recent Aspen Institute conference, an American assumption of a new international order, headed by the United States and Soviet Russia, "was rudely shattered by ... a Soviet analyst. He said it simply did not take into account the fact that 'my country is collapsing and my government is losing control.'" Nor did the Russian delegation "have pat answers, nor can these be expected any time soon. As one of the Russians observed, with typically crushing candor, 'Do not expect us to define our national interests. We do not know what our nation will be five or ten years from now. We may be a much smaller country ....'" David S. Broder, Washington Post Writers Group, Wye, Md., "New generation wrestling with altered world order," in the Kansas City *Star*, May 2, 1990, C-9.

Author's Note: The greater portion of sources used in this chapter came from the personal library of younger son, Jeff.

Chapter XV

AN HISTORICAL INTRODUCTION TO AMERICAN DEMOCRACY

"I seem to remember a time when we did not believe lying had a public place in this democracy, where the processes of decision-making are based on a well-informed people, which obviously means a truthfully informed people. People my age grew up thinking - naively ... there was always one big difference: They [the enemy] lied, but we didn't."

"We were shocked ... in 1960 ... when it turned out that President Eisenhower was lying ... over whether the United States was sending spy planes over Soviet territory. ... A couple of years later ... an intense national debate was triggered by the careless assertion by an assistant defense secretary, Arthur Sylvester, that the government had the right to deceive the press in the name of national security. ...

Lies themselves have eroded into just
another category of news. ...
      We call it a crisis of leadership. It is
much worse than that: it is a crisis of authority.
No one believes anyone in power now; we take
lying for granted. The trick is to find the lie and
the reason for it."

      Richard Reeves, Universal Press
      Syndicate, New York, "President Bush is a liar,
      but that's no surprise," in the Kansas City *Star*,
      July 2, 90, B-7.

For the next three chapters, our inquiry centers on attempted answers to three questions: 1) By the standards of operational definitions, are we really a democracy? 2) Since 1945, could an informed outsider justifiably regard us as a peaceful nation? and 3) Is our modern industrial system both efficient and benign, or relatively inefficient and ready to sacrifice national welfare in order to show a profit for the next quarter?

A fourth factor enters as soon as we decided to give the reader a bird's eye view of our history, or that involving democratic and anti-democratic events and trends in time. It was Tom Urban who first felt its necessity. Otherwise, one would be discussing current tendencies in an historical vacuum.

Since the Reagan administration was recently in the saddle for eight years, it was inevitable we were forced to consider what happened to America during this period, both domestically and abroad. Because of time and space limitations, we chose to concentrate on three facets: 1) What happened to the once popular welfare state and why? 2) Why the tremendous acceleration of the national debt, and one to foreigners and not ourselves? and 3) What impact did this have upon worsening our adverse balance of trade and its threat to our standard of living, and hence to the American dream of progress?

Finally, in the Epilogue, FULL CIRCLE, we confront implications of the fact that the two "legitimate" excuses for the reduction and decimation of native cultures the world over - the idea of progress and Christianity - no longer compel the allegiance they once did. Let Robert Nisbet tell it: "For just as the century especially in its second half is barren of faith in progress, so it is almost barren of wide-spread and life-permeating religious faith." This movement, however, does not catch him by surprise because, in his opinion, the idea of progress has always been dependent upon "religion or intellectual constructs derived from religion." As both erode, irrational and mystical elements survive and prosper so that Nisbet is justified in calling the present age "the revolt against reason."[1] To us, however, we see much of which the primitive would be in empathy with, assuming he were still here to pass judgment upon the new age.

At the suggestion of my co-author, we begin these final chapters on the same theme which characterized our first. That was the insistence by Karl Mannheim on the essential difference between the event world and the way it is perceived culturally, or that interaction between the fact itself and the mind-set of the beholder.[2] With us, democracy poses such a problem, precisely because it means so many different things to Americans themselves. We think that a former editor of the Detroit *Free Press* spoke words of wisdom when he declared: "We are absolutely up to our necks in groups and blocks and religious and economic interests certain beyond all reason that they are correct and actively interested in imposing their rules and values and selected morals on the rest of us. They prattle about democracy, and use it when it suits them without the slightest regard or respect for what it means and costs and requires. These people are - please believe me - dangerous."[3]

Since the matter of conceptualization is a cultural one for all, and Americans possess many different notions, let us say what democracy means for us. We plea a Jeffersonian bias in that we not only believe that all should vote - all males, for him, all adults for us - but the voter should not be economically dependent upon another because that could easily cloud his or her judgment. (For Jefferson, the ideal basis for a democratic society was the small farmer who, without considerable indebtedness, owned land. Unfortunately, in our day that individual is fast disappearing and no other ideal basis immediately comes to mind.) Just as importantly, that "independent" voter must be educated, politically and economically, to that point where he understands the issues to be decided upon by the electorate. And if he is to be the master, rather than the public servant, the latter must not lie to nor deceive him. This deprives him of ample and fair ground on which to make a fair and intelligent judgement. Let us resort to Jefferson himself to explain the relationship between the individual and the state. Education is the business of the state because it is essential to the happiness, prosperity and liberty of the people. The state itself exists for these purposes.[4] The education of the poor is to be subsidized by the wealth of the nation.[5] Finally, the purpose of education is not the development of nationalism by propaganda. It is in order for the people to know their rights.[6]

However, democracies are not simply the rule of the majority; the problem really is how to reconcile majority rule with the rights and privileges of the minority not trampled upon. Here civil, as well as property rights, come to the fore. While democracy relies upon law for its sanction and authority, the law must be the same for all. One cannot apply Orwell's famous principle: "All animals are equal but some are more equal than others" without corrupting the basis of the democratic structure.

Finally, democracy stands for the principle of the worth and dignity of every individual and his right of dissent, or the art of striving to be a self-directed or autonomous man. And this in front of and in full view of the public. Not as naive as we sound, we know that this is very difficult concept to approach when people are complacent, if not happy, and are not worried about this thing called "national security." But, when that spectre is invoked - whether justifiably or not - we have wholesale incursions into the civil rights of persons by the government. Even more deplorably, citizens applaud, instead of writing angry letters to the editor. In recent times, one need only note the Red Scare of 1919, the Sacco-Vanzetti affair of the mid-Twenties, the post-World War II trial and execution of Julius and Ethel Rosenberg, and the witch hunts of Senator Joe McCarthy in the Fifties. The principle these events had in common was that all invalidated some of the presumptions we emphasized.

We agree with Robert Nisbet when he observed if we seek causality, we must turn to history.[7] Contrary to conventional wisdom, disciplines which stress "presentism" cannot help us in our mission. When perceived rationally or unemotionally, one can see how frail a reed democracy is today in America. We offer no hope to those seeking inspiration and guidance from the supposedly better model in the past - some ill-defined golden age - because it never existed. While it is easy to dispel the notion of the democratic intentions of the authors of the Constitution, there are still three eras in our history which possibly could rival our own with regard to progress on the democratic ideal: Jacksonian Democracy, the Progressive Era, 1900-1916 and the New Deal. Since, in our investigation, we are prepared to crowd much of American history into a few pages - that concerned with democratic or anti-democratic tendencies - we felt it wise to eliminate footnotes rather than to bury the general reader under a plethora of them.

While it is customary to eulogize the works of our "Founding Fathers," the most fulsome, or offensive, praise is voiced by those who invariably know the least about their intentions. It is certainly no reflection upon those "fathers" that they had not the slightest notion of setting up a democracy. Indeed, that was the one thing they were determined to avoid. And circumstances made that plausible. They were in fact the "new elite." The traditional elite, the Tories, had been crushed, exiled and stripped of property rights as a result of the Revolution. These new rulers were not only comparatively young men, but successful ones. They represented commercial interests in the north and landed ones in the south. Among the professions, the law appeared to predominate and, as in England, lawyers served men of property. Now the price the South exacted for its share in forming "a more perfect union" was the assurance that slavery would not be disturbed by the national government and the slave trade might continue until 1807. The definition of voting rights was also left in the hands of the states. That insured a majority of white males would be disenfranchised in many, if not most, of the states. If, however, a man succeeded in establishing his property credentials, he was allowed to vote for only the members of the House of Representatives – the least prestigious of all chambers of government - and not for members of the Senate and the presidency itself. These were chosen by indirect election. Members of the Supreme Court -

whose real job it was to break any residue of the people's authority which manifested itself - were chosen by the president and the Senate, none of whom were elected directly by the people. Finally, the Constitution itself contained no Bill of Rights. This was passed a couple of years later at the insistence of the Jeffersonian Republicans. Many Federalists - those of the party of George Washington - insisted that no such bill was necessary. The people could trust their rulers not only to be discreet, but fair.

Despite the fears of the wealthy that Jefferson's election in 1800 meant the French Revolution of 1789 all over again, no radical changes in government were effected until after the election of the people's champion, Andrew Jackson, in 1828. His most spectacular triumph, breaking the monopoly of the Second United States Bank as a repository of public funds, was more symbolic of democracy's distrust of special privilege than anything else. Immediate beneficiaries were state banks in the north and east. Now that there was no longer a monitor or regulator of banking in a national sense, it led to wildcatting and wide-scale failures in banking. Re-chartered under the laws of Pennsylvania, the ex-Second National Bank was one of these casualties. Meanwhile, although the common white man was given the ballot everywhere in the decade of the Thirties, slavery was left undisturbed. The rights of women were conspicuously ignored. As for the red man, he was treated as a non-person and his tribe as a conquered nation. This callous and inhuman policy led to a host of broken treaties, stolen lands, the forced exodus of agricultural and civilized peoples like the Cherokee. Mass genocide occurred wherever feasible on the grounds that "The only good Indian is a dead one." Save for the consciences of a few, notably the hapless Supreme Court, Jackson's Indian policy was extremely popular among the newly enfranchised masses.

The so-called Progressive Era of 1900-1916 was in reality a middle class reform period, one which altered situations by law displeasing to that class. Its interest in reform was limited to things like banking, monetary affairs, taxation, transportation, "pure food" and such weighty matters. It was not concerned with the problems of the immigrant poor, like adequate housing, fair wages and hours, safe and healthy working conditions, unions and other such trivial affairs. It was Upton Sinclair, author of the poignant book about the terrible living and working conditions of Chicago's stockyard workers, who said something like: "When I wrote *The Jungle*, I was aiming at the public's heart, but instead I hit it in the stomach." This occurred because, while the Pure Food and Drug act followed the publication of the book, nothing was done to alleviate the deplorable living conditions of the workers and their families.

It was during this period that presidents of both parties openly and cheerfully practiced the Bad Neighbor policy in the Caribbean. Historians charitably called it the era of Dollar Diplomacy. Both the State department and the Marines were at the beck and call of American investors in the entire Caribbean. Their steady dollar returns were far more important than the development of democracy there. Indeed, it often seemed to threaten profit. It was Teddy Roosevelt who laid down the most monstrous policy under the innocuous title of the Roosevelt Corollary of the Monroe Doctrine. Behind the fine verbiage, what it meant was this: if Catholic countries in the region could not live by the Protestant ethic - always save a portion of your income or spend less than you make - and thus ran up debts to Europeans they could not pay, then Uncle Sam would seize their customs houses and pay off their creditors. And if Mexico could not capture a bandit on our most wanted list, then Woodrow Wilson felt it his duty to order General "Black Jack" Pershing to invade the sovereign state of Mexico in search of Pancho Villa. Only Socialists and other crack pots ever dared question this self-righteous behavior.

In many respects the New Deal under Franklin D. Roosevelt approached the democratic ideal of rule by the people. It was perhaps for this reason that he and Eleanor were so hated by bankers, industrialists, stock brokers, big and little businessmen who looked to their superiors for political advice and behavior. While it was frequently bandied about the Country Club crowd that Franklin D. Roosevelt was "a betrayor of his class," it is far more likely he succeeded in saving capitalism from capitalists themselves. The New Deal reformed the worst excesses of the system. Thus, it was made more palatable to those who exacted the least returns from it.

While Murphy's law was in operation i.e., if something can go wrong, it will, the government's intentions were good. These were to help the farmer make a decent living, to allow the industrial worker fair wages, hours and working conditions with unions to effect those rights, to protect the investor from unscrupulous stock market promoters, to provide decent housing for the poor, to aid dependent children and, finally, to protect the victims of unemployment, old age and illness.

Now all these aspirations were not part of a master plan to bring Socialism to America and sack capitalism. It was rather the result of day-to-day, hit and miss propositions. It might be argued that the New Dealers were too busy to think. Americans themselves did not want long range plans, but rather immediate solutions.

A completely new and ethical foreign policy was inaugurated by Franklin D. Roosevelt in the Caribbean and Western hemisphere, one called the Good Neighbor. It consisted of two precepts: 1) That no country intervene in the internal affairs of another and 2) Mutual consultation and cooperation by all nations in the event of an attack upon one or more by powers outside the hemisphere. It meant the United States voluntarily renounced the principle that the Caribbean was nothing more that a lake of ours and our Marines might "peacefully invade" petty nations like Cuba, Panama, and Nicaragua any time American presidents so stipulated, and for whatever reason. A new principle of national equality was substituted. Such a generous gesture more than paid for itself a few years later under the Nazi menace. All countries, with the single exception of Argentina, cooperated against the foe.

Unfortunately, the Thirties was marred not only by class hatred - witness the terrible passions and violence attached to the prolonged and bitter strikes in the steel, textile, and auto industries - but by the prevalence of deep racial divisions everywhere. The cooperation of the South throughout the experimentation of the New Deal was based upon the understanding Washington was not going to interfere with the hallowed principle of racial segregation. As a consequence, lynchings in the South continued to be commonplace. While there was less racial violence in the North, its cities were carefully segregated. Democracy there was thwarted by big city political machines and their joint alliance with business and crime. Big Business could easily recruit thugs as strike breakers, as did Bennett for

Henry Ford. Meanwhile, Anglo-Saxons on the West coast were equally prejudiced against its Asian minority. In the public eye everywhere the red man was regarded as inferior to the white.

World War II abruptly ended America's attempt to solve its democratic dilemma in isolation without class violence and racial suspicions and hatreds. Somewhere between the end of the war itself in August, 1945 and two years later, an entirely different mood and life style was substituted. In a great seizure of optimism, America launched into a tremendous effort to save capitalism and the "democratic" way of life, first in Western and Central Europe, than in Greece and Turkey and, finally, in Asia itself which had never experienced either in any real sense.

It is this post-World War II era then which serves as our social laboratory in which to examine the reality of Veblen's early assumptions about us as a democratic, peaceful, and efficiently industrialized state.

However, Veblen's disillusionment with Western democracy became apparent when the victor's peace was imposed upon Germany in 1919 at Versailles. "The light-hearted crusade to make the world safe for democracy by open covenants openly arrived at has come to a tragic end because Bolshevism is a menace to the vested interests of privilege and property." Consequently, the world was made safe for "Mid Victorian commercialized democracy, that is, a democracy for the safeguarding of the vested interests of property."[8]

122

Footnotes

1   *History of the Idea of Progress* (New York, Basic Books, 1980), 352-355.

2   "Even today open, frank, and 'objective' inquiry into the most sacred and cherished institutions and beliefs is more or less seriously restricted in every country in the world. It is virtually impossible ... even in England and America, to inquire into the actual facts regarding communism, no matter how disinterestedly, without running the risk of being labelled a communist. That there is an area of 'dangerous thought' in every society, is, therefore scarsely debatable. ... the subjects marked with the danger signal are those which the society of the controlling elements of it believe to be so vital and hence so sacred that they will not tolerate their profanation by discussion. Since every assertion of a 'fact' about the social world touches the interest of some individual or group, one cannot even call attention to the existence of certain 'facts' without courting the objections of those whose very *raison d'etre* in society rests upon a divergent interpretation of the 'factual' situation." Louis Wirth, "Preface," to Mannheim, *Ideology and Utopia*, xvii.

3   Kurt Luedtke, Los Angeles Times-Washington Post News Service, "A right to speak, but no one listens," in the Kansas City *Star*, January 18, 1987, K-2.

4   Charles Flinn Arrowood, *Thomas Jefferson and Education in a Republic* (New York, McGraw-Hill Book Company, 1930), 60-61.

5   *Ibid.*, 23.

6   *Ibid.*, 49.

7   Immanual Wallerstein, "The Rise and Future Demise of the World Capitalist System: Concepts for Comparative Analysis," 387-415 in *Comparative Studies in Society and History*, vol. 16, 1974, 388.

8   Joseph Dorfman, *Thorstein Veblen and His America*. With New Reprints of Economic Classics (New York, August M. Kelley, 1961), 432-433.

Chapter XVI

HISTORY
VERSUS
THE DEMOCRATIC, PEACEFUL
AND
INDUSTRIALIZED STATE:
DEMOCRACY?

While we have borrowed heavily from the Jeffersonian agrarian concept of a model democratic state, we do not think this act, by itself, does violence to an industrialized version. This is particularly true if, like Peter Drucker writing in the mid-Fifties, one could predict that for the next two decades there would be an industrial labor shortage. Meanwhile, the chief problem would be that of checking inflation when monetary, if not real wages, are always going up.* This scenario sustains the illusion of both progress and the American dream. However, the problem of sustaining democracy suddenly becomes quite serious when *prognosticators have to confront current facts: a horrific national debt - and to foreigners this time instead of, as in the Thirties, to ourselves - an ever-increasing adverse balance of trade, a national exodus of American industry, or its decay at home and ultimate absorption by foreign nationals, a steady wage decline due to the shift from productivity to service trades. All of these factors together point not only to a steep decline in international prestige and power abroad, but to a crisis at home. The latter will be due to the fact that, unlike aristocracies, democracies are not content with the economic welfare of a few, but stress the greatest good to the greatest number. This is an old egalitarian urge, one characteristic of democracies. Once a sharp and prolonged economic decline occurs - and the masses yield up their belief in the American dream as myth - they may resort to politics to do for them what their economic skills no longer do, i.e., give them a piece of the action. And there will be many who call this reaction socialism. And for those who do, it heralds the end of democracy. This, when and if it comes, will mark the beginning of class warfare. Another alternative, the development of a permanent underclass, is a negation of all serious thinking about democracy.*

*America's Next Twenty Years (New York, Harper and Brothers, 1955), pp.3.

A fascinating question, and one which keeps occuring, is when was the age of innocence terminated for the thinker, the philosopher, the intellectual, and why? When did he cease to believe we were without sin in foreign affairs and, meanwhile at home, steadily making advances both in democracy and benign industrialism and technology? When did he - and we almost shudder to say this - abandon his faith in the perfectability of man? Of course, this is impossible to say, but one may point to certain landmarks.

From a foreign policy standpoint, Kurt Vonnegut believed the loss of our innocence originated with the horror and disgust felt by the thoughtful at the dropping of the A-bomb on Japan.[1] We believe, - for reasons made evident in the following chapter - by the summer and fall of 1947 a general feeling of disillusionment set in among the closest observers of the foreign scene.[2]

From a domestic point of view it was Seymour Martin Lipset who astutely pointed out the dilemma for modern man: he cannot have the extremely large institutions he is dependent upon - such as the nation state, trade unions, political parties, churches and such -without at the same time "turning over effective power to a few who are the summit of these institutions." Thus, he concluded, democracy and large-scale management were incompatible.[3]

However, the researcher is duty bound to point out two difficulties at the outset. In capitalistic democracies, where class representation is the mediated product of a visibly pluralistic society, the complicated process often obscures the power of property, even to the capitalists themselves.[4] Further, and perhaps most important of all, it is very painful and threatening for a man to believe what is powerful in his own society is not at the same time benign. His behavior is akin to that of a religious man asked to believe that his god is evil.[5]

Nevertheless, in any extended analysis as to why belief in the existence of a democratic, peaceful, and industrialized state eroded, one cannot avoid the danger that de Tocqueville called attention to about a century and a half ago. He called it the tyranny of the minority and thought the new manufacturing class might prove one of the harshest ever. Unlike landed aristocrats, they did not wish to own or govern the person of their workman. Rather they preferred to use him in his productive years and abandon him to public charity in his non-productive ones. If ever a permanent condition of inequality pervaded this land, it would occur at the hands of this new elite[6] and its allies of the paper aristocracy, i.e. bankers and stock market devotees. The power of this remarkable triad swept away any illusions about the political influence of Jefferson's small and independent farmer. In recent times Charles A. Beard made this all the more meaningful by his observation that, in the absence of military force, property dominates.[7]

In any prolonged investigation into the extent of democracy, and its inherent respect for individualism in our society, it becomes apparent, like both primitive societies and socialist countries, we are guilty of the social manipulation of the individual in the greater interest of the whole. Allan Bloom phrased this in inoffensive terms: "Democratic education whether it admits it or not, wants and needs to produce men and women who have the tastes, knowledge and character supportive of a democratic regime."[8] In brief, we have invested in conformity and not individual diversity.

One skilled observer thought the kindergarten classes he observed were managed to induce immediate social conformity, even when the children did not understand why something was being asked or required. Even in the sixth grade, children could not rationalize intelligently about class prayer and the swearing of allegiance to the flag because they had been nothing more than rote exercises. Operationally, the function of the school appeared to be to turn out highly disciplined products for industry who, while patriotic, also believed in God. Since problem children were those who did not neatly fit these categories, kindergarten was called one's first exposure to boot camp.[9]

Another expert came to the reluctant conclusion that a healthy child deviant in school might be diagnosed as one suffering from hyperkinesis. Children most vulnerable were those with excessive motor activity, low attention spans, low frustration levels, delayed speech and, finally, aggressive behavior. That child in effect became the ward of medical authorities who were free to administer psychoactive drugs for the purpose of making individual behavior conform to that of the group. This intolerant approach blocked out the possibility that the fault might lie in the way dull school classes were conducted. This technique had ominous implications. It reminded those knowledgeable of the way Soviet Russia treated its adult dissenters and non-conformists, declaring them mentally ill.[10]

For those familiar with the earlier work of Eric Fromm, there is little room for surprise here. Based on such studies as undertaken at the Sarah Lawrence Nursery School and elsewhere, it was obvious that our culture, like all others, deliberately fosters a tendency to conform, one begun at infancy.

By the time a child has arrived at nursery school or kindergarten, he is waging a last-ditch fight to preserve some sense of individuality. As a weaker contender in life's struggle, he has been forced to surrender one position after another to the "enemy." About all he has left is a sense of hostility and rebelliousness to those outside forces who seek to prevail over him in a contest of wills. Naturally, one of the primary aims of the educative process is to eliminate this antagonistic reaction. From the very start, therefore, elementary schooling discourages individual thinking and aims at supplanting this with a larger social thought process supplied by the adult world. The child is kept so busy and bombarded with so many facts so often that he has no time or energy left for individual reflection.[11] That such training must have been highly successful is indicated by Fromm's hypothesis. While modern man lives under the illusion that he knows what he wants, the fact of the matter is that he has been socially conditioned to want what he does.[12]

This may help explain why a decade later David Riesman found that Americans may be characterized as getting their values from others. They seek to gain and keep social approval by the observation of those values. The inner-directed man received his values from the preceding generation - his parents, teachers and the like - who in effect planted a gyroscope in his brain to enable him to detect "right" from "wrong." Even when unobserved, therefore, he tends to behave as taught, else he suffers from a guilt feeling. Consequently, he is relatively independent of social situations later in life as the other-directed man is not.[13] The latter, because of a more permissive upbringing, ultimately adopts his peer group, or contemporaries, as models of behavior or comportment. Much more adaptable and sensitive to suggestions and changes in comportment and ethics than the inner-directed person, he is more anxiety-prone. Instead of an internal and "independent" gyroscope, he is armed with a sort of radar. It allows him to be in tune or harmony with the latest socially-approved or in-thing. This enables him to be at home everywhere and, consequently, at no place in particular, and to be sensitive to others but only in a superficial sense.[14] The third type, the odd man out, or the autonomous man, is capable of freedom, or of setting his own behavioral goals of a high order. Yet, he is not necessarily capable of martyrdom, often incurred by open deviation from socially approved goals.[15] Like Fromm, Riesman understood that America did not educate with the autonomous man in mind, unless, of course, for the purpose of eradicating him.[16]

The most frightening thing of all, however, was the callous treatment on a national level of prison populations, particularly radical blacks, homosexuals and hallucinating schizophrenics. They were subjected to extreme sensory deprivations - solitary confinement in a perpetually dark room - electric shocks, powerful tranquillizers and, finally, psychosurgery. All of these are associated with the treatment of intellectual dissenters in the Soviet Union. The aim, bluntly stated, was to reduce the individual to that very low intellectual level where he could no longer differentiate between his own ideas and those imposed upon him from without by Big Brother. Furthermore, this was not even being done with the "noble" intent of sending the individual back to society, stripped of his antisocial tendencies. It was rather to render fractious prison populations easier to manage or manipulate.[17]

The whole bizarre episode rests upon a psychologically chilling theory which, if accepted, would justify Soviet behavior. It has been advanced by James V. McConnel, a behavior psychologist at the University of Michigan. No one, so the argument runs, makes his own personality. It was shaped socially. Therefore, if society discovers, for whatever reasons, an individual's personality is an antisocial one, he may be run through the cookie cutter again. He has no right to resist being re-shaped or done over.[18] Both we and the Soviet Union, therefore, have pronounced social conformity as "good" and deviations from it as "bad." The chief difference is in Soviet Russia the principal class of dissidents are urban intellectuals and here they are products of black ghettos.

A perusal of our legal system may help clarify the unconscious distinctions we make between blacks, the very poor, and ourselves. Defendants in capital punishment murder cases, where represented by court-appointed lawyers, were found guilty 93 percent of the time. Those with private counsel were judged guilty only 65 percent of the time. Nationwide, killers of whites, according to the Dallas *Times Herald,* were nearly three times more likely to be sentenced to death than killers of blacks. The Atlanta *Constitution* observed black men were twice as likely to go to jail for the same crimes, writing bad checks and armed robbery, than white men. Indigent offenders "are frequently represented by ill-trained, unprepared court-appointed lawyers so grossly underpaid they cannot afford to do the job they know needs to be done."[19]

Recently, in the states of Louisiana and Alabama, two mentally-retarded black men were executed by white juries because their counsel failed to produce crucial mitigating factors. In the Alabama case, one juror said later she would never have voted for the death sentence had she known the defendant was mentally retarded.[20] The same prejudice pops up in the so-called war on drugs. It has become a war against blacks and the poor because they are more visible and easier to arrest. Although the great majority of cocaine users are whites, they make purchases in more prestigious and affluent areas and are harder successfully to prosecute. Thus, the "huge arrest figures have become a dubious way to keep score in our new drug war while drugs proceed along on their merry way with little interruption." Meanwhile, the first casualities of war, often at the request of crime-weary black communities, are civil rights and liberties.[21]

Finally, one must recognize the question of how the group induces the individual to want to fit into the whole, and be like his fellows, is a primitive one. Uniformly primitive societies were able to do this with the minimum of coercion. Only very occasionally was it necessary to drive a recalcitrant member from the tribe. By a subtle educative process which was never relaxed, every member of the tribe was psychologically conditioned to want to gain and keep tribal approval. This made for a homogenous group with common goals.[22] Needless to say, such societies could tolerate no intellectuals who, like Socrates, subjected their own fellow citizens, and the social order itself, to frequent and public criticism.

Also explored was the larger issue of the grave social danger to the American community of allowing medical practitioners to have a monopoly over cases where they pronounce it a question of mental health or illness, despite having no key to its cure.[23] Baffled by the increasing complexity of many social problems relating to alcoholism, drug usage and exotic illnesses, the lay public rapidly retreated in the fact of the supposedly neutral and objective medical profession. Once the labels of health and illness are openly used, the issue is suddenly depoliticized and even the question of what freedom, if any, an individual should have over his own body is ignored or regarded as not pertinent.[24] The social effects of this were sometimes startling, even horrifying. For example, medical men under contract with the Defense Department had for eleven years deliberately exposed their dying patients to massive doses of radiation. The purpose supposedly was to study the physical and psychological results of nuclear fall-out.[25] Subsidized by NASA, which was very interested in discovering how much radiation human beings could take before they became nauseous,[26] scientists at Oak Ridge Laboratories bombarded in a sea of radiation ninety-four cancer victims over a fourteen-year period.[27] Patients who came to the free clinic unwittingly became human guinea pigs. They were not informed that the doctor's interest in the degree of nausea after treatment took precedence over the strategy and tactics for their recovery.[28] Even some of the doctors, like the director of the Health Physics program at Oak Ridge, felt they were misled and betrayed.[29] In retrospect, the significant fact is that Americans involved in that episode were no more critical of their doctors than primitive societies were of their shamans. Magic was expected of both.

Perhaps the greatest blow to the supposed objectivity of the medical profession was given when it was revealed the U.S. Health Study of blacks with syphilis at Tuskegee, Alabama, extending over forty years, was motivated and sustained by Social Darwinism and assumptions of inherent racial inferiority. The experimenters appeared to share the fears of common white folk. One example: the black male, much more generously endowed sexually, presumably wanted nothing so much as to violate the white female.[30] Likewise, doctors involved in the extended case openly postulated syphilis affected blacks entirely different than it did whites. Further, the universal supposition by white doctors that ignorant blacks would not seek proper medical treatment in any event was the justification for a program of outright deception and a pretended treatment of 400 patients.[31] At the same time the experimenters successfully sought to block the treatment of their human guinea pigs elsewhere.[32] Despite wide medical publication since 1936 of these experiments on the untreated results of syphilis, they met with no protests by the medical fraternity and were not stopped until outside pressure by the media in 1972. Meanwhile, much needless individual and community suffering by blacks were the unhappy results of a study which produced, as predictable, nothing of scientific merit.[33]

Furthermore, that same government had a basic indifference toward workers and soldiers it exploited during World War II and thereafter. With regard to the present and obvious menace to public health and safety by asbestos, the foremost expert, D.I.J. Selikoff, may be correct in his insistence it was not the result of a callous desire for profits over human safety, but of ignorance and apathy.[34] His contentions seem supported by the fact, relatively late in World War II, the government astonishingly dictated the use of asbestos clothing for workers in dangerous places like steel plants where they faced a daily threat of severe burns.[35]

Nevertheless, there remains the disturbing contention which arose in the law suit of Johns-Manville. It was one designed to force the government to share in the recompense of individuals and families hurt by early and prolonged exposure to asbestos. During the course of the legal proceedings, both parties alleged the other was long aware of the pernicious effects of asbestos fibers, but chose to suppress the truth.[36] Moreover, the recent attitude of the Navy toward three million shipyard workers in World War II re-enforces suspicions raised by the Johns-Manville charges. As early as 1970, reports came from Great Britain about the fatal illness from cancer in stomach and chest among former shipyard workers. Despite prodding by the American Cancer Society and the Mt. Sinai School of Medicine, the Navy made no attempt to locate and alert the three million. On the contrary, it kept the affair a hush-hush one, while making as few pay-offs as possible to the victims.[37]

The behavior of the Veteran's Administration towards its own wards is even more shocking. Despite the fact, from 1946 to 1954, the military command foolishly exposed somewhere between a quarter to a half-million servicemen to radiation effects from nuclear explosions, the sad fact remains, by November, 1982, the VA granted only sixteen of 2,883 radiation-related claims by veterans or their widows.[38] Consider, for example, the celebrated case of John Smitherman. Now over fifty-five, legless and with one hand twice the size of the other, he is suing the VA. In 1977, it not only failed to diagnose his cancerous condition, but it wanted and tried to avoid such findings. His exposure to atomic radiation in the Bikini tests of 1946 was horrifying, even unbelievable, but true.[39] Once again, the VA's attitude towards American servicemen victimized by the use of Agent Orange in Vietnam was equally callous. In 1966, an Army handout assured the troops the chemical was non-toxic to man and animals.[40] Since then it has been well established that dioxin is one of the most harmful chemicals manufactured by man and is cancer-inducing. However, the VA apparently has been more concerned over the question of legal damages than about the health of its exposed veterans. Thus far it has provided little in the way of either counsel or medical attention.[41] Its position is that the diseases suffered by the veterans, and the birth defects of their children, may well be caused by totally unrelated agents. It is up to the ex-servicemen to prove it was the result of exposure to Agent Orange.[42]

In 1979, Congress ordered the VA to conduct a major study of this issue and, after Veteran protests, transferred research to the Centers for Disease Control. Following a preliminary study which showed almost non-existent differences between troops which had been heavily exposed to Agent Orange and those which had not, the CDC declared it could not find enough exposed cases to ensure the validity of the study itself.[43] If this outcome were a favorable one for the VA, the same can scarcely be said for its attitudes and methods toward its own wards. A federal judge in San Francisco ordered the Veterans Administration to pay $115,000 in fines and legal costs because it destroyed pertinent documents and gave evasive replies to lawsuits by veterans who had been exposed to radiation while in service.[44] It also leaves nagging questions of why did the Marines serving in Vietnam die of lung cancer and lymph cancer at significantly higher rates than Marines who did not.[45] One might be forgiven for concluding that the answer remains elusive because, in part, the Veterans Administration did not care enough. Only in 1990, after a decade-long fight, did that body admit for the first time exposure to Agent Orange "may have caused cancers among the 3.1 million U.S. military personnel who served in Southeast Asia."[46]

In August of 1990, a bipartisan committee from the House blamed the Reagan administration because it "obstructed" such health studies. The latter feared an adverse report would force the government not only to compensate veterans, but would set precedent of having the U.S. "compensate civilian victims of toxic contaminant exposure too." Nine of fifteen Republicans agreed with the majority report.[47]

Nor was the general public to escape the government's callous disregard for its safety during wartime. This occurred at the Hanford nuclear weapons plant in the state of Washington. A recent federal report confessed that radioactive iodine "was allowed to escape over a three-year period in the mid-1940s.... But the news got even worse. The government knew the plant was operating in a dangerous fashion, poisoning people in the area, and did not reveal that fact. The very officials charged with protecting human life were endangering it instead."[48]

It is when we reflect upon the mass protest of the young against the war in Vietnam, one understands the criticism of the democratic West when engaged in a prolonged war. Hilaire Belloc likened its offenses to those religious ones of the thirteenth century Inquisition.

Rather than physical torture, think of cross-examination and public dishonor. For the sacrifices of all civic guarantees to the preponderant interest of one religion, substitute the similar sacrifices of all such guarantees to the preponderant interest of a united nation engaged in total war. Instead of clerics using every means for the preservation of religious unity think of civil officers using every means for the preservation of national unity in a time of peril. This eventuates in a sorry spectacle of universal conscription for young men who may or do not believe in the war itself. They are faced with the distasteful choice of risking being maimed or killed on the battlefield, or subjected to public dishonor in the courts. These civil infringements on individual liberty would cause a fourteenth century citizen to recoil in horror as we do at the Inquisition itself.[49] What Vietnam showed was the government could utilize the apparatus Belloc described almost as effectively on the unfortunate draftee when the nation itself was sharply divided upon the necessity and morality of the war effort.

All these illustrations have one thing in common. That is their disregard for the principle of the sanctity of the individual personality with which the democratic principle has always been allied.

Since World War II, one lamentable feature about the democratic and industrialized state is in any contest between profit margins for capital and possible long-term harm to its citizens, it has characteristically come down on the side of the former. Charles Beard meant that when he said, in the absence of military force, property tends to dominate. A more recent explanation concerned extraordinary favors covertly shown by Defense department officials to private contractors at the expense of the American public. In return for allowing suppliers to write contracts in a way to insure excess profits, government officials hoped to curry favor and thus insure themselves of jobs in the private sector following their government "service."[50]

If one thinks of a particular industry where one might best see this principle at work, it would be the automobile. The industry's popularity, wealth, and power overawed all those in Washington who were supposedly vested with authority for establishing and maintaining safety standards. During the Eisenhower administration, for example, Congressman Kenneth Roberts of Alabama found it extremely difficult to obtain any information from federal agencies dealing with highway safety standards. He was forced to conclude the auto was a taboo subject for them.[51] Ralph Nader offered a convincing explanation. Civil servants tailored their jobs so as to avoid stirring up controversy, and the strong reaction which accompanied it. This meant more work for them. The auto industry was quite capable of generating such pressure whereas the unorganized consumer was not.[52] Nor was the conservative character of such regulatory agencies as the Federal Trade Commission to change, despite the political turbulence and reform zeal manifested during the Sixties.[53] Its chairman, Paul Rand Dixon, appeared more concerned with defending the integrity and patriotism of businessmen than in protecting the public from those whose concern for immediate profits placed its health and safety at some risk.[54]

Such complacency in regulatory institutions no doubt existed when the Ford Motor Company decided to market the 1973 Pinto as it was, although aware rear collisions might collapse the gas tank and result in fires trapping the occupants. Apparently company officials thought this would be cheaper and less trouble than meeting any possible lawsuits resulting from such tragedies.[55] While *Consumer Reports* overlooked that crucial aspect of safety standards, it rated the 1973 Pinto poorly on a half-dozen equally crucial safety aspects. These were poor drive visability, rough ride and directional instability, unstable drum brakes, throttle response and general drivability. It was a poorly engineered car.[56] Nor was this Ford's only major offense. After several years of investigation, the Department of Transportation cancelled its case against Ford's transmission in 1980, although still maintaining its original position that the part was faulty. The car had a history of shifting from park into reverse gear with very serious consequences when parked on an incline. The department settled for Ford's offer to dispatch a warning to all car owners to be sure the gear was in park with the brake on and the engine off.[57]

However, the record of GM in this respect was no better. More than two years after GM and the National Traffic Safety Administration were first alerted to faulty engine mounts, which might jam the throttle and cause severe accidents, GM instituted a recall of seven million Chevies and light trucks in December, 1971. But even this belated effort was partially nullified when, in letters to the car owners, GM insisted there was no accident risk if they did not bring the car in for "repairs." Many dealers contributed to the messy situation by failure to possess the needed part.[58] *Consumer Reports* was quite critical both of the company's refusal to admit structural defects and the NHTSA's reluctance to release full details to the American public. The magazine concluded the entire episode suggested the danger of the government's reliance upon the auto manufacturers to maintain adequate safety standards.[59] In October, 1983, the Department of Transportation released GM documents indicating the company produced and sold more than one million X-body cars in 1980 with the full knowledge they had defective brakes. This produced over seventeen hundred official complaints, three hundred accidents, and fifteen deaths.[60] Stubbornly refusing to admit fault, General Motors succeeded in getting arbitration over single cases of complaints. Although the attorney general for the state of New York called it a "sellout" to the auto company, the FTC defended its action on the grounds it would otherwise be in litigation for the next decade.[61]

Chrysler's known sins feature the odometer scandal of 1987. That company for many years followed the policy of allowing its executives to drive 60,000 new cars up to four hundred miles with the odometer detached and then selling the cars as new. Much more alarming was the fact some of these cars had been wrecked, fixed and still sold as new. When first charged with these facts, Chrysler officials declared the charges were outrageous. Later, Chairman Iacocca admitted the action was "dumb," but did not admit dishonesty. He promised compensation for those sinned against, but no mention was made of any guilty or "dumb" executive being fired.[62] Such action induced two different editorial writers to contrast our national failure to hold corporate executives responsible for their stupid or dishonest decisions with that of the Japanese who would demand the resignations of their executives. Instead, when our big corporations finally unload an inadequate executive, the same board which fires him makes him rich for life.[63]

That same year Chrysler was fined $1.5 million by the Labor department for deliberately exposing its workers at its Newark, Delaware plant to the health hazards of lead and arsenic without so informing them. Agreeing to pay the fine, the motor company did not admit to breaking the law.[64]

Enough has been said to establish general principles: while government agencies may not have been given enough powers by Congress to do a good regulatory job, they were and are timorous about using what they have. They fear offending big business and incurring its wrath, while becoming a deep source of embarrassment for the incumbent administration. This naturally puts to hazard both the public's pocketbook and its health.

Both Detroit and Washington understood, despite any pious talk of a better distribution of wealth and income and the primacy of health and safety of the public, the success of any administration was determined by its ability to promote economic growth in quantitative terms, or the Gross National Product. The tremendous importance of the auto industry in effecting these goals was obvious to all. If, in their zeal to protect public health and safety, legislatures, or their agencies, undermined public confidence in the domestic auto industry by revealing too many of its defects, the economy might slide into a recession. One almost certain outcome would be the same administration voted out of power at the next election.[65]

The triumph of private property over public interest was "finalized" as a consequence of the victory of the "free" enterprisers in 1980. The magazine, *Motor Trends,* reported the Reagan administration quickly kept its promises to the auto industry by delaying, modifying and eliminating many auto safety standards, such as air bags, emission standards, noise levels, and warranty information.[66]

If the causal connection between the clout of big business and the caution of timorous officials, elected and otherwise, is vague, the focus is sharpened by a survey of the ever-increasing influence of money upon our supposedly free elections. It is immediately apparent that its darling is the Republican party. Their money raising advantages over the Democrats, always large, have now become grotesque.[67] Because the candidates have to spend so much time raising money, they have little time to spend with the electorate, depending instead on television bits and flashes. Perhaps as a consequence an increasing number of voters do not bother to exercise their right of franchise. It all bodes ill for the future prospects of democracy, but it is a problem which even conservatives admit exists.[68]

In 1958, Robert Byrd and a companion senator from West Virginia raised a combined total of $50,000 for their campaigns, but in the last election Byrd had to raise $2 million for his alone. As late as 1976, total spending on Senate elections was $38 million, but rose to the alarming figure of $182 million in 1986.[69] While the Republican party outspent Democrats by nearly a 5 to 1 ratio,[70] the power of money was reflected

everywhere and by a great many candidates of both parties. In staid
Missouri, for example, the Republican Kit Bond spent $5.31 million
successfully pursuing the Senate seat while Harriet Woods, Democrat,
spent $4.35 million. *Common Cause* reported that Jack Kemp of New York
spent over $2 million in a successful defense of his seat in the House while
young Joseph Kennedy laid out $1.5 million to win one in Massachusetts.[71]
In brief, what this means is simply this: the notion in a democracy anyone
can legitimately aspire to high office is simple piety rather than an expression
of reality. "Nobody," wrote a well-known conservative columnist, "likes
the situation. For members the incessant hunt for campaign contributions is
stultifying and degrading. For the big donors, the constant dunning gets
expensive. The voting public reads of breakfast clubs and political action
committees and its cynicism deepens."[72] And what did all that money buy
in the elction of 1986? Tom Wicker said it best when he wrote: "Surely the
nastiest, least relevant, most fraudulent campaigns - by statesmen of both
parties - in the history of a long-suffering nation." It was all capped by the
lowest voter turn-out since 1942 when the nation was engaged in war.[73]

The most recent national election, that of 1988, hit new lows in
campaign integrity and morality and voter participation. Republican
Chairman Lee Atwater was probably as responsible as any for the callous
and Machiavellian approach. Appearance, not substance, was the Republican
theme. Everywhere, their candidate, George Bush, campaigned draped in
the flag. Leading us all daily in the Pledge of Allegiance, he dropped
innuendoes that his opponent was not patriotic. Instead, he was alleged to
be pre-disposed to free black criminals from prison - the Willie Horton
variety - to prey upon innocent white middle classes.[74] Meanwhile, he
constantly appealed to the pleasure-pain theory: stress the pleasure of your
public and avoid pain. Thus, George played the old Reagan shell game to the
hilt. He promised not to increase taxes.

His opponent, Michael Dukakis, Governor of Massachusetts, played
everything so cool he was suspected of having no emotions. He did not get
angry when President Reagan clearly implied he was an emotional cripple,
having undergone psychiatric care. He also - and fatally this time - played
it cool when asked at the last presidential debate how he would react if his

wife were raped. Meanwhile, he tried to avoid the liberal tag, stressing competence instead. This too, was an appearance ploy, i.e., Herbert Hoover, the competent engineer.

Thus, anxious to avoid a Cassandra-like role of truth telling, neither candidate hammered away at the real issues: America's rapid economic decline, its staggering foreign debt, the decay of our cities, roads, bridges and infrastructure, mass poverty, homelessness, the public health crisis, and the sad state of public education in grade and high schools.[75] Of course, if we were not going to raise taxes and vastly reduce spending in the destructive category, military spending, there was no need. There would be no money for social programs.

On safe issues - or those upon which almost everybody agreed -like drug abuse, better educational opportunities and a clean environment - both candidates assumed a like stance: " ... there was not much difference between them in their concern ... or how they would approach them [problems] in the future. This agreement struck many people as a lack of concern for the issues."[76]

When Bush managed to push past glittering generalities, or points of light, he seemed to concentrate on matters like the pollution of Boston harbor. Here he threw words at his opponent rather than the promise of federal money for the project itself. He ignored the fact, despite frequent appeals from Massachusetts, the Reagan administration had given no money for the clean-up project.

Here, as always, the entire campaign seemed to be an advertising man's dream of word and image. George Will later gave an apt summary of Bush's performance: "His campaign showed little promise and he has kept that promise."[77] In electoral politics, "personality always counts more than issues."[78]

Typical Republican behavior was manifest in the strong stance taken by Bush against abortion and his promise of federal action to make it illegal. Of course, this raised the possibility of criminal liability either on the part of mothers aborting or their physicians.[79] It tied in neatly with the old conservative and Republican accent upon outlawing individual sin and holding the individual accountable and not society. The stress upon individual patriotism, the emphasis on more cops and prisons in the so-called war against drugs, restoration of the death penalty for certain crimes, the emphasis on longer sentences for the Willie Hortons, even the so-called thousand points of light (charity) for local welfare, all would have made a great deal of sense to the wealthy and powerful who shaped the Republican planks of 1920 and thereafter.

Perhaps the greatest tour de force of the entire campaign was the way in which Bush successfully stonewalled any questions about his all-too-apparent involvement in the Nicaraguan contra supply problem at a time when Congress outlawed it. Had he admitted his undoubted participation, he would have disqualified himself. During the New Hampshire primary, Senator Bob Dole challenged him to discourse about it while among friends. Bush declined. Throughout the presidential campaign itself, he issued nothing more informative than denials. From a democratic standpoint, the strategy was, unfortunately, successful. Once again, the electorate was kept in the dark, kept ignorant.

As we see it, the public outcome that mattered most was not the election results themselves. It was the dual fact that, while more money was spent than ever before, Americans boycotted the election. "The turnout - less than half of the voting age population - was less than it had been since 1924" (the Keep Cool with Coolidge one).[80] Particularly disturbing is the fact that the participation of young people from eighteen to thirty "has declined in every presidential election since 1972," when the Watergate scandal turned them off. Today, it is not political scandals which are responsible for the low turn-out among that group. Rather, it is their indifference to public affairs.[81]

If this is what we mean by democracy in action - and we write this particular section after the demise of communism is eastern Europe and the Soviet Union - one would be hard put to urge its emulation. At best we win by default.[82] Writing in the New York *Times,* Michael Oreskes came to a devastating conclusion: "The result is a political system that is becoming dangerously close to brain dead."[83]

Let us admit it is not easy to obtain a general agreement as to what this means.[84] In part, this is because the problem is not universally recognized among theorists of political science and democracy.[85] However, let us consider an immediate view and another of long-range historical perspective. Of the former, recent studies indicate the classes boycotting elections were the economically disfranchised ones, or the poorest. They are precisely the ones who need the clout that a few political triumphs might bring. With regard to the ghettoes of Detroit, let a prominent journalist speak: "Could it be that we are in the process of creating a permanent underclass, without education, without skills, without jobs, without hope - state-of-the-art urban despair...."[86] According to Robert Nisbet, the problem is larger and spaced out over time. He argues the appeal of politics to the Westerner has been in a visible state of decline ever since the tremendous miscalculations of politicians produced the great devastation of World War I. In recent years this sentiment has mushroomed.[87]

Perhaps the supreme example of the close nexus between the influence of big money in recent elections and fraud and corruption in high places in the private sector is the $500 billion Savings and Loan Scandal. According to a report issued by the General Accounting Office, "fraud and insider abuse existed" at all the failed savings and loan outfits. While bank examiners knew the perils, their superiors hesitated to act in the public interest. "Political pull reined in the regulators. Corrupt thrift owners and bankers discovered how easy it was to beat the system with a call from a friendly congressman, and congressional friendships were easily purchased. The fix was in." Campaign contributions and unsavory business deals were determined by political power, not ideology. Its trail led everywhere, even to the White House.[88]

While the tragedy has many distressing facets, the historian concentrates on two. First, he is reminded of its similarity with the disastrous banking scandals of the great depression from 1929-1933. Both were produced by the easy optimism generated by the business and financial leaders of the country, and the false confidence reposed in them by a gullible public. Politicians, therefore, were under no pressure to check fraud and chicanery, inevitable under any system where the players have daily opportunities to make a fortune with other people's money. Secondly, the sad fact is, ignorant of monetary manipulations, the public neither understands nor is interested in a matter which should be of vital concern. Therefore, the public learns nothing. Economic tragedies in a supposedly democratic system tend to perpetuate themselves. A little rhetoric in the right places about the glories of democracy and free enterprise dissipates the justifiable criticism.

Underlying it all is the sad fact one-third of our citizens are functionally illiterate. Among the literate, the average ability to read is too low. There is more than mere sentiment attached to this question. Only highly literate societies can prosper economically.[89] Complicating our problem is for the first time in history high school graduates are less knowledgeable and skilled than the previous generation.[90] That great exponent of democracy, Thomas Jefferson, recognized the *sine qua non* of that experiment was an educated electorate.[91] It is, unfortunately, impossible to argue this is any longer the case. Among experts, there is general agreement education is sinking in a "tide of mediocrity."[92]

Meanwhile, supposedly the best and brightest of our youngsters turned their backs on the traditional liberal arts courses - literature, philosophy and history - for so-called practical ones like prebusiness which promises immediate jobs after graduation, as well as those commanding higher salaries.[93] Twenty percent of America's undergraduates are now estimated to be majoring in economics and accounting, hoping for an advanced degree in business. Like students in prelaw and premedicine, they manifest little interest in the social sciences, being at best casual visitors. Some maintain they are unnecessary. Obviously, there is even less regard for the humanities.[94] Some authorities maintain that these attitudes were carefully nurtured by educators in the nation's high schools. There history was degraded into social studies, English into language arts and other scholarly content into process, towards skill rather than substance.[95]

What these students have sidestepped - whether consciously or not - has been ably expressed by Allan Bloom: "True liberal arts education requires that the student's whole life be radically changed by it, that what he learns may affect his action, his tastes, his choices, that no previous attachment be immune to examination and hence re-evaluation."[96] When put in these terms, it is understandable why the modern day student is not prepared to put his promising career at hazard.

What has been the cost of this insistence by students upon the relevancy, or practicality, of subject matter? By that we mean constantly putting the question of what it promises to do for them tomorrow in terms of status, power and money? Two examples immediately come to mind. The first is the conspicuous lack of a concern for ethics in business schools. This is something Veblen anticipated over half a century ago.[97] It was typified by a recent episode which apparently occurred at the Wharton School of Business, but which could just as easily have occurred at any of the other high-ranking ones. Before the Wall Street scandals, Ivan Boesky was invited to speak there by the students. When he publicly praised "the vitality and the salutary advantages of greed ... they applauded enthusiastically."[98] This is precisely what Bloom meant when he observed these students were not, as typical liberal arts devotees, motivated by the love of the discipline itself, but rather by the love of money which their chosen discipline promises to return. Of course, the sooner the better.[99] Secondly, as surveys repeatedly reveal, modern-day students have cut themselves off from history. The "major national traumas of the past quarter century -civil rights, Vietnam and Watergate - have been reduced to ancient, irrelevant history ....the young are being deprived of the lessons of history - history so recent that it might as well be yesterday."[100] And behind it all lies the grave warning of the philosopher, George Santayana. Those who neglect history are condemned to repeat its recorded mistakes.[101]

Thus, even the smart set of our young men and women does not qualify, by Jeffersonian standards, as the stuff of which democracy is made and maintained.

Perhaps, therefore, it should not come as a source of surprise if, "besides their academic problems, America's colleges are losing their place as havens for tolerance and understanding." Instead a research team for the Carnegie Foundation investigating eighteen campuses "found a level of campus tension and conflict that is truly alarming." Instead of tolerance, good will and mutual respect, "student life is being increasingly scarred by racial tensions, sexual harassment, campus crime, intolerance for competing ideas and persistent abuse of drugs and alcohol. It seems that many colleges are just not very nice places to be."[102] These, of course, are the same ills from which our society suffers. Having lowered America's colleges to the level of the public, is it any wonder they reflect the same ugly visage?

It is possible these lamentable outcomes were the result of a surrender by administrators and faculty in the Sixties of the old -and perhaps aristocratic - principles of liberal arts institutions. In a speech in the college chapel of the University of Chicago in 1951, Robert Redfield set forth two which had a great appeal for me. First, when a university is no longer criticized by right-wing segments of the public as being subversive, it is no longer doing its proper job. Second, when liberal arts faculty no longer seeks to advise, guide and even instruct its business-minded president, it is no longer doing its job. In effect, Redfield modernized Socrates' gadfly. While both forms of behavior were dangerous, it was the latter which got me into trouble at my own institution.[103] Today, one can safely say, if God is not dead, Redfield certainly is.

These elite principles were sharply challenged in the Sixties by democratic ones, championed by newly-admitted and subsidized minorities. Everyman's opinion is as good as the next one.[104] "Who says what the universities teach is the truth rather than just myths to support the system of domination?"[105]

According to Bloom, the tragedy of the Sixties was, confronted by the threat of violence on campus, the university compromised its traditional autonomy "in the desire to be more useful, more relevant, more popular." As a consequence of yielding to the imagined needs of the comparatively ignorant, this "democratization of the university helped to dismantle its structure and caused it to lose its focus."[106] When the dust of the conflict settled, the university had been virtually levelled to the standard of public opinion outside it. Now, like other public servants, it was there to do the public's bidding, or to give it what it thought was needed to surmount today's problems.[107]

Turning once again to the question of a close alliance between town and gown - one dominated by a joint acceptance of the commercial mentality - one must conclude that it produces a miasma for the traditional liberal arts. These cannot survive without the independence and autonomy enjoyed since the twelfth and thirteenth centuries in Europe. The liberal arts, therefore, must resist monetary impulses to concentrate almost exclusively on turning out the sort of graduate who can be immediately helpful to businessmen, while also striving not to attract attention as being too liberal, or left of center, i.e., un-American. Further it must not be sucked into the maw of the military-industrial complex because this siren song promises greater publicity, research grants to natural scientists, and larger and better equipped science labs. As Bloom himself puts it: "The university must resist the temptation to try to do everything for society." Instead, it must preserve its mission and sacred quest and resist the impulse to compromise itself "in the desire to be more useful, more relevant, more popular."[108] But enough of day dreams! Since the glory years of the Thirties, the American university has done all these things. That is perhaps why it is not apt to produce the sort of educated youth America will need in the next generation to solve the kinds of social problems anticipated for it.

At this juncture younger son, Jeff, himself a product of the radical left Sixties, voiced a caveat. If we are not careful in our claims for the university, we are apt to present it clothed in a sort of Protestant "papal infallibility" and perceive its liberal arts professoriat as a "pure" priesthood. History belies this for any institution. Since its birth the university has been endowed by church, king, nobility and bourgeois. Thus, its tilt has, consciously or unconsciously, been toward its benefactor. Ironically, Higher Education served as the training center for those cultural anthropologists of which this study has been critical. Finally, when violence came to the campuses and offices were stormed, we learned how intimate the involvement had become between the university itself and the military-industrial complex. At the outset, older son Tom had been inclined to dismiss Allan Bloom as an elitist and observed I had a few such symptoms myself. At this point, therefore, family disagreements become apparent.

Undeterred, however, by these youthful reservations, one of my age and training finds it reflects the perception of Alexis de Tocqueville. American democracy meant the triumph of mediocrity. It was essentially distrustful of one of perceptible intellect and independent mind. Such an individual was free to express his own views only as long as public opinion itself was divided upon the issue. Once the public was united, it exercised a tyranny of the majority, forcing a universal compliance. Those few who defied the majority were "tormented by remorse for having spoken the truth." It led the author to over-generalize: "... there can be no literary genius without freedom of opinion, and freedom of opinion does not exist in the United States."[109]

In more recent times, the celebrated journalist and foreign correspondent, Harrison E. Salisbury, concluded that mankind seeks, not truth, but instead the useful or, better, the comforting. "Once again," he concluded, "I had violated the rules. I had reported an important but unpalatable truth."[110] Of course, Salisbury did not spend any time in the Gulag. Instead of him, his story, his baby, was killed. That is the democratic way.

Other professionals share his alarm at the degeneration of the information and news segment of the media. The longtime dedication to informing the public yielded to the demands of business school graduates. Budgets must be balanced. The way to do that is to cut drastically, or eliminate, expensive news in favor of mass entertainment. As one disillusioned expert put it: "We have lost our commitment to what we believe people should know and just give them what they want." An underlying, but undeclared, theme of the entire piece is the legitimate fear the American public, like the old Romans, wants little more than bread and circuses.[111] David Brinkley made the same charge against a news director of NBC who was frequently trying to jazz up his appearance, attitude and delivery. Be light, be peppy, and be happy, he was admonished.[112] A recent theory, and one which appears plausible, is TV moguls decided to cater to the eighteen to thirty year old age group whose capacity for hard news is sharply limited. At the same time, they are heavy consumers. "Catering to this new generation has spawned a new kind of news media, offering lighter fare and 'infotainment' a hybrid of information and entertainment."[113]

What, then, have we done with democracy's precious heritage of free speech? "We like it well enough when it occurs in Latvia or Czechoslovakia or Poland, but it tends to make us uncomfortable closer to home."[114] Racial, ethnic and special interest groups discourage polite, but serious discussion of problems they regard as their private preserve. "Why has a quarter-century of genuine racial progress left us in what is most charitably described as a state of racial disquiet? Why has calumny rather than conciliation become our preferred method of political dissent? Why is there so much meanness in the air?"[115] Legislative concern is divided by a host of "persistent and inflammatory" issues such as abortion, racism, flag desecration, obscenity laws, assault weapons and drug enforcement.[116] Here intolerance is frequently manifested, as when the editors of the Fort Worth *Star-Telegram* were branded as traitors because they opposed tampering with the First Amendment.[117]

Anti-abortionists threaten excommunication for the pro-choice proponents,[118] deny them the sacrament,[119] talk about Satan being the enemy,[120] and promise a "lake of fire" awaits their foes in Hell.[121] This makes their cause appear as a fanatical theological exercise. It is hard to believe they really accept the American experiment of the separation of church and state.

As for causality, we think David S. Broder came close to the heart of the matter: "These cultural disputes preoccupy us now because we are floundering. No American leader in twenty-five years has discovered or articulated a popular goal to focus the nation's energy and attention. As we drift in our debt-financed prosperity, we are losing confidence in our future. So we let ourselves be upset by fringe characters whose goal is simply to shake us up."[122]

While we were searching for an appropriate way to terminate this chapter, Tom called attention to a scholarly article which referred to a subject in our opening summary. This was the possibility of an ever-sharpening division among Americans likely to result in class conflict. His argument can be summarized as follows. The earning gap between rich and poor in this country is greater than in any other industrialized nation. Expenditures for the so-called welfare state are lower than any other industrialized state, save for Japan which has a much stronger traditional family-supported system. However, the inequities in this system do not appear to have lasting qualities. An ethical and cultural metamorphosis is occuring which promises to change things. This is the relatively high reproduction rate among blacks and Hispanics, as well as the recent immigration of non-Anglo-Saxon whites. All lack the old Protestant ethic of individualism and private charity, if available, for all the disadvantaged. This situation is aggravated by the loss of millions of jobs in the relatively high-paying industrial area and, simultaneously, the creation of poorly paid ones in the service trades. The blue collars, obviously enough, are absorbing the blow. When working at fifteen dollars an hour, they were as individualistic as any union people could be but, with a permanent shift in economic conditions, there is bound to be an ideological one. Thus, "it may be unwise to assume that the prevailing norms of the American political economy (such as low government social expenditures and low taxes on the rich) would be maintained if the nation entered a period of sustained economic difficulty caused by a plunging dollar and slow economic growth."[123]

This updates, and in a sense fulfills, an old prediction by the German sociologist, Ferdinand Tönnies. Despite the fact that a capitalist middle-class society continually stresses the theme it is interested in and represents the whole of the community, it cannot change the ever-widening hiatus between the few who possess a virtual monopoly of the wealth and the relative poverty of the people themselves. Thus, ultimately deprived of a faith in individualism which has brought them little in a material sense, the "people come more and more to think of the state (community) as a means and tool to be used in bettering their condition, destroying the monopoly of wealth of a few, winning a share in the products."[124]

In brief, we can no longer ignore the future prospect of a people's revolt against the "capitalist market discipline, in action again - establishing the conditions in which more babies in poor families will die; in which poor people will be unhealthier and live shorter lives."[125]

Let us summarize some of the ways in which we fall short of being a genuine democracy. We live in a social order so large and diverse that its leading institutions are always in the hands of a small elite. As de Tocqueville rightly observed, the interests of that group does not lie in the development of a real democracy. As a culture, we are guilty of indoctrinating the young to believe in God, democracy and patriotism. Mavericks are troublesome to us. On the contrary, everyone is free to be like his fellows, to have the same likes and dislikes. On the contrary, justice is perverted to the disadvantage of minorities and the poor. That government which advises its citizens "to ask what you can do for your country," exploits them in war-time and then abandons them. When it is forced to choose between public safety and those who profit by putting it to hazard, it characteristically comes down on the side of property, economic prosperity, and "progress." These illustrations reveal the government's frequent disregard for the principle of the sanctity of the individual, a principle with which the democratic process is always allied.

Meanwhile, irresponsible government is promoted. Big money for thirty-second TV emotional messages increases the distance between candidates and voters. Personal and vicious attacks replace meaningful dialogue. Even the thoughtful person, nay especially so, feels helpless. That may in large measure explain the voter boycott.

Meanwhile, our educational institutions in grade and high schools are a study in mediocrity. Low prejudices, as well as academic standards, invaded the bastion of the liberal arts, our colleges and universities. At the same time the TV media dilutes its hard news in favor of the entertainment factor.

To disguise the fact it does not have the courage to tackle real issues, our legislative bodies focus attention on sexual, moral, theological and patriotic issues. Republican presidents initiate this, as well as encourage it. It reminds the historian of Massachusetts, circa 1690. Meanwhile, in the absence of leadership at the top, public acrimony is the order of the day.

We try, nevertheless, to ignore evidence of the creation of a permanent underclass, something entirely foreign to the thinking of the leading exponents of American democracy prior to World War II. We refuse to think about the fact this unproductive class - whose welfare is perennially neglected - is reproducing itself at a greater rate than those capable of producing in a highly technological and sophisticated society. Early in the next century, it will represent one-third of the work force and, later in the same century, probably a majority. This means the surrender of the last vestige of our international economic hegemony.

Finally, as we shall see in the next chapter, our presidents, and their entourage, habitually lie to the American people. This prevents intelligent action on the part of the voter, the *sine qua non* of democracy.

Democracy's prospects, therefore, are not good. Other than as a matter of rhetoric, our top echelons are really not interested in it. Our lowest orders seem presently incapable of it, and every year it seems farther removed from them. Meanwhile, our middle classes apparently want to avoid any serious discussion of the matter.

Such failures, or flaws, in our democracy are not surprising. Perhaps democracy, like communism and Christianity, is not something actually to be achieved in historical space and time. It is, instead, mythological, or something for which its adherents perpetually strive and never achieve. We suspect that democracy to us is something like the green light at the end of Daisy's dock was to Gatsby on the other side of the bay. It just points out the direction rather than a promise of the unattainable.[126] But, we would all be lost if the green light itself were extinguished! For, to paraphrase Winston Churchill, though democracy is not a very good kind of government, it is "more good" than any other kind we know about. And that is why we are devoted to it.

However, if a small, homogenous, and isolated people - primitive, in other words - manifested but a few of these pernicious symptoms we have just described, that society would disintegrate overnight. It would do the same if there were a tribal disregard for the Ten Commandments, something which every tribe discovered in a practical manner for itself, independently of Moses. Strictly, therefore, on the basis of internal or "tribal" ethics and behavior, we find the primitive superior to our so-called democratic society. It is difficult, if not impossible, to reconcile that conclusion with the idea of progress and the perfectability of man.

Footnotes

1   See vol. I, Chapter II, ft. 30.

2   See vol. II, Chapter XVII, pp. 168-170

3   "Introduction," 5-39 in Robert Michels, *Political Parties, A Sociological Study of the Oligarchial Tendencies of Modern Democracy.* Translated by Eden and Cedar Paul (New York, The Free Press, Collier-Macmillan, 1962), 15.

4   Maurice Zeitlin, *Classes, Class Conflict, and the State. Empirical Studies in Class Analysis* (Cambridge, Massachusetts, Winthrop Publications, Inc., 1980), 23.

5   Alvin W. Gouldner, *The Coming Crisis of Western Sociology* (New York, Basic Books, Inc., 1970), 486.

6   *On Democracy in America in The People Shall Judge,* vol. 1, The Staff Social Science 1 (Chicago, University of Chicago Press, 1949), Second Book, 549-550.

7   *The Economic Basis of Politics* (New York, Alfred A. Knopf, 1934), 39. Property as such is not always recognized as a status obligation, but in the long run it is and with extraordinary regularity. For example, in the so-called pure democracies, like the United States, where aristocracy is prevented by law, a pseudo-aristocracy appears and is made up of persons of diverse occupations who only dance with others at the top. Max Weber, *Selections from His Works,* with an introduction by S. M. Miller (New York, Thomas Y. Crowell, 1968), 49.

8   *The Closing of the American Mind* (New York, Simon and Schuster, 1987), 26.

9   Harry L. Gracey, "Learning the Student Role: Kindergarten as Academic Boot Camp," 215-226 in *Readings in Introductory Sociology,* 3rd edition (New York, Macmillan, 1977).

10   Peter Conrad, "The Discovery of Hyperkenesis: Notes on the Medicalization of Deviant Behavior," 12-21 in *Social Problems,* v. 23, No. 1, October, 1975.

11   *Escape from Freedom* (New York, Farrar & Rinehart, 1947), 246-248.

12   *Ibid.,* 252.

13   *The Lonely Crowd. A Study of the Changing American Character.* Abridged edition with a 1969 preface (New Haven, Yale University Press, 1973), 16, 23-24.

14   *Ibid.,* 21, 24-25.

15   *Ibid.,* 250-251.

16   *Ibid.,* 251.

17   Wayne Sage, "Crime and the Clockwork Lemon," 16-23 in *Human Behavior,* v. 3,

152

No. 9, September, 1974, 18-21.

18   *Ibid.*, 22.

19   Rhonda Chriss Lokeman, of the Editorial Staff, The Kansas City *Star*, June 10, 1990, J-1, 4. The Constitution "also makes it virtually impossible to execute someone who has enough money to hire a really good lawyer, This makes for an Execution Gap between the rich and the poor." Donald Kaul, Tribune Media Services, "Circumstantial opinions about absolute matters," in *ibid.*, July 7, 1990, C-9.

20   Gerald Uelmen, Los Angeles Times News Services, "Rush to Injustice," in the Kansas City *Star*, May 29, 1990, B-5.

21   Clarence Page, Tribune Media Services, "Dubious Drug War," in *ibid.*, May 4, 1990, C-15.

22   Mead, *Cooperation and Competition Among Primitive Peoples*, 493. See also Spencer, *North Alaskan Eskimos*, 162, 238 and Grinnell, "The Cheyenne Indian," in *The Golden Age of American Anthropology*, edited by Mead and Bunzel, 144.

23   Irving Kenneth Zola, "Medicine as an Institution of Social Control," 511-526 in *The Sociology of Health and Illness*, edited by Peter Conrad and Rochelle Kern (New York, St. Martin's Press, 1981), 516.

24   *Ibid.*, 511, 523.

25   *Ibid.*, 523-524.

26   Merely discomforting to a man on the ground, nausea could prove fatal to a man with a space suit and oxygen mask on. Howard L. Rosenberg, "Informed Consent," 31-44 in *Mother Jones*, September-October, 1981, 32.

27   *Ibid.*, 31.

28   The doctors themselves were not sure that radiation would be effective for the patient, but the experiments provided the best opportunity to monitor the radiation sickness syndrome. *Ibid.*, 33-34. The parents of six-year-old Dwayne Sexton were not told the umbilical monitor attached to their son during the radiation experiments was for the purpose of collecting data for NASA. *Ibid.*, 36.

29   *Ibid.*, 44. Later Congressional investigations were rendered innocuous by the fact that NASA's records on the affair had been destroyed and that a key medical witness at Oak Ridge was deceased. Eliot Marshall, "Gore Investigates Radiation Clinic," 423-424 in *Science*, v. 214, October 23, 1981, 423.

30   "Racism and Research: The Case of the Tuskegee Syphilis Study," 186-195 in *The Social World*, edited by Jan Robertson (New York, Worth Publishing Company, 1981), 187.

31   *Ibid.*, 188-189.

32   *Ibid.*, 191.

33   *Ibid.*, 191, 193.

34   "Asbestos," 2-7 in *Environment*, vol. 11, No. 2, March, 1969, 7.

35   "Safety Clothing," 51-52 in *Scientific American*, July, 1945, 51.

36   "Manville Suit Asks U.S. to Pay Asbestos Claims," New York Times, July 20, 1983, D 1-2; "U.S. Fights Manville Suit," in *ibid.*, September 17, 1983, A-34; "Manville Files Suit," in *ibid.*, November 17, 1983, D-4. Johns-Manville of Canada admitted 43 deaths since 1969 of workers who had manufactured asbestos-fiber building materials in their Toronto plant. Since 1942, Ontario's Workman's Compensation Board has processed 279 claims for asbestos-related deaths. "The Asbestos Hits the Fan," 26-27 in *Macleans*, April 14, 1980, 27.

37   "A Grim Legacy from World War II," 31 in *Business Week*, September 29, 1975, 31.

38   Vernon Lee Hawthorn was one such victim. He died of cancer in 1962 because he participated in the A-bomb test at Eniwetok in 1950. Only in May of this year did the Army admit he had been there. Meanwhile, it refuses to turn over any documentation. "Wrongful Death," 9-10 in *Progressive*, vol. 44, No. 11, November 10, 1980, "As a radiated veteran, I am not against building arms to protect us. I am against the most hideous crime of our government, covering up the truth ... of what nuclear particles do to the human body." Eldon D. Praisewater, Chairman, National Association of Atomic Veterans, Missouri Chapter, "First-hand knowledge," in The Kansas City *Star*, October 31, 1983, A-10.

39   Within hours after the first test shot at Bikini atoll in a 1946 test known as Crossroads, Smitherman and others were ordered aboard the target ships to fight fires. Since there were absolutely no restrictions, they then took a swim in the polluted lagoon waters. Later, clad only in shorts on the fantail of a vessel, and told not to look directly at the blast, Smitherman was hit with debris from the second test shot. Tom Wicker, New York Times News Service, "Vets of atomic blasts still paying for service to nation," in The Kansas City *Times*, September 1, 1983, A-19.

40   "Where is My Country?" 20 in *Time*, vol. 115, No. 8, February 25, 1980, 20.

41   *Environment*, 2-4 in vol. 21, No. 5, June, 1979, 2-3.

42   "Where is My Country?" *loc. cit.*, 20; "Deadly Legacy: Dioxin and the Vietnam Veteran," *The Bulletin of the Atomic Scientists*, 15-19 in vol. 35, No. 5, May, 1979, 18.

43   Joan Beck, Chicago Tribune, "Veterans won't easily let grievance go," in The Kansas City *Star*, September 8, 1987, A-8; The New York Times News Service, Washington, "Veterans health study hits snag," in The Kansas City *Times*, September 1, 1987, A-1.

44   The Associated Press, San Francisco, "VA fined for destroying papers," in The Kansas City *Times*, January 9, 1987, A-4.

45   The New York Times News Service, Washington, "Study links cancer, Vietnam

154

duty," in The Kansas City *Times*, September 4, 1987, B-9. "Two months ago, through the legal efforts of the Vietnam Veterans of America, a VA study was brought to light which showed a 110 percent higher rate of non-Hodgkins lymphoma and a 58 percent higher rate of lung cancer among Marine veterans of the Vietnam war. The VA suppressed this study for six months." Michael Baxendale, Chairman, Veterans Affairs, Vietnam Veterans of America #317, Kansas City, "Veterans neglected," in The Kansas City *Times*, December 28, 1987, A-16.

46   Washington Post, Washington, "Effects of Agent Orange acknowledged," in The Kansas City *Star*, May 19, 1990, A-7. "The department said ... it would compensate veterans for non-Hodgkin's lumphoma and for another rare cancer called soft tissue sarcoma. However, the government maintains that exposure can't be documented." The Associated Press, Washington, in *ibid.*, June 27, 1990, A-5.

47   The New York Times, Washington, "U.S. blocked study, says House panel," in the Kansas City *Star*, August 10, 1990, A-1.

48   Yael T. Abouhalkah, of the Editorial Staff, "Federal officials can't be trusted on radiation," in the Kansas City *Star*, July 29, 1990, J-1.

49   "Preface," xxix-xli in Hoffman Nickerson, *The Inquisition. A Political and Military Study of its Establishment* (Port Washington, New York, Kennikat Press, 1968), 2nd edition, xi.

50   United Features, Washington, "Public pays for Pentagon profligacy," in The Kansas City *Times*, September 17, 1983, A-15. Only about six percent of Pentagon contracts were let after open bidding. Charles Mohr, New York Times News Service, Washington, "Great Plains Rebels don't like Pentagon ways," in *ibid.*, October 14, 1983, A-21. According to a government audit, Pratt-Whitney made a profit of $900,000 by charging the Air Force nearly triple what the items were actually worth. From the Knight-Ridder Newspapers, Washington, "Audit finds huge profit on tools for military," in The Kansas City *Star*, November 2, 1983, A-1. When the public outrage forced an investigation into the much-inflated charges, the Navy proposed to let a contract to Pratt & Whitney to conduct an investigation. "Outrage of the Week," in The Kansas City *Star*, December 20, 1983, A-11.

51   Ralph Nader, *Unsafe at Any Speed. The Designed-in Dangers of the American Automobile* (New York, Grossman Publishing, 1965), 295.

52   *Ibid.*, 304-305.

53   Perhaps the most telling criticism was the one that the main enforcement technique of the FTC was merely an assurance of voluntary compliance: the business man merely promised, not even under oath, that he would not repeat the same specific act of deception against the public. *The Nader Report on the Federal Trade Commission, 61-62.*

54   "Statement of Chairman Paul Rand Dixon," 179-191 in *The Nader Report on the Federal Trade Commission* by Edward F. Cox *et al,* (New York, Richard W. Baron, 1969), 182, 184; Nader, *Unsafe at Any Speed*, 123-124.

55   Ford Motor Company escaped on the judge's controversial decision to exclude presentation in court of their internal documents which demonstrated that company officials were aware of the gas tank defect. See "Pinto Precedent," 356-357 in The *Nation*, March 29, 1980; "A Local D.A. Charges the Pinto with Murder," 36-38 in *People*, February 4, 1980, 37; "Blessed be the Name of Ford," 29-30 in *Maclean's*, March 24, 1980, 30. For cost reasons the gas tank was designed to withstand crashes at only twenty miles an hour "which would make it unsafe even at relatively low speeds." The car itself was built to withstand them at forty or fifty miles per hour. So testified Harley Copp, ex-highranking Ford engineer. "A Dead Stop in the Ford Pinto Trial," 65-66 in *Newsweek*, February 25, 1980. The company, however, was not so lucky in similar suits against the Mustang. Company documents admitted into a trial at Corpus Christi, Texas, apparently showed that company officials knew in 1970 there were problems with the gas tank but balked at spending from $4 to $24 per car to remedy the matter. Heavy damages were also awarded the family of the victim as occurred in a similar Los Angeles trial over a defective gas tank. Corpus Christi, Texas, "Court finds Ford guilty in fiery crash," in The Kansas City *Times*, November 23, 1983, A-4; Los Angeles, "Crash victim family awarded $1.1 million," in *ibid.*, December 24, 1983, A-4.

56   "Comments and Ratings. Subcompact Cars," 274-275 in *Consumer Reports*, vol. 38, No. 4, April, 1973, 275. The Pinto also had a history of shoddy workmanship. "The Little Cars," 8-17 in *ibid.*, vol. 36, No. 1, January, 1971, 13.

57   *Consumer's Research*, vol. 64, No. 3, March, 1981, 4.

58   "Faulty Engine Mounts and Faulty Recall Program," 83-84 in *Consumer Reports*, vol. 38, No. 2, February, 1973, 83-84.

59   "Chevrolet's Failing Engine Mounts," 118-121 in *ibid.*, vol. 37, No. 2, February, 1972, 120.

60   From Times News Service, Washington, "GM was aware brakes were flawed, documents indicate," in The Kansas City *Times*, October 21, 1983, A-1.

61   By the Associate Press, Washington, "Better business bureau to rule on complaints of faulty GM cars," in The Kansas City *Star*, November 17, 1983, C-2.

62   Donald Kaul, Tribune Media News Services, "The buck never stops where the bucks flow," in The Kansas City *Times*, July 9, 1987, A-15; New York Times News Service, Highland Park, Michigan, "Iacocca says Chrysler sorry," in *ibid.*, July 3, 1987, A-1.

63   Kaul, "The buck never stops...." Kansas City *Times*, July 9, 1987, A-15; Jerry Heaster, the Star's business and financial editor, in the Kansas City *Star*, July 6, 1987, H-6.

64   By the Associate Press, "Chrysler gets $1.5 million safety fine," in the Kansas City *Star*, July 6, 1987, A-6.

65   Nader, *Unsafe at any Speed*, 324-325.

66   "Rules Roundup," 111 in *Motor Trend*, vol. 33, No. 11, November, 1981, 111.

156

67   From January 1, 1985, through September, 1987, the national Republican fund-raising committees raised $179 million while the Democrats raised a mere $35 million. Anthony Lewis, New York Times News Services, Boston, "Grotesque deparity in party resources," in the Kansas City *Times*, November 4, 1987, A-7.

68   Tom Wicker, New York Times News Services, New York, "Political Consultants are no asset," in the Kansas City *Star*, November 23, 1986, C-5.

69   James J. Kilpatrick, Universal Press, Washington, "Senators agree on one point: something has to be done to curb campaign spending," in the Kansas City *Star*, March 27, 1987, A-15.

70   Washington, "Republicans spent more" in the Kansas City *Times*, February 16, 1987, B-8.

71   Stephen C. Fehr, Washington Correspondent, "Bond-Woods race among the costliest," in the Kansas City *Times*, February 13, 1987, C-7; Wicker, "Political Consultants no asset," *loc. cit.*

72   James J. Kilpatrick, Universal Press, Washington, "Eggs Bentson may bring action," in the Kansas City *Times*, February 13, 1987, A-11.

73   "Political consultants no asset," *loc. cit.*

74   "Bush criticized Dukakis for having vetoed a bill to require Massachusetts school teachers to lead their students in a Pledge of Allegiance, for having supported a furlough program that allowed a convicted murderer to escape from prison, for having boasted of being a 'card-carrying member' of the American Civil Liberties (a liberal interest group), for opposing capital punishment, and for not favoring a strong national defense. ... portraying him as a person who did not share the core social values of the swing voters in the states that held the key to success in the electoral college. It worked. ... Whereas only 31 percent of the voters surveyed in June thought Dukakis was a liberal, by September 46 percent saw him that way - and for many of those voters, the liberal label was harmful." James Q. Wilson, *The 1988 Election* (Lexington, Massachusetts, D.C. Heath, 1989), 9. Such tactics have aptly been called Bush's "scurrilous presidential campaign...." Donald Kaul, Tribune Media Services, "Confusion reigns in nation's capital," in the Kansas City *Star*, January 25, 1990, A-11.

75   "On many issues the American people do not know what they want or are so divided in their opinions that any candidate who takes one side runs the risk of alienating a lot of potential supporters. For example, most Americans are worried about the deficit. But most Americans also oppose raising taxes or cutting spending on expensive domestic programs. Those who favor some cuts are divided on what should be cut. This being the case, neither candidate can say much more than that he 'deplores' the deficit and promises to devise a 'plan' to solve it." Wilson *The Election of 1988*, 13. The same principle applies after a man has been elected to the presidency. "The more a president does or even tries to do in difficult domestic affairs, the more he is likely to outrage one or more powerful interests or constituencies; but the less he attempts, the less he risks rocking the boat or pulling down his approval rating." Tom Wicker, New York Times News Service, "President's polls reinforce lesson often ignored by Democrats," in the Kansas City *Star*, January 24, 1990, A-7.

76   Wilson, *The Election of 1988*, 13.

77   "... his administration illustrates ... the echoing emptiness at the core of contemporary politics. Its intellectual and moral flaccidity reflect ... the sagging of America deeper into a peripheral role abroad and self-indulgence at home." Washington, "Poor George began tumbling down hill at his inauguration," in the Kansas City *Times*, January 22, 1990, A-9.

78   Tom Wicker, New York Times News Service, "President's pools reinforce lesson," in *loc. cit.*, A-7.

79   The penalties anti-abortionists had in mind were revealed when the Louisiana legislature approved a bill which denied abortion even to victims of rape and incest. Doctors performing such abortions might be imprisoned at hard labor for up to ten years. The Associated Press, Baton Rouge, Louisiana, "Abortion showdown set in Louisiana," in the Kansas City *Star*, June 28, 1990, A-6.

80   Wilson, *Election of 1988*, 10. See also The Associated Press, Washington, "Apathy, acceptance permeated 1988 election, panel says," in The Kansas City *Star*, May 6, 1990, A-4.

81   Los Angeles Times, Washington, "Young Americans don't care about public affairs, study says," in The Kansas City *Star*, June 28, 1990, A-1, 11. "The authors term this 'the age of indifference,' adding that 'the ultimate irony is that the Information age has spawned such an uninformed and uninvolved population.'" David S. Broder, "Encouraging words from youth group," in *ibid.*, July 3, 1990, B-9.

82   A panel of eight prominent figures from politics, the media, political science faculty and public policy analysis concluded: "Even as enthusiasm for democracy ignites around the globe, it is waning in the very nation whose political traditions inspire others." The Associated Press, Washington, "Apathy, acceptance permeated 1988 election, panel says," in The Kansas City *Star*, May 6, 1990, A-4. The Markle Commission also believed, because of the degeneration of political campaigns, voters saw themselves as "distant outsiders with little personal consequence at stake in national elections." Little wonder as "politicians try to hack their opponents to pieces with innuendo, tawdry distortions or tangential attacks that obscure the real issues." Rich Hood, "Tactics say voters' ardor for democracy, in *ibid.*, May 13, 1990, B-2.

83   Carolyn Barta, Dallas Morning News, "American politics becoming dangerously close to brain dead," in The Kansas City *Star*, April 1, 1990, K-4.

84   Not trusting myself to report on this dreary affair of the election of 1988 alone, I solicited the cooperation of my colleague, Ron Brecke of the Political Science department at Park College. I have been ruthless in exploiting him as a sounding board throughout this monograph. The least I can do is to acknowledge my indebtedness to him.

85   For example, in an otherwise brilliant analysis made recently, one young scholar made no mention of the pernicious influence of big money on the elections of 1986 and 1988, or of the consequent boycott itself. See Emily Hauptmann, "When Politics Makes Choices Disappear: Marcel Ophuls' France and Rational Choice Theories America." Paper read in March, 1990, at the Western Political Science Association in Newport

158

Beach, California.

86   Donald Kaul, Tribune Media Services, "Let's save Detroit," in The Kansas City *Star*, August 13, 1987, A-15.

87   *History of the Idea of Progress*, 356-357.

88   James Ring Adams, *The Big Fix. Inside the S & L Scandal. How an Unholy Alliance of Politics and Money Destroyed America's Banking System* (New York, John Wiley & Sons, 1990), 274-275. While there appears to be general agreement about the causes, we believe Edward Hill of Cleveland State University said it as well as anyone. While special-interest contributions to legislators were in part responsible, the "bailout is the direct result of the mindless deregulation of the Reagan era." Randall D. Smith, "Who'll pay for the S & L mess?" in The Kansas City *Star*, June 28, 1990, B-1.

89   Anthony Lewis, "Whole host of problems plague us," in the Kansas City *Star*, February 25, 1980, I-5; Roger Thompson, Congressional Quarterly, "Illiteracy takes toll in lives and dollars," in *ibid.*, July 18, 1983, A-15; E. D. Hirsch, Jr., "Cultural Illiteracy," in *ibid.*, July 8, 1987, A-15; James Flanagan, "Competition will change U.S. education in 90's," in The Kansas City *Times*, January 29, 1990, A-6.

90   John Naisbitt, *Megatrends. Ten New Directions Transforming Our Lives* (New York, Warner Books, 1982), 31. About a third of the youth is ill-educated, ill-employed and poorly equipped to make a decent living in America. *Ibid.*, 31, 250. From 1972 to 1982, college entrance examination scores fell in every state, rising only in the District of Columbia. By the Associated Press, Washington, "News stats highlight decline in U.S. education," in The Kansas City *Star*, January 5, 1984, A-1.

91   How else explain his preference for newspapers without government to that of government without newspapers? *The Political Writings of Thomas Jefferson* with an Introduction by Edward Dumbauld (New York, Liberal Arts Press, 1956), 93. Or of his confidence in reason in the free market place of ideas? "First Inaugural Address," 426-428 in *The People Shall Judge*, I, 427.

92   This stunning conclusion came in a 1983 report of the National Committee on Education entitled *A Nation at Risk*. Almost seven years later, the Secretary of Education confessed "little progress" had been made. See James Flanagan, "Competition will change U.S. education in '90s," in The Kansas City *Times*, January 22, 1990, A-6. A bipartisan report of twelve governors concluded: "Our nation is facing a major crisis in education, one larger and more significant than was realized a few years ago." Will Sentell, Jefferson City Correspondent, Mobile, Alabama, "A dozen governors give education reforms bad marks," in the Kansas City *Star*, July 29, 1990, A-5.

93   Haynes Johnson, Washington Post, Knoxville, Tennessee, "Best and brightest of college set know exactly what they want in life," in The Kansas City *Star*, April 23, 1987, A-15. The National Endowment for the Humanities reports the following alarming statistics: "From 1970 to 1982, the number of college students graduating with bachelor's degrees in English dropped by 57 percent; in philosophy, by 41 percent; in history by 62 percent, and in modern languages by 50 percent. At the same time the total number of degrees awarded rose by 11 percent. ...A student can get a bachelor's degree from 72 percent of all U.S. colleges and universities without having studied American history or

literature; from 75 percent without studying European history; and 86 percent without studying about classical Greece or Rome." From Times News Services, Washington, "Report criticizes colleges for decline in the humanities," in the Kansas City *Times*, November 26, 1984, A-1.

94   Bloom, *Closing of the American Mind*, 370.

95   Jonathan Yardley, Washington Post, "Schools undone by 'process' sophistry," in the Kansas City *Times*, September 9, 1987, A-17. A national report on what eleventh graders know about history and literature concluded that "the student's knowledge was deplorably poor." It was contained in Diane Ravitch and Chester E. Finn, Jr.'s book entitled *What Do Our 17-Year Olds Know*. Citing several other studies, all of which came to an identical conclusion, James J. Kilpatrick rightly came to the conclusion that the "typical 11th grader, culturally speaking, is an ignoramus." See Universal Press, Washington, "Another devastating report on deterioration of U.S. schools," in The Kansas City *Times*, September 18, 1987, A-14.

96   Bloom, *Closing of the American Mind*, 370.

97   *The Theory of Business Enterprise* (New York, Charles Scribner's Sons, 1935), 382-384.

98   Sally Gaines, Chicago Tribune, "Business schools re-evaluating offerings to students," in the Kansas City *Star*, May 24, 1987, F-1. Another popular and influential columnist, noting the same speech and student reaction, claimed it originated at a New York University. Flora Lewis, New York Times News Services, Paris, "Money the measure of prestige," in the Kansas City *Star*, April 26, 1987, K-5. The point is, we believe that the incident could have happened at any one of the prestigious business schools.

99   Bloom, *Closing of the American Mind*, 371.

100   Jonathan Yardley, Washington Post, "Civil rights, civil wrongs," in The Kansas City *Times*, March 25, 1987, A-13. A defense of the modern college student has been written by Kelley Griffin in a book entitled *More Action for a Change* (Debner Books). College apathy or indifference is nothing but a myth. Inspired by Ralph Nader, college youth has been actively engaged in issues having to do with the preservation of human health and safety, consumer and environmental hazards. Public interest research groups, Nader said, were "using lobbying, litigation, referenda, all the mainstream ways to change society. But that isn't considered news (by a media which defines activism in terms of the more overt student activities of the Sixties)." Lee Mitgang, AP Education Writer, "People are wrong to think students aren't concerned," in the Kansas City *Star*, September 2, 1987, A-17. All such issues, of course, can be said to lie within the student's realm of experience - whether at first hand or vicariously through the press, TV and such - and thus may be said to be independent, or innocent, of history as a discipline.

101   *The Life of Reason or the Phases of Human Progress* (New York, Charles Scribner's Sons, 1922), 5 vols., I, 284. According to Flora Lewis, journalism students at the University of Missouri - oldest school its kind in America - would agree with Santayana. "... several complained privately that they were not being taught enough about the past and the world outside that confronts America. For them, the Vietnam war is already history, but they said it is skipped over with a bare mention in their classes. They

wanted deeper probing into how and why it happened, what went wrong, what to watch out for as the nation moves ahead. They criticized what they considered excessive American inwardness, self-congratulation, ignorance of other countries. ... But when the talk turned to democracy, it was clear that subject had been skipped over, too. ... If anything they were asking for more, not less, substance in their education ...." New York Times News Service, Columbia, Missouri, "Missouri journalism students belie image," in The Kansas City *Times,* November 15, 1987, A-15.

102   Brian Dickinson, Providence Journal, "No haven from strain of society," in The Kansas City *Star,* February 6, 1990, C-1. The National Institute Against Prejudice and Violence found 250 colleges and universities where racism, sexism, anti-Semitism and homophobia flourished this year. Barbara T. Roessner, The Hartford Courant, in *ibid.,* May 25, 1990, C-9.

103   Later, when attempting to perform the gadfly role at Park College, I received from its president a sharp reprimand in a hand-written letter on three pages of legal size paper. By both internal evidence, and dated memos in the same file, it was written in the late summer of 1954. But, much more important is the expressed hope of the president that the resident gadfly would go away: "Whenever anything basic comes up in faculty or student affairs, you can be counted on as the spokesman for counter-action. ... You seem to give ready assent to all the critics of our way of life. If we were looking for an interpreter of the college, you would think we could call on the head of the social sciences. ... Time after time, you let us down by what can be called only an incorrigible attitude - the almost professional objector.... This fact places you in a very ambiguous position with many of your colleagues. If there were not so many good things in contrast ('Conscientious, able and hard working'), it would be an intolerable situation. As it is allowances are continuously made for your eccentricities." This undated memo, signed Zwingle, suggested, since "we are about to begin a new year," a joint meeting. Subsequent and dated memos between us indicate that the meeting, due to the president's ill health, was not held until the first week of October, 1954. Obviously, I was much more diplomatic than usual at this verbal session for the meeting was apparently congenial. In addition to the original copy of President J.L. Zwingle's letter, I possess signed and dated correspondence between us for the month of September and final memo from me to him dated 8 October, 1954.

104   Bloom, *Closing of the American Mind,* 256, 329. My own life-time experience with conservative friends, who were businessmen, engineers, lawyers and the like, was that the principle of equality of opinion did not apply to their professions, but only to mine. Whereas I accepted their expertise in their respective fields, they did not return the same courtesy. Not only were they prepared - as they had a right to do - to challenge my views on current domestic and foreign events, but, much more importantly, to argue about events long past, say those of ten, twenty, or even thirty, years ago, events which only the historian continued to study and ponder. On one occasion - two decades after the deed - I observed that in some measure, President Truman plunged us into the Korean "war" in June of 1950 in order to enable his party to avoid the effective charge of being "soft on Communism" in the coming presidential election of 1952. A friend and successful lawyer then declared: "If that is what you are telling your students, then you have no *business* teaching." You see to him, even teaching was a business in this business-dominated society. Naturally, I was aware of the traditional, even standard, explanation: "Recalling how 'appeasement' in the 1930s had brought on World War II, President Truman felt that 'if this was allowed to go unchallenged it would (ultimately) mean a third world war.' .. 'the foundations and principles of the United Nations were at stake.'" Anthony Cave

Brown, *"C" The Secret Life of Sir Stewart Graham Menzies, Spymaster to Winston Churchill* (New York, Macmillan, 1987), 700-701.

105   Bloom, *Closing of the American Mind*, 94.

106 *Ibid.*, 65. The U.S. Secretary of Education, Bill Bennett, put the matter bluntly and clearly when speaking at Harvard's 350th anniversary: "At a minimum, a real education embraces the classical and Jewish-Christian heritage, the facts of American and European history, the political organization of Western societies, the great works of Western art and literature, the major achievements of the scientific disciplines - in short, the basic body of knowledge which universities once took it upon themselves as their obligation to transmit, under the name of a liberal education, from ages past to ages present and future." Today, because the student gets to opt from such a proliferation of courses, liberal arts at the universities, including Harvard, has lost its meaning. James J. Kilpatrick, Universal Press, Cambridge, Massachusetts, "Harvard gets a sample of education," in The Kansas City *Star*, October 28, 1986, A-17.

107   Bloom, *Closing of the American Mind*, 319.

108   *Ibid.*, 254.

109   *On Democracy in America*, I, 253-255.

110   *A Journey for Our Times. A Memoir* (New York. A Cornelia and Michael Bessie Book, Harper and Row, 1983), 375-376.

111   Richard Reeves, Universal Press, New York, "Journalism has suddenly become another business without value," in The Kanss City *Star*, June 30, 1987, A-6. In the Forties and Fifties "the idea in TV news was to tell people not only what they wanted to know, but what they ought to know. It is an approach that is all but discarded now in network prime-time specials." Rick Du Brow, Los Angeles Times, "Up next; big changes for the big newscasters," in *ibid.*, August 13, 1990, D-1, 4.

112   Marian Christy, The Boston Globe, "Brinkley has the last laugh," in *ibid.*, January 25, 1990, D-1.

113   Los Angeles Times, Washington, "Young Americans don't care about public affairs, study says," *loc. cit.*

114   Donald Kaul, Tribune Media Services, "River of patriotic bilge let loose," in The Kansas City *Star*, June 18, 1990, C-11.

115   Jonathan Yardley, The Washington Post, "If these are happy times, why do Americans seem to hate each other so much?," in *ibid.*, June 24, 1990, J-4.

116   Claude Lewis, Philadelphia Inquirer, "Persistent, inflammatory issues shaping U.S. future," in *ibid.*, June 15, 1990, C-9. "'Republicans are really facing an identity crisis,'" said Burdette Loomis, a political scientist at the University of Kansas. "'You've got abortion, you've got taxes, you've got no real communist threat. So what do they do? Flag burning didn't seem to make it. Is obscenity going to make it? I don't think so. For Republicans, you've got a real question of where to go.'" Jake Thompson, Washington

Correspondent, Washington, "New national issues and easy times for GOP," in *ibid.*, July 8, 1990, A-1, 8.

117   Tommy Denton, Fort Worth Star-Telegram "Freedom kept alive and well by its exercise," in *ibid.*, June 27, 1990, C-11.

118   John Cardinal O'Connor defended the bishop who warned Governor Mario Cuomo he was "in serious risk of going to hell" because of his support for abortion. "The Bishops' view, the Cardinal said, are consistent with Church teaching." "O'Connor: the real issue," in The New York *Times*, February 1, 1990, A-1.

119   San Diego's Bishop Leo T. Maher barred California Assemblywoman Lucy Kilea from receiving communion "because of her pro-choice stand in abortion." "A Mistake in San Diego," in *America*, v. 161, December 9, 1989, 416.

120   "Our enemy is Satan," said Debbie Delaney at a rally sponsored in Kansas City by the Missouri Citizens for Life. See Diana Williams, Staff Writer, "Abortion opponents celebrate anniversary of Webster decision," in The Kansas City *Star*, July 4, 1990, C-6.

121   The age-old Christian conviction of a horrible death for the unbeliever probably motivated fundamentalists who consigned to "the lake of fire" all who defied Jesus by signing a recent planned parenthood petition in the Kansas City *Star*. I personally received such a threat in a postcard signed "Hanovers, 606 N. 1st, Burlington, Ks. 66839."

122   Washington Post Writers Group, "Flag flap signals loss of purpose," in The Kansas City *Star*, June 18, 1990, B-5. President Bush merely epitomizes presidents who do not lead. While calling himself an "education president" and an "environment president," he has done little or nothing. The same is true for matters of public health and homelessness. "His record in office is a particularly graphic example of the current American habit of talking about problems without doing anything that would be really difficult." Anthony Lewis, New York Times News Service, "Whole host of problems plague us," in *ibid.*, February 25, 1990, I-5.

123   Paul Kennedy "The (Relative) Decline of America," 29-38 in *Atlantic*, vol. 260, No. 2, August, 1987, 32-33. In Kansas City, as in a great many other cities, there is clear evidence of the creation of a permanent underclass. In its school district, 50 percent of the children are from single parent homes, 68 percent from poor homes, 70 percent blacks and 4 percent Hispanic. "The majority of our kids live in neighborhoods where drugs or drug addiction are heavy." However, black and Hispanic populations are reproducing themselves at a faster rate than whites are doing. "By the year 2010, one of every three employees will be a minority." From the testimony of George Garcia, Superintendent of Schools. Jean Haley, of the Editorial Staff, "So many of the young at risk," in The Kansas City *Star*, May 13, 1990, I-1, 4. "Time magazine recently announced that whites will become a minority in the 21st century. Already in California, African-Americans, Latinos, and Asian-Americans represent a majority of the children. This multiracial diversity is increasingly visible in cities everywhere...." Ronald Takaki, "Economic disparity breeds contempt," Newsday, in The Kansas City *Star*, July 8, 1990, J-1, 4.

124   Ferdinand Tönnies, *Community and Society (Gemeinschaft and Gesellschaft)*. Translated and edited by Charles P. Loomis (East Lansing, The Michigan State University

Press, 1957), 259. Such a tactic is perhaps best explained by Michael Burawoy. Far from the modern state merely being agents of the bourgeois, as Marx charged, it must be autonomous of it to preserve the real interest of capitalism itself, i.e., their class interest in the maintenance of capitalism itself. "For to preserve these political interests, the state must frequently act against the capitalists' economic interests by granting concessions to other classes." *Manufacturing Consent. Changes in the Labor Process under Monopoly Capitalism* (Chicago, University of Chicago Press, 1979), 196-198.

125   The Quality of Life Index by the U.N. Development program reveals a drop in social spending in the United States for the last ten years from 17% of the total government expenditures to 10%. The criteria used were literacy, life expectancy and social services as well as average income and wealth created. Alexander Cockburn, Los Angeles Times, "The harsh discipline of capitalism," in the Kansas City *Star*, June 24, 1990, J-5. A report authorized by the American Medical Association concluded: "Never before ... has one generation of teen-agers been less healthy, less cared-for or less prepared for life than their parents were at the same age. ... Our political system allowed 2 million children to fall into poverty in the 1980s while the number of billionaires quintupled." Anthony Lewis, New York Times News Service, Aspen, Colorado in *ibid.*, July 9, 1990, B-7. ... the nation's leaders in the 1980s behaved as if societal breakdown was really none of their business. ... The major Republican thrust was to reduce social service budgets. ... According to present federal definitions, 32 million Americans live in poverty. That is no cause for alarm in Washington; the administration has not found their condition a topic to be seriously addressed." "Paint them a little shinier," (editorial), in *ibid.*, July 9, 1990, B-6.

126   F. Scott Fitzgerald, *The Great Gatsby* (New York, Charles Scribner's Sons, 1953), 182.

Chapter XVII

HISTORY
VERSUS
THE DEMOCRATIC, PEACEFUL AND
INDUSTRIALIZED STATE:
PEACEFUL?

"There is ... no war within memory, however nakedly aggressive ... which has not been presented to the people who were called upon to fight as a necessary defensive policy, in which honour, perhaps the very existence, of the State was involved."

John Hobson, *Imperialism. A Study* (London, George Allan & Unwin, first publication 1902, fifth impression 1954), 47.

* * *

It seems clear that we are in for a very bad time, so far as the economic and social position of the country is concerned. We cannot go through another ten years like the ten years at the end of the twenties and the beginning of the thirties without having the most far-reaching consequences upon our economic and social system ....

... We may say it is a problem of markets .... We have got to see that what the country produces is used and sold under financial arrangements which make production possible.... You must look to foreign markets.

The first theory I want to bring out is that we need these markets for the output of the United States. If I am wrong about that, then all the argument falls by the wayside, but my contention is that we cannot have full employment and prosperity in the United States without foreign markets.

Testimony of Dean Acheson, Assistant Secretary of State, before the Hearings on Post-War Economic Policy and Planning, Select Sub-Committee on Post-War Economic Policy and Planning, House, 78th Congress, 2nd session, 1944, in *The Pentagon Watchers. Students Report on the National Security State,* edited by Leonard S. Rodberg and Derek Shearer (Garden City, New York, Anchor Books, Doubleday and Company, 1970), 4.

* * *

First, a caveat. Since the subject matter is far too staggering for the confines of a single chapter, we limit it to our relations with the Third World. Our detailed illustrations relate to Latin America because it affords a fertile area in which to separate our rhetoric about democracy from the hypocrisy of power politics.

When discussing the origins of a tendency in history, it is difficult, for example, to say precisely when it was the United States in effect abandoned its priority upon democracy at home and subordinated it to an aggressive and imperialistic policy abroad. However, we emphasize the words and thoughts of four prominent Americans. They are symptomatic of a deep national transition of thought and action in this regard.

The first was Henry Luce, millionaire, owner and editor of the tremendously influential *Life* and *Time* magazines. Even before America's entry into World War II, he recognized the luxury of isolation from European affairs was something we could no longer afford. Rejecting the socialism which he thought inherent in the New Deal,[1] he believed America was confronted with the hard and inescapable truth that the twentieth century must belong either to Nazi Germany or the United States.[2] Of course, few at the time realized that World War II would crush the former and the consequent political vacuum in Central Europe would suck the victors in from both east and west. At any rate, Luce postulated we would, after the war, insist to the fullest on the freedom of the seas: "The right to go with our ships and our ocean-going planes where we wish, when we wish and as we wish." We have, he concluded, the opportunity and the duty to accept the fact that the United States is the most powerful and vital nation in the world. "We can exert upon the world the full impact of our influence, for such purposes as we see fit and by such means as we see fit."[3] It would be hard to find a better prophet for the self-righteous use of armed force by us in all corners of the post-war globe.[4]

About the same time another prominent journalist, Herbert Agar of the Louisville *Courier Journal,* had almost identical thoughts. America had to enter the war against Fascism. Agar then "talked out a blueprint for the 'Pax Americana,' under which the American vision would be extended into an 'Atlantic community.' In turn, it would wage war against anyone threatening peace and freedom. John Foster Dulles' aggressive defense treaties of the 1950s were direct descendents of Agar's ideas, as was John F. Kennedy's policy in Vietnam."[5]

In 1944, when we were still in the midst of war, our Assistant Secretary of State, Dean Acheson, provided an economic justification for the policy which Luce promulgated. Before a select post-war planning committee, he confessed that America could not risk another ten year depression as experienced since 1929 without devastating effects upon the economy. On the contrary, he saw any post-war prosperity as essentially dependent upon foreign markets. To produce was one thing, but to sell our surplus quite another. Only the certainty of the control and disposition of overseas markets as purveyors of essential raw materials and buyers of our manufactured products could yield the desired outcome, i.e., full employment and prosperity. Confronted with this overpowering fact, it was clear that the depression policy of peace and isolation was out. We willingly immersed ourselves in power politics on a global level.[6]

Only one thing now needed was the willing consent of the minority party, the Republicans. That was provided for by Senator Arthur Vandenburg of Michigan. By 1947, President Truman and Dean Acheson were worried as to how to get the American people to abandon the Monroe Doctrine. Issued in 1823, it said America did *not* intervene in Europe, and, therefore, did not countenance further intervention of Europe in the Western hemisphere. Now, however, we were prepared to take up England's historic economic and political burdens in Greece and Turkey. Vandenburg was present at the briefing session at the White House and came up with sound advice. If you want the American people to take this monumental departure from traditional national policy, then you are going to have to scare Hell out of them with the communist menace.[7]

While it was easy for Truman and Acheson to follow Vandenburg's advice with regard to something they planned to do anyway, the celebrated journalist, James P. Warburg, had serious reservations. As far as Soviet Russia was concerned, this may have sealed the fate of the Marshall Plan, a cooperative scheme for the economic recovery of Europe. At that point the Cold War became winter.[8] My own limited experience tends to bear this out. In the summer of 1947, when teaching at the University of Maine, I was asked to give a campus-wide lecture. Because of the then widespread concern, I chose Soviet-American relations. One of my colleagues, a well-known historian of the American West, thought it was a good speech but too pessimistic. In the light of subsequent history, it was not nearly pessimistic enough. More significant, however, was the vast internal change within me, from the euphoria of the summer of 1945, and the surrender of Japan, to the gloom voiced at Orono. Gone was that sublime confidence in the innocence of one's own country, one which provided such a superb rallying cry when Pearl Harbor was bombed.

Despite these early signs of uneasiness, the Truman cult prevailed among historians for the next two decades. Beginning with a transition in tone in 1966-1967, however, there emerged by the mid-Seventies the prevalence of a revisionist theory, one which abandoned the stance of injured innocence. It "forced us to be aware of the United States' atomic blackmail, search for markets, support for corrupt and reactionary regimes, maintenance of colonial subserviency, misrepresentation and suppression of the Left both at home and abroad, and the desire to expand the American way of life throughout the world. In this light, almost all Cold war interpretations ... have been stood on their heads." At the heart of it all was the Truman policy of "cynically exaggerating the threat of Russia and communism in order to legitimate its refusal to work out a detente."[9]

This national leap into the quest for a Pax Americana fascinated many able historians. Barbara Tuchman appeared to stress the psychological factor. In a kind of fuzzy way, we visualized ourselves as "a Paul Bunyan straddling two hemispheres."[10] This illusion of omnipotence, and the accompanying absence of calculated reason, led to the squandering of American power in grand folly in sharp disproportion to the national interest involved. All this naturally flowed from our unilateral decision to make ourselves the police, judge and jury of world order.[11] To Immanuel Wallerstein there was a kind of curious logic about it all. First of all, the successful conclusion of World War II allowed the United States for a brief time "to attain the same level of primacy as Britain had in the first part of the nineteenth century."[12] Further, the aspirations of capitalism were never limited by national boundaries.[13] Finally, the managers of such a system, believing that their own well-being is wrapped up in its survival, not only propagate myths in their own self-interest, but believe them. This, naturally enough, makes it easier to convince a public to follow where they led.[14] "Soviet policy," concluded David Cute, "challenged America's claim to offer itself, or impose itself, as the model on which the future of world civilization would be based." Assuming that prosperity could obtain only from a long-term dominance of free enterprise, then peace and stability could be assured only in terms of our dominance. This necessitated a massive presence of the world's strongest democracy as a guarantor of a free world.[15] A similar view worth noting was that of Stuart Ewen who described the immediate post-war years in these terms: "During this period of broad commercialism and suburbanization, the idea of a *free world* characterized by goods established itself as a pacific social ethic." Yet the reverse side of the same coin revealed "a more traditional and compulsory ethic to enforce it: the strict rule of conformity maintained by the patriotic imperatives of anti-communism, the cold war and McCarthyism."[16]

According to Robert Borsage, there were serious miscalculations in our post-war foreign policy which brought unexpected outcomes. First of all, under the impetus of Pax Americana, our global policies, generally speaking, could be summarized thus: "The American leadership equated peace with order, and order with stable capitalist regimes."[17] Despite the fact that in Yugoslavia, China, Greece, and Korea, the communist parties worked for national goals in the face of Russian opposition, the mythology was that the Kremlin masterminded every upset in the political status quo anywhere in the world. Within Europe, we believed that military pressure, through such agencies as NATO, would weaken the Soviet grasp upon the central and eastern sectors. Instead, the enemy remobilized after its formation.[18]

One cannot refrain from pointing out the predictive power of Thorstein Veblen. Business men, he wrote, favor an aggressive foreign policy and, when in government, they direct one which is both patriotic and warlike.[19] "The quest for profits," he concluded, "leads to a predatory foreign policy."[20]

Searching for a plausible theory as to why, since World War II, this democratic and industrialized state can no longer be considered peaceful, but imperialist instead, we reluctantly settled for one which attributed it to the nature of the capitalist system, or one subordinating everything else to profit and growth. Bluntly put, the argument is that our overseas imperialism was a natural consequence of the maturation of domestic capitalism. Its spillover in search of markets for raw materials and capitalist investment necessitated a vast military establishment. It also meant a complicated alliance system throughout the world to contest with international communism for the mastery of the world market.[21] While not forgetting the paranoia of Stalin and the Kremlin itself, this hunger of our multinational corporations for Lebensraum is indispensable in accounting for major struggles throughout the world since World War II. They want the area of their operations to be as large as possible. They want its laws and institutions to be favorable to the unfettered development of private capitalist enterprise. They want a world of nations which operates unhampered by local obstacles to their making and disposing of the maximum available profit.[22] It must be understood, however, that this was not due to individual greed but rather to the capitalist method of production, or the entire economic system, which itself generated inexorable pressure for greater profits and expanded sales.[23] But this is not surprising when one recalls the insistence by Karl Polanyi. Under the modern capitalist system, the economic aspect dominates the rest of society and everything is ultimately measured in marketing terms.[24]

This makes more meaningful the object lesson undergone by Western capitalism during the depression of the Thirties. As Tom Urban pointed out, the only two countries whose manufacturing in that decade dramatically exceeded the figure for 1929 were Nazi Germany and Japan. Both of these nations were virtually on a wartime footing. Before World War II, for example, production in the United States failed to achieve the 1929 level. This was unprecedented because never before had it taken a full decade to recover from a major depression. This gave rise to a permanent body of the unemployed throughout the Western world. Even in Great Britain, which by 1935 exceeded the production figure of 1929, there remained over ten percent unemployed in 1938, an exceptionally high figure. Worse, in the United States unemployment reached an almost unheard of figure of twenty percent of the labor force, or over ten million workers. World trade, naturally enough, manifested the same symptoms of disorder, having plunged dramatically following 1929 and, save for a brief period in 1937, never recovered its health and vigor. The conclusion, therefore, was while the welfare state was a palliative, it did not solve crucial economic problems. The Western world entered upon World War II without having conquered the most deep and widespread economic crisis in the history of capitalism. Fortuitously, the war itself and the great devastation it wrought in Europe and Asia proved a tremendous boon to American business. It did not suffer another recession until just before the Korean war of 1950.[25]

Supplementing this modern theory, however, is a much older one by de Tocqueville which re-enforces it. This also deals with imperialistic self-interest generated by profit and growth from a different group of influential men in democracies. He pointed out the strange paradox that, while democracies tend to be peace-loving, their armies, on the contrary, have a clear stake in war itself or the perpetual threat of it. He attributes this to the fact when aristocrats enter their army as officers, status depends more upon their inherited aristocratic title than army rank. They can always look forward to retirement upon ancestral estates. Whereas in democratic armies, officers have no such property and thus status depends upon army rank. And no breed of men suffer more from a long sustained peace - and no threat to it - than officers and men because rank is frozen and life boring. We witnessed this in the United States in the two decades from the termination of World War I to our forced entry into World War II. On the contrary, war, or the immediate threat of it, invariably means a sudden expansion of the military as jobs open and both ideas and promotions flow rapidly. So, as de Tocqueville concluded, democratic armies have a vested interest in this, just as business men have a vested interest in prosperity.[26]

This possibly helps explain why President Eisenhower left office deeply distrustful of advice received from his Chiefs of Staff, made up of the highest raking officers in all the services. He thought its personnel habitually too aggressive. Their picture of the foe's strength and purpose had something to do with their desire to witness growth in their own service.[27]

How else may one explain the dramatic increase in our military presence throughout the world from three countries in the Twenties to thirty-nine in World War II, and approximately twice the latter figure since the war? In 1969, we maintained more than 1,500,000 men in uniform in over one hundred countries and had eight treaties to help defend forty-eight nations if they requested it, or if we chose to intervene. Forgetting Vietnam, we possessed 429 major and 2,972 minor military bases throughout the world, covering 4,000 square miles in thirty foreign countries as well as Alaska and Hawaii.[28]

Certainly the technique of using our armed forces to protect investments of American corporations had been well worked out in the Caribbean prior to World War I.[29] This merely underscored the point made decades ago by the authors of the celebrated book, *Dollar Diplomacy*. They argued that American intervention and violence followed from the refusal of Caribbean nations willingly to conform to the economic and strategic demands of the Colossus of the North. Apparently our executives and the State department felt these weaker neighbors had no rights we were bound to respect.[30] Naturally, our legal and ethical justification for intervention in the Caribbean rested on the Monroe Doctrine of 1823. It was proclaimed unilaterally by us and, though discouraging further European inroads, did not carry any explicit promise on our part to abstain from them.[31]

While currently this vast military establishment throughout the world must be supported by an industrial system which maintains a logistic flow of arms and supplies to them, the system itself is dependent upon our continued ability to import crucial raw materials, like bauxite, iron ore, copper, lead, zinc, rubber and tin. Of sixty-two vital materials for our military-industrial complex, we must depend upon imports of eighty to one hundred percent on more than half of these.[32] But, if the military establishment is dependent upon our industrial system, the latter is equally dependent upon our armed forces to safeguard the delivery of these crucial raw materials to the United States so that our industrial apparatus can deliver the necessary goods to keep them in operation. This prevents any perceptible shrinkage of strategic areas under capitalist management and control.

Nor is it surprising that the large and monopolistic firms, or multinational corporations, undergird this entire structure, whether it be in the area of arms production at home or investment capital in crucial raw materials throughout the world. In 1964, for example, of the 500 largest manufacturing firms, at least 205 were significantly involved in military contracts; all but five of the largest twenty-five in 1968 were among the one hundred largest contractors for the Defense department.[33] Of the fifty largest industrial firms in the United States involved in the international economy and the supply of military goods, twelve were in oil, five in aviation, three in chemicals, three in steel, three in autos, eight in electronic equipment and three in rubber.[34] Likewise, the multinational corporations dominated the field of international investment. Although in 1965 the income from foreign trade and investment was less than one percent of the gross national income, thirteen corporations from among the top twenty-five listed by *Fortune* magazine received more than forty percent of the total foreign earnings.[35] Our expenditures for plants and equipment of subsidiaries abroad more than doubled from 1957 to 1965. That figure was in terms of domestic investment by the same corporations. What this meant was the United States controls over half of the auto business in Great Britain, forty percent of the petroleum industry in Germany and over that amount in the French telegraphic, telephone, electronic and statistical ones.[36]

Between World Wars I and II, the United States and England dominated the field of monetary investment and the extraction of strategic materials around the world, with the United States as the dominant partner.[37] Thus, our actions since World War II may be perceived primarily as defense efforts against threats, real or imaginary, that certain nations on our side might opt out of international capitalism.[38] More aggressively, on the other hand, has been the extension of the power of the United States to fill the vacuums in Asia and elsewhere, created by the military collapse of Japan, as well as the weakened military power of Western Europe and England.[39]

One of the reasons why there is such public reluctance to accept the charges of imperialism against the United States is that, by nature, ours lacks the open and brutal exploitation of the Soviet model. Take our penetration of the Third World, or the undeveloped countries for example. This new imperialism of ours does not demand open domination of the penetrated country. Nevertheless, whereas earlier foreign investors were interested in the right to mine and export raw materials, modern ones are more intimately involved in the national economy itself. This leads to a greater influence in that government. Rather than merely requesting a minimum of intervention in their businesses, Western investors now require the local government to create a "favorable investment climate," designed to further the spread of capitalism in an integrated international system.[40] In return for the engagement not to depart significantly from accepted practices by international bankers and giant corporations, the government of the host country gets military supplies and assistance, corporate investment and foreign aid programs. In Latin America, for example, it is at least legitimate to question whether the military aid is intended for use against external communist foes, or to enable the rich and privileged few to maintain their power. They return the favor to us by maintaining an hospitable environment for our business men and investors.[41] In this sense imperialism is merely the internationalization of the economic relations of capitalism.[42]

This post-war quest or mission of ours was much more successful in enhancing capitalism rather than democracy. Take, for example, the high points of foreign policy since World War II. Try to explain them either on the basis of democratic outcomes or that of human rights. What have the following episodes to do with either: aid to Chiang Kai Shek in China, 1945-1949, and afterwards in Taiwan, to the Shah of Iran, beginning in 1946, to Greece and Turkey in 1947, to the French in Indo-China in 1950 and to South Vietnam from 1955 to 1973, to President Marcos for decades in the Philippines, to right-wing revolutionists in Guatemala in 1954 and Chile in 1973, and, finally, to the less successful maneuver of the CIA under Eisenhower and Kennedy at the Bay of Pigs?

If one follows the lead of scholars like Seymour Melman, and explores what he calls our counter-revolutionary reflex, one discovers in assessing whether a revolution ought to be supported by us or opposed, our sole criterion is whether or not it is infiltrated by communists. That poses a menace because it may shrink the area of international capitalism. Therefore, it is opposed. If not, no matter how unpalatable its right-wing or Fascist component, it is supported in the international battle against communism.[43] Melman's generalization was supported by the authors of *Elite Deviance* when they concluded: "The chief characteristic of such regimes is that they are right-wing, military dictatorships, and, hence, friendly to the goals of international capitalism."[44]

Writing after the covert intervention of the Nixon administration resulted in the death of President Allende in Chile in 1973, and bloody reprisals against his followers, Richard R. Fagan correctly predicted an aggressive United States foreign policy against the Third World. We would be drawn into covert actions and military interventions as long as we continued to insist our vital interests, including national security, were jeopardized by Third World politico-economic experiments not under our control. This was a by-product of a quarter of a century struggle on a global level against both communism and Communism and one which accepted both fair means and foul as legitimate. The corollary of this was the status quo was "good" in the Third World, even though it was accompanied by the persistence of large-scale misery and repression of the masses by the favored few, the local elite.[45]

Reagan's ambassador at the United Nations, Jeanne Kirkpatrick, fulfilled the prophecy of Richard R. Fagan. Beginning with her article in *Commentary* in 1979 on "Dictatorships and Double Standards," she was noted for a well-reasoned argument which would have justified turning the clock back to the era of Dollar Diplomacy. At that time our State Department used the Monroe Doctrine as an excuse to intervene in any country which threatened the well-being of any United States corporation or rolled up debts it could not pay to international bankers. The United States then preferred dictatorships to bargain with, rather than the uncertainties of doing so with democracies. Kirkpatrick condemned the Carter administration for abandoning that tried and true policy. Friendly goverments in Central America were weakened whenever we refused to grant them money, arms, logistic support and counterinsurgency experts to train their armed forces.[46] Significantly, she extended our legitimate sphere of influence - meaning the right of military intervention - from the Caribbean to Bolivia and the heart of South America.[47]

But, as critics charged, the chief difference the amoral Kirkpatrick saw between dictators of the right and left was not that the former were only moderately repressive of human rights and liberties. They were willing allies of international capitalism.[48] Meanwhile, her obsession with the communist menace blinded her to the genuine causes of unrest throughout Central America. While Castro and Cuba might eventually go away, local miseries and instabilities would remain.[49]

Perhaps nothing reflects our moral blindness in recent decades more than our policy in El Salvador. Anthony Lewis posed the crucial question: "When will the U.S. government get serious about stopping the murderous behavior of the armed forces we train and finance in El Salvador. In the last 10 years, the United States has spent nearly $5 billion...$1 billion of it for military aid. In that time the Salvadoran forces have killed more than 40,000 civilians, most of them because someone thought they were politically suspicious. Not one officer has been convicted of those crimes. ... The murder of six Jesuit priests has brought the issue forward again. ... The head of the Salvadoran military academy .. has been arrested.... But no one thinks he will be convicted. The murder of the Jesuits was almost certainly ordered at a higher level than colonel." Part of the elaborate coverup took place in the United States where an El Salvadoran colonel was allowed to bulldoze the housekeeper witness of the murders until she recanted her testimony. Meanwhile, our ambassador there denied the military was involved. This charade, however, was exploded days later when President Cristiani charged it with the foul deed.[50]

As for the perennially alleged American interest in the growth of democracy in Central and South America, we find it a contradiction in terms. Democracies are supposed to represent sovereign nations and thus act as their people wish them to do. It is a matter of historical record that democracies in this hemisphere are not permitted to be sovereign to the point they nationalize IT&T or interfere with the capitalistic interests of Americans, as in Chile under Allende.[51]

For example, our decade-old sponsorship of contra rebels to destabilize the Sandinista regime in Nicaragua finally brought the political triumph of the opposition there. As one journalist so graphically put it: "The [Madame] Chamorro victory is a vindication of the Reagan doctrine which, briefly stated, is: 'No country is too small to be invaded if it is close by.'"[52] Perhaps Reagan's greatest achievement was that he made most of us proud to be the Ugly American.

Meanwhile, President Reagan's disregard for international law frequently embarrassed even his strongest supporter, Margaret Thatcher. For example, her government was not informed of the invasion of the tiny island of Grenada in the Caribbean, a member of the British Commonwealth, until after it was under way in November of 1983. Then the Reagan administration forced the governor-general to say he asked for an armed invasion. The British government knew it was a patent lie, but one useful before the Organization of American States.[53]

This was the first of several military operations, culminating in the dispatch of troops to Saudi Arabia in the Kuwait crisis of 1990, which denied all access to the media. Reporters were warned they would be shot if they sought to collect news where they chose and by their own devices. Thus, the only reporter in all these operations was "the U.S. government - covering the world from behind a gun, burying its own mistakes."[54]

With this kind of secrecy, it is extremely difficult to try to sort out the facts and we have not the time nor space here. What is clear is that the Grenada operation was a Cold War tactic, inspired by the fear of further encroachment into this hemisphere by Soviet Russia and Castro's Cuba. If our official explanations are to be trusted, the invasion was necessary to save hundreds of our medical students from becoming hostages of the revolutionary government. It also prevented the completion of a large airport facility which had crucial military possibilities.

The other fact which soon emerged with clarity was that it drove off the front pages and TV primetime the disaster suffered only days earlier in Lebanon where over two hundred Marines lost their lives in an enemy bomb explosion.[55] Thus, we were spared the pain of having to ponder the consequences of another national blunder in the Middle East.

These valuable lessons were not lost upon the Bush administration, particularly Lee Atwater, in the invasion of Panama. He understood "the rally-round effect that always bolsters a president who sends the troops into action abroad - never mind the reasons, the resulting casualities or the ultimate consequences. ... This national glorification of violence ought to give supposedly peace-loving Americans pause; but it never does."[56] We think a fair summary of the irony of that situation best put by Tom Wicker:

"As indications of brutal overkill in the illegal invasion of Panama keep turning up, the Bush administration is mounting only a weak case against the invasion's prime target, the alleged drug kingpin, Manuel Antonio Noriega. ... President Bush needs a Noriega conviction to bring some faint color of legitimacy to an invasion that resulted in at least four times more Panamanian civilians killed than Panamanian soldiers. Yet the evidence against Noriega is so weak ... government prosecutors may be resorting to dubious, if not unconstitutional tactics to get a guilty verdict."[57]

The bitter truth, of course, was that the Reagan administration previously enlisted the aid of drug runner Noriega because he assisted us in the fight to oust the Sandinistas in Nicaragua. All over the world we have "been willing to pay for anti-communist activity by ignoring or even facilitating narcotics traffic by what are laughably called 'freedom fighters.'"[58]

Today, our patronage of right-wing regimes in the Third World is somewhat shaky. While providing a haven for some capital investments abroad, they are scarcely adequate to the needs of those with the capital itself. First of all, there are limits to the capital these friendly dictators can absorb, or with which to be trusted. Further, the very safety of the funds is illusory because of political instability. Force and terror cannot make their regimes permanent. Finally, once the capital and the plant it builds is installed in-country, the big corporations are held hostage because of their immobility.[59] It is just these "peripheral" regions which, by joining the system of international capitalism, helped preserve the stability of monopoly capitalism in the United States.[60] Now, ironically, they menace it because they themselves are jeopardized as never before.

As many see it, "the organization and needs of capitalism are not appropriate for a [Third] world of scarcity, overpopulation, ecological disasters, and vast inequities."[61] And to continue to play our game is as often for it to emerge the loser. That is why, until recently, socialism was very much on the agenda throughout the Third World and this independently of either Soviet Russia or Red China.[62]

Jeff, however, was always unimpressed by such logic, believing that, aside from sheer rhetoric, communism offered no solution for the ills of the

Third World. Its ploy was the purely ideological one that scarcity, overpopulation, vast inequities and ecological disasters were a product of capitalism. "It can't happen here," was their bold but idle boast, as if poverty and misery were not independent of existing political systems and their seductive but empty slogans.

We borrow heavily here from Peter F. Drucker to underscore our concern and fear for democracy in the Third World. He places a great emphasis upon the necessity of government - legitimate government - to give the individual social status and function. When the people cannot sense this "society to them is nothing but a demoniac, irrational, incomprehensible threat. ... any legitimate authority appears to them as tyrannical and arbitrary. ... As social outcasts the masses have nothing to lose - not even their chains." Thus, any society "which cannot prevent the development of masses is doomed."[63] However, the problem is compounded for him by the fact within industrialized nations in this century, "the individual has steadily been losing function and status in society. Society has slowly been disintegrating into anarchic masses in all industrial countries."[64] Consider, then, the monumental problem of Third World countries. They are generally made up of separate, disparate, suspicious and even hostile masses, like British India in 1947.

Let us advance a postulate which would be difficult for a reasonable and enlightened person to deny. Prospects for the establishment and maintenance of democracy - or even stable government which is less than authoritarian - is not bright where one must deal with the fact that for several hundred years two or three percent of the populace, or even five, read and ruled and where the remainder were illiterate and exploited. And, unfortunately, that is why we cannot get excited at the battle cry: "Democracy is on the march everywhere."

Furthermore, our political and military seismographs in Washington are super sensitive to turmoil and change everywhere in the world. This is precisely why we cannot remain peaceful, but must somehow react with a threat to raise and expand the level of violence.

The naivete of Americans with regard to our aggressions against the Third World were more than adequately summarized by Ronald Steel: "We long ago stopped behaving like innocents abroad. It is time we stopped thinking that way." He rightly traced the beginnings of our encroachments on foreign turf around the world to the old - and still lively - obsession of evangelical Protestantism: believers have a God-given duty to convert non-believers to the true faith. This was the justification for sending missionaries "into distant lands on self-defined godly missions, an intrusion into the lives of people who never sought our presence. We went there for their own good."

Meanwhile, every American abroad, no matter how bellicose he or they appear to the natives, is an innocent in our eyes. Shocked surprise greets every counter act of violence against them. We invariably fell back on our good intentions, while ignoring our actions which may appear aggressive to outsiders. Steel's conclusion is a masterpiece: "Today, after 40 years of global involvement in other people's quarrels, and a century of intervention in Central America, we can still be shocked that others see us as the enemy. We want to order the world our way - but not to be held personally responsible by those against whom we apply our power. We seek the benefits of imperialism while hoping to enjoy all the conveniences of pacifism."[65]

There are, of course, times when our paternalistic attitude toward Latin American countries does more than bolster our reputation as the Ugly American; it threatens nothing less than our own Constitution.

Although we shall probably never know all the seamy details of the sordid Irangate affair - due to conscious forgetfulness, lying, conflicting versions by different witnesses and, above all, a clear desire to protect the president - one can identify the chief threats to the Constitution and to the maintenance of our democracy. Like Richard Nixon before him, Ronald Reagan and his principal advisers acted as if they were above the law.[66]

The matter was probably rooted in Reagan's political desire to win big in the off-presidential elections of 1986. If he could get the eight hostages back - those in the hands of terrorist Iran - and have his picture taken with them in the Rose Garden before election day, that should carry the day for him and the Republican conservatives in the Senate.[67]

So, despite repeated denials to Congress, the American people and our allies that we would never negotiate with terrorists for the hostages, Reagan authorized the move of selling arms to Iran, warring with Iraq, for hostages. He got three of the eight released but Iran seized another three Americans. So, that ended in inglorious failure, but the administration's lies followed the deception. Reagan's theme apparently was: "Well, would you believe this one?"

Then either the president himself or his number-one-man, Admiral Poindexter, authorized the use of the Iranian monies to pass on to the contras in their revolt against the legitimate government of Nicaragua, the Sandinistas. Unfortunately, they did so at a time when Congress had forbidden such aid, and Reagan signed the bill. Somebody at a high level broke a national law. James Reston concluded "the administration acted with contempt for Congress if not for the law, and avoided the principle of accountability for its actions."[68]

Because of a decision to abandon normal political channels, rather than abide by constitutional checks and balances, the administration turned over foreign policy to bureaucrats, obsessed with their own patriotism, and businessmen concerned with the profit motive. The disastrous consequences were adequately summed up by Representative Lee H. Hamilton, Democrat from Indiana: "Our government cannot function cloaked in secrecy. It cannot function unless officials tell the truth. The Constitution only works when the ... branches trust one another and cooperate. Privatization of foreign policy is a prescription for confusion and failure. The use of private parties to carry out the high purposes of government makes us the subject of puzzlement and ridicule."[69]

Perhaps the most alarming constitutional note was struck by Col. Ollie North, Poindexter's subordinate, who in a curious sense seemed to wow the American public. This would have been less surprising had we known that polls show that by almost a 2-1 margin the general electorate, contrary to more politically aware persons, thinks that "there are times when it almost seems better for the people to take the law into their own hands rather than wait for the machinery of government to act."[70] North's shady behavior was, of course, a perfect example of such a situation.[71] In addition to the act itself being illegal,[72] he took part in and defended actions which were also stupid and unfair to his fellow soldiers. As Col. Harry Summers wrote: "As a fellow officer ... can you tell me how I explain to young soldiers in my platoon that if we have to go into battle in Iran, they might be killed by the Tow anti-tank missiles you sent to the Iranians. I know you wanted to look good to your boss, but how could you do that to your fellow soldiers?"[73]

But our principal concern, fear, if you like, came when North confessed his great love and admiration for his wonderful president for whom he would do anything upon command. At the same time he manifested his genuine contempt for Congress, particularly those unsympathetic with the contras. Suppose in a crisis state an impasse arose between the president and Congress. For patriotic motives, the president ordered Colonel North to pull an Oliver Cromwell, i.e., to cordon off Congress and only let in those members who could be trusted to vote massive aid to the contras? What would North do? It is evident to us that, whatever his choice, including that of the application of force, North would act with a clear conscience. That realization makes the man dangerous in our eyes.

Back in the turbulent Sixties one recalls good conservatives admonishing young radicals of the Left in language such as this: "If you don't like the law, work peaceably within the system to change it. Meanwhile, obey it. Don't act as if you are above the law. If you only obey the laws you approve of and I do the same for myself, anarchy results."

Although many ponder the question of whether or not Reagan knew of these shady maneuvers, Donald Kaul wisely proclaimed it made no difference: "It might be better if he *had* known about the diversion of the funds to the contras; then he'd only be guilty of violating the Constitution. If he truly didn't know anything, he has to be the biggest dummy to sit in the White House since Warren G. Harding."[74] The best explanation for why this administration "is not only so duplicitous, but so blandly and morally unrepentant" when caught in a reprehensible act came from Richard Reeves: "The administration is not governed by the old ethic of government and public service; it functions according to the ethics of American business, which are lower than the traditional ethical standards of government. ...public officials generally have higher and more rigorous ethical standards and codes than men of power in private life."[75] Although the celebrated journalist and autobiographer, Lincoln Steffens, stressed this fact over a half-century ago,[76] the American people still do not believe it. That, of course, is a large part of the problem of why there were so many scandals in both the business administrations of Harding and Reagan.

Our own personal opinion of the Irangate tragedy, and illicit aid to the contras, is that its origin lay in Reagan's obsession to get rid of the Sandinistas, lock, stock and barrel. We are reminded of Jean Anouilh's *Becket* when Henry II in 1170 cried out to his knights and courtiers about that monster Becket: "So long as he's alive, I'll never be able to do a thing. ... Will no one rid me of him? ... Are there none but cowards like myself around me? Are there no men left in England?"[77] Then, after the awful deed, Henry piously expressed surprise and promised an official investigation which would ferret out the murderers of the sainted archbishop.[78] Had men like Poindexter and North been in Henry's entourage, we think they would have arranged for the foul deed, had they not wielded the sword and axe themselves. For they knew that it was all in a "good cause."

We shall spare the reader the dreary details of the subsequent trials of these men. Suffice to say that none have gone to prison yet, despite the fact Poindexter was sentenced to six months in jail and a $250 fine. He has, of course, appealed.[79] It was Seymour Hirsch, writing in the New York Times Magazine, who first let us see through his crystal ball. It was, he wrote, a cardinal blunder for the congressional investigating committee to grant immunity to both North and Poindexter for their testimony.[80] Very recently, two Reagan judicial appointees on a Washington appeals court took advantage of this. They overturned one of three of North's convictions and returned the other two to judge Gerhard Gesell. Had these verdicts been based upon North's testimony before the congressional committee? "Such tainting could mean a new trial or the dropping of all charges...." The article ends with a reference to Hirsch's prediction: "Did the lawmakers haste to hold sensational hearings guarantee that the culprits would go unpunished."[81] It looks like a fiasco of the worst sort.

From the outset one other factor mitigated against the application of impartial justice. That was a general reluctance to entertain any thought of the impeachment of President Reagan. Why? First of all, he was a very popular president and nearing the end of his term. Beyond this, Congress did not want to impeach "a president deemed pathetic rather than abusive," i.e., a complete character opposite of Richard Nixon.[82]

Everything written so far pertains to the Cold War. Its continuance for almost a half century had a few pluses and many more negative consequences. First, the good news, the military and political variety. The proponents of nuclear power are fond of saying it acted as a deterrent to war in Europe and the West. Since it is not clear democracies are any better at keeping the peace than authoritarian states,[83] some look forward to nuclear deterrence to keep the peace in post-Cold War Europe.[84] According to those in a position to know and the disposition to speak frankly, the chief purpose of NATO was not in reaction to any alleged Soviet threat. Its object was "simple - to keep the Yanks in, the Russians out and the Germans down."[85] Whatever the motives, this strategy and tactics coincided with peace in an area deemed most crucial by us all, precisely as Southeast Asia was not.

However, the disadvantages of the Cold War are more obvious and appear to be at least four in number: 1) the diffusion of sophisticated weapons in a growing number of countries 2) possible irreversible damage to the environment 3) growing desperation of the world's poor and 4) the obvious weakening of the American economy.[86]

While points one and three would never occur to the American public, and we deal with the adverse effects upon the environment elsewhere, we confess a preoccupation with the last one.

It is the most immediate threat to the American Dream. "That the United States," concluded Anthony Lewis, "has paid a heavy economic price for Cold War militarization is hardly necessary to argue - not when we see the boom in the two countries that avoided most of that burden, Japan and Germany. We have a military-industrial complex that limits our ability to compete in the civilian goods the world wants."[87] Even prior to the collapse of international communism, Paul Kennedy argued in a similar vein. If the Pentagon continues to siphon off more than its share of talented scientists and technicians from their natural task of designing and producing useful goods, while our competitors resist that impulse, then our share of the world's markets, already in perceptible decline, will continue on that disastrous course. History shows that to be the chief tendency of number one powers when in a state of relative decline, economically speaking.[88]

Nevertheless, what is astonishing - at least until one thinks about it - is the fact the military-industrial-political complex tried to maintain Cold War mechanisms in place when peace broke out. It was, as one columnist wrote, "still determined to carry on business as usual after V-C Day, the muted celebration of victory in the Cold War."[89] While the glue holding the conservative coalition together, fear and hatred of Soviet Russia, dissolved almost overnight,[90] conservatives seemed instinctively to sense, as did more perceptive critics, that the "price of peace will be economic hell." Swollen unemployment would be the immediate cost for closing factories dedicated to military purposes.[91] Since we are unprepared to make an extended analysis here, we are content to endorse the judgments of Donald Kaul. Congress, he observed, "is absolutely ingenious in its efforts to protect the military budget from the scourge of peace." In turn, the Bush administration "has been unconscionable in its reluctance to make significant cuts in the military budget." Meanwhile, the military itself was frantically trying to find some new mission, any mission, which would justify the $300 billion it devours each year. Kaul's conclusion was a masterpiece. "That can't go on indefinitely. Sooner or later the public will figure out that we're spending $300 billion to protect ourselves from an enemy who has lost interest in us."[92] Finally, the hypocrisy surrounding the entire Cold War was best summarized by the following declaration: "The West can no longer blame the Soviets, just as the Soviets can no longer blame the West. An urgent need has thus risen for a new villain. The quicker we can fool ourselves into finding one, the happier all of us will be."[93] It will constitute a remarkable justification for no longer being peaceful. We can resume belligerency, our normal post World War II position.

It was at this crucial juncture the armies of Saddam Hussein of Iraq invaded and annexed the oil-rich, but tiny feudal nation of Kuwait; this presented the world with its first global crisis since the termination of the Cold War. While we have no intention of pursuing it, we cannot refrain from comments on its background and causality.

Despite the stringent oil crisis of 1973, and again in 1987 when we threatened war with the fanatical Ayatollah Khomeini of Iran, neither we nor our allies - especially the latter - eliminated our dependence on the free flow of oil from the Persian Gulf.[94] Had London in 1912 threatened to exchange British lives for foreign oil, it would have surprised few perceptive observers. The fact the United States did the same in 1987 and 1990 underlines the fact history may not permit big industrial powers to be peaceful, especially if they insist on being prodigal, as we did, with the consumption of oil. Peace is also unlikely if we continue to insist upon the sanctity of boundaries drawn by imperialist Britain in the Arabian desert in 1922. Out of a desire to keep Iraq in a state of dependency, the English purposely denied it a sea port on the Persian Gulf.[95] Are we fighting to maintain that aspect of the status quo?

Despite the protestations of George Bush that we acted out of concern for principles, the truth was better expressed by a prominant journalist: "... we are embarking on this war for the least noble of reasons. This is not a war to make the world safe for democracy. This is not a holy war against godless communism. It is not a war to protect our borders. It is a war for cheap oil."[96] Several other perceptive commentators said virtually the same thing in equally colorful language.[97]

A second observation is the invasion came just in time to spare our military-industrial complex from agonizing budget cuts.[98] The end of the Cold War, said the hawks, created the illusion, or the nonsense, "that there was no longer any need for the world's leading superpower to maintain a strong defense capacity. ... Even without the East-West conflicts ... there is no shortage of international turmoil; there is no shortage of villains to menace peace-loving nations."[99] Saddam Hussein was merely the first to rise to the occasion.[100] "And it may have been just in time. On a euphoric 'peace is at hand' binge, we were about to slash our defenses to the bone, convinced that with the breakup of the Warsaw Pact and the improvement of relations with the Soviet Union there was no longer any need to concern ourselves about military threats to our worldwide interests."[101] Had Hussein delayed his attack another two or three years "with our planned reduction of forces, we may not only have lacked the will but also the capacity to project any forces. The United States today is really the only country that has the force and the ability to project it in a timely manner."[102]

Thirdly, the old, old lesson of history was repeated: today's "monster"[103] was yesterday's ally. Despite the fact Hussein started the war against Iran in 1980, and badly damaged our frigate, the *Stark,* in the Persian Gulf[104], we were his steadfast ally in that eight-year war.[105] We remained so until the very eve of his invasion of Kuwait.[106]

Our fourth point is that the Iraq affair "may involve what experts call 'oil geopolitics,'" or "the balance of power in the Middle East." If Hussein took control of Saudi Arabia, he would have mastery of 25 percent of our oil supply.[107] The Middle East, therefore, is to the United States what Europe was to Great Britain from the days of Napoleon to the Kaiser, to Hitler and, finally, to Stalin. Britain practiced a continental policy of divide and rule. Whenever a single state, or individual leader, threatened to alter that balance of power, that entity was Britain's enemy. It had to be checkmated, or destroyed. Yesterday, our enemy in that region was Iran, today Iraq, and maybe tomorrow, Syria. If we continue to respond as Pavlov's dog, how can we keep the pretense we are a peace-loving nation? What we love instead is the status quo, especially where oil is involved. A considerable number of small, independent nations - or princely families even - producing oil in that region tends to keep prices down.

Finally, what disturbs some commentators the most about those who seek a quick military end to the impasse is "their assumption that future events can be predicted and controlled." On the contrary, war "nearly always brings an avalanche of unforseen consequences, even for the victors."[108]

What these lovers of direct action cannot tolerate is the possibility "the age of the superpower is over. From now on history will be driven by economic rather than military power. The future leadership of the world lies in Europe and the Pacific rim. The American century is history."[109]

To conclude, I, as historian, made an error which the reading of Gore Vidal's *Empire* forces me to correct. Although he has written a novel, his historical sense is quite accurate. Therefore, intead of men like Henry Luce and Herbert Agar as original architects of Pax Americana, and the concept of the twentieth century as an American one, we must concede that dubious honor to a little coterie of men at the beginning of the twentieth century itself. They clustered around the persons and expansive ideas of Admiral Alfred Mahan, author of *The Influence of Sea Power on History,* and Brooks Adams, who wrote *The Law of Civilization and Decay* and *The New Empire.* The charmed circle included such luminaries as that giant intellect, Henry Adams, Henry Cabot Lodge, a Boston Brahmin, and the celebrated activist and politician, Theodore Roosevelt. John Hay, biographer of Lincoln and Secretary of State under Teddy, must also be included, despite the fact his views are harder to summarize.

Let's start with Brooks and his "laws" of history. "All civilization is centralization. That is the first unarguable law. All centralization is economy. That is the second - resources must be adequate to sustain the civilization, and give it its energy. Therefore all civilization is the survival of the most economical system."[110] Turn now to Mahan. "The logic is overpowering. Maintain a fleet in order to acquire colonies. Then, in turn, the colonies will provide you with new wealth in order to maintain an even larger fleet in order to acquire more colonies."[111]

Now lend an ear to Henry Adams as he expounds on the philosophy of his brother, Brooks. This new world mission of expansion found its way to America' doorstep because only England and the United States were devoted to freedom and the common law. History dictated that England drank her cup a round or two before. Since she faltered on the sacred mission of civilizing the world, it was left to her young and vigorous successor to do it. The acquisition of the entire Philippines was necessary because that gave access to China and its vast coal fields: "... whichever power has the most and the cheapest energy will dominate the world."[112] In the epochal struggles of the twentieth century, Germany, like England, would be crushed and reduced to a second rank of powers, leaving the two colossi, Russia and the United States, to confront one another. It was unreasonable to suppose that we would allow the superstitious and barbaric Russia to preempt our historical mission.[113]

Finally, we round out our case by listening to the volatile and bombastic Teddy. "Everywhere that we are needed [I am for expansion]. It is to take the manly part, after all. Besides, every expansion of civilization - and we are that, preeminently in the world, our religion, our law, our customs, our modernity, our democracy. Wherever our civilization is allowed to take hold means a victory for law and order and righteousness. Look at those poor benighted islands without us. Bloodshed, confusion, rapine ... Aguinaldo is nothing but a Tagal bandit."[114]

This philosophy would have been immediately understood and endorsed by American believers in Manifest Destiny a half century before, or prior to the Civil War. While they generally confined their claims for territorial dominance to all of North America and the Caribbean, some were generous enough to include Central America and, indeed, the entire Western hemisphere. Naturally, they were armed with the same racial arrogance and contempt for persons of color, as well as for those not blessed with a belief in Protestant Christianity. When applied to our expansion at the expense of less civilized people, force was justified, if only because it speeded up the inexorable law of progress. Finally, it was a part of a providential and masterful plan in which the godly and the pious should be happy to participate.[115]

All this reminds the historian of the essential truth of the assertion made by the Athenians to the Melians in 416 B.C.: "Of the gods we believe, and of men we know, that by a necessary law of their nature they rule wherever they can. ... we found it existing before us, and shall leave it to exist forever after us; all we do is to make use of it, knowing that you and everybody else, having the same power as we have, would do the same as we do."[116] And we would add that the strong and the pious attribute the deed to the will of the gods or God.

Neither Mahan, nor Brooks, nor Teddy would have doubted for a moment where the necessary, the good and the just stood in all of this. For they were one and the same. It meant progress and led toward the perfectibility of man. It was the same philosophy used everywhere to sanctify the act of the obliteration of the primitive.

Finally, it was Christopher Lasch who observed the remarkable persistence throughout our history of "a self-aggrandizing impulse, a secret determination to convert the world to its own 'anti-ideological' ideology...."

Thus, "liberalism in America, no less than communism in Russia, has always had a messianic creed, which staked everything on the ultimate triumph of liberalism throughout the world."[117]

In conclusion, as far as the idea of progress and the perfectibility of man is concerned, it is difficult to argue that the civilization afforded by American democracy has been more peaceful than the so-called "savage" tribes it usurped in this hemisphere.

192

Footnotes

1   *The American Century.* With comments by John Chamberlain, Quincy Howe *et al* (New York, Farrar & Rinehart, 1941), 14.

2   Dorothy Thompson in *ibid.*, 47.

3   *Ibid.*, 23, 36.

4   Two prophetic observations were contained within this book. John Chamberlain wrote that hopes for the United States were uncommonly high "provided we do not waste too much of our blood and substance trying to control the course of events in parts of the world beyond our effective control." *Ibid.*, ft. 82. "If," declared John Spivack, "we embark upon a world-wide program of Yankee imperialism we shall find ourselves more hated at the end of the century than Great Britain is now at the end of hers." *Ibid.*, 77.

5   Peter Drucker, *Adventures of a Bystander* (New York, Harper and Row, 1979), 328-329.

6   *The Pentagon Watchers,* Rodberg and Shearer, editors, 4.

7   Robert Lasch, "The Origins of American Postwar Foreign Policy," 34-37 in *America Since World War II. Historical Interpretations,* edited by Jean Christie and Leonard Dinnerstein (New York, Praeger Publishing, 1976), 42. See also Lawrence S. Wittner, *Cold War America. From Hiroshima to Watergate* (New York, Praeger Publishing Company,, 1947), 33. See also Robert Borosage, "Making of the National Security State," 3-63 in *Pentagon Watchers,* 45-46.

8   "Onset of the Cold War," 958-966 in *Shaping of American Diplomacy,* edited by William Appleman Williams (Chicago, Rand McNally, 1965), 961-962.

9   Harvard Sitkoff, "Years of the Locust. Interpretations of the Truman Presidency Since 1945," 75-112 in *The Truman Period as a Research Field. A Reappraisal, 1972,* edited by Richard S. Kirkendall (Columbia, University of Missouri Press, 1974), 77.

10   *The March of Folly. From Troy to Vietnam* (New York, Alfred A. Knopf, 1984), 292.

11   *Ibid.*, 375. It was the celebrated Swedish anthropologist, Gunnar Myrdal, who observed that foreign policy decisions "are in general much more influenced by irrational motives" than rational and domestic ones. *Ibid.*, 336.

12   "The Rise and Future Demise of the World Capitalist System, Concepts for Comparative Analysis," 387-415 in *Comparative Studies in Society and History,* vol. 16, 411.

13   *Ibid.*, 402.

14   *Ibid.*, 404.

15   *The Great Fear. The Anti-Communist Purge under Truman and Eisenhower* (New York, Simon and Schuster, 1978), 29. "Truman was in fact digging deep roots for the double standard that have obscured the motives of American foreign policy for the last thirty years. While committing men and money to the support of the bitterly reactionary elements in Greece, and while insuring that the Communists were squeezed out of the French and Italian coalition governments, Truman on April 5 sanctimoniously deplored 'the atrocious violations of the rights of nations in the interference of anyone in the internal affairs of another.'" *Ibid.*, 30-31.

16   *Captains of Consciousness. Advertising and the Social Roots of the Consumer Culture* (New York, McGraw-Hill, 1976), 191.

17   "The Making of the National Security State," 3-63 in *The Pentagon Watchers*, edited by Rodberg and Shearer, 7.

18   *Ibid.*, 7-8.

19   *The Theory of Business Enterprise* (New York, Scribner's, 1935), 391.

20   *Ibid.*, 398.

21   *The Capitalist System. A Radical Analysis of American Society.* Written and Edited by Richard C. Edwards, *et al* (Englewood Cliffs, New Jersey, Prentice-Hall, 1972), 98, 393.

22   Paul Baran and Paul Sweezy, "The Multinational Corporation and Modern Imperialism," 435-442 in *The Capitalist System*, edited by Edwards, *et al*, 441-442.

23   "Thus, not only does the capitalist firm *want* to expand production and profits, it is *forced* to expand production and cut costs to *retain* profits. The firm cannot stand still, It must push on." Richard C. Edwards, "The Logic of Capitalist Expansion," 98-106 in *ibid.*, 102.

24   "The Self-Regulating Market and the Fictional Commodities: Labor, Land and Money," 68-76 in Karl Polayni, *The Great Transformation* (New York, Farrar & Rinehart, 1944), 68-76.

25   Maurice Zeitlin, *Capitalism and Imperialism. An Introduction to Neo-Marxian Concepts* (Chicago, Markham Publishing, 1972), 26-29.

26   *Democracy in America*, II, 281-283.

27   Interview by Carl Sagan of George Kistiakowsky, "Confessions of a Weaponeer," September 8, 1987, Channel 19, PBS.

28   Henry Magdoff, "Militarism and Imperialism," 421-426 in *The Capitalist System*, edited by Edwards, *et al*, 425. See Also Zeitlin, *Capitalism and Imperialism*, 102-103; Richard Halloran, "Uncle Sam pays a high price for being in 359 places at once," in the New York *Times*, July 24, 1983, E-5.

29   *The Capitalist System*, edited by Edwards, *et al*, footnote, 415.

30   Scott Nearing and Joseph Freeman, *Dollar Diplomacy. A Study in American Diplomacy* (New York, Modern Reader Paperbacks, reprint 1966), 171-172.

31   "The Monroe Doctrine," in *Documents of American History* in 2 vols., I, edited by Henry Steele Commager (New York, Appleton-Century-Crofts, 1963), 235-237.

32   *Capitalism and Imperialism,* 103-104.

33   Michael Reich and David Finkelhor, "Up Against the American Myth," 393-406 in *The Capitalist System,* edited by Edwards *et al,* 394.

34   Zeitlin, *Capitalism and Imperialism,* 115.

35   Arthur MacEwan, "Capitalist Expansion, Ideology and Intervention," 409-420 in *The Capitalist System,* edited by Edwards *et al,* 419.

36   Zeitlin, *Capitalism and Imperialism,* 105-106.

37   William Appleman Williams, "The Legend of Isolation," 657-663 in *The Shaping of American Diplomacy,* edited by W. A. Williams (Chicago, Rand McNally, 1956), 661.

38   Harry Magdoff, "Militarism and Imperialism," 421-426 in *The Capitalist System,* edited by Edwards, *et al,* 424; MacEwan, "Capitalist Expansion, Ideology and Intervention," *loc. cit.,* 418; Zeitlin, *Capitalism and Imperialism,* 121.

39   Magdoff, "Militarism and Imperialism," *loc. cit.,* 424.

40   Thomas B. Weisskopf, "United States Foreign Private Investment: An Empirical Survey," 426-434 in *The Capitalist System,* edited by Edwards, *et al,* 431.

41   *Capitalism and Imperialism,* 109.

42   "Capitalist Expansion, Ideology and Intervention," *loc. cit.,* 417.

43   *Pentagon Capitalism. The Political Economy of War* (New York, McGraw-Hill, 1970), 140.

44   David R. Simon and D. Stanley Eitzen, *Elite Deviance,* 2nd edition (Boston, Allyn and Bacon, 1986), 155.

45   "The United States and Chile. Roots and Branches," 297-313 in *Foreign Affairs, An American Quarterly Review,* January, 1975, 310. See also Gabriel García Márquez, "The Death of Salvador Allende," translated by Gregory Rabassa, 46-55 in *Harper's,* vol. 248, No. 1486, March, 1974, 46.

46   "U.S. Security & Latin America," 29-40 in *Commentary,* vol. 71, No. 1, January, 1981, 30-31, 35.

47   *Ibid.,* 39.

48   Margaret Wilde, "Jeane Kirkpatrick; Utilitarianism as U.S. Foreign Policy," 226-

229 in *Christian Century*, Vol. 97, No. 7, 226-228. See also Anthony Lewis, New York Times News Service, Boston, "Lessons from Argentina on conduct of American foreign policy," in the Kansas City *Times*, January 27, 1984, A-13.

49   Robert Pastur, 4-6 in "Letters from Readers. U.S. Security & Latin America," in *Commentary*, 4-20, vol. 71, No. 4, April, 1981.

50   New York Times News Service, Boston, "Time for hard questions on El Salvador," in the Kansas City *Star*, April 29, 1990, J-3. Rep. Joe Moakley of a House task force "fresh from a trip to El Salvador, found nothing to indicate that an investigation exists at all. He charged that Salvador's military high command has conspired to silence witnesses to the killings and destroyed evidence." Rhonda Criss Lokeman, of the Editorial Staff, "Salvador getting away with murder," in *ibid.*, August 20, 1990, B-5. See also the New York Times, San Salvador, "Salvadoran evidence vanishes in deaths of priests, 2 women," in *ibid.*, May 7, 1990, A-8.

51   The CIA made Chile safe for IT&T, not democracy. The Pinochet regime is a "poor testament to the belief in the link between capitalism and freedom." Wachtel, *Poverty of Affluence*, 265.

52   Donald Kaul, Tribune Media Services, "Tragic Victory for Chamorro," in the Kansas City *Star*, March 1, 1990, C-19. "In disregard of treaties ... the Reagan administration made war on Nicaragua. When Nicaragua sued in the World Court, the Reagan administration rejected the court's judgment and withdrew from its jurisdiction." Anthony Lewis, The New York Times News Service, Boston, "Reagan folly led the way to imminent war in the desert," *ibid.*, October 8, 1990, B-7.

53   William V. Shannon, Boston Globe, "Thatcher has her doubts about Reagan," in the Kansas City *Star*, June 11, 1987, A-20.

54   Richard Reeves, Universal Press, New York, "What's news any day depends on what else is news," in *ibid.*, August 15, 1990, C-13.

55   Typical news reporting - which sounded as if released by a PR man at the White House - may be seen in the following: "Americans at War," 52-58 in *Newsweek*, vol. 102, November 7, 1983; "The Invasion Countdown," in *ibid.*, 75; "D-Day in Grenada," 22-28 in *Time*, vol. 122, No. 20, November 7, 1983.

56   Tom Wicker, New York Times News Service, " President's polls reinforce lesson often ignored by Democrats," in *ibid.*, January 24, 1990, A-7.

57   New York Times News Service, "Trial isn't likely to lend legitimacy to Panama raid," in *ibid.*, June 20, 1990, C-9. "I am shocked at our indifference at having killed 4,000 people in Panama City. We are a heartless people." Donald Kaul, Tribune Media News Services, in *ibid.*, May 14, 1990, B-7.

58   Richard Reeves, Universal Press, Washington, "These vicious killers work for us," in *ibid*, May 16, 1990, C-9.

59   Pliven and Cloward, *New Class Warfare*, 148.

196

60   Burawoy, *Manufacturing Consent*, 203.

61   Simon and Eitzen, *Elite Deviance*, 253.

62   Burawoy, *Manufacturing Consent*, 203.

63   *The Future of Industrial Man* (New York, John Day Company, 1942), 39-40.

64   *Ibid.*, 25, 28, 275.

65   United Features Syndicate (Reprinted from the *New Republic*), "U.S. has a troubling naivete about how the world works," in the Kansas City *Star*, February 22, 1987, K-3.

66   "... the Iran-contra hearings have quickly brought us to a radical constitutional claim. It is that the president has plenary power in foreign policy, not subject to limitation by law. ... The whole argument is staggering to someone brought up in a day when conservatives feared autocratic powers in the presidency. Conservatives thought then that law was the great protector of American freedom." Anthony Lewis, New York Times News Service, Boston, "Something like divine right," in the Kansas City *Times*, May 11, 1987, A-9. See also Haynes Johnson, Washington Post, Washington, "Everything to excess in this land of plenty," in the Kansas City *Times*, May 8, 1987, A-15; William V. Shannon, Boston Globe, "Reagan offense basically same as Nixon's," in the Kansas City *Star*, February 19, 1987, A-14.

67   David Nyhan, Boston Globe, "Hooked on Iran-contra scandal," in the Kansas City *Times*, September 2, 1987, A-8; By Tip O'Neill with William Novak, "Friendship not leadership," first of five parts, in the Kansas City *Star*, September 13, 1987, A-1, 16.

68   New York Times News Service, Washington, "Now Congress is angry," in the Kansas City *Star*, June 11, 1987, A-21.

69   David S. Broder, Washington Post Writers Group, Washington, "Additional restrictions on the president won't help," in the Kansas City *Times*, June 17, 1987, A-15. The real tragedy, obscured by this "comedy of error," lies in the public's sense of values. "Even about the factual information that we Americans do have in mind, most of us seem unable to think very well. We as a people seem not to recognize that truth-telling by public officials is absolutely indispensable to the functioning of free societies, for we give it a lower priority than 'national security' as defined (or asserted) by North and company." Kenneth S. Davis, Los Angeles Times, "Public values security over truth," in the Kansas City *Star*, August 2, 1987, M-3.

70   William F. Woo, St. Louis Post Dispatch, "It's galling to watch erosion (of morality)," in the Kansas City *Times*, August 5, 1987, A-13.

71   North believed that "the end justifies the means, just as long as he had authorization from his boss, whom he 'assumed' had the approval of the commander in chief. ... He is our latest antihero, bent on expanding democracy abroad even if he violates it at home." James Reston, New York Times News Services, Washington, "Oliver North is not on trial," in the Kansas City *Star*, July 14, 1987, A-9. " ... each in their own way, the men under President Reagan believed that Americans are lazy fools, sissies, dupes, or traitors.

...[It is] another manifestation of the irrational super-patriotism that leads eager beavers such as Lt. Col. Oliver North to think they have the duty to protect Americans against themselves." Richard Reeves, Universal Press, New York, "Patriotic paranoia grows in the dark," in the Kansas City *Times*, August 1, 1987, A-23.

72   "However poorly drafted and ambiguously stated, the Boland Amendment was clearly intended by Congress to stop the United States from engaging secretly in an undeclared war. It is specifically intended to cover those engaged in intelligence activities." Haynes Johnson, Washington Post, Washington, "That isn't smoke ... that's fire," in the Kansas City *Times*, May 22, 1987, A-16. "Congress was repeatedly told by high officials that the Boland Amendment was being punctiliously observed." However, the Irangate testimony "left no doubt that he [Reagan] wanted his subordinates to circumvent the Boland Amendment, and that they acted on that understanding." Anthony Lewis, New York Times News Services, Boston, "Best argument for the Reagan defense was made in 1977," in *ibid.*, May 25, 1987, A-23.

73   Los Angeles Times Syndicate, "Wrong questions, wrong answers," in the Kansas City *Times*, July 15, 1987, A-19.

74   Tribune Media Services, "Russians must think this Iran-contra thing is some kind of trick," in the Kansas City *Times*, May 16, 1987, A-13.

75   Universal Press, Washington, "'Business is business' mentality reigns," in the Kansas City *Times*, March 1, 1984, A-11.

76   "When he [Richard Corker] confessed ... that he 'worked for his own pocket all the time' he was denounced and politically doomed. But W.L. Strong, as a merchant, had done that all his life, and he was not condemned for making profit. That was a matter of course in commerce. ... I drew another, more interesting, tentative theory, viz.: that the ethics and morals of politics are higher than those of business." *Autobiography*, 408.

77   *Becket; or the Honor of God*, translated by Lucienne Hill (New York, Coward-McCann, 1960), 121. When the Irangate Congressional report was finally issued - on or about November 19, 1987 - the majority report concluded: "The president created or at least tolerated an environment where those who did know of the diversion believed with certainty that they were carrying out the president's policies...." By the Associated Press, Washington, "Actions subverted the Constitution's check on executive branch," in the Kansas City *Times*, October 19, 1987, A-8. Three Republican senators joined in that conclusion. They were Warren B. Rudman of New Hampshire, William S. Cohen of Maine and Paul S. Trible of Virginia. "They [White House coterie] say no laws have been broken, and they are certainly wrong. That is why they are also thinking about pardons." Otis Pike, Newhouse News Services, Washington, "Iran-contra report teaches nothing new," in the Kansas City *Star*, November 23, 1987, A-9.

78   Anouilh, *Becket*, 127-128.

79   José Armas, Albuquerque, New Mexico, "Poindexter fiasco cost U.S. $100 million," in the Kansas City *Star*, June 29, 1990, C-11. The U.S. District Court jury convicted Poindexter of lying to Congress and conspiring with North to deceive Congress and destroy government documents. Stanley Meisler and Robert L. Jackson, Los Angeles Times, "Poindexter found guilty," in *ibid.*, April 8, 1990, A-1.

198

80   Anthony Lewis, New York Times News Service, "Institutions that worked in Watergate failed in Iran-contra," in *ibid.*, May 14, 1990, B-7.

81   "A Big Break for Ollie; Will a court ruling mean that North goes free," in *Time*, v. 136, No. 5, July 30, 1990, 20.

82   Anthony Lewis, New York Times News Service, "Institutions that worked in Watergate failed in Iran-contra," in *loc. cit.*, B-7. See also Thomas Collins, Newsday, "Iran-contra; The press meekly trips away," in the Kansas City *Star*, May 9, 1990, C-9.

83   John J. Mearsheimer, "Why We Will Soon Miss the Cold War," 35-50 in *The Atlantic*, v. 266, No. 2, August 1990, 47.

84   *Ibid.*, 50.

85   The spokesman was none other than "Pug" Ismay, British general on Eisenhower's staff and the first secretary-general of NATO. Brian Dunning, a Special Correspondent, "Truth is hidden under history," in the Kansas City *Star*, April 1, 1990, K-1.

86   Alice M. Rivlin, The Washington Post, Washington, "A new world order presents Americans with new challenges," in *ibid.*, April 15, 1990, I-4.

87   New York Times News Service, "Cold war years did terrible damage to real sources of U.S. security," in *ibid.*, July 16, 1990, B-5.

88   The (Relative) Decline of America, 29-38 in *The Atlantic*, vol. 160, No. 2, August 1987, 33.

89   Richard Reeves, Universal Press, Brookhaven, New York, in the Kansas City *Star*, July 16, 1990, B-7.

90   Dan Balz, Washington Post Writer, "If Happy Days are Here, Why Aren't Conservatives Singing," in the *Washington Post Weekly Edition*, June 4-10, 1990, 14.

91   Scott Bennett, Dallas Morning News, Dallas, "'Morning in America' is over; here comes the night," in the Kansas City *Star*, July 27, 1990, C-11.

92   Donald Kaul, Tribune Media Services, "Environment in bad enough shape without military aid," in *ibid.*, July 14, 1990, C-11.

93   Brian Dunning, A Special Correspondent, "Truth is hidden under history," in *ibid.*, April 1, 1990, K-1, 4.

94   "... America has come full circle. Its dependence on foreign oil is back to the levels of the late 1970s. This has happened in the face of persistent warnings from all sides .... The government has continued its desultory support for research into alternative energy sources, albeit at lower levels in the 1980s .... But the free market approach [of President Reagan] had one inherent defect: It led inexorably to the cheapest and most adaptable fuel - foreign oil, most of it from the Gulf. ... Bush has an understandable distaste for doing it [conservation] by regulation: for example, through setting average fuel standards for cars." The Economist (London), Washington, "America has come full

circle on energy," in the Kansas City *Star*, August 19, 1990, J-4. "... dependence on Middle Eastern oil, underscores the failure of that last two administrations to develop an energy policy that would achieve the long-expressed U.S. goal of energy independence." Carl P. Leubsdorf, Dallas Morning News, "Public support for Persian Gulf action could erode," in *ibid.*, August 31, 1990, C-9. See also Yael T. Abouhalkah, "U.S. has spent 17 years not prepared for this moment." in *ibid.*, August 6, 1990, B-7.

95   Glenn Frankel, The Washington Post, London, "Is history on Hussein's side?," in *ibid.*, September 4, 1990, A-1, 8.

96   Donald Kaul, Tribune Media Services, "Shiny statements of principle aside," in *ibid.*, August 13, 1990, B-7. A 48-hour war with the Iraq military machine destroyed, a new and moderate president of Iraq, and a Saudi Arabia deeply in our debt, would see oil prices dropping rapidly, perhaps to $15 a barrel, maybe even less. Robert Unger, National Correspondent, "A war wouldn't bolster business in U.S. this time, economists say," in *ibid.*, August 27, 1990, A-1.

97   "We may go to war over petroleum. We are still dependent on the rulers of the Middle East as a drug addict is on the lords of Columbian cartels. Oil, black and slick, has spilled over the greening of politics (concern for global environment)." Ellen Goodman, "War story intrudes on chronicle of change," in *ibid.*, August 13, 1990, B-5. "The United States has not sent troops to the Saudi desert to preserve democratic principles. The Saudi monarchy is a feudal regime.... This is about money, about protecting governments loyal to America and punishing those which are not, and about who will set the price of oil." Thomas L. Friedman, "Why defend Saudi Arabia," in *ibid.*, August 12, 1990, A-1, 13. "For the international financial community to keep its 1980s speculative balls in the air, any renewal of inflation and commodity prices had to be beaten down. Oil could not be allowed to rise again. Hussein threatened that balance far more than Joe Sixpack's romance with the Great American gas guzzler. But it's not a politic reason for sending the 101st airborne." Kevin Phillips, Los Angeles Times News Service, "Worst of Vietnam, Iran crisis combines," in *ibid.*, August 27, 1990, B-5. "... we probably wouldn't have made a big stink about it except that Kuwait's full name is Tiny Oil-rich Kuwait, and if there is one thing we stand for, it's the democratic dream that people everywhere have a right to obtain gasoline for their automobiles and recreational vehicles and luxury motorboats of their choice." Dave Barry, Knight-Rider Newspapers, "They probably hate us in Kazoot, too," in *ibid.*, August 28, 1990, E-4.

98   "... Saddam invaded tiny Kuwait ... at just the right moment to save the Pentagon budget. ... In terms of fiscal salvation, Saddam's invasion came just after the House and Senate Armed Services Committees lopped about $20 billion off the Pentagon's $306 billion budget request for fiscal 1991.... As one Pentagon staffer remarked: 'Before the invasion of Kuwait, the services were staring into the fiscal abyss.'" David Evans, The Chicago Tribune, "Saddam to the rescue," in *ibid.*, September 4, 1990, B-5.

99   Bill Thompson, Fort Worth Star Telegram, "Trouble in the world didn't end with culmination of the Cold War," in *ibid.*, August 9, 1990, C-7. Hussein invaded "because both superpowers were preoccupied with the disengagement from their mutual hostility and because Congress was contemplating deep cuts in defense." Casper W. Weinberger, New Perspective Quarterly, "All combat criteria met," in *ibid.*, August 10, 1990, C-7.

100   "We've had so many devils lately. In the Mideast alone we have faced Moammar

Gadhafi, Hafez al-Assad and the late Ayatollah Khomeini. Saddam Hussein is only the latest Great Satan." Joseph Sobran, Universal Press, Washington, "Melodrama in the desert, in *ibid.*, August 20, 1990, B-7.

101　Harry Summers, Los Angeles Times Syndicate, "Let Saddam Hussein's action be a lesson to us," in *ibid.*, August 8, 1990,　C-9. "Also, things are looking up for the Pentagon budget, which has been in trouble because of the threat of lasting peace. For example, we've decided to go ahead with the B-2 bomber, even though we don't actually need it and it has certain technical problems such as it can't fly." Dave Barry, "They probably hate us in Kazoot, too," *loc. cit.*

102　Elmer D. Pendleton, Special Correspondent, "Iraq Threat Must be Contained," in *ibid.*, August 19, 1990, J-1, 4. If Hussein waited another year or so, "he might have faced nothing more lethal than empty words for the United States, the one nation ... capable of projecting power into the area, would more than likely have disarmed itself and retreated into neo-isolation." Harry Summers, "Hussein's colossal miscalculation," in *ibid.*, August 15, 1990, C-11.

103　"What can you say about an understanding of history so shallow that it allows its perception of every new challenge to be governed by a single stereotype (George Bush's declaration that Saddam Hussein was another Hitler who had to be stopped in his tracks for the good of mankind)." Joseph Sobran, Universal Press, Washington, "Turns out there's only one lesson in the sum total of history," in *ibid.*, August 27, 1990, B-7.

104　37 sailors were killed in the attack. Donald Kaul, Tribune Media Services, "A great and roaring example of incompetence at every level," in the Kansas City *Times,* June 18, 1987, A-17. See also Helmut Pickel, Nurnberger Nachrichten (Reprinted from the *German Tribune*), "Saber-rattling is too dangerous to be indulged," in the Kansas City *Star,* July 5, 1987, A-1; editorial in the Kansas City *Star,* "Mission impossible in the Persian Gulf," June 23, 1987, A-14.

105　U.S. ships attacked Iran's patrol boats which were menacing Kuwait oil, sold to finance Hussein's war effort. The American move, coming when Iranian troops were advancing, may have saved Hussein from defeat. This all came after the Stark episode of May 17, 1987. "The Making of a Monster," in *Newsweek,* Vol. 116, No.8, August 20, 1990, 29, 32.

106　On July 25, 1989, Saddam received official assurances from the American ambassador to Iraq to the effect that the United States had "no opinion on the Arab-Arab conflicts, like your border disagreement with Kuwait...." Jim Hoagland, Washington Post Writers Group, Washington, "U.S. all but invited Saddam to go ahead and take Kuwait," in the Kansas City *Star,* September 15, 1990, C-9. "Indeed, the very week that Saddam moved into Kuwait, the administration was trying to weaken congressional sanctions on the Iraq dictator." Carl P. Leubsdorf, "Public support for Persian Gulf action could erode," the Kansas City *Star,* August 31, 1990, C-9.

107　James Flanigan, "Oil is only 1 factor in Gulf maze," in The Kansas City *Star,* August 27, 1990, A-11.

108　Joseph Sobran, Universal Press Syndicate, Washington, "Our 'warrior pundits' assume even events can be controlled," in *ibid.*, September 3, 1990, B-5.

109   Donald Kaul, Chicago Tribune, "One last hurrah for American gunboat diplomacy," in *ibid.*, August 30, 1990, C-9.

110   Gore Vidal, *Empire. A Novel* (New York, Random House, 1987), 37. Compare the above, for example, with Preface to Brooks Adams, *The Law of Civilization and Decay* (New York, Macmillan, 1896), v-xi.

111   Vidal, *Empire*, 45. See *The Influence of Sea Power on History in The People Shall Judge*, II, 260-265.

112   Vidal, *Empire*, 37.

113   *Ibid.*, 35. Even before the publication of *The New Empire* in 1902, Brooks sounded the same theme: "A survey, written in 1900, of the international situation ... containing a reasoned and gloomy forecast of the crackup of Britain as the fortified outpost of the Anglo-Saxon world, of the decay of France as a major nation, and of the rivalry of the United States and Russia for the control of the world." Brooks Adams, *America's Economic Supremacy;* with a new evaluation by Marquis W. Childs in *Book Review Digest*, 1947, edited by Mertice M. James and Dorothy Brown (New York, H.W. Wilson, 1948), 4-5. *The New Empire* itself was finally traced to the Washington University Libraries in St. Louis but, unfortunately, the volume does not circulate on interlibrary loan.

114   Vidal, *Empire*, 129. Brooks thought of Roosevelt as "a man who understood the forces of history and could accommodate American policy accordingly. As the leader of the Progressive movement, he had forseen the dangers of an unchained capitalism and had thwarted the masters of finance in their ruinous schemes. As a formulator of foreign policy, it was Roosevelt who detected the drift of civilization that dictated American expansion in the Far East and opposition to the latest enemy, Russia. Undoubtedly, the fact that Roosevelt listened to the advice proferred by Brooks inclined the latter to think highly of Roosevelt's prescience." Timothy Paul Donovan, *Henry Adams and Brooks Adams, The Education of Two American Historians* (Norman, University of Oklahoma Press, 1961), 175.

115   See C. Stanley Urban, *Slavocracy and Empire: New Orleans and the Attempted Expansion of Slavery, 1845-1861* (1976), edited by Robert W. Wadsworth, 352 pp. (Revision of a Ph.D. dissertation, 1943, entitled *The Idea of Progress and Southern Imperialism, 1845-1861*). Both volumes are available at Northwestern University Library in Evanston, Illinois.

116   *The Complete Writings of Thucydides: The Peloponnesian War*. The unabridged Crawley translation with an introduction by John H. Finley, Jr. (New York, The Modern Library, Random House, 1951), 334.

117   Louis Menand, "Man of the People. The True and Only Heaven. Progress and Its Critics," 39-44 in *The New York Review of Books*, vol. 38, No. 7, April 11, 1991, 39.

Chapter XVIII

HISTORY VERSUS THE DEMOCRATIC, PEACEFUL AND INDUSTRIALIZED STATE: PUBLIC WELFARE?

About ninety years ago Lincoln Steffens discovered the ethic of investment capitalism: profit, profit, and more profit! It occurred when his editor told him to investigate a story which alleged that New Jersey "had enacted statutes under which the antitrust laws of other states could be evaded and American public opinion defied." His informant, James B. Dill who masterminded it all, "opened up the criminal inside of the practices under the New Jersey legislature, a picture of chicanery, fraud, of wild license and wrong-doing...."

Sometime later, Steffens asked Dill why he had been so frank with him. "When you [Dr. Innocent] wrote as charges against us what financiers could and did actually do in New Jersey .. you were advertising our business -

free. ... what you wrote as 'bad' struck business men all over the United States as good, and they poured in upon us to our profit to do business with us at their profit."

The Autobiography (New York Literary Guild, Harcourt-Brace, 1931) 193-195.

Steffens later graduated to the more sophisticated position that you "can't run a railroad without corrupting and running the government." Since an honestly-run railroad could not produce the kind of revenue which would attract investors, the natural reaction of the railroad president would be to resort to fraud and chicanery, while paying for political protection. He would do this in order to lure capital to his enterprise. According to knowledgeable sources, such strategy always had a pay-off. The Autobiography, 608-609.

The same ethic explains why industry deserted New England for the South following World War II and why in the last decade it has abandoned the United States for Mexico and elsewhere. It explains why investment capital has gone into promoting mergers, buying stock to wreck perfectly good companies and then saddling them with the cost of their adventures, rather than concentrating upon quality production. It explains your dismay when learning that your favorite health bread has become part of a financial empire dominated by a glue-making outfit.

"Capitalism as a social order and as a creed is the expression of belief in economic progress toward the freedom and equality of the individual in the free and equal society." That observation came from Peter Drucker. We know of no better way to get immediately to the core of the problem addressed here. "But the capitalist creed," he continued, "was the first and only social creed which valued the profit motive positively as the means by which the ideal free and equal society would be automatically realized."[1]

This chapter consists of an analysis why the dream itself was doomed to failure. If we appear critical of our capitalistic and industrialized society today - thinking it neither benign, nor rational, nor efficient - this has not always been true.

In my case, I recall in the depression Thirties being a staunch advocate of progress, technology and industrialization. One instance I can never forget occurred at Louisiana State University in 1936. There I met an engaging chap, a southerner from Washington, Georgia, first capital of that state. On one occasion he confided that his aristocratic mother wept the day she heard that the first factory located there. While he smiled, I was almost convulsed with laughter. How could anyone wish to cling to an agricultural and rural life when they could have the blessings of industrialization, civilization, and all the goods and services which went with it? Even later, when I read "I'll Take My Stand," a book by twelve learned and prominent southerners who advocated resistance to the idea that the South ought to emulate the industrial North and East,[2] I was equally unsympathetic. How, you ask, could I be so naive? Well, for one thing, if we ever gave industrial pollution any thought, we believed it confined to say, strip mining and life in grubby cities like Pittsburgh and perhaps Detroit. No one had any notion that we in the Gentile world would do to ourselves what we falsely accused the Jews of doing in Europe in the Middle Ages. For we were dutifully, even cheerfully, to go about the dirty business of poisoning our own wells. That is hubris with a vengence.[3]

When one begins an investigation into the matter of whether industrialization in America is benign or not, the first concern is to put the matter into proper perspective: in the last one hundred years, under the banner of free enterprise, two-thirds of American manufacturing has been metamorphosed into a "closed enterprise system."[4] Since the termination of

World War II, the movement has vastly accelerated. In 1945, for example, 200 of our largest corporations controlled about 45 percent of the total business assets. That had increased to 61 percent in 1982 and to a whopping 70 percent by 1985, including 72 percent of all profits. Shared monopolies dominate the following key industries to this extent: motor vehicles, 93 percent; turbines and generators, 86 percent; primary aluminum, 76 percent; photographic equipment, 72 percent, and guided missles and spacecraft, 62 percent. This was a natural consequence of a desire for monopoly power, and not for technological advancement.[5]

The great significance of this was grasped by John Kenneth Galbraith when he wrote: "The important thing is that the doctrines of a monopolistic or imperfect competition paved the way for a destruction of the old assumption of competition on which the competitive model was erected."[6] This was because the incentives in a typical American industry, one dominated by a few firms only, do not in fact work in the direction of a maximum output at the lowest prices. The market power of these firms is used to subvert those old postulates of capitalism.[7] Instead, what obtains as a result of competition within a concentrated industry is "price stabilization."[8] That which makes this economic crunch all the more fascinating is the realization Karl Marx predicted it well over a century ago.[9]

Since World War II a psychological revolution simultaneously occurred, one which represented the spirit of consumerism over the older Protestant ethic. It had a tremendous impact upon the rate of our economic growth. While Americans still stress productivity at the work place, so much that in effect we turn ourselves into machines, at home we behave as if it is our patriotic duty to help consume what we produce.[10] This of necessity meant the abandonment of the Protestant ethic. It stressed delay in self-satisfaction, or saving, until one had the necessary money in hand for the purchase of the desired article. That instinct began to erode in the Twenties under the lure of installment buying and credit innovations, but the idea of spend and borrow did not achieve universal compliance until after 1945.

Advertising was probably the key to the transition as it sensed the new mood of social and political conformity which swept the nation under the post-war Communist scare. At the same time that advertisers told us how to buy and how to live while doing it, they warned against looking, thinking, and acting different than fellow Americans. Advertising, therefore, "relegated people to consumption, passivity and spectatorship. Those who questioned this chain of command were labeled 'communist.'"[11] Creators of advertising copy cleverly created discontent within the consumer market - planting worry about yellow teeth, bad breath, perspiration, thinning hair, flab, ring around the collar, and a host of other ailments - and then clearly implied that their product could alleviate that miserable condition. It was like the old-time evangelist who first acquainted us with the terrors of Hell and then promised a way out if we would blindly follow him.[12] In a more positive sense, advertisements made us see, for example, that buying the "proper" motor car [theirs] "could serve us as a symbol of freedom, strength, speed and adventure." This adult fairy tale was a form of romantic escapism: "Cars are our personal dream machines and dreams are private experiences."[13] The triumph of consumerism was best reflected by the fact that shopping had become our chief cultural activity. So important was it that the lack of daily challenge at the work place, or even the health and safety of the workers, was considered a small price to pay for the maintenance of such a productive system.[14]

For us the best empirical evidence that the old Protestant ethic is dead, and long live consumerism, is the current TV advertisements. If a family wants to go on a vacation but does not have the cash, no problem. Simply borrow the money. Enjoy now, pay later. Well-known actors advise one to obtain their credit card so "you too" can travel around the world with no money in pocket. Borrowing merely to have fun was and is anathema for that individual who clings to the Protestant ethic. But the overriding consideration of the average American is that he *not* be considered an "odd ball" by his colleagues, friends and neighbors. That character is obviously someone who does not worry about consumer trends.

When and if one attempts to compare and contrast the American economy since World War II with that which existed before, the stark contrast lies in the emergence of the military-industrial complex. While this has, no doubt, contributed in a superficial sense to economic growth and prosperity, it carries a much more somber message. By the time that President Eisenhower called our attention to it upon his retirement in 1961, the constant and ever-increasing movement of personnel from the higher ranks of the armed forces and government procurement offices to huge munitions firms, or vice versa, was already under way. While in 1959, 721 retired officers were employed by the hundred largest defense firms, by 1969 there were over 2,000 such exiles with the rank of colonel or higher in the Army and that of captain or above in the Navy. From eight leading contractors in the Seventies, 2,000 employees either transferred from industry to government or the other way around. Of almost 500 civilians in this group, 34 percent had worked in key research and development offices of the armed services or the Department of Defense.[15] In 1968, Senator Young of Ohio observed that, immediately following retirement, at least 3,600 officers became associated with defense industries. David E. Sims explained the inner motivation responsible for such a movement. An officer still in service, but approaching retirement, must view a transfer to defense industry as one of his better options. Even the most ethical soldier would find it difficult to refuse to help a particular company land a lucrative contract in the face of such a potential reward.[16] Even the Wall Street *Journal* had sharp reservations: "The movement of weapons experts between industry and government jobs, frequently on the same project ... tends to blur the distinction between national security and corporate goals.[17]

It was Tom who called attention to the iron triangle. It was the unholy alliance between the Pentagon, the defense industry, members of the armed forces committees, defense appropriation subcommittees, and Senate and House members from those states boasting a high concentration of defense spending.[18] In the Seventies, eight leading research and development contractors got over $20 billion in contracts. Another authority estimated that two-thirds of total defense contracts went to the hundred largest corporations and that the top twenty-five roughly got half.[19] Using the mythology that the Soviet Union was constantly outspending us[20] this team was not only enabled to gloss over conspicuous defense failure - like tanks which would not drive or amphibious vehicles which sank.[21] It was also capable of reversing President Carter's decision in 1977 to abandon the controversial Rockwell B-1 bomber. Rockwell spent $1.35 million on such efforts, an amount opponents could not hope to match. Rockwell concentrated its campaign contributions for re-election to members of defense appropriations and armed services committees in both houses. When President Reagan revived the program in 1981, nearly all voted for it.[22] "Behind the veil of national security the defense iron triangle has unusual power." With the Reagan administration, it reached its zenith. Between 1980 and 1984, the defense budget doubled in current dollars and projections called for it to have tripled by 1988. "The Reagan military build-up has been the most dramatic peacetime increase in defense spending this nation has experienced. By 1985, defense spending will be at a higher constant dollar level than at any point since the Second World War.[23]

According to a report from the Justice department in the summer of 1987, the continual rape of the Treasury by private "defense" contractors was done with the consent of the Pentagon. A perusal of the contract with General Dynamics served as a model. In 1978, both signed a contract for the delivery of a self-propelled anti-aircraft weapon, later called the Sergeant York, at the supposed cost of $39 million. However, the contract did not stipulate delivery of the weapon in good-working order, but merely that the company exert its "best efforts" at the same. According to a Pentagon official, if the money ran out before delivery, the company could have "delivered a bucket of bolts without breaching the contract." In August, 1986, Secretary of Defense Weinberg scuttled the abortive affair. This result was predictable because Pentagon officials anticipated an expenditure of $60, not $39, million, which was all Congress appropriated.[24] One might even hazard a guess that the fiasco ran "according to plan."

By virtue of a Senate subcommittee report in late September, 1987, we are enabled to get behind the screen of this often nefarious activity, focusing on the celebrated Wedtech scandal involving Ed Meese. He served both as an aide to President Reagan and as Attorney General. Months before Meese invested $55,000 in Wedtech, he knew that the company had been awarded a $135 million contract to build pontoon bridges for the Navy. Although the company had absolutely no experience at this sort of thing, it was given the no-bid Army and Navy contracts while several qualified companies were passed over. When, several months later, Meese became Attorney General, he invested the aforementioned money and made a profit of $40,000 in about a year and a half. Even more significantly, it had been Meese's White House aide, James Jenkins, who had been responsible for the initial Navy contract. A year, after being instrumental in swinging it for Wedtech, he went to work for the company. Since bankrupt, Wedtech has been accused of bribing about twenty officials when it was posturing as a legitimate Hispanic-run company.[25]

The dawning of the computer age merely underscores the political death of the democratic ideal of a more perfect society for all. This is because it promises to mechanize or robotize a great many unskilled and semi-skilled jobs out of existence. For example, a large body of the unemployed in heavy industry today, like steel and autos, will never return to work there.[26] This trend has been in effect ever since America's factories produced far beyond the line of scarcity while not utilizing all available machines. The problem, thus, for decades has not been how to produce more, but rather how to dispose or consume that which has been produced. In such an affluent society, the labor force tends to be quite vulnerable.[27] The tragedy is compounded by the fact that, as a society, we have yet to face the problem or, worse, even to acknowledge it.[28]

A prominent journalist explained this best in terms the layman can understand. While twelve million new jobs have been created since President Reagan took office, a high percentage of these were in service trades, or about ten million, whereas two million manufacturing jobs have evaporated during the same period. A third of the jobs in the service sector were attributed to a rise in retail trade and nearly half of the new ones were in eating and drinking establishments. There the average wage is a mere $4.39 an hour. Meanwhile, the number of minimum wage jobs at only $3.35 an hour increased by almost three million. On the contrary, the $15 dollar an hour unionized wage was a casualty of the economic slow-down of the early '80s, foreign competition, plant relocation and the general decline of our manufacturing sector.[29]

Experts predict the new era of high technology will emphasize the problem to the point where the tragedy can no longer be ignored. This is much more than a gloomy guess. In July, 1983, the heads of major business corporations, or those attending a meeting of the Business Council, affirmed that few of the workers laid off in heavy industry would be rehired with the lifting of the depression because they would not be needed.[30] Later reports verified earlier predictions. Late in 1986, the Joint Economic Committee declared that 60 percent of the 8 million jobs created since 1979 paid less than $7,000 a year. This proliferation of low-wage jobs "pointed to growing income inequality in the United States."[31] Likewise, it threatens the standard of living of the bulk of the work force.[32] Ultimately, of course, it threatens our national ability to consume what we produce and that implies a deep depression.

Further, the computer revolution now adds a new threat or that of the loss of jobs by the middle class. Many observers believe this movement could lead to a dangerous polarization between the new elite of highly trained professionals and that of the great mass of unskilled laborers. It is predicted that, as factories are without hired hands, so offices will be without paper, and the people to process it. This transition will sharply reduce the demand for middle-income positions.[33] It should make for a situation dangerously close to that predicted by Karl Marx. He was one of the first to call attention to the fact of the dehumanization of the worker, and his alienation from work. This came as a consequence of capital investment in technological innovations which, routinizing the productive process, required less work skill.[34] The history of industrialization, wrote Lilian Breslow Rubin, has, unfortunately proved him correct.[35] The computer age merely exacerbates an old problem.[36] With know-how a monopoly in the hands of management, it seeks and demands obedience as the most desirable trait of the labor force.[37] A privileged position falsely encourages it to try "to maintain profits by reducing the living standards and increasing the labor efforts of working people."[38]

If, however, one assumes that the individual remedy lies in good training, aptitude and the determination to rise to a highly-paid job, and the satisfaction which success yields, this is belied by two nationally prominent psychologists. Because we are a rootless society, it is harder to see the fruits of our individual efforts in any meaningful sense. The nature of the work of the eminently successful is that it is meaningless and boring. It is because it has no social utility that labor at the top of the task heap is so handsomely rewarded.[39]

The computer revolution may also present us with a regrettable historical first: more people unemployed than employed.[40] Quite aside from the dreadful economic consequences is the fact that people derive their identities or statuses from their jobs. Without them, their personalities wither on the vine. The most encouraging hope is that unemployment may be somewhat curtailed by the sharing of these glamorless jobs. And even when people have jobs, if they are low paying and low status ones, their recipients share the same low esteem of themselves as does the public. Nothing so destroys the feeling of equality as this situation. One cannot maintain a democracy without at least the illusion of equality.[41]

All such events and movements occurred simultaneously with the sharp decline of the American labor movement. It began with the breaking by President Reagan of the Air Traffic Controller's strike in the summer of 1981, and the business recession, which marked his first two years in office. A great many large corporations in many different fields, including steel, autos, transportation, mining and airlines, took advantage of rising unemployment to force unions to agree to lower wages. If that did not work, they successfully used, or threatened to use, federal bankruptcy laws to get out from under existing wage contracts. [42] It is expected that management will demand further union concessions.[43]

Such strategy and tactics reminds the historian that the chief reason for the hostility to labor unions by Big Business was its natural desire to retain a single soft spot upon which immediately to dump its losses in an unexpected recession. Given a sudden business crisis, management could not lower contractual costs as far as interest rates, rents and prices for raw materials and parts from other business firms. However, if there were no strong labor organizations, lay-offs and sharp pay reductions could occur immediately. Naturally, costs of operation would be lower and the firm would be in a better position for competitive bidding. It promised an opportunity for survival that no sound business mind could resist.

This gloomy economic forecast for the American worker, whose only capital is his labor whether in a white or blue collar, strikes directly at the basis of the American dream: a good job at a high wage which enables the purchase of a detached home in a suburb, a college education for the young, a couple of family cars and other gadgets so dear to a materialistically-minded society. What is substituted instead is a sense of powerlessness on the part of the American worker. The final price of this is the pink slip and the feeling that the individual is expendable, just like a machine part.[44]

"Sooner or later," concluded Tom Wicker, "a falling living standard will be political dynamite, too. When it dawns on enough Americans that they can no longer expect to do better economically than their parents, or even as well, their reaction is likely to be outraged, maybe even dangerous."[45]

Another alarming trend since World War II has been the tendency of the multinational corporation to move its fabrication centers from the United States to take advantage of cheap labor costs and thus enhance profits. Its hallmark is not merely that it does business in many nations, but that its managerial decisions about production, marketing and research are made in the interest of the corporation as a unit, rather than that of the host nation. Declining domestic profits in the face of rising ones for investments abroad were responsible for the initiation of that trend.[46] A dramatic illustration was the announcement by the Ford Motor Company it would make Escorts in Japan, assemble them in Mexico and sell its product in the United States.[47] However, this was preceded by a decade of the assembly of electronic components in Taiwan, IBM punch cards in Hong Kong, shoe fabrication in Italy and hand typesetting in many countries.[48] A plausible argument can be made for the fact that this shift of money, time and energy overseas has come at the expense of the domestic economy, resulting in a lagging economic growth rate and rising unemployment.[49]

Nor has this decade-old trend been reversed or even slowed. A fair judgment of the change of American business practices in 1990 was this: while nineteenth century businesses brought labor in from all over the world, "today they take their factories to foreign, low-wage markets." GE shut down the Providence, Rhode Island, factory where workers were paid $5.84 an hour and relocated in Nogales, Mexico, where the hourly wage was less than $2.00. Litton, Fairchild and RCA have joined this "border industrialization program."[50] Zenith of Springfield, Missouri, affords a typical case in the Midwest. In the late 70s and early 80s, it lopped off about 800 workers. "Then we were told in 1986 to accept an 8.1 percent wage cut or 600 more jobs were going to a plastics plant in Mexico. We took the pay cut."[51]

The situation deteriorated to the point the intelligent consumer can easily tick off the stuff he used to buy American-made but not longer can: typewriters, radios, cameras, shoes, and now even shirts and jackets. "The flight of the typewriter," wrote one critic, "was part of a general exodus of American manufacturing that began in the 1950s. Unions squawked, but our prophets assured us that we would build a brave new industrial world around the computer chip. Now those high tech industries are leaving too."[52] And much of that "industry" which has not left is now owned by foreigners. Recently, Richard Reeves wrote in dismay: "I had just spent $384.75 for a new General Electric dishwasher - $40 of that was for a mandatory two-year service contract - when I read the news that GE had sold its consumer electronics business to Thomson of France."[53] That, however, would have come as no surprise to Ernest Conine: "Carnation Co. is Swiss. Doubleday, RCA Records, Celanese and General Tire are all German. Zale Corp., the giant jewelry retailer, is Canadian. Purina Mills, Smith and Wesson, and J. Walter Thompson advertising agency are British. The list goes on."[54]

This significant economic trend becomes understandable if we postulate that, with regard to the host nation, the modern corporation is a kind of mid-nineteenth century merchant. As Adam Smith correctly anticipated, he was not really the citizen of any particular country. On the contrary, he was "as much as possible, isolated from all necessary relationships, duties, and prejudices." He was thus free to calculate economic self-interest and, as a rational man, based everything he did upon this single principle.[55]

Nevertheless, as Jeff pointed out, the early followers of Adam Smith, like David Ricardo and John Stuart Mill, developed their concepts of comparative advantage and free trade under the false assumption that capitalists would remain at home. "These pioneers never envisioned that capital would become mobile. They could not imagine that American television manufacturers might set up shop in Taiwan to take advantage of lower labor costs.... Modern economists so love the old logical argument for comparative advantage that they have ignored that its foundation, capital immobility, has crumbled, and that, as a result, absolute advantage will increasingly rule."[56]

The comparative inactivity of our national productive apparatus sharply contrasted with that of a frenetic one on the stock exchange. It was fueled by Reagan's tremendous tax cut on corporations in 1981, and highlighted by recent scandals sweeping through the highest quarters of Wall Street. Executives at Kidder Peabody, as well as Goldman, Sacs & Co., were arrested early in 1987 on charges they illegally traded stocks to make millions of dollars. Insiders expect the scandal to spread.[57] It has even extended to include the use of cocaine as a business proposition.[58]

At this point the historian is reminded of Louis Brandeis' warning when he wrote that remarkable little book in 1913, entitled *Other People's Money*. It examined the promoter's art of buying something with other people's money and ending up with the property purchase without having parted with his money.[59] Essentially, this was part of the magic or trickery practiced on a large scale by J.P. Morgan and other investment bankers.

The betrayal of fiduciary trust is precisely what our experts admit has swept the big bank and stock markets in recent times. For example, one financial journalist observed that the scandal is not limited to inside trading, but that the larger crime is widespread and "unrestrained greed." Since a premium is placed upon doing deals, and dispensing with moral values, it is but one step further toward ignoring client interest and substituting one's own by investment bankers. Take the celebrated instance in 1984 of the sale of Lehman Brothers Kuhn Loeb, an old-line investment banking firm, to Shearson/American Express, another huge company owned by the American Express Company. These secret manipulations were undertaken because they promised as much as $15 million for each of the Lehman Brothers' 77 partners. But what occurred in this betrayal of the public trust was merely "a microcosm of what's going on in Wall Street."[60]

Nor dare we neglect the fantastic aspects of what is called the leveraged buy-out, a practice which deserves special citation in any book

whose proper title ought to be *Alice Through the Business Looking Glass*.
That was what happened when Campeau Corporation of Canada took over
the highly successful giant, Allied Stores Corporation. The purchase came
from funds Campeau did not have but bankers did, about four billion. After
the transaction, Campeau tried to pay back that money by saddling all the
debt to the company it bought out. Bankers themselves were indifferent as
long as their money is out at a high interest rate and returns are prompt and
steady.[61]

As Lee Iacocca explained, such financial rip-offs have had much to
do with America's industrial decline: "I see billions of dollars tied up in new
corporate debt to keep the raiders at bay while research and development
goes begging. I see billions going for greenmail that ought to building high-
tech factories. ... I also see a huge share of America's best management
talent wasted on takeover games when it should be devoted to strengthening
the industrial base of the country. But I don't see the raiders creating jobs.
I don't see them increasing productivity. And worst of all, I don't see them
doing a thing to help America compete in the world."[62] More briefly put, the
same idea was advanced by Representative Richard A. Gephardt:
"Corporations have become chips in a casino game, played for high stakes
by people who produce nothing, invent nothing and service nothing."[63]

Louis Brandeis was correct in his assertion that bankers were ill-
advised to own and operate railroads merely because they had, by financial
manipulation, obtained a majority of the voting stock. How much more
irrational is the current practice of combining, under one directorate, many
companies which made their original reputation and fortune in entirely
different areas? The only tie which binds is a common bookkeeping system,
one which makes the accountant the master and the engineer his servant.
This entire sequence of historical events was more than adeuately summarized
by Thorstein Veblen. He affirmed that the Captain of Industry (the founder,
the builder, the productive genius) was unfortunately succeeded by the
Captain of Business (front office white collars) and he by the Captains of
Finance (J.P. Morgan and the manipulators of paper on Wall Street).[64]

Perhaps the most dramatic result of our decline in industrial
productivity lies in the revolution of the Japanese attitude toward us, i.e.

from the subservience of the late Forties and early Fifties to their attitude of superiority today. "Many an American exporter has had his produce dismissed because the Japanese consider it to be poor quality. The trend is to view the United States as a place where lawyers overrule engineers and where comsumption, not production, is king."[65]

Another distressing aspect of our industrialization is that, when coupled with capitalism and a world market, it is in the final process of liquidating the small freeholder or farmer. It was this individual breed Jefferson relied upon to attain and maintain democracy. However, the independence of that farmer was at hazard ever since he abandoned self-sufficient farming, and opted it for a world market. Here prices fluctuate rapidly and often due to the law of supply and demand and artificial manipulation by speculators. Both a rapidly accelerating technology, as well as his forced competition with corporate farming, meant an ever-increasing tendency to suppy more agricultural products than could be consumed under the pricing system. Unfortunately, however, the farmer fell victim to the same tendency Veblen declared periodically waylaid the businessman.[66] When times are good and prices high for the product, bankers encourage one to borrow in order to be able to produce more and to pay for the expansion with the profits incurred from the bold move. When the inevitable recession occurs, however, the borrower finds he cannot repay the loan at its high interest. This is especially true because the demand for his product has been sharply curtailed and prices drop even further. Nothing deters his own sacrifice. Bankruptcy presents itself as an uninvited guest.[67]

The irony of these trends was captured by Richard Reeves: "Our problem is that we got what we wanted after World War II [that for which Henry Luce first asked]. We created a world in our own free enterprise image, and established an expensive American-controlled military structure to defend it against communism." As the free world's hired gun, we worked hard and persistently to create our own problems, or those which flowed from our creation of "a capitalist world of free global markets."[68] David Vogel summarized our present dilemma: "America can never hope to dominate the world as it did in the quarter-century after World War II. Nor should it want to."[69] The best explanation of why this cannot be done came from Senator Daniel Moynihan of New York: "We will soon learn that the world's largest debtor nation does not decide world policy and that deindustrialized America can no longer be the arsenal of democracy."[70] Our very concentration on armament contributed to the erosion of the economic base of the United States. While many of our brightest engineers focused research on the development of new weapons systems, Japan and Germany devoted their efforts to commercial research and development.[71]

Recent events in the Middle East dramatized that dichotomy. When the Reagan administration challenged the Iranian navy in the Persian Gulf in 1987, critics declared "Reaganite dreams of restoring the Eisenhower-era U.S. clout are unaffordable and unrealistic for a country losing its old hegemony."[72] And when, in 1990, President Bush rushed many thousands of troops to defend Saudi Arabia from the menace of Iraq, Germany and Japan - our great economic rivals - were fortunately barred from doing this by law.[73] Germany at first declined to contribute to the cost of occupation on the ground the affair was rooted in a bi-lateral agreement between the United States and Saudi Arabia. Japan was less stingy, offering to pay one billion dollars, enough for a month's occupation. Although its prime minister planned to send a medical team of one hundred, a few weeks later he had only three volunteers.[74] The plight of the United States as a sort of "Have gun, will travel" person is beautifully capsulated in the following " ... the Persian Gulf crisis has laid bare how incapable America is of paying for such a military operation, and how reluctant our allies are to chip in, even if they benefit. If the countries we are defending weren't oil kingdoms like Kuwait and Saudi Arabia, which have promised to pick up most of the tab, the administration would be in big, big trouble. So if the vision of 'the new world order' involves American playing global policeman, the Persian Gulf crisis seems to have proven that this won't work, if for no other reason than that we are broke."[75]

All these lamentable conditions, arising from the combination of capitalism and industrialization, make it easier to comprehend the following declaration: "Many businessmen have begun to fear that capitalism and democracy may be incompatible in the long run." This somewhat surprising conclusion came from observers at a recent meeting held by the Conference Board, a forum for big business leaders to exchange candid views.[76]

What, then is the price that America must pay for the self-indulgence of eight years of Reaganomics, or that which virtually promised to eliminate corporate taxes, sharply reduce those on the wealthy, spend $1 trillion over five years on defense and still yield a balanced budget by 1983?[77] Even before the mid-October stock market crash of 1987 some experts sensed the doom inherent in these policies. In the interest of economy, we single out but two, ie., the tremendous debt incurred and the extremely adverse balance of trade. From the world's largest creditor nation in 1982, we plummeted to that of the world's largest debtor. In 1986, our debt stood at the all-time high of $140.57 billion. That was almost 20 percent higher than the imbalance of the previous year.[78] Installment debt has virtually doubled since Reagan assumed control. The money we send to Japan to make up for our trade deficit is re-invested by them in the United States. The Japanese buy government bonds which means they supply the money to keep our economy going while our government spends $200 billion a year more than it collects.[79] In California, where five of the largest 11 banks are Japanese-owned, foreign investors now own more than half of 170 banking firms. The number is 300 in New York.[80]

Experts estimate that by 1990, interest payments on that debt will amount to between $40 and $50 billion annually and that our living standards will certainly be lowered. It also puts us at the mercy of the whims of the foreign investor. As Wright Investors Service put it: "Foreign buying should not be counted on as a lasting support since a weakened dollar, a faltering economy, or declining foreign stock prices could each send foreigners for the exit."[81] According to official sources, foreigners are already demanding higher interest rates because of lost confidence in our ability to solve our financial problems. If foreign investment were curtailed, the government's continued demands for money would displace private investment, push interest rates up, as well as inflation, while contributing to a recession and increased spending. The shock to our stock market might rival that of 1929.[82]

It was the foreign investment dollar which financed our consumption binge of the last seven years. "If it weren't for a flood of foreign capital we long ago would have faced the choice between higher interest rates, which would have throttled the recovery, or printing money, which would have reignited inflation." But, writes Michael Kinsley, the day of judgment can no longer be postponed. "To keep attracting foreign capital we must either let the dollar sink, which means inflation, or raise interest rates, which probably means a recession."[83]

What seems clear, however, is that Reagan killed the growth, if not the very existence, of the once popular welfare state. That fact was confessed to in 1987 by the celebrated conservative columnist, George Will: "The government which is energized by money, is out of energy, thanks to Reagan's shrinkage of the government's revenue base."[84] Liberals like senators Ernest Fritz Hollings and Daniel Patrick Moynihan predicted that probability well before Reagan's re-election in November, 1984.[85]

Economists conclude the United States will not recover from its declining trade problems until matters of the deficit have been resolved. Our recent plight can be measured in terms of three factors: rate of economic growth, growth of gross national product per capita, and productivity per worker annually. In terms of these, from 1979 to 1985, the American economy grew half as rapidly as that of Japan, but a little better than that of West Germany. Based on the other two factors, America was clearly in third place. Our average growth in gross national product was one-third of Japan's and her productivity was five times that of ours. West Germany was also ahead of us, although not that dramatically.[86]

It is worth noting here that none of these successful competitors of ours, including Sweden, did it by "free enterprise." For example, our government absorbs about 30% of the gross National Product while in West Germany it is over 50% and larger than that elsewhere.[87]

This unhappy domestic situation was a consequnce of the ever-increasing federal deficit, which resulted in the equally dramatic adverse trade balances we suffered during the Reagan years. Barry Bosworth, economist for the Brookings Institute, explained it: "This is a country that's on a consumption binge and is forced to borrow overseas."[88] Kenneth McCay of the House Budget Committee agreed: "We are consuming more than we produce, borrowing more than we save." But, our national plight was dramatized when he added: "...we're borrowing -[since 1979] at roughly ten times the rate we're increasing our productivity."[89] In detail, the system worked something like this. Because our government is spending far more than it takes in, it has to borrow money. It does this by issuing attractive rates on Treasury bonds but, in order to buy this fancy product, foreigners need to buy U.S. dollars. This increases the value of currency in relation to all others. It makes it cheap for Americans to travel abroad and to buy there while at the same time it raises domestic prices to scare off foreign buyers. In other words, it sharply increased both our deficit and our adverse trade balance. And while this remarkable invasion of foreign investment was an important factor in reducing inflation, it hurt domestic industries. It meant both wage cuts and lay-offs for American workers.[90]

Meanwhile, our adverse balance of trade admits of no easy solutions, certainly not that of deliberately cheapening our dollars. We have already demonstrated a preference for foreign-produced goods. Now, if the dollar were to sink low enough, foreigners would find our domestic goods more attractive but our money would buy far fewer of these desired overseas goods. Our standard of living would, therefore, suffer. Likewise, we could narrow the trade balances provided American workers accepted substantially lower wages and salaries. But the result would be the same: a decline in our standard of living.[91] There is no evidence that our consumption-ridden society would accept these sacrificial solutions. And, further, policies that have been tried have not worked. Two years after the deliberate tinkering with the dollar's worth, the U.S. trade deficit is higher than ever, or about $175 billion.[92]

Finally, the Alice in Wonderland economic approach - standard operational procedures both at the White House and on Wall Street -was succeeded by a stock market bubble burst even more dramatic than the one in 1929. On October 19, 1987, the market's bottom dropped out with a loss of over 500 points or 22.6 percent of stock values. By comparison, on Black Tuesday, October 29, 1929, the Dow-Jones Industrial Average dropped 20.57 points or 12.8 percent decline in the value of total stocks.[93]

Whatever the subsequent history of the stock market, it cannot ignore a catastrophe of this scope and depth. "There was this pre-Monday world and now there is this world," concluded the chairman of Solomon Brothers.[94] For example, it produced almost immediate and equal agonies in Japan and West Germany, as well as in London and Hong Kong. As one expert explained it, in 1929, under international capitalism, there were five or six separate stock markets and now there is one with five or six main branches.[95] A week after the initial crash, the market had not recovered. There were far more sellers than buyers. By December, the market still had not levelled off. Investors stayed on the side lines, in part because of concern over the dollar's slide and administrative inactivity.[96]

While the big moguls of the Exchange called for immediate government action to trim national deficits and lower interest rates,[97] in Washington, it was only necessary that something *appear* to have been done.

President Reagan sacrificed his nap time. Congress milled about a bit and they had a meeting to negotiate a compromise deficit reduction. "They met and they met and they talked and they talked and finally came up with as slim and puny a plan as they could get away with." Supposedly, they were to cut the budget by $30 billion but, instead, they cut it out of the new or proposed budget. So, if ratified by Congress, the deficit will be $149 billion whereas last year it was a billion less. "See. You've got to cut $30 billion out of the budget just to keep from getting further behind. It's a mess."[98] Once Reagan excluded Social Security from any cuts, the result was predictable because entitlements, defense and interest make up 85 percent of the budget. Since it appears politically impossible to raise the maximum tax rate of 28 percent on the nation's top money earners - down under Reagan from 70 percent - any projected cuts are apt to be in the vulnerable areas of "child welfare, food stamps, school lunch and other such programs."[99]

By 1990 it was clear the stock market no longer reflected the real state, or health, of the economy, if indeed it ever did. The United States is in a topsy-turvy period "in which bad news is often treated as good news by financial experts." This is ridiculous but true. The answer lies in the heavy indebtedness of the entire country, including the consumer and private companies as well as the government. Thus, our interest payments are huge. When the government acknowledged its debt was much greater than previously reported, it was believed by many to be a further depressant to the economy. The fear of a recession, however, might prompt the Federal Reserve to try to prop up the economy by lowering the interest rates. That would be very good at sponsoring further speculation, further investment, further growth. Therefore, stocks went up because the investors have their eye on prices six months from now and not today. "What's driving the stock market is the expectation of lower interest rates...."[100] Thus, what we are witnessing is a tug of war between corporate profits and interest rates in the stock market. When corporate profits are off, that tends to pull the market down. "But that has been more than offset by optimism regarding low interest rates. Now it seems we're not likely to get low interest rate, the focus is back to profits."[101]

The reason, of course, for the paralysis of the Fed was the wretched state of our indebtedness. If it lowered interest rates, that would make U.S. bonds less attractive to the foreign investor. International money markets already viewed the United States as having abandoned the value of the dollar. It borrowed from abroad to finance a government deficit and ran up a huge trade deficit "because it refused to curb domestic consumption." Thus, the world was flooded with our dollars and its value declined almost 40 percent against the German mark and the Japanese yen. The logical conclusion, therefore, was that the Fed would have to keep interest rates high to "defend" the dollar. Although its falling value would help exports, it would also bring higher inflation in a country which imports half its oil while burdened with interest payments on a huge indebtedness.[102]

Thus, although Merrill Lynch may be bullish on America, predictions are the stock market must eventually respond to the gloomy industrial news. The loss of 45,000 private industrial jobs contributed to the huge overall job loss of 219,000. The slumping construction industry lost 50,000 jobs. The manufacturing industry, which dropped 32,500 workers since the post recession peak in March, 1989, lost another 7,000. The national production grew at the annual rate of only 1.2 percent in the second quarter of 1990. The general fear is the economy is stalling after eight years of faulty expansion.

In early August, 1990, for example, traders flooded the market with stocks to sell, causing the Dow Jones average to fall more than 120 points before closing down 55 points.[103]

It was the bullish feeling about America which was responsible for the S&L crisis which experts called "the biggest financial scandal in American history."[104] After World War II, these savings and loan institutions performed a public service, giving married couples loans on new homes. However, the inflation of the 70s led to demands they lend on development schemes as banks did.[105] In 1980, the government raised the guaranteed deposit limits to $100,000, and a depositor could have that much in several different institutions. By offering unusually high interest rates, the S&Ls in Texas and California attracted much outside capital in purely speculative ventures in land, shopping malls and office buildings. Some critics believe "the primary cause of the S&L cancer," rather than deregulation *per se* "was a destabilizing increase in deposit insurance." It encouraged money to flow into the coffers of the worst run institutions. Government examiners cannot give banking stability when wealthy speculators "are completely shielded from risk" while earning the highest possible interest rates from a number of S&Ls.[106] When the real estate bubble burst, it became apparent that raw land - much of it speculative lots without clear titles - morgage loans and junk bonds made up questionable assets.[107] In 1989, criminal fraud was discovered in 60 percent of the savings institutions seized.[108] Since the government got so much worthless "property," the liabilities of the seized institutions "far surpass the ability of the assets of the [federal] insurance fund to finance an immediate solution." It is not surprising that politicians elected not an immediate solution - one that cost $11 billion or so - but a piecemeal solution, one that will probably take another thirty years. No one knows its real cost.[109]

Finally, we get the gloomy prognosis from the budget office that, even without a recession, six or seven hundred commercial banks will fail within the next four years. This will drain the government's deposit insurance fund by more than $20 billion. Like the failed S&Ls, this will require a multibillion dollar bailout by the taxpayer.[110]

Despite evidence of the effectiveness of the welfare state in

America,[111] we must now discuss the sharp decline of its popularity. While in the past, as Tom observed, capitalism permitted the simultaneous development of production and political democracy and social rights, this no longer obtains. Since 1973, a tension has existed between market profitability and social services to the disadvantage of the latter. As the material basis for social and economic reforms was visibly shaken, so was the Keynesian model after three decades of commitment to full employment and the welfare state.

Its successor was laissez faire with Milton Friedman as the new prophet.[112] The latter identified state encroachments on the private economic sector as the source of the problem. He would instead rely on market forces. Openly, this was accompanied by an insistence on both cutting taxes and social welfare, and on the covert strategy of higher unemployment. This was in order to discipline the work force while at the same time limiting the right to strike and subverting the strength of unions.[113]

The ultimate dilemma was a capitalistic nation had to choose between either economic growth and financial accumulation, or political democracy and the need to improve levels of social consumption and living standards by the masses. Those dedicated to the economic principles of the new order would certainly choose the financial approach over the social one. Either way the nature of the welfare state would be transformed and there would be a revival of class conflict.[114]

The withering away of the welfare state has been explained as an essential part of Ronald Reagan's limited social vision: "Reagan appears to believe that the 'rabble' has captured the state and is plundering its resources, both to avoid work and to live better than those who do work. Productive people (like the self-made millionaires who surround Reagan) must be restored to honor, and to power. Thus does the indulgence of ideological animus nicely fit the calculation of class interest."[115] This is because people in different social classes have different natures and thus respond differently to rewards and punishments. Whereas the affluent respond best to incentives, the lower classes react best to the threat of punishment, or to the economic insecurity which will result from reductions in income support programs. Only when these are withdrawn will they voluntarily go to work.[116]

Thus it was that the significance of the victory by Ronald Reagan in the presidential election of 1980 meant that we were projected back into the pre-New Deal era. So-called democratic governments in the West were then either helpless or indifferent towards high unemployment and the inequitable distribution of wealth and income.[117] Reagan's admiration for Calvin Coolidge is well-known. The latter was the high priest of the laissez faire state which Keynes attacked.[118] Ironically, however, the Reagan administration, by virtue of its elimination of corporate taxes and heavy tax cuts for the affluent, plus its huge military expenditures, has run up a super Keynesian deficit. Momentarily it is highly stimulating to the economy, but eventually inflationary.[119] While all presidents quite naturally tend to reward their supporters, Reagan disguised his pay-off to corporations and the affluent citizenry under the neutral guise of supply side economics.[120]

As soon as the outsider is immersed in the economics of Reaganism, he recognizes the familiar terrain of the magical and the mystical. One does not have to depend upon the primary foes of Reagan in 1980, like George Bush, who properly called the whole thing "voodoo economics." One relies on the confession of the man who was primarily responsible for the presentation of the original budget, David Stockman. Stockman confessed the key question of John Anderson, Independent senator from Illinois, had never been answered: "How could one cut taxes, vastly increase military expenditures and balance the budget, all at the same time?" It depends on faith, Stockman said.[121] And so does primitive medicine. Furthermore, he added, it was necessary to do the terribly complicated thing so fast that the numbers lost their significance for everyone involved. In short, nobody knew what he was doing. But Stockman knew one thing not to do. When an OMB computer correctly predicted an unprecedented peace time deficit, if the Reagan program were implemented as conceived, Stockman merely abandoned that computer for one which promised to spin a different story.[122] It is much as if Caesar, when told to "Beware of the Ides of March," merely resorted to another soothsayer in order to obtain a more reassuring picture of the immediate future. When Reagan's policy makers knew their plan was fallacious, or at least inadequate, their chief cheerfully proceeded to convey the opposite impression to the gullible public.[123]

As the budget was hammered out in Congress, Stockman later confessed his distaste at the economic greed of the big money operators. They wrung special tax concessions for oil lease holders and tax shelters for real estate and generous loop holes which virtually eliminated the corporate income tax. The level of lust, of opportunism, simply got out of hand. The biggest loser of course was the one who could afford it the least, welfare mothers.[124]

Despite the fact, due to inflation, the actual dollar value of welfare shrank by almost thirty percent during the Seventies, an estimated fifteen million women were further harassed economically. This came as a result of the Reagan cuts in aid to dependent children, Medicaid, food stamps, subsidized school lunches and dozens of other valuate programs.[125]

To Jeff, the dilemma apparently cannot be solved within the traditional thought patterms. While it is true the Reagan mentality is going to produce economic dislocation and social unrest, one cannot improve the living standard for the masses without the process of capital accumulation. Meanwhile, the principal error of the Left in fashioning the welfare state was to assume that social and economic needs in a democracy create a right and that demand creates supply. By definition, as well as reality, capitalism has to grow, and, at the same time or, as a consequence, create capital accumulation. How is America to do this, given the increased scarcity of our natural resources and increased international competition in the market place where we have less to sell and more to buy and will be increasingly preoccupied with the difficulty of servicing our huge debt? Where, then, are we to get the capital to do either: 1) to experience economic growth and financial accumulation, or 2) to improve levels of social consumption and living standards by the masses? Either strategy is based upon wishful thinking or on a willful oversight of our worsening economic situation.

Meanwhile, public attitudes toward social programs and increased taxation remain ambivalent. True, support for welfare programs remains high: 78 percent say aye to governmental medical care for everyone as opposed to 19 percent no; 71 percent say the govermment should guarantee a job to everyone who wants one as opposed to 26 percent negative; 62 percent favor federally-sponsored child care programs to 35 percent who object; and, finally, 60 percent reject cuts in social programs to effect a balanced budget as opposed to 33 percent. On the other hand, 60 percent reject the idea of increased taxation on themselves in order to cut the federal deficit.[126]

Furthermore, despite all breezy talk of income redistribution since the New Deal, no perceptible change occurred. If one were to divide Americans into five brackets from low to high, and count all the known income, the top fifth gets forty cents of every dollar while the bottom fifth receives but five cents. That ratio of eight to one has been constant every year since the termination of World War II. On the contrary, income distribution has grown more regressive. While corporate taxes were down from twenty-seven cents of every dollar in 1950 to only sixteen by 1970, security and payroll taxes increased from nine to twenty-six cents.[127] And, despite the fact that ownership trails have purposely been obscured, at least sixty percent of the top 500 corporations are "probably" (236) or "possibly" (64) under the control of an identifiable close-knit group, such as family or a core of associates. Nor can true distinctions be made between the ownership and management of America's giant corporations. Key representatives of both have become in effect a common class, much as England's "horsey set" prior to World War I. They live, work and play together while their offspring do likewise, whether as toddler, children, adolescents or young married.[128]

When discussing the emergence and persistence of class in America, Robert L. Heilbroner said it as honestly and well as anyone: "Despite sweeping claims of the democratization of ownership associated with 'People's Capitalism,' there is very little, if any, evidence of a significant widening of the concentrated ownership and control of the American corporate structure."[129].

Instead, the change which has clearly emerged is the birth of classes, via income distribution, in a society which has been most reluctant to admit their existence because of their threat to a democracy. At the same time that the average real hourly earnings for production workers - the lifeblood of roughly 80 percent of all employees - declined by 6 percent from 1979 to 1985, income going to families earning more than $250,000 a year increased by more than 6 percent. Currently they control about one half of the total net worth in the economy. Between that fortunate class and that of the affluent - or those households earning more than $40,000 a year - they control almost all the personal net worth in the United States. In sharp contrast, householders in the lowest 80 percent of income distribution - seventy million of them - with median annual earnings of $18,000, boast, on the average, no net worth.[130] To complete the distressing picture of class inequality to a nation which has never admitted it is the fact that, after twenty-five years of declining, proverty is once again on the increase. In 1985, over thirty-three million persons were below the government's official poverty line. Perhaps the most alarming fact is that the new poor descended from the old middle class. A great many of these were white women heading up broken families or those without husbands.[131]

Consequently, even when bolstered by President Reagan's Alfred E. Neuman's "What, me worry?" approach, Americans recognized the sharp decline of the old dream of freedom, equality and prosperity. Significantly, there was a loss of confidence in the future. On the contrary, in the past no matter how bleak the situation appeared, Americans were always confident that happy days lay before them.[132]

By 1990 it was clear the "income gap between the rich and the rest of America grew so fast during the last decade that the wealthiest fifth of households will get as much after tax revenue as everyone else combined this year...." While the poor got poorer and the middle class "struggled to stay even," income returns for the wealthiest increased over thirty percent. Thus, "the 2.5 million people at the top 1 percent now get nearly as much of America's total income after taxes as the 100 million people on the bottom 40 percent...." This disparity is a "relatively recent trend." It narrowed in the 50s and 60s. Widening somewhat in the 70s, the "gulf grew fastest in the 80s."[133]

Thus, "the illusion of rising living standards is proving impossible to maintain." Since 1940 employment outstripped population increases, but that movement has been reversed. First to go were the part-time jobs which middle class families resorted to in order to keep afloat. "Hence, achieving a rising standard of living at the rate experienced from 1984-89 does not appear possible."[134]

"No one now challenges the truism that theirs [youth's] is the first generation since the Great Depression to inherit a living standard lower than that of its parents." Translated into more specific terms, it means that "home ownership, health insurance and in many cases even adequate shelter are beyond their financial reach."[135]

Thus, it is not surprising that a study released in 1990 showed people had "even greater alienation toward their government and politics than they did three years ago, and virtually all the increase has been among people from families earning less than $50,000 a year...." The greatest degree of increase in frustration, both personal and in the public sector, was noted among whites, middle class as well as poor. Over some issues "they express levels of despair almost as great as blacks, traditionally among the most alienated of Americans."[136]

To summarize, capitalism and its free market system have not, and seemingly cannot, produce a free and equal society. The greater the economic freedom of the individual, the greater the economic inequality of the masses. And democracy cannot flourish without the freedom and equality of the individual in a free and equal society.[137]

While all the material data amassed appears to menace the American dream, we dare not dismiss the permanent element of fervent hope which lodges deep in the national breast. While the skeptic may dismiss it as irrational, he cannot deny its existence. America's dream was reflected on a more personal level by F. Scott Fitzgerald's protagonist in *The Great Gatsby*. He dreamed of consummating his old love affair with a girl lost and found:

> *I thought of Gatsby's wonder when he*
> *first picked out the green light at the end of*
> *Daisy's dock. He had come a long way to this*
> *blue lawn, and his dream must have seemed so*
> *close that he could hardly fail to grasp it. He did*
> *not know that it was already behind him,*
> *somewhere in that vast obscurity....*
>   - *Gatsby believed in the green light, the*

> *orgiastic future that year by year recedes before*
> *us. It eluded us then, but that's no matter -*
> *tomorrow we will run faster, stretch out our*
> *arms still further .... And one fine morning——*
> *138*

What we found to be positively uncanny was the virtual oneness between Gatsby's obsession with Daisy's green light and de Tocqueville's analysis of the American pursuit of the perfectibility of man: "Thus, for ever seeking - for ever falling, to rise again - often disappointed, but not discouraged, - he tends unceasingly towards that measured greatness so indistinctly visible at the end of a long track which humanity has yet to tread."[139]

Dreams aside, reality does little or nothing to justify the reduction and/or obliteration of the primitive in the name of progress and the perfectibility of man. By virtue of the application of history and operational definitions, we concluded that America was not really democratic. Nor in the light of recent history could it be considered peaceful. Finally, its vaunted system of private property and capitalism was neither benign, nor rational, nor efficient. Instead of meaningful progress, one merely senses change, however dramatic, influential and pervasive. Change itself, however, should not be deified. That is to say, it should not be attributed to some supernatural being or force which has its own designs or plans for man's destiny. For sooner or later worshippers are bound to be disillusioned. We believe we have already entered that age.

Footnotes

1   *The End of Economic Man; a Study of the New Totalitarianism* with an introduction by H.N. Brailsford (New York, John Day Co., 1939), 34-36.

2   Even the book by the champions of agrarianism failed to mention pollution as a reason to fear industrialization. Evils cited were the traditional ones of over-production, unemployment and the growing inequality of wealth. Exponents of the system of industrialization expected economic solutions to come in the wake of bigger, better and more machines, the very thing which created the problem in the first instance. The closest the agrarians came to the pollution charge was this one: "We receive the illusion (under industrialization) of having power over nature, and lose the sense of nature as something mysterious and contingent." "A state-ment of Principles," ix-xx in *I' ll Take My Stand. The South and the Agrarian Tradition.* By Twelve Southerners (New York, Harper & Brothers, 1930), xiii-xiv.

3   See volume II, Chapter XIX. beginning p. 269

4   Simon and Eitzen, *Elite Deviance,* 77.

5   This conclusion was drawn by Eugene Rostov. *Ibid.,* 74-75.

6   *American Capitalism, the Concept of Countervailing Power* (Boston, Houghton Mifflin, 1952), 46.

7   *Ibid., 90-91.*

8   Alfred A. Berle Jr., *The Twentieth Century Capitalist Revolution* (New York, Harcourt Brace, 1954), 25, 51.

9   Harold J. Laski on *The Communist Manifesto. An Introduction.* Together with the Original Text and Prefaces by Karl Marx and Friedrich Engels. Foreword for the American Edition by T.B. Bottomore (New York, Pantheon Books, Random House, 1967), 31, 135-138.

10   Paul L. Wachtel, *The Poverty of Affluence. A Psychological Portrait of the American Way of Life* (New York, Free Press, Macmillan, 1983), 45.

11   Ewen, *Captains of Consciousness,* 213-214.

12   Wachtel, *Poverty of Affluence,* 287.

13   *Ibid.,* 34.

14   *Ibid.,* 23, 43.

15   David E. Sims, "Spoon-Feeding the Military - How New Weapons Come to Be," 225-265 in *Pentagon Watchers,* 244-245.

16   *Ibid.*, 254-255.

17   Gordon Adams, "The Department of Defense and the Military-Industrial Establishment: The Politics of the Iron Triangle," 320-334 in *Critical Studies in Organization and Bureaucracy,* edited by Frank Fischer and Carmen Sirianni (Phildadelphia, Temple University Press, 1984), 329.

18   Gordon Adams, *The Iron Triangle*, 326-328.

19   Sims, *"Spoon-Feeding the Military,"* loc. cit., 225.

20   Simon and Eitzen, *Elite Deviance*, 145.

21   Adams, *The Iron Triangle*, 322.

22   *Ibid.*, 330-331.

23   *Ibid.*, 321.

24   Washington, "Pentagon and Contractors Said to Agree to Understate Cost of Weapons," in the New York *Times*, July 30, 1987, A-16.

25   By the Associated Press, Washington, "Meese saw Wedtech Report before investing, memo says," in the Kansas City *Star*, September 29, 1987, A-1, 2.

26   According to Secretary of Labor Bill Brock, such lay-offs and plant shut-downs have impacted on about a million workers a year for the last seven years. Results are disastrous. One-third are left permanently jobless. The average term of unemployment is four months and for those who then find jobs, earnings are down from ten to fifteen percent. David S. Broder, Post Writers Groups, Washington, "Brock treatment another symptom of ailing White House," in the Kansas City *Star*, January 19, 1987, A-9. An identical situation has already occurred in Scotland where old jobs in steel, shipbuilding and coal were labor-intensive and rested upon adult male labor. The new jobs in high technology are fewer, offering those to women at considerably less money. Fay Moseley, Chicago Tribune, Glasgow, Scotland, "Scots have an edge in high tech," in the Kansas City *Times*, January 6, 1984, A-11. The American prospect of less work and much larger unemployment has hit our allies in Western Europe and England where shared work, a shorter work week and earlier retirement were offered as solutions. Less pay for a shorter week, has not yet been made explicit. Richard Reeves, Universal Press Syndicate, Annecy, France, "Europeans doing some trail-blazing on jobs," in the Kansas City *Times*, September 2, 1983, A-15.

27   Richard Sennett and Jonathan Cobb, *The Hidden Injuries of Class* (New York, Alfred A. Knopf, 1972), 261. Walter Reuther wrote the following just after World War II was over: "We suffer .. from what Thorstein Veblen called the 'inordinate productivity' of the machine. ... But our productive genius has always been stalemated by our failure at the distributive end." "Our Fear of Abundance," the New York Times Magazine, September 16, 1945 in Walter P. Reuther, *Selected Papers*, edited and with an Introduction by Henry M. Christman (New York, Macmillan, 1961), 14.

28   Paul Wachtel, *Poverty of Affluence*, 248. Three factors have generally obscured

the fact that the average American worker has now gone two decades without any increase in pay. "The increase in Social Security payments, the growth in the number of families in which both adults work and the decline in the number of children per household thus have effectively masked the real erosion of wages." Only superficially have the 1980's been better than the 70's, which produced double digit inflation and unemployment, for it was during the current decade that the U.S. went from the world's greatest creditor to the greatest debtor and our trade deficit increased more than six times. All these facts are indispensable when attempting to answer the following question: "How is it possible for real wages to have declined and most Americans appear to be living better?" David Vogel, Washington Post-Los Angeles Times News Service, "Changing family situations in America," in the Kansas City *Star*, January 16, 1987, A-11.

29   Tom Wicker, New York Times News Services, New York, "America's Standard of Living is falling (yes, falling)," in the Kansas City *Times*, August 18, 1987, A-9. "Middle class families find the growth in their real incomes by sending their women out to work, not by higher salaries. Real average wages rose steadily from 1947 to 1972, in all by more than half. They have fallen, less sharply but almost as steadily, ever since, so that they are back to the level of 1962." From The Economist, London, "A frown is visible on America's face," in the Kansas City *Star*, September 27, 1987, H-1.

30   According to a Carnegie-Mellon University study, robots, by the end of the Eighties, will have replaced about 75 percent of factory labor. Clayton Fritchey, Newsday, "Shorter Work Week," in the Kansas City *Star*, July 18, 1983, A-7. Already, U.S. Steel has closed several major plants, eliminating over 15,100 jobs. The New York Times, "Plant closings are ominous," in the Kansas City *Times*, December 28, 1983, A-12. This is, or was, 15% of its payroll. Editorial, "Steel's woes deepen with job cutback," in the Kansas City *Star*, December 29, 1983, A-10.

31   Associated Press, Washington, "Poverty report faults economy," in the Kansas City *Times*, December 22, 1986, A-3.

32   The two political economy professors who did the study - Barry Bluestone at the University of Massachusetts in Boston and Bennett Harrison at MIT - concluded: "If this pattern of development continues the standard of living of a growing proportion of the American work force will be significantly jeopardized." Associated Press, Washington, "Wages low in most new jobs," in the Kansas City *Times*, December 10, 1986, D-1.

33   Rex Julian Beaber, Los Angeles Times-Washington Post News Service, "Computer age brings spectre of unemployment," in the Kansas City *Times*, August 15, 1983, A-12. See also Mary H. Cooper, Congressional Quarterly, Washington, "High tech and permanent unemployment," in *ibid.*, August 2, 1983, A-9. A typical example was that of Charles Connor of Kansas City. He was laid off in January, 1983, from his $12 an hour job as yard clerk when the Milwaukee Road and Kansas City Southern installed a computer system, eliminating the job itself. Charles Pluckhahn, Labor Writer, "Jobless begin to cope as the work place changes," in the Kansas City *Star*, September 18, 1983, K-1.

34   *Laski and the Communist Manifesto*, 140-142. Prepared with the help of scholars at four prominent universities, the AFL-CIO released a study predicting that four to six million workers "may become a permanent labor surplus in a polarized two-tiered society." Charles Pluckhahn, "Jobless begin to cope as work place changes," *loc. cit.* See also Mary H. Cooper, "High tech and permanent unemployment, *loc. cit.* Labor forecasts

were that future jobs will require less skill and that job growth will be in service trades like nurses' aids and janitors. Bruce Cooperstein and Art Pearl, Knight-Ridder Newspapers, "It is in society," in the Kansas City *Times*, September 19, 1983, A-9.

35   *Worlds of Pain. Life in the Working-Class Family* (New York, Basic Books, Inc., 1976), 159, 161.

36   Mass unemployment was the decisive historical factor in the downfall of the laissez faire economy of the 20s and 30s. Edward Hallett Carr, *The New Society* (Boston, The Beacon Press, 1951), 47. A minority view, an optimistic one with regard to the computer is entertained by John Naisbitt who thinks that one of its benefits will be to destroy the present "hierarchial pyramid of authority," and help revitalize worker participation in decision-making and productivity. *Megatrends. Ten New Directions Transforming Our Lives* (New York, Warner Books, 1982), 250-252.

37   Ewen, *Captains of Consciousness*, 133-134.

38   Pliven and Cloward, *New Class Warfare*, 147. Reliable reports indicate that management will be in an excellent position in 1988 to work its will upon labor. The Conference Board, a prominent business research group, predicted that the number of new jobs would tumble to 1.5 million, roughly half of those produced in 1987. Most jobs created will be part-time service positions in such occupations as janitors and hamburger jockeys, positions of low pay, few benefits and no long-term security or promise of advancement. Changing population patterns, tougher management practices and the October stock market crash were presumed to be causal factors. An authority for the AFL-CIO stressed a growing inflation rate, declines in housing construction and auto sales, continued growth of imports and government budget cuts. The Associated Press, New York, "Economists predict number of new jobs will decline in '88," in the Kansas City *Times*, December 30, 1987, D-1.

39   Los Angeles Times, Washington, "Baby Boomer Madness: amid success there is happiness?" in the Kansas City *Times*, November 27, 1986, K-2.

40   Rex Julian Beaber, Los Angeles Times-Washington Post News Service, "Computer age brings spectre of unemployment," *loc. cit.*

41   In a class society, laborers know that as a group they are regarded as "nobody special," and they tend to assume that same low opinion of themselves. Richard Sennett and Jonathan Cobb, *Hidden Injuries of Class*, 213. This same group is actually insecure even in good times. Easy access to credit means that they perpetually live upon the brink of economic disaster. Any lay-off or even cut-back in overtime threatens to precipitate them into financial turbulence. Rubin, *Worlds of Pain*, 205.

42   The United States Supreme Court eased the problem for companies to break union contracts by filing for bankruptcy under Chapter II of the Bankruptcy Code of 1978. Companies no longer have to prove bankruptcy is imminent unless relieved of union contracts, but merely that said contracts "burden" them in efforts to avoid it and that they made "reasonable efforts" to negotiate changes with the union. Once such a plea has been filed, the company is free to destroy its union contract prior to a court decision as to the contract itself. Ernest Conine, Los Angeles Times, "Court hands corporate managers another big stick," the Kansas City *Star*, February 29, 1984, A-13.

236

43   James Strong, Chicago Tribune, "Reagan stance on PATCO hurt all labor," in the Kansas City *Star*, January 29, 1984, E-5, 7. In the construction trade in Washington, D.C., for example, the unemployment rate in 1983 was about twenty-five percent. Consequently, there was a plethora of scab labor for non-union construction. Lars Erik Nelson, New York Daily News, Washington, "Nation's capital isn't a blue-collar town," in the Kansas City *Times*, January 10, 1984, A-9.

44   The layoff of 17,000 at McDonnell Douglas was probably due to the "arrogance and short-sightedness of the top leadership." C.W. Gusewelle, "And the meek shall inherit the pink slip," in the Kansas City *Star*, July 21, 1990, D-1. Tragedies also occur on the individual level. Vivian, now about sixty, was a victim of the decade of business cannibalism. Her firm was absorbed and, though competent, she was fired so that younger and cheaper help could be hired. Mike Royko, Tribune Media Services, "To get job age has no privileges," in *ibid.*, July 20, 1990, C-11.

45   New York Times News Services, New York, "America's Standard of Living is falling (yes, falling)," in the Kansas City *Times*, August 18, 1987, A-9. "I don't want to be an alarmist, but that confused crowd in Washington known as Our Leaders had better begin thinking beyond what the slumping Dow Jones means to next year's elections and their corporate contributors. They might start by renting a video movie called 'Road Warrior.' But they shouldn't look at it as a piece of fiction. Think of it as a documentary. One of these days it could be." Mike Royko, Tribune Media News Service, "It's horrible to think what might happen," in the Kansas City *Star*, October 29, 1987, A-19.

46   Paul Baron and Paul Sweezy, "The Multinational Corporation and Modern Imperialism," 435-441 in *The Capitalist System. A Radical Analysis of American Society*. Written and edited by Ricard C. Edwards *et al*, (Englewood Cliffs, New Jersey, Prentice-Hall, Inc, 1972), 438-440.

47   A $500 million dollar plant will be built at Hermosillo, Mexico. From Times News Services, Mexico City, "Ford to build plant in Mexico to make autos for export," in the Kansas City *Times*, January 14, 1984, F-1. The Ford Escort story provided one major theme for the CBS TV broadcaast of Dan Rather on January 10, 1984.

48   Arthur MacEwan, "Capitalist Expansion, Ideology and Intervention," 410-420 in *The Capitalist System*, edited by Edwards, 412.

49   Baran and Sweezy, "The Multinational Corporation and Modern Imperialism," *loc. cit.*, 441. The vice president of United Auto Workers estimated that the Ford move to Mexico would result in the loss of 25,000 jobs in the United States and Canada. Mexico City. From the Times News Service, in the Kansas City *Times*, January 14, 1984, F-1.

50   Ronald Takaki, Newsday, "Economic disparity breeds contempt," in the Kansas City *Star*, July 8, 1990, J-1, 4.

51   Robert Unger, National Correspondent, "Has U.S. lost jobs? Depends on point of view," in *ibid.*, April 28, 1990, A-16.

52   Guy Wright, San Francisco *Examiner*, "Buying American is becoming harder," in the Kansas City *Star*, March 26, 1987, A-11.

53   "Remember when GE could successfully compete," in the Norwich, Connecticut *Bulletin*, July 29, 1987, A-7.

54   Los Angeles Times, "'Buy American' sounds good," in the Kansas City *Star*, August 16, 1987, K-3. The outgoing Senator Thomas Eagleton from Missouri summed up the problem in this way: "Factories are shifting operations overseas, foreign management has found greater efficiency, and America is becoming a service nation." John A. Dvorak, Missouri Notebook, "Eagleton offers harsh advice for liberalism's troubled times," in the Kansas City *Times*, December 13, 1986, B-3.

55   Tönnies, *Community and Society*, 80-81. For the twentieth century couterpart of this, consult Baran and Sweezy, "The Multi-national Corporation and Modern Imperialism," *loc. cit.*, 441.

56   Paul R. and Anne H. Erlich, *The Population Explosion* (New York, Simon and Schuster, 1990), 290.

57   By the Associated Press, New York, "Wall Street trader enters guilty plea," in the Kansas City *Star*, April 23, 1987, A-1; from the *Star's* Wire Services, "New arrests stun Wall Street," in *ibid.*, February 13, 1987, A-9; The Associated Press, White Plains, New York, "Levine gets two years," in the Kansas City *Times*, February 21, 1987, E-10.

58   From the Times News Services, New York, "Drug ring broken on Wall Street," in the Kansas City *Times*, April 17, 1987, A-1.

59   *Other People's Money. And How They Use It*. Edited with an Introduction and Notes by Richard M. Abrams (New York, Harper Torchback, Harper & Row, 1967), 14-15.

60   Ken Aulleta was the expert observer. By Jim Davis of the Business Staff, "Ethics, scandals tied, writer says," in the Kansas City *Times*, September 23, 1987, D-1.

61   Sidney Rutberg, Fairchild News Services, "Bargains like this are few indeed," in the Kansas City *Star*, January 20, 1987, A-4.

62   Lee Iacocca, Guest Columnist, "Tactics of takeover artists, arbitragers hurt U.S. business," in the Kansas City *Times*, January 29, 1987, C-1, 3.

63   Haynes Johnson, Washington Post, Washington, "'Teflon Years' closely resemble '20s," in the Kansas City *Times*, March 20, 1987, A-17.

64   *The Engineers and the Price System* (New York, Viking Press, 1921), 27-82 *passim*.

65   Dick K. Nanto, Los Angeles Times News Service, "U.S. boosts Japan's rising arrogance," in the Kansas City *Times*, April 29, 1987, A-11.

66   *Business Enterprise*, 92-114.

67   Kennedy, "Economic Decline of the United States," *loc. cit.*, 29-30.

238

68   Universal Press, Tokoyo, "U.S. suddenly out of step in world of new realities," in the Kansas City *Times*, April 19, 1987, A-15.

69   Special to the Los Angeles Times, "Trade deficit only a starting point in making U.S. competitive again," in the Kansas City *Star*, May 3, 1987, M-2. The Joint Economic Committee's Democratic-controlled staff arrived at the same conclusion. By the Associated Press, Washington, "Debt level threatens U.S. status," in the Kansas City *Star*, August 10, 1987, A-1.

70   William V. Shannon, Boston Globe, "A certain extravagence of objectives," in the Kansas City *Times*, May 28, 1987, A-15.

71   Ronald Takaki, Newsday, "Economic disparity breeds contempt," in the Kansas City *Star*, July 8, 1990, J-1, 4. Compared to nations like Japan, Germany and even Italy, our economy has been drifting for the last decade. There has been a slow down in the development of new technology, in upgrading manufacturing facilities and the introduction of new commercial products. So wrote Michael E. Porter, professor at the Harvard Business School. The Baltimore Sun, Washington, "Standard of living is suffering, according to a professor's report," in *ibid.*, May 14, 1990, A-7.

72   Kevin Phillips, Los Angeles Times-Washington Post News Services, "U.S. is over-committed to the world," in the Kansas City *Star*, July 5, 1987, C-1, 6.

73   Both nations "still cite Allied-imposed restrictions on their military as reasons for opting out of the burdens of the Gulf crisis." Lars-Erik Nelson, Tribune Media Services, "Saudis come out ahead any way you look at it," in the Kansas City *Star*, September 12, 1990, C-11. "The chancelor (Helmut Kohl) said the West German Constitution ... prohibits sending troops and warships to the gulf." The Associated Press, Ludwigshafen, West Germany, "German pledge aid in crisis," in *ibid.*, September 16, 1990, A-1, 10.

74   Donald Kaul, The Chicago *Tribune*, "With friends like this, who needs muggers?" in the Kansas City *Star*, September 10, 1990, B-7. See also the Economist (London), "Lying low or falling down may be the best Japan can do," in *ibid.*, September 11, 1990, B-7. Later, saying the forces in the gulf "are also defending our interests," Kohl pledged almost two billion in economic and military assistance. The Associated Press, Ludwigshafen, West Germany, "Germans pledge aid in crisis," *loc. cit.*

75   Trudy Rubin, Philadelphia *Inquirer*, "New world order easier said than achieved," in the Kansas City *Star*, September 17, 1990, B-7.

76   Wachtel, *Poverty of Affluence*, 267.

77   Carl T. Rowan, North American Syndicate, Washington, "Chuckholes on Reagan road to greatness," in the Kansas City *Times*, April 17, 1987, A-13.

78   By the Associated Press, Washington, "Figures to reinforce U.S. slide into debt," in the Kansas City *Star*, June 22, 1987, B-7. See also By the Associated Press, Washington, "U.S. maintains largest debt," in *ibid.*, March 17, 1987, A-1. "The budget deficit has not been all bad for America, or for its trading partners. It helped to lift the economy out of the recession of 1982, and to give America two years of cracking growth. By then it was outliving its usefulness, serving mainly to swell the trade deficit.... It has turned the

world's richest country into its biggest debtor.... From the Economist, London, "A frown is visible on America's face," in the Kansas City *Star*, September 27, 1987, H-1.

79   David Nyhan, Boston Globe, "Japanese investors are buying a lot more," in the Kansas City *Star*, April 14, 1987, A-9.

80   Tony Coelho, "The Foreign Greening of America. Outsiders Banking Moves Threaten our Ability to Compete," in the Los Angeles *Times*, March 26, 1987, Part II, 5.

81   John Cunniff, Associated Press, New York, "U.S. economy feels foreign influence," in the Kansas City *Star*, June 23, 1987, A-5.

82   Elizabeth Wehr, Congressional Quarterly, Inc., Washington, "No dire predictions from the seers - yet," in the Kansas City *Star*, July 29, 1987, K-3. See also the New York Times, Washington, "Study says deficits, foreign debt will longer," in the Kansas City *Times*, November 6, 1987, C-1.

83   United Features, "Some confusion between president, supporters on nature of Reaganomics," in the Kansas City *Times*, November 3, 1987, A-9. "Americans consumed more goods than they produced, and the deficit became America's pawn ticket. The new fear is: What happens if Japan and Western Europe recall their loans? The conventional answer to that question: A lower standard of living for future generations of Americans as they are forced to reverse the current trend and produce more than they consume." Chris Reidy, Orlando Sentinel, Washington, "Foreign money pays for America's standard of living," in the Kansas City *Star*, December 6, 1987, K-3.

84   Washington Post Writers Group, Washington, "President's budget will control future debate, agenda," in the Kansas City *Times*, January 12, 1987, A-9.

85   Senator Ernest Hollings, presidential candidate in 1984, believed that Reagan's purpose of piling up such a huge deficit was to make it impossible for the welfare state to operate again, even if the Democrats were returned to power. Tom Wicker, New York Times News Service, New York," Are big deficits part of Reagan plot?," in the Kansas City *Times*, February 8, 1984, A-17. Whether conspiracy or not, such strategy promises to be very effective in crippling the welfare state. For example, the Congressional Budget Office estimated that the total savings Reagan made by slashing welfare programs was $110 billion dollars. His initial position was that such cuts would enable him to balance the budget, while allowing for sharply increased military expenditures. It is now clear that this saving from public welfare is far less than the increase in interest payments, or $124 billion. Since Reagan's sacred cow is the military, it is obvious that there must be further attacks on the residue of the welfare state. See the New York Times News Service, Washington, "Rising interest swallows Reagan budget cutbacks," in the Kansas City *Star*, February 5, 1984, A-1. As early as 1983, Senator Daniel Patrick Moynihan of New York predicted that the astounding rise in the Reagan deficits would eventually mean that a Republican administration and Senate would use "the budget deficit to force massive reductions in social programs." See "U.S. economy is at stake in mounting deficit crisis," in the Kansas City *Times*, December 22, 1983, A-23.

86   David Vogel, Special to the Los Angeles Times, "Trade Deficit only a starting point in making U.S. competitive again," in the Kansas City *Star*, May 3, 1987, M-2. For the final three months of 1986, the U.S. economy grew at a rate of 1.1 percent annual rate,

even weaker than previously supposed. For all of 1986, the growth rate was 2.5 percent. By the Associated Press, "GNP grows weak," in the Kansas City *Star*, March 18, 1987, A-17. " ... there's rising evidence that the solutions of the last few years - the deficits and currency devaluations that have breathed vigor into an anemic economy - are now the dangers. Our national borrowing spree is catching up with us. International fear of Washington's inability to deal with the deficit, coupled with concern about a trade and budget deficit-linked collapse of the dollar, hang over the financial markets like a guillotine. Financial crises could now conceivably develop overnight, threatening recession without the lead-time necessary in previous cycles." Kevin Philips, Los Angeles Times-Washington Post News Service, "Economic boom of 1983-1988 may yet go bust," in the Kansas City *Star*, January 24, 1988, H-3.

87   Paul Wachtel, *Poverty of Affluence*, 277.

88   By the Associated Press, New York, "U.S. deficits blamed for trade lag," in the Kansas City *Star*, January 23, 1987, A-13.

89   William R. Neikirk, Chicago Tribune, Washington, "'Competittiveness' a meaningless word," in the Kansas City *Star*, August 6, 1987, B-6.

90   The Washington Post, Washington, "Why should Americans mind if dollar drops?" in the Kansas City *Times*, January 22, 1987, A-1. See also Associated Press, New York, "U.S. deficits blamed for trade lag," in the Kansas City *Star*, January 23, 1987, A-13.

91   Martin and Kathleen Feldstein, Los Angeles Times-Washington Post News Services, Washington, "Bitter medicine in store for U.S. consumers," in the Kansas City *Times*, March 6, 1987, A-11; David Vogel, Special to the Los Angeles Times, "Trade deficit only a starting point," in the Kansas City *Star*, May 3, 1987, M-2. Of course, currency devaluation can have temporary effects which are much valued by the administration in power: "The real threat of a major slump, apparent in 1986, was avoided as currency devaluation began to take hold." Kevin Philips, Los Angeles Times-Washington Post News Service, Washington, "Economic Boom of 1983-1988 may yet go bust," in the Kansas City *Star*, January 24, 1988, H-3.

92   Richard Reeves, Universal Press, Paris, "Beware the falling superdollar," in the Kansas City *Times*, January 26, 1987, A-7. European experimentation with currency depreciation suggests that "it causes higher inflation instead, which in turn offsets the helpful price effects of the currency depreciation and leaves the exchange rate little changed in real terms." It can only work with a system of expanded production which appears unlikely at the present time in America. From the Economist in London, "One thing sure: America's feast is coming to an end," in the Kansas City*Times*, December 29, 1987, A-7.

93   Lance Gay, Scripps Howard News Service, "Time to worry, when important folks say it can't happen," in the Kansas City *Star*, October 21, 1987, A-19. See also Los Angeles Times, New York, "Dow sinks 108.36 in frantic 'blowout'," in the Kansas City *Times*, October 17, 1987, A-1.

94   The New York Times, New York, "Wall Street can never be the same again," in the Kansas City *Times*, October 26, 1987, A-1. "'Tuesday was the most dangerous day we

had in 50 years," Felix Rohatyn, of the investment firm of Lazard Feres & Co. told the financial newspaper (The Wall Street Journal). Rohatyn, a general partner at Lazard Feres, said the market might have come 'within an hour' of disintegrating as the panic reached a climax by midday on October 20." The Associated Press, New York, "Terrible Tuesday examined," in the Kansas City *Times*, November 21, 1987, A-1, 15.

95   The source of this perceptive statement was Barbara S. Thomas, a senior vice president of Bankers Trust and a former member of the Securities and Exchange Commission. Los Angeles Times, "Worldwide panic travels like lightning," in the Kansas City *Times*, October 27, 1987, A-1, 12. In an article in *Foreign Affairs* magazine, W. Michael Blumenthal, former secretary of the Treasury, made an almost identical observation: "Purely national action of domestic policy and exchange rates has been rendered essentially obsolete by the growth of a true world capital market of gargantuan size and many interconnections - the vast range of financial innovation with its array of new money and moneylike instruments criss-crossing through the world's computer and telecommunications net-works, without regard to borders, as fast as the speed of light." William R. Neikirk, Chicago Tribune, "World affairs weaken U.S. economic policy," in the Kansas City *Star*, February 16, 1988, A-5.

96   Reagan's comments - that he did not want a further decline in the value of the dollar - "followed three weeks of decline after the administration decided to shift policy and allow the dollar's value to drop with the interest rates." New York Times, Washington, "Dollar resumes fall," in the Kansas City *Times*, November 11, 1987, A-1, 21. As late as early December, the news from Wall Street was discouraging: "The dollar fell to new lows Monday amid conjecture by experts that the Reagan administration was content with the currency's recent slide. Even as the dollar continued to decline ... stock prices slumped ... in heavy trading. ... the Dow Jones industrial average closed with a loss of 76.93 points, or 4 percent, at 1,833.55." The New York Times, Washington, "Dollar's nose dive batters market," in the Kansas City *Times*, December 1, 1987, A-1. On December 4, the Dow Jones average fell to 1,766.74 only a few points better than the big plunge to 1,738.41 on Black Monday, October 19. By the Associated Press, New York, "Dow near crash level," in the Kansas City *Times*, December 5, 1987, B-1.

97   A typical remark was the following from Peter Solomon, vice chairman of Shearson Lehman Brothers: "The winds have got to change and the only way that is going to happen is if the administration shows some real leadership. They don't seem to sense the real urgency that exists here." The New York *Times*, October 27, 1987, A-1, 12. A senior vice president at the same firm agreed on the necessity of leadership from Washington. From the Times Staff and the Associated Press, "Dow declines in heavy trading," in the Kansas City *Times*, November 5, 1987, E-1.

98   Donald Kaul, Tribune Media Services, "Titanic metaphor resurfaces," in the Kansas City *Times*, November 28, 1987, A-21. Conservatives entertained a like opinion: "For thirty days the mountain labored. It brought forth a mouse. The deficit reduction plan ... scarsely can be called a 'plan' at all. It is all flab and no bones. ... We should properly say of such a government that it is impotent, indecisive and lacking in leadership...." James J. Kilpatrick, Universal Press, Washington, "Miserable performance on deficit reduction," in *ibid.*, November 30, 1987, A-11. "The summit accord covered two years and was supposed to lower the budget deficit to $66.9 billion by 1989. ... In 1989, the deficit remained at the triple-digit-billion level." E. Thomas McClanahan, of the Editorial Staff, "Deficit politics as usual," in the Kansas City *Star*, October 3, 1990, C-7.

99   Richard Reeves, Universal Press, Boston, "Recovering from Reagan revolution will be painful," in the Kansas City *Times*, November 25, 1987, A-11. "So there is no escaping the fact, says [Felix] Rohatyn" - senior partner of Lazard Feres, investment banking firm - "that the money will come out of 'the consumer side of the economy.' That means reductions in Medicare, or veterans benefits or taxing Social Security. It means hard work but few wage increases. ...Longer term, it means higher taxes ...." James Flanigan, "Lean economic times await U.S. consumers," in *ibid.*, November 30, 1987, A-9.

100   Charles R.T. Crumpley, Staff Writer, "In a strange market, bad news can be good," in the Kansas City *Star*, July 21, 1990, A-1, 16. The economic reports, investors hoped "would show a weak economy that would convince the Federal Reserve that it could trim short-term interest rates." New York Times, New York, "Stocks take a 53.71-point fall," in the Kansas City *Star*, June 19, 1990, D-1.

101   New York Times, New York, "Stocks take a 53.71-point fall," in *loc. cit.*, June 19, 1990, D-1.

102   James Flannigan, "The dollar is losing its muscle," in the Kansas City *Star*, August 13, 1990, A-9. Economic experts from seven major industrialized countries agreed on the necessity to maintain high interest rates to check possible inflationary pressures as a result of the Persian Gulf crisis. Most Americans in that category "want to keep a tight rein on credit to fight inflation, even if it means running a greater risk of an economic downturn...." Los Angeles Times, Washington, "Oil prices pose two threats," in *ibid.*, September 23, 1990, A-17.

103   Los Angeles Times, Washington, "Jobless report is grim news," in *ibid.*, August 4, 1990 A-1, 12.

104   Richard Reeves, Universal Press, Washington, "Ongoing S&L debacle demonstrates bankruptcy of American government," in the Kansas City *Star*, April 19, 1990, C-7. See also The Associated Press, Washington, "Tax increase will be needed in thrift bailout," in *ibid.*, April 9, 1990, A-7.

105   Even international banks cannot survive holding six percent mortgages when new interest rates approach twenty. Richard Reeves, "Ongoing S&L scandal demonstrates bankruptcy of government," *loc. cit.*

106   E. Thomas McClanahan, of the Editorial Staff, "Savings and Loans, They need more help than Congress is giving," in the Kansas City *Star*, September 23, 1990, K-1, 4. See also Paul Craig Roberts, Scripps Howard News Services, "How did S&L bill mount up?," in *ibid.*, May 31, 1990, C-7. According to the Durham-based Southern Financial Project, thirty percent of the total deposits in twenty-two insolvent S&Ls were in individual accounts of more than $80,000. On the other hand, "from a quarter to half of all Americans have no financial deposits at all. Of those who do, the average account contains only $8,000." David Morris, St. Paul Pioneer Press, "Beneficiaries of thrift crisis should pay the bailout bill," in *ibid.*, August 16, 1990, C-11.

107   James Flannigan, "S&L mess just keeps growing," in *ibid.*, April 9, 1990, A-7.

108   This conclusion was arrived at by L. William Seidman, chairman of the Resolution

Trust Corporation, the new agency created to run the rescue program. New York Times, Dallas, in *ibid.*, April 12, 1990, A-1.

109   Jerry Heaster, "Why no outrage on S&Ls," in *ibid.*, April 11, 1990, B-1.

110   The Associated Press, "700 banks may fail, budget office warns," in *ibid.*, September 13, 1990, B-1.

111   President Johnson's War on Poverty reduced infant mortality by 33 percent between 1965-1975 and among blacks from 40.3 to 24.2 percent. Whereas one in five Americans once endured poverty, that figure was reduced to one in fifteen by 1980. Tom Wicker, New York Times News Service, "President's Domestic Policy Council says 'let them eat cake,'" in the Kansas City *Star*, July 27, 1990, C-9.

112   Ian Gough and Anne Steinberg, "The Welfare State and Crisis," 141-171 in *Political Power and Social Theory*, 2 vols., edited by Maurice Zeitlin (New York, Jai Press, 1980-1981), II, 145.

113   *Ibid.*, 164-165.

114   *Ibid.*, 168-169. One of many typical examples lay in the field of education. Reagan took office with the avowed intent of liquidating the Department of Education. In 1982, he proposed $12.9 billion for education but Congress raised it to $14.7. Early in 1987, his administration proposed to lop off $5.5 billion from a budget of $19.5, but members of two Congressional committees notified Education Secretary Bennett that Congress would not permit such crippling cuts. Educational authorities warned that the acceptance of the Reagan proposal would "result in fewer students taking out loans, fewer students going to college, or students going to the cheapest institution." Carl T. Rowan, News America, Washington, "Education budget blunder may be bigger than Iran mistake," in the Kansas City *Star*, January 19, 1987, A-9.

115   Frances Fox Pivan and Richard A. Cloward, *The New Class War. Reagan's Attack on the Welfare State and Its Consequences* (New York, Pantheon Books, 1982), 38-39.

116   *Ibid.*, 39.

117   John Maynard Keynes, *The General Theory of Employment Interest and Money* (New York, Harcourt and Brace, 1936), 372.

118   William Safire, New York Times News Services, Washington, "President should retire while he is ahead," in the Kansas City *Star*, October 4, 1983, A-10.

119   Robert G. Kaiser, Washington, "Reagan's '84 prospects tied to economy," in the Kansas City *Star*, October 23, 1983, F-1, 5. John Kenneth Galbraith, Los Angeles Times-Washington Post News Service, Cambridge, Mass., "Economic truth surrenders to politics," in the Kansas City *Star*, December 15, 1983, A-15. While in 1976, corporate income tax paid one-sixth of the national taxes, under Reagan it was reduced to one-twelfth. The 16 percent rate paid typically by the large corporation is the same rate as that levied on a family of four in the $12,000 to $16,000 income category. David S. Broder, Washington Post Writers Group, Washington, "Reagan team has strange concept of the 'public interest,'" in the Kansas City *Times*, December 5, 1983, A-10.

120   Charlotte Curtis, New York Times News Service, New York, "Effects of poverty in America aren't as well hidden as they were 25 years ago," in the Kansas City *Times*, November 25, 1983, A-15.

121   William Greider, "The Education of David Stockman," 27-54 in *The Atlantic*, vol. 248, No. 6, December, 1981, 29.

122   *Ibid.*, 32.

123   *Ibid.*, 40. There are at least two explanations for this. First, it is reminiscent of what Weston La Barre observed about Platonism when it reversed the values of Greek democracy. It depended, he concluded, not upon reason but upon "an authoritarian faith in a new myth, or the consciously fabricated Noble Lie." *Ghost Dance*, 546. The other explanation is postulated upon the lack of understanding of human events, particularly in the tricky economic realm, by Reagan himself. Some of his intimates believe he is most effective in convincing the American people of something when he himself believes in what he is saying. It is like he is reading the script of a new movie and it has to make sense to him before he will play the part. He is a man who responds primarily to symbols rather than to facts or logic. David S. Broder, Washington Post Writers Group, Washington, "Reagan approach is substitute symbols for substance," in the Kansas City *Times*, February 13, 1984, A-11. An explanation somewhat akin to that of Broder's is that of Anthony Lewis who concluded that a cheerful manner is chronic with Ronald Reagan, even when he was responsible for a disaster like intervention in Lebanon. When things go wrong, he smiles, ducks his head and murmurs, "Who, me?" New York Times News Service, Washington, "U.S. paying dearly for president's cheerfulness," in the Kansas City *Times*, February 21, 1984, A-11.

124   Greider, "The Education of David Stockman," *loc. cit.*, 51-52. "...as a result of the 1981 Tax Act - the quintessential 'supply side' program of the Reagan years - taxes of the poorest 10 percent of the people went up by 2.5 percent between 1977 and 1984, while those of the richest 1 percent went down by a whopping 7.8 percent. That is a fairly routine irony of recent years: The most vulnerable are punished by government policy, the most secure are made more secure." Michael Harrington, Los Angeles Times News Service, "Tax inequality haunts U.S.," in the Kansas City *Times*, January 25, 1988, A-7.

125   Barbara Ehrenreich and Karin Stallard, "The Nouveau Poor," 217-223 in *MS.*, July-August, 1982, 223. An itemized list is provided on page 221. States, such as Kansas, were hard hit for it lost twenty-five percent of federal aid for programs like day care, home help for the handicapped and adoption services. In general, the biggest Reagan cuts to the states were in such areas as federally financed job training, health programs, child nutrition and aid to dependent children. Richard Tapscott, Kansas Correspondent, "Pinch on welfare mothers in states," in the Kansas City *Times*, January 21, 1984, A-1.

126   New York Times News Service, "Reagan's popularity slides, survey says," in the Kansas City *Times*, December 1, 1987, A-3. "To sum up, here are the public's marching orders to Congress: Balance the budget, but don't raise taxes and don't cut services to the hinterlands, and for goodness sake don't do anything to hurt the elderly's economic life-support systems. Right. No problem. No wonder things are so messed up in Washington." Yael T. Abouhalkah, a member of the editorial staff, "When it comes to taxes, Americans aren't so bright," in the Kansas City *Star*, December 6, 1987, K-1.

127   Maurice Zeitlin, "Who Owns America? The Same Old Gang," in *The Social World,* edited by Ian Robertson (New York, Worth Publishers, 1981), 169. The same thing seems to be true of most capitalistic societies and may be assumed to be a part of a comparatively inflexible system. Thomas E. Weisskopf, "Capitalism and Inequality," 125-133 in *The Capitalist System,* edited by Edwards, 132-133.

128   Zeitlin, "Who Own America?" *loc. cit.,* 172.

129   *The Future as History* (New York, Harper & Brothers, 1960), 125. The same authority called attention to Frederick Lewis Allen's revelation that, at the very height of America's prosperity in 1928, virtually sixty percent of America's families were living below what the Brookings economists set as the $2,000 income "sufficient to supply only basic necessities." *Ibid.,* 119-120.

130   David M. Gordon, Special to the Washington Post, Washington, "Average citizens losing key fights to affluent class," in the Kansas City *Star,* November 9, 1986, K-1.

131   From Consumer Reports, "Minimum wage puts family of four below poverty line," in the Kansas City *Star,* November 4, 1986, A-8. A two decade follow-up of the celebrated Kerner Report in 1968 on America's slums concluded: Menacing the nation today are "quiet riots" in the form of poverty, unemployment, crime, school desegration and such. "These quiet riots are not as noticeable to outsiders ... but they are more destructive of human life than the violent riots of 20 years ago." The problem is clear to point to, though extremely difficult of solution: "the increasing concentration of poverty in an isolated urban underclass from which it is increasingly difficult to escape." "Kerner report revisited," The Washington Post, Racine, Wisconsin in the Kansas City *Times,* March 1, 1988, A-1, 4.

132   Since the hopes for American democracy have been so closely associated with equal aspirations for economic competency and comfort - not greed - the American dream is threatened, as revealed by a recent poll taken by the Wall Street Journal. 45 percent of Americans believe the American dream will "be harder to achieve than in the past, and 55 percent think it will be harder still." From the *Economist,* London, "A frown is visible on America's face," in *loc. cit.* According to a senior analyst for the Roper Organization, the specifics are these: "Ranking high in the American dream index are a high school education, freedom of choice, home ownership, a child's college education, and a happy marriage.... Less important is being rich or becoming president of the country or of a corporation...." $20,000 was understood to be a survival wage, $30,000 should afford reasonable comfort and a majority would be happy to settle for $50,000 a year. Ignacio Lobos, staff writer, "Wealth's importance diminished, poll says," in the Kansas City *Star,* April 14, 1987, A-3. 53 percent of Americans think the dream will be harder to achieve a generation from now. *Ibid.* "We still live well, but fewer of us see a continuing prospect for 'more' each year, and consequently fewer think of themselves as affluent or comfortable." Wachtel, *Poverty of Affluence,* 181.

133   From Star News Service, Washington, "The rich get richer in U.S.," in the Kansas City *Star,* July 24, 1990, A-1, 8. See also Tom Wicker, New York Times News Service, "President's Domestic Council says, 'Let them eat cake,'" in *ibid.,* July 27, 1990, C-9 and Virginia Hall, "Bush stuck without if, ands and buts," in *ibid.,* July 3, 1990, B-7.

134   Marc Levinson, Journal of Commerce, "Queasy economy," in the Kansas City

246

Star, July 25, 1990, C-9.

135   Jim Fain, New York Times News Service, "Nation split by shift in tax burden from wealthy to middle class," in *ibid.*, September 11, 1990, B-5.

136   The study "Alienation a threat to political system," was conducted by the Times Mirror Center for the People and the Press. Michael Oreskes, New York Times News Service, in *ibid.*, September 23, 1990, K-4.

137   "If the income share of the rich is rising at the expense of the rest of the population (it is), if the government is directly altering its policies to augment the income share of the rich (it has), if the campaign contributions of special interests increasingly dominate the political process (they do), if fewer and fewer middle-income and lower-income individual vote (it's happening), America is, under the cover of supply-side economics, rapidly moving toward becoming - dare we say it openly? - a plutocracy. History tells us that as a social and governmental system, plutocracy does not work for long." Lester C. Thurlow, Dean of MIT's Alfred P. Sloan School of Management, "Economic Mythology Underlies Budget Fiasco," in the Kansas City *Star*, October 14, 1990, L-1, 4.

138   *The Great Gatsby*, 182.

139   deTocqueville, *On Democracy in America*, II, 33.

Chapter XIX

FULL CIRCLE:
THE ULTIMATE HUBRIS

*"Myself when young did eagerly frequent
Doctor and Saint, and heard great argument
about it and about: but evermore came out by
the same door as in I went."*

Rubáiyát of Omar KháyyamTranslated
into English Quatrains by Edward Fitzgerald.
Edited with an Introduction by Louis Untermeyer
(New York, Random House, 1947). p. 27

As Tom maintained from the outset, the primary concern of our work
was not so much the primitive as man himself. We used the primitive as a
mirror through which we might see ourselves more clearly. The theme
which gave form to the entire edifice was struck in the opening chapter of
the first volume. It began with the hubris of the West - and its anthropologists
- regarding the primitive everywhere with prejudice, this justifying his
physical and cultural reduction in the name of Christianity and progress.

The greatest folly of the conquerors was they ignored the lessons of
archaeology, anthropology and history. Scorning the laws of nature, they

placed their hopes instead on the prospect of progress, measured by continual, even infinite, growth in terms of population and material things. In this essentially irreligious atmosphere, nature was perceived as nothing more than a willing and obedient slave to science and technology. On the contrary, the machine that these two spawned was glorified. There was a pervasive feeling that none of our resources, labors and skills "should be wasted - that is, employed so as to yield less than they might yield in [immediate] human satisfaction."[1] When the system ultimately failed to work as planned, the remedy sought was simply more and better machines. In our eyes, however, the machine was merely another god that failed.

In this chapter we try to analyze new trends whose common denominator was either an abandonment of a belief in the nineteenth century version of progress, or of the traditional mainline Christianity of the same era. One notes a recent revival by environmentalists and scientists of the primitive's efforts to live in harmony with nature, a rejection of progress. Simultaneously, there was a burst of irrational love of Oriental mystical beliefs and symbols, negating Christianity. Accompanying the latter, although at odds with it, was the dramatic rise of Christian fundamentalism which rivaled ninth century Europe in its emphasis on miracle, mystery and authority. This came at the expense of mainline Christianity, both Protestant and Catholic. Throughout it all, runs a central thread: the theme bonding the primitive and the ritualist in the West today is a mutual dependence on cosmology and ritual. But, if the primitive could instinctively harmonize the two by use of art forms the modern could not reconcile both with history and science. The result leaves a pervasive schism between the rational and scientific personality and the ritualist. The bifurcated society naturally lacks both logic and harmony. Consequently, a great many individuals suffer a sense of spiritual loss.

Recently, for example, no sooner had Henry Ford witnessed the demise of the rural farm culture of America, as it existed in the nineteenth century, than he sensed a nostalgia for that which he helped efface. Accordingly, he sought to atone by building a museum for that obliterated culture.[2]

Concerning the most perceptive of modern thinkers, more than nostalgia was responsible for their resurrection of the primitive's basic philosophy of life, or his reverence for nature and its component parts. The essence of this religious attitude is that man is not lord and master of all the animals, and of nature which sustains them. He is instead merely a part of a complex food chain, which includes both plants and animals, and all are subject to nature's laws. Perhaps the most revolutionary corollary of this is that nature, and not man, with all his science and technology, determines both the growth and activity rate of the tribe or nation. This is true both as regards population of man and his livestock and their utilization of the environment of land, sea and sky, whether by proper use or misuse. When nature's maximum has been reached and exceeded, whether out of man's ignorance, necessity or greed, it is only a question of time until nature exacts a severe penalty.

This modern view recognizes that the wisdom of the primitive was he willingly conformed to the dictates of nature. This meant limiting total population to that which the terrain would support in the leanest years, and not engaging in the over-kill of animals, part of the indispensable food supply. It also meant not destroying forests, thus altering climate and rainfall, and not hopelessly scarring the landscape, producing devastating erosion. To so conform to the dictates of nature is what the primitive meant by seeking and maintaining tribal harmony and contentment. He thus felt himself to be at one with the Great Spirit.[3]

While the born-again Christian phenomenon and the New Age movement present us with an astounding variety of unscientific beliefs and behavior, the link between the two was the escape from freedom theme. The emphasis in each instance was a surrender to some great cosmic force. Previously denied the individual about to bow the head and knee, it would then immediately assume the care and custody of the body and soul which had just capitulated. Great rewards would tumble upon the head of the humble confessor and spiritual suitor both in this world and the next. It was an updated version of David's twenty-third psalm where God supposedly prepared a meal for him in the presence of his enemies. It reminds the historian of the nineteenth century Vision Quest by our Indian tribes in the West.

Unattractive as both are to the intellectual and rational person, they often appeared dangerous for democratic as well as scientific principles.

Underlying a great deal of it was the search for an authority figure, or one who, possessed of a charismatic personality, had a simple and dogmatic solution for a host of infinitely complex problems. As in the days of Merlin, these exponents - whether followers of some guru or swami or TV revivalist - appear to believe in both magic and magicians. Recognizing the truth may perpetually elude us all, one may nevertheless observe that all these so-called "modern" religious practices and beliefs are not a whit more sophisticated, or akin to college physics, biology and chemistry, than those of the primitive shaman whose strange and exotic maneuvers we described in volume I, Chapter IV. SHAMAN, SORCERER AND PRIEST.

Intellectual allegiance to a system, whose significance was rightly stressed by Crane Brinton,[4] long ago evaporated with regard to the impersonal technological, urbanized, contractualized, individualized money economy so dominant in recent times in the West. A few examples suffice. Pitirim Sorokin rightly credits Ferdinand Tönnies, writing in 1887, with predicting the coming crisis and decay of what he termed this *Gesellschaft* type of society.[5] Utterly lacking in the type of emotional appeal so characteristic of folk societies in pre-capitalistic times, the system doomed itself. Rather than doing away with social and class inequalities, by virtue of the machine as slave rather than man, it rapidly accelerated them and was thus incompatible with the idea of progress which emphasized social and economic benefits for all.[6]

Writing in the first decade of this century, George Simmel thought the modern age was shaped by the mathematical character of money which removed the personal element from human relationships.[7] "Man," he concluded "has thereby become estranged from himself; an insuperable barrier of media, technical inventions, abilities and enjoyments has been erected between him and his most distinctive and essential being."[8] Its end product was not only an isolated individual but a lonely, frustrated and alienated one. "If we consider the totality of life," he concluded, "then the control of nature by technology is possible only at the price of being enslaved by it and dispensing with spirituality as the central point of life."[9]

Since that time experts stressed individual alienation - from work, the machine, society itself. In an age of materialism, of bigness, of interlocking directoriates, huge bureaucracies, both public and private, individuals on all levels "feel increasingly frustrated and powerless, unable to exert any control over our lives."[10] It yields a broken sense of belonging, an abandoned sense of place, a mutilated sense of self.[11] Peter Berger aptly concludes that this alienation is the price of individualization. Even religion has been privatized because none speaks for the whole community anymore. As a result, the sense of homelessness pervades the cosmos.[12]

Currently, Kathleen Agena, contributing editor of the *Partisan Review,* has given us a classic analysis of our present social malaise at the dawning of the computer age. This features at least two equally alarming truths: 1) the sense of the bewilderment and powerlessness of the individual, which Eric Fromm bemoaned,[13] is now pervasive throughout the social fabric and 2) this has been dramatically increased by the computer which, so far beyond the understanding and control of the individual, has put so much power "out there" as to seem like magic.[14] The almost sudden revival in many art forms of the world of enchantment, featuring mystical beliefs and symbols that seek inspiration from the simple religious, social and political precepts of Medieval Europe, are seen as a manifestation of the decay of the age of the Enlightenment. The centuries old belief in a rational world which obeyed sensible and definable rules in a mechanistic universe is breaking apart and with it the idea of progress which insisted that man could control his own fate or destiny. Instead, the universe has been revealed as quirky - with even time defying absolute measurement - leaving one with a feel of wonderment and mystery which in turn caused a breakdown of rational cosmology. With the demise of the confident spirit of the Enlightenment, technology -which on the one hand gives us a barrage of facts which itself defies understanding and, on the other, exposes us to the clear danger of becoming economic robots - looks more and more like Frankenstein. There is, unfortunately, no uniform view which gives understanding and meaning to life. What the individual is left with is a sense of the loss of vitality of self and a sense of the emptiness of the universe.[15]

In retrospect, it was Robert L. Heilbroner who in the late Fifties accurately predicted the social malaise which would accompany the computer age. "Meanwhile, we must anticipate," he wrote, "a further rise of the impotence and incompetence of the individual vis-à-vis the social environment which modern technology creates. ...the individual will find himself increasingly forced to adapt to technological changes whose advent he did not order but must nevertheless accept, whose operation is beyond him, and whose ultimate impact he does not understand."[16] On the contrary, the primitive was happily at home with and understood perfectly all the technology by which he sustained life on a daily basis.

An understanding of this social cul-de-sac is extremely important because so many individuals were desperately seeking meaning and a personal identity in a fellowship of believers. It gave rise to the anti-intellectual cults.

A somewhat different view, but one quite complimentary, was voiced by the European libertarian socialist, Cornelius Castoriadis. He thought the contemporary Western crisis was a result of social decomposition, or the death of vision by that society. This decay occurs in periods of continuously rising unemployment, the stagnation of workers' standards of living and the appearance of a substantially large body of permanently poor. In such a fragmented society, as we have had since the mid-Seventies, materialistic hopes slowly faded and with it the American dream. Society loses its élan vital and becomes meaningless as it is deprived of a meaningful past and a hopeful future. Lost is the desire by the social order to maintain itself as it is and the individual, feeling abandoned, assumes antisocial attitudes.[17] He, too, is ripe for cult conversion.

A popular historian dramatized our fall from innocence which occurred between the assassination of President Kennedy and Nixon's disgrace as a result of Watergate. While he listed ten beliefs which were fractured in those days, more interesting was the fact that at least six were clearly based on the idea of progress. These were the worship of technology and beliefs in the health and virtue of the American economy, as well as our military might. Furthermore, small nations needed our care and guidance. Happily, our environment and resources were virtually unlimited. All this made us a worthy model for the rest of the world to emulate. It is important to realize these were the very assumptions which not only led Admiral Mahan, Henry Cabot Lodge, Teddy Roosevelt and their coterie into our first imperialist plunge in 1898 in both the Caribbean and the Pacific, but in much more recent times into our impetuous and extremely costly forays on the mainland of Asia itself, i.e., Korea and Vietnam. The other four related to our domestic life. These involved the conservative postulates of the sanctity and legitimacy of our leaders, minorities staying in their "place," youth playng its customary role and the supremacy of the nuclear family.[18] While one or more of these ten assumptions will still have their champions in the Nineties, the glue which held them together throughout the twentieth century has itself dissipated.

The loss of faith in our own time was widespread. Since the Twenties, when religious fundamentalism was routed by science, "our secular culture has lost confidence. How can you believe in the beneficence of science, that '20s verity after Hiroshima? How can you believe in progress after the Holocaust?"[19] However, it was the latter which had such terrible implications for those who believed the Bible unerring and thus that the Hebrews were God's chosen people. As Mark Ellis concluded: "The Holocaust represents the severing of the relationship between God and person, God and community, God and culture. The lesson of the Holocaust is that humanity is alone and there is no meaning in life outside of human solidarity."[20]

Amidst the skepticism produced by the followers of empiricism and reason, the cult of the true believer alone appeared to thrive upon the social disorganization and alienation. Eric Hoffer agrees the cult does not usually rise until the prevailing order has been discredited.[21] He proceeds to explain why the new one breeds fanaticism, fervent hope, enthusiasm, hatred and intolerance, all of which are vast energy sources.[22] First of all, the cults offer the convert what he has been searching for fruitlessly: a sense of identity, discipline, knowledge and power.[23] "People who see their lives as irremediably spoiled cannot find a worthwhile purpose in self-advancement. ...Nothing that has its roots in reason or self can be good and noble. Their innermost craving is for a new life -a rebirth ... by an identification with a holy cause."[24] The crusader has now found his Holy Grail. "All questions have already been answered, all decisions made, all eventualities forseen. ...The true doctrine is a master key to all the world's problems."[25]

Let the author of *Cults in America* cap this description: "Their vision is absolutist, their promises as well: absolute redemption, absolute fulfillment in exchange for absolute loyalty. It is ... this quality of absoluteness that is their hallmark."[26]

However, we are particularly indebted to Marvin Harris who questions whether this movement signals the end of concern for America's materialistic quest, or a last-ditch effort to secure materialism and consumerism by the magical and mystical means of the shaman. He thinks it represents a desperate effort to save the beleaguered American economic dream.[27] "The point is that humankind's religious impulses are more often than not as much instrumentalities in the struggle for worldly wealth, power, and physical well-being as manifestations of the search for spiritual salvation."[28]

The so-called New Age movement originated late in the turbulent Sixties among the young people of America who had lost faith in the Establishment, but had seen the fires of social idealism burn themselves out in Vietnam and the Civil Rights crisis. In retrospect the one-time zealots felt that none of these national episodes provided "any unique vehicle for discovering meaning and purpose in life."[29] Now without another social crusade to fire their imagination and enthusiasm, they were willing to give their allegiance to anything new and exotic provided it promised a spiritual orgasm. This profound urge to touch base with an extremely elusive thing called a "soul,"[30] and to find certainty in the modern world where intellectuals despaired of it,[31] had a common denominator. This was in the pious hope that "there must be some secret and mysterious shortcut or alternative path to happiness and health."[32] Other than this naive optimism there was "no unanimity of New Age belief in anything, but many New Agers do believe in unidentified flying objects, crewed by oddly shaped extra-terrestials who have long visited earth from more advanced planets, spreading the wisdom that created ... Stonehenge and the pyramids of Egypt."[33] Add to that beliefs in reincarnation and the use of mediums in channeling or conversing with dead spirits. When considering their faith in the magical healing powers of crystals, colors, triangles and such,[34] one sees that "modern" cults have come up with the equivalent of the magical properties attributed to holy relics and bones of saints by the medieval Catholic church.

Prominent among all this spiritual unrest was the natural appeal of Oriental mysticism which many experts believed involved not only a rejection of Western empiricism and materialism,[35] but also of the cherished precepts of Christianity.[36] It was the Christian theologian, Nels Ferre, who put the matter philosophically: "The supernatural, personalistic, classical Christian faith is now being undermined by an ultimately nondualistic, impersonal, or transpersonal faith."[37] Edmund D. Soper, historian of religion, put the matter on a simpler level. Oriental religions have influenced a great many "who have thus turned away from their loyalty to ancestral faith and who are led to doubt the validity of the Christian claim that the revelation of God in Jesus Christ is the one completely adequate message for mankind."[38]

Added to the confusion of all this is the certainty that "New Age fantasies often intersect with mainstream materialism, the very thing many New Age believers profess to scorn."[39] This fulfills the prediction made several years earlier by Marvin Harris. Take, for instance, Scientology, founded by L. Ron Hubbard, who simply confessed: "Money is a symbol." Such candor merely demonstrates a "definite yearning for control - which contradicts the notion that the current religious awakening is best understood as an Asian-inspired 'critique of the expansion of wealth and power.'"[40] Despite the personal renunciation of wealth, and even physical comfort, demanded of converts by other Oriental religions, such as the "Moonies," the "Hare Krishnas," and the Divine Light Mission, the same worldly preoccupations characterize these organizations. "Not surprisingly, the New Age condones Big Business because the New Age is Big Business. In 1986 New Agers spent $100 million on crystals and $300 million on audio and video tapes. There are channelers and hypnotists and self-help groups.[41] The Werner Erhard - or EST - seminars represents but another example of the L. Ron Hubbard affirmation that worldly success is yours once you are determined to achieve it. There is virtually no limit to the imagination and power of the human will.[42] To skeptics, however, there is little difference between this and the childhood tendency to wish upon a star.

Early in this decade Marvin Harris claimed there were ten times as many born-again Christians in this country as those New Agers who gravitated toward Asiatic spiritual messages;[43] however, a Hollywood actress, Shirley MacLaine, may have radically changed that situation. The executive editor of Bantam Books observed that she "suddenly made it respectable ... to deal with reincarnation, out-of-body experiences, spiritual messages, channeling." According to a poll in 1987, *American Health* magazine reported that two-thirds of American adults believe they experienced psychic experiences. That magazine declared that ever since the actress "revealed her personal contact with extraterrestrials and spiritually channeled wisdom, with a book and TV mini-series last year, the New Age has come out of the closet - and so have the crystal gazers."[44]

Originally, she was attracted to Oriental values because she was distressed with American materialism: "...my traditional American value system got knocked into a cocked hat as I traveled the world.... Having addressed myself to success, money, getting property, getting things.... What did that have to do with living really? ...so few people understood when 'enough' was theirs. Most always wanted more ... so that living got lost ...."[45] She observed that there was nothing in the trade papers "about what had really gone wrong. Nothing about Vietnam, our poverty, or racism, nothing about the way the whole brave American dream seemed to be crumbling about us." Her friends who accompanied her to mainland or Mao China worried about the overwhelming prevalence of dope in America, crime in the streets, government surveillance of private citizens and a host of other vices which indicated a sharp deterioration of the system.[46]

It is likewise true that Shirley perceived much that was wise and true in the Oriental religions and worthy of personal incorporation. First, she began to understand that truth itself is relative and that it changes as culture changes.[47] The Buddhist philosophy of never hurting your neighbor appeared much more realistic than the Christian injunction of loving him.[48] She admired the Yoga aim of union with the universe because we all are merely a part of nature and not separate and apart from it as we imagine in the individualistic and materialistic West. "And it is folly and stupid, because nature will work her quiet and silent will inevitably." If we cooperated with nature, we would "find life not only easier but miraculous."[49] Instead of the irrational dread of death, as in Western eyes, the Buddhist viewed it as but a part of the cycle of life. That put an end to another perennial battle between the individual and nature.[50] One of her interviewers described her Hindu aims: "Peeling away fear, insecurity, material possessions, jealousy, despair and sorrow" which, if achieved, would allow Shirley to become who she really was and not how she might be presented in some Hollywood publicity bit. Her ultimate goal was "to try to achieve what the Hindus call a 'dharmic' existence, living in the service of others, loving them without judging or criticizing them."[51]

Levitation, an ancient practice of the primitive shaman, was one of the first "miracles" to attract Shirley. An instructor in Calcutta first told her that levitation was possible. The trick is to reverse the poles of gravity within oneself and one is enabled to do this by concentrating upon another planet. It is a question then of mental energy, or to bring oneself within the gravitational pull of another planet and thus rise off the ground. She herself first experienced it at the Taksang monastery at 14,000 feet. She felt as if her spirit was the wind above and disengaged from herself. "I felt fused and part of all things. It felt as though I wasn't only me any longer - I was everything."[52] That was probably the root of Shirley's later emphasis that she was God, that everyone was God.[53] Gloria Steinem, a friend though not personally a believer, summed it up: "Love is an understanding that you are part of everything. ...And fear comes from the feeling that there may indeed not be any God there, which is really the feeling that there is no self there. So fear is really based on this feeling of self-abandonment."[54]

It was the same Gloria Steinem who concluded the reason most of Shirley's followers were patently women was that "many women have long felt discriminated against by the organized [Judeo-Christian] religions."[55]

Finally, MacLaine was forced to reconcile her new-found spirituality with the basest of American materialism, greed. In 1987, in a huge ballroom at the New York Hilton, one crowded with 1,200 of the faithful, who parted with $300 apiece to listen to this modern female shaman, she told them what they had come to hear. The basic message of the New Age contained but a simple yet powerful truth: "you can be whatever you want to be." As for Shirley herself, she got to the bottom line quickly: "I want to prove that spirituality is profitable." Here she was in complete accord with the entire crowd inside the ballroom and with all the TV evangelicals outside, as well as the hopeful millions who watched at home. In yet another crucial regard she was also in complete accord with the evangelicals: "It is a complete surrender and trust, the key words for this new age."[56] Once again, it was the escape from individual freedom theme. Shirley might as well have advertised it all as a born-again variety, this time emphasizing individual identity with pantheism.

Despite MacLaine's appeal, one cannot surrender and trust someone's fantastic accounts of extraterrestrial, or non-human "visitors" from another planet, who follow, terrify and subject one to frightening biological experiments; apparently, however, that is the way both to the best seller list and the amassing of a private fortune. William Morrow gave Whitley Strieber a million dollar advance for the recitation of such "experiences" in *Communion*. When Avon came out with a paper back edition, it sold almost two million copies and was on the best seller lists. The author claims more than 4,000 other people throughout the world have written to say they have had similar abductions.[57]

One dare not abandon this analysis of what Robert Nisbet called "the revolt against reason,"[58] without attention to the born-again Christian movement which has such mental and spiritual compatibility to the New Age trend.

Both received a great impetus from the social and political upheavals of the Sixties; both insisted on surrender and trust to a simplistic formula or belief, one utterly unconnected to reality as the Enlightenment defined it, and both promised great and immediate spiritual and financial rewards. Predictably, because both were devoid of an intellectual and rational appeal,[59] they swept through Middle America like a prairie fire.

We know that differences exist between fundamentalists and pentecostals, particularly on the behavioral level. The latter are much more emotional, apparently experiencing religious ecstasy virtually on a daily basis and fraternizing with God almost as often. They wouldn't have batted an eye, we suspect, when pastor Pat Robertson claimed to have deflected a hurricane, following prayer. Their *Weltanschauung* is akin to that of Old Testament prophets who operated on the same intuitive level as that of the primitive shaman (vol. I, Chapter IV, SHAMAN, SORCERER AND PRIEST).

Being more "code" bound in Biblical study, and more apt to attempt a rational case for it,[60] fundamentalists conceivably could have had problems with Robertson's assertion which pentecostals never experienced. But here, concentrating upon the TV revivalists, what we are struck with are the similarities between all parties.

Listen, for example, to Billy Graham, presumably one of the most respected fundamentalists, describe the Second Coming of Jesus. "Jesus," he wrote, "repeatedly taught he would come again to bring history as we know it to a close and establish his kingdom. To his disciples he said, 'When the Son of Man comes in his glory, and all the angels with him, he will sit on his throne in heavenly glory. All the nations will be gathered before him.'" And, presumably, the prophecy of Jesus was verified in the sacred words from Acts: "When he was miraculously taken into heaven the angels promised those who watched, 'This same Jesus, who has been taken from you into heaven, will come back in the same way you have seen him go into heaven.'"[61]

As we have previously seen, it is not necessary to believe in this prophecy of magic in order to be a Christian. Mainline Protestant churches no longer maintain this postulate as an article of faith (see Chapter XII. SCIENCE AND HISTORY VERSUS CHRISTIAN COSMOLOGY).

Ever since their gospel was clearly stated at Niagara Falls in 1895, however, Protestant fundamentalism managed to restore the same emphasis on miracle, mystery, and authority which historically characterized the Catholic church. If true, their world picture is one whose magic and mysticism are quite compatible with that of the primtive shaman. The 1895 declaration demanded complete and utter dedication to the following: 1) Virgin birth 2) literal payment for the sins of mankind by Christ substituting himself in death on the cross 3) the physical resurrection of Jesus 4) his visible and bodily return and 5) absolute inerrancy of the Scriptures.[62]

Because of their low or pessimistic view of human nature, what was required for the salvation of man was that the individual renounce the control over his or her own life and surrender it to the care and custody of their Lord and savior, Jesus Christ. Required also was the acceptance of the Bible as the word of God and most often that of the preacher as the authoritarian dispenser of the sacred text.[63] Such insistence on a flight from rationality and the spirit of critical inquiry could not have been stated with more vigor by Dostovesky's Grand Inquisitor, although he did make the case more poetical.[64] Catholics always preferred beauty in their religious ceremonies while early Protestant reformers were quite skeptical of it. Their heirs appear, quite naturally, blind to beauty, although not to sheer pageantry or showmanship.

This, plus the inevitable fundamentalist emphasis on evil personified by the sins of the flesh,[65] was the heritage of the TV revivalist. So preoccupied were they with it a skeptic might be forgiven for concluding they were fascinated by it, charmed by it. That is probably as good as any other theory to explain why a couple of Elmer Gantrys, Jimmie Bakker and Jimmie Swaggart, were eventually exposed as the biggest sexual sinners of them all. Swaggart especially distinguished himself by hating and scorning so many different groups and individuals, all of whom were sinners. Thus, his abject plight when caught, and his moisty plea for forgiveness, struck the secular humanist as a bit ironic.[66]

One new and advantageous element was given the "modern" fundamentalist preachers that their predecessors did not have in 1895. This was hatred for the Godless Communists, centered in the Kremlin. It apparently is not enough for a society to love, especially in times of crisis. There must also be someone to hate, a scapegoat for all the nation's ills, for all revolutions against the status quo in far-off places and like misfortunes. We know how useful - even indispensable - for national unity it was in this country when the Japanese hit Pearl Harbor in December, 1941, without an official warning. But America has not been able to sustain a "good and just" war with a high level of national hatred since then.

Fortunately, however, for the governing classes and the armed services, at least here and in the Soviet Union, the glorious victory over the Fascist foe in 1945 quickly dissipated. By 1948, we had a new national menace to put the nation *en garde,* international communism. Even our governors were not immune from the charge of conspiracy after Chiang Kai

Shek lost China through his incompetency and the corruption inherent in his own organization.[67]

Religious leaders, particularly Catholics and fundamentalists, cooperated wholeheartedly and without stint in the "noble" endeavor. Thus, as in primitive communities, Christians gave an excellent example of loving their country, if not their neighbor, while hating the foreigner, or, in this case, the Commie who was pretty much spread over the globe. The old song, "Onward Christian Soldiers" captures this dual relationship between love and hate. It reminds one that not only was Christianity historically indebted to the sword for its spectacular advances throughout history,[68] but "that the idea of a military-messaniac apocalypse lies at the very base of the Judeo-Christian tradition."[69]

On the other hand, it has been suggested by an exponent of fundamentalism that evangelicals in the post-war world emphasized national security and the fear of communism because that was the price of a national hearing.[70] The same authority points to a dependence since 1945, and the first Billy Graham spectacle in Chicago, on the electronic media of radio and TV, a streamlined and entertaining program, slick promotion, and pungent preaching, laced with current events.[71] One wonders whether this is an unconscious argument for the show biz theme.

As was characteristic of the whole "roll back the Iron Curtain" movement, evangelicals were victims of an historic optimism. This, as Robert L. Heilbroner observed, "has given us the notion that history is only, or largely, the product of our own volitions. Thus it has deluded us as to our power when the forces of history run not with, but counter to, our designs. It has filled us with a belief that everything is possible, and has made it not a sign of wisdom but a suspicion of weakness to think in terms of what is impossible."[72]

Instead our ideologues ignored three crucial facts. In the Fifties, technological changes in weaponry made a military conquest over communism impossible.[73] In the Third World traditional capitalism itself was on the defensive.[74] Most frustrating of all, however, was the realization the only way to halt "creeping socialism" in our own country was "to return to an atomistic economy with small-scale technical and economic units," as in the days of Adam Smith. "This is obviously impossible for us to attempt without a degree of historic intervention which is entirely alien to our social philosophy."[75]

Authorities are in general agreement that the TV revivalist has his greatest appeal among the social and economic losers, the psychologically deprived, or those under the stress of estrangement, loneliness, depression, and who are desperate to substitute meaning and identity for that undesirable condition.[76] Eric Hofer stated it simply but well: "Faith in a holy cause is to a considerable extent a substitute for the lost faith in ourselves."[77] Lowell D. Streiker said it most dramatically: "If his freedom has not brought him an intense sense of failure and self-dissatisfaction, conversion would not have occurred in the first place. Therefore, the convert places his life in the hands of a higher authority."[78] And one of the most attractive facets of it all is that he or she can do this at drastically reduced rates from those in the time of Jesus. The TV media offers the unique opportunity to "follow" Jesus without ever leaving home.[79]

When a prominent journalist analyzed Pat Robertson's nostalgic societal lament, we think he gave an apt description for millions of his evangelical followers; "...one in which divorce does not end half of all marriages, in which more than 1 million 'therapeutic' abortions do not take place every year, in which teen-age pregnancy is not epidemic among inner-city girls, in which drug rites are not an inevitable rite of passage for the affluent and poor youths alike, in which homosexuality is still the love that dare not speak its name and not just another lifestyle."[80]

It is impossible to discourse for long about the TV revivalists without getting snarled up in their preoccupation with money. "All of the leading figures in the electronics ministry have rags-to-riches stories to tell and their congregations hope to follow the same road...."[81] Constantly harping on the theme that Jesus cannot capture a man's heart until he has his pocketbook, Jerry Falwell asks his congregation for a tenth of their income. Nor will his followers be the loser in this transaction. "Put Jesus first in your stewardship and allow him to bless you financially."[82] One is forced to conclude that these TV personalities are either con artists or blessed with faith of the simple themselves. Bakker affirmed that on two occasions he wrote checks for $20,000 without the money, armed only with the assurance that God would somehow provide it.[83] One can only trust that his listeners do not have an equality of faith, else a lot of Christians are going to be arrested as bad-check artists. However, the biggest horror story came from a Robertson 700 Club performance. He told of a woman in California with all sorts of health problems who was already sending half of her disability income to him. But, having made her decision to back God to the hilt, she sent all of her cancer money, $120 a month, to Robertson. Three days later, from an unexpected source, she received a check for $3,000.[84] Now, first of all this story, and others like it, are never verified. But, even if she did "luck out," it is quite probable that in every one hundred such cases scientifically studied, no more than two or three at most would have the same happy ending. Even a stock market which endured the terrible beating of October, 1987, or the slot machines in Las Vegas would no doubt have better percentages than that.

Even the church historian who appeared most appreciative of the aims and aspirations of fundamentalists, Martin E. Marty, confessed himself bewildered by the many forms of cultural adaptations it has recently assumed: "The sudden intrusion into politics, the attempts to replicate secular culture with Jesus-expressions (television talk shows, Christian rock music, fellowships of athletes and beauty queens, proclamations of the gospel of success, political partisanship, the promise of healing and material abundance) signal that fundamentalism is coming to a new phase whose limits we cannot yet assume. It may be 'gaining the whole world and losing its soul' through this astonishing cultural adaptation. It may simply be going through the inevitable compromise that movements need by their third or fourth generation."[85] This ties in with something the perceptive must realize after seeing Tammy Bakker who is obviously over-devoted to make-up. It is okay for God's women to be fashion-conscious and to employ all manner of beauty aids in order to be attractive to their husbands.[86] It is possible that these maneuvers point to an unconscious acceptance of the fact that the Christ is not scheduled for an imminent Day of Judgment. Meanwhile, there is no risk of salvation in being a little more comfortable and more like the image of white middle Americans have of themselves.

Finally, we must address ourselves to one of the most curious but fascinating aspects of the born-again Christian movement: that is its undoubted attraction for young people whom one assumes have scarcely lived long enough to regard themselves as failures. Thus our original hypothesis was to view it as a sort of adolescent Head Start program for personal success and happiness. The buyers could largely be categorized as young, white, of middle class origins and affluent parents and apparently well educated[87] (meaning, one presumes, some college experience). They found mainline churches, both Protestant and Catholic, not to be relevant to their emotional needs: the music was centuries old, the sermons were uninspiring, and opportunities for lay participation limited and routinized. In other words, they did not feel part of the show. They believed themselves neither liked nor understood by their parents.[88] Thus, both bastions of conservatism and the status quo had failed them. Of course school had done likewise because at best it merely explained what the outside world was like and nothing about ultimate meaning and purpose. A sunset was simply there. It had little meaning other than to explain the time of day, color variations, weather prospects and - on the basis of the heliocentric theory - when to expect the next sunrise. To put it another way, a sunset told us nothing about a countdown for the Second Coming. A great many converts, therefore, among the young, looked to Jesus as a father figure to provide the authority, love and understanding they never received at home or anywhere else.[89]

Anyone, however, who has pondered the relationship between nature and nature's God is apt to discount the claims of those who boast of a born-again status despite an abject knowledge of nature. But, as Suzanne K. Langer reminded us: "Nature, as man has always known it, he knows no more." Modern Western man, city dweller that he is, can muster up nothing more than a pathetic knowledge of nature.[90] But, when has that prevented the affluent urban and suburban youth from claiming that he has vaulted straight into the arms of Jesus? As for us, we will take the spiritual musings of Henry David Thoreau any time over those of the religious tracts of persons "saved" in our time.[91]

It was, however, precisely at this juncture we became aware these post-war kids were, and had been all their lives, under terrific social and psychological pressure. They were, as a consequence, depresssed and bewildered. Quite naturally, they were seeking to shed or shut out that portion of the world's adversity they themselves could not change or amend. Let the designated successor of Dr. Benjamin Spock tell their story. It has only been in the last two decades psychologists have recognized stress symptoms in the very young, some of the physical ones now being detectable as early as six to ten years of age. One of the earliest pressures comes from parents who want their child to excel at school. Sexual pressure comes later in adolescence. But many if not most of the anxieties of youth "arise from the instability of society. For example, the 1 million divorces each year lead to splintered homes, reconstituted families and frequent changes of neighborhoods and schools." However, concluded Dr. Michael Rothenburg, the "most frightening stress of all is living in an era when global destruction is possible, if not likely. ...Older children acknowledge a direct danger to themselves, and adolescents become inclined to pessimism and the loss of a sense of the future; they may question the need for studying or staying healthy if they have a good chance of dying before reaching adulthood."[92]

Factual information finally dispelled the earlier notions of psychiatrists that only adults, not children or adolescents, could be depressed: adolescent suicides are the second greatest cause of death among that group.[93] In the last three decades these tragedies have increased three-fold.[94] However, it was from the feminine director of the Youth Suicide Center in Washington, D.C. that we learned the most salient feature of this phenomenon: typical cases "tend to be both impulsive and poor problem solvers."[95]

The conclusion to be inferred is that in this electronic age the family is no longer able to do the job it once did rather well. That was to insulate or protect the child from an outside world, one that by nature appears forboding and threatening, until such time as maturation occurs and he or she can take it on, as the parents had once done. If, however, outside pressures upon today's child are much greater than upon those growing up prior to World War II, and if typical suicide cases are both impulsive agents and poor problem solvers, it is obvious that the Youth for Christ movement is a natural. If this young and tormented mind receives a timely invitation to throw all off his burdens upon Jesus, the result is predictable. Like an addict, he or she cannot - nor should he - resist a "quick fix."

These restless and unhappy souls were also searching for some religious institution staffed by a young and charismatic leader whose sermons were simple but dynamic, where the music was contemporary and where, amid a fellowship of believers and peers, one could experience a spiritual up-beat.[96] Like the New Age phenomenon, the basic interest of the new assembly they joined was to help the individual become part of a group seeking meaning and purpose in life.[97]

In what we assume to be a typical situation in America - one which occurred on or near the Irvine campus of the University of California - there was a general admission the born-again movement concentrated exclusively on the spiritual needs of the convert while ignoring larger social and economic needs of society. The Catholic priest and leader of the Interfaith Center at Irvine expressed the concern of a great many religious leaders about the born-again concept: "This can be a very selfish style of religion ... where there is no interest in social justice, only personal spirituality."[98] Even more to the point, the young and hip leader of the Santa Anita Calvary church, admitted with regard to his new converts: "They live for themselves and what they want and need. They don't want to be burdened with social problems, and they're not at all embarrassed about acknowledging this. There's no war to involve kids today, and they're bored politically. They make their statements by the way they dress and their music. And more and more often, by their church."[99]

In our eyes, however, both the New Age and Youth for Christ exponents have set themselves a task which will ultimately prove impossible. Both are attempting, with a privileged minority, to accomplish in an urban, heterogeneous and secular society - and in a news sense, a global one - what primitive man found easy to do in a small, homogeneous and isolated society, one dominated by the charismatic shaman. This was to give identity, fellowship, discipline and insight into the meaning and purpose in life. Both American subgroups are attempting to achieve this by isolating themselves from the larger social problems of their own society, i.e., poverty, misery, despair, homelessness, unemployment, lack of job satisfaction, crime in the streets, drugs and a multitude of other dismaying facets in the lives of the masses, plus fraud, corruption or even indifference on the part of our supposed leaders. But our guess is that in the long run, they will not be able to do this. The universe is not interested in your personal health, welfare and happiness. TV sends this global message to us on a daily basis. The primitive, fortunately, was spared this or, if he knew about it, it always happened to his enemy and, therefore, to any enemy of the gods. It was but a just punishment. We, however, cannot be so naive. Even if we cannot go so far as John Donne - "when the death bell tolls, it tolls for thee"[100]- we are forced to admit that these terrible tragedies continually happen to people like us and to those in no lower favor in God's eyes than we.

Science, on the contrary, has pursued nature, and its many mysteries, with the same intensity and persistence that ritual man has God. But, if we may, as Rainmundo Panniker confessed, ignore or deny God without peril in this world,[101] we may not do so with nature. God may, to be sure, exact retribution in the next world, but nature manifests its extreme displeasure in this one. For all those of us who are not natural scientists, it would be hard to improve upon the four simple concepts - or nature's ecological laws - which we must all live by or suffer from. Barry Commoner explains them thus: 1) Everything is connected to everything else 2) Nothing (solids, fluids, gas and vapors) is ever obliterated for it must go somewhere in our ecological system 3) Nature knows best (the introduction of an artificial compound made by man and placed in a natural environment is more apt to produce harm than good) and 4) There is no such thing as a free lunch (every gain is won at some cost and the payment can only be deferred, not avoided).[102]

And when scientists study nature, they come up with vastly different answers than the religiously-minded to crucial questions. The reason is simple enough. It lies in the realm of causality, as postulated by the ancient Greek physician, scientist and philosopher, Hippocrates. Nothing happens without natural cause. Natural, not supernatural.[103]

On the contrary, religions make "not so much objective statements about the universe as subjective statements about people ... collectively or individually."[104]

The very presuppositions of science are at war with those of ritual man throughout the ages. Science "assumes that there are no transcendent, immaterial forces and that all forces which do exist within the universe behave in an ultimately objective or random fashion. The nature of these forces, and all other scientific knowledge, is revealed only through human effort in a dynamic process of inquiry."[105] Scientists must assume that the universe or nature: "does not play favorites, that miracles do not happen, and that there is no arcane or spiritual knowledge open only to a few."[106] Jacques Monod stated this truth even more dramatically. Science "assumes the universe ... is dispassionate of, indifferent to and unswayed by human concerns and beliefs about its nature."[107]

Even if one assumes the Big Bang theory coincides with the idea that God at least started the mechanism, it leads us nowhere. The hypothesis itself offers two outcomes, diametrically opposed physically, but united in the proposition that, in any event, the end will be disastrous. Either there is not enough matter in the universe to slow down its continual expansion, in which event, as the rest of the universe draws away from us, we will eventually be confronted by the cold and the dark. Or, there is enough matter not only to slow expansion down but to cause it all to converge on the point of origin and thus implode the universe.[108] One cannot obtain any kind of sensible master plan from a universe which is fated eventually to self-destruct.

And yet, as Lévi-Strauss reminds us, a great many men have not abandoned morality or hope of working for improving the conditions for mankind, even though they believe life for them ends with the grave.[109] To be honest, however, one of the brightest of those hopes was the secular idea of progress and it has been pretty much demolished. If the religious person seizes upon this to ask: "And where does that leave you, or the secular humanists?," we have to confess uncertainty. Some questions cannot be solved before nightfall and others not at all.

Just as Shirley MacLaine popularized the obscurities of the New Age religious and philosophical bent to the general public, so Jacques Cousteau perhaps did more to acquaint the laymen with the proper relation between science and nature than any other public figure of our time. He was at work prior to the Sixties with a plea which might be translated to mean: "Help keep the Mediterranean Sea alive." His divers discovered large areas off the coasts of Monaco which, once housing a teeming source and large variety of sea life, were now turned into a virtual desert. He proposed an inviolable sea museum of six square miles off Monaco. But this did not interrupt the progressive deterioration of a hundred sick beaches off the Côte d'Azur near Nice. Hundreds of tourists were bathing where the city's sewers emptied human feces and urine, threatening thirty or more forms of illness. Cousteau constantly trumpeted the threat that one day there would no longer be any living fish, nor crustaceans, nor sea urchins, nor jellyfish. Nothing would exist save fungi, protozoa and pathogenic viruses. Then no one will dare put a toe in the poisonous mess.[110]

From reading the reflections of this gentle and learned man, we can identify at least three of the major causes of this creeping pollution of Paradise: 1) the right-to-life movement, or the right of overpopulation, 2) the profit motive and 3) the right to pollute unless and until authorities can prove it is disastrous for public health.

By 1960, Cousteau had distinguished himself as a conservationist operating upon scientific principles at a time when many celebrated scientists were behaving in a non-rational manner. Even then, it was the problem of disposing of nuclear wastes. First of all, he had faith in knowledge, not faith in faith: "The only remedy is knowledge which has pulled man through so far."[111] Second, he cautioned French politicians "about the dangers inherent in placing poison in the sea without knowing what the effect would be."[112] But, meanwhile, at a scientific convention in 1959, "a scientist gave a paper advocating burying irradiated material in the desert. Another wanted to parachute it onto the Greenland icecap. Others destined it to guarded caves and abandoned salt mines. However, the most popular refuse dump with the scientists was the ocean." Not to worry overmuch, thought Cousteau. The next day a celebrated marine scientist was to speak and all would be set to rights. Much to his chagrin, however, this marine specialist also favored the sea as the garbage dump for atomic materials. Later he explained to

Cousteau his reasons for the curious reversal of form. The biggest problem for the future was the population explosion which eventually would reach 100 billion persons. The natural resources of land and sea to feed that many would fall alarmingly short. But, if we concentrated on atomic energy we would have enough energy to run factories to produce the protein needed to feed all mankind. That is why we have to go all out on atomic energy even if it means closing the sea to all human uses, including navigation.[113] It would be difficult to identify a more dramatic illustration of the dangers posed to humanity.

Cousteau's fears for the Mediterranean Sea affect us all deeply. Since 1960, a laboratory in the museum at Monaco has taken daily readings of radioactivity in the atmosphere and rainfall. When both major powers resumed bomb testing in that year, the measurement of radioactive content of rain at Monaco jumped to more than a thousand times the previous levels. At least two-thirds of the atmospheric fall-out goes directly into the oceans and more soon follows in land drain-offs.[114] Furthermore, a little-known fact which should be understood by all is that water moves: in ninety years not a drop of water currently in the Mediterranean will still be there. Meanwhile, poisons like DDT are found in the livers of penguins in the Antartic, pollution-free to this point.[115]

Finally, Cousteau placed the blame indirectly upon capitalism in the West: "But those in power make only short-term decisions. They put a Band-aid where there is cancer. *For them the only thing that counts is economic productivity during the next four or five years* (Italics ours). While they are obliged by public opinion to do something, they cheat. They commit to something and don't do it or do it badly."[116] Curiously, however, Cousteau was thereby describing the behavior of Soviet bureaucracy just as accurately as that in the West.

While a great many scientists now openly share Cousteau's view, it was William T. Blackstone who best delineated the major errors in our assumptions which gripped us all both on the eve of World War II and after: 1) the belief that we can exploit the environment without restriction 2) that the production of goods is more important than the people who make and use them 3) that nature will provide unlimited resources 4) we, therefore, have no obligation to future generations to preserve them 5) the continual increases in human population are desirable and there is an inviolable right to have as many children as one pleases 6) the answer to the few problems about technology is more technology and 7) the gross inequality in the distribution of goods and services is acceptable.[117]

It is imperative to understand virtually all the fallacies in the above paragraph rested upon Biblical Genesis. The ethical and/or religious justification for man's exploitation of both his environment and animal life, concluded Arnold Toynbee, lay in the Biblical injunction: "Be fruitful and multiply and replenish the Earth and subdue it." As that authority sadly confessed, for people brought up in the Judeo-Christian tradition, it is going to be difficult to regain the necessary awe and respect for nature which was shattered by pronouncements in Genesis.[118] But, unfortunately, science had given these Hebraic injunctions respectability. In 1940, in a magazine article entitled, "Boundless Frontiers of Science," appeared seven irreligious words: "Man must outdo nature in the laboratory."[119]

It is difficult to say when the great bulk of scientists swung around to viewpoints of the Sierra Club, Greenpeace and others,[120] but Barry Commoner adequately explained the difficulties in the process. Scientists were trained to observe or speculate about what happened in fairly simple events, i.e. "how one particle bounces off another, or how moledule A reacts with molecule B. Confronted by a situation as complex as the environment ... we are likely ... to attempt to reduce it in our minds to a set of separate simple events, in the hope that their sum will somehow picture the whole. The existence of the environment crisis warns us that this is an illusory hope."[121]

What we can do, however, is to point out highlights in the conversion process and Arnold Toynbee's admonition is one of the first called to mind. "We have discovered," he wrote, "that, in the last resort, we are still as much at nature's mercy as our pre-human ancestors were. If man de-natures the air and water and soil of this planet, he is not going to be able to survive. Nature is still our mistress; she, not man, has the last word."[122] Lévi-Strauss put the same attitude in the form of a question. Like maggots in a flour sack who become so numerous they poison the flour and bring on their own extinction, will man eliminate himself the same way through poisoning his environment?[123]

This deep psychological change on the part of science may have been due to the slow but increasing realization that there was a basic fallacy in the old assumption that nature was infinitely malleable, responsive and inexhaustible in her capacities and resources as a handmaiden to technology.

Although the conservation movement in America had its origins with George Perkins Marsh in 1864, his book contained an ambiguous message. He did warn in tampering with nature men might destroy himself through wanton destruction and proliferous waste, thus making the world an unfit habitation for man. From our standpoint, however, he seriously compromised the entire conservation movement when he confessed a belief technology could adequately feed the world's population, however large that might be.[124] That fiction persisted for the next hundred years. As late as the Seventies in this century the argument was popular that, since we demonstrated our ability to go to the moon, we could solve any problem, given enough money and brain power.[125]

Only recently has that fiction been exposed. Charles Hartshorne stated the unpalatable truth. Now it is clear that not only does technological man expand at the expense of others - the history of Western imperialism - but in principle he faces limits beyond which his own expansion is impossible or self-defeating.[126]

Empirical studies also attacked the specious notion future productivity was unlimited under the aegis of technology and a pliant nature. One of the most reliable concluded the "central message is that in the past decade the 5 billion inhabitants of the world have reemphasized their ability to strain ecological systems to the breaking point."[127] As one might expect, the biggest increases in population "are in the poorest countries where environmental erosion and pollution will continue." To the present 5.3 billion world population, almost 100 million are added each year, thus creating another China by the year 2000. This will be accompanied by an exhaustion of natural resources, malnutrition and poverty.[128] Since 1970, for example, Africa's steadily declining ability to feed itself was dramatized by famine in Ethiopia. Its chief causes were human overpopulation and widespread erosion and desertification caused by forest clearance and excessive cattle population.[129] Likewise, famine in the Sahel was the result of overpopulation on the borders of the Sahara by both nomads and their livestock. Once grasses were cropped out, the desert rapidly advanced. As fast, nomads drifted southward with their destructive livestyles intact.[130] In Brazil, which suffers both from overpopulation and mass poverty, the systematic industrial attack upon tropical forests threatens the regenerative source of a quarter of the oxygen in the world's air.[131] Similar misguided practices elsewhere resulted in the loss of 40 percent of the world's diversity of species which live in tropical forests.[132]

Naturally, not all grievous offenses against nature originated in the poverty-stricken countries in the Third World. These were borrowed from the practices of advanced nations. For example, under the private property system, agriculture in the United States had the impact of a destructive or extractive industry. Between 1882 and 1952, it destroyed half the top soil on 38.5 percent of all cultivated land. This forced out of cultivation 3.45 billion acres. Since 1952, the level of violence to nature has rapidly accelerated, due to the fact that in a market system high agricultural yields per acre are very desirable. But these "are obtained at a price of increasing the expenditure of energy and the disturbance of water, nitrogen, and carbon cycles, which is untenable in the long run. There are water shortages everywhere. The dilemma is further aggravated by the energy crisis."[133] Currently, sulphuric emissions from industrial plants in the Midwest are believed to be destroying forests, streams and animal life in Canada and northeastern United States.[134] Skeptics think emissions from automobiles - or organic solvents - produce ozone which may be more responsible for the sickness evident in German forests, and inferentially for those in the United States.[135] While nature may produce about half of the world's acidity,[136] the damaging aspect of the acid rain problem belongs, unfortunately, to man. The same is true with regard to the threat of extinction in the next decade to the Everglades National Park in Florida. This 150-mile marsh river from Lake Okeechobee to the Gulf of Mexico has been killed by real estate development, farming and overpopulation in the last twenty years. The present lack of water threatens to turn the marsh into prairie-like grass and trees that could make it into a plains area.[137]

Not surprisingly, devastating practices like this the world over have reached the point they may be causing very undesirable climatic changes.[138] For four billion years nature had "a queer kind of rationality and expectedness about it," accompanied by a "slow pace of inorganic life." Now, man, however, has succeeded in altering climatic change at a rate of from ten to sixty times that nature set and maintained.[139] Indeed, the invention and extended use of nuclear devices "may have actually marked the beginning of the end of nature." By thus polluting the atmosphere, we changed the weather and "deprived nature of its independence."[140] Man-made chlorine is believed by scientists to be responsible for alarming decreases in the atmospheric ozone since 1969. Since ozone filters out damaging ultra violet solar rays, a sharp increase in skin cancer is predicted.[141] Scientists report that Antarctica experienced another gaping hole in the protective ozone layer again in 1990, one which is almost as bad as in the previous years of 1987 and 1989.[142] They have also discovered a 15 percent decrease in protective layers over Macquarie Island, 800 miles south of Tasmania.[143] Since the penetration of ultra violet rays increase temperatures at earth levels, it seems logical that in 1989 the world's average temperature of 57.6 degrees Fahrenheit was the highest "in 130 years over which reliable records have been kept." This rise in earth temperature jeopardizes precious water supplies. It is predicted that, at present rates, deforestation, top soil erosion and desertification "will eliminate one-third of the world's productive land over the next ten years."[144] Meanwhile, coral reefs all over the world appear to be starving due to warmer seas. This will have a drastic impact upon all life there.[145]

It was data such as this which caused scientists and environmentalists to write off the idea of progress in a materialistic sense, the essence of the philosophy itself. They predicted "increases in consumption at the rate of the last hundred years is wholly impossible for the next twenty years, let alone the next hundred. A century ago, there were just over one-quarter as many people alive as today. Each person ... used only one-tenth ... of the fuel we use today. So the earth has to consume and recycle waste products forty times the tonnage of a hundred years ago. ... It is possible that mankind will drown in his own ordure; this will be true if the causes of pollution are not arrested and reversed rapidly. There are not only too many people in many parts of the world, but they are consuming too much...."[146] Instead of worshipping perpetual growth as the economists did in rich countries, scientists likened it to the spread of a cancer cell. Normal growth, they concluded, "must cease at maturity."[147]

While it is not believed checking human population, or reducing births to less than deaths, would eliminate all environmental problems - such as global warming, acid rain, depletion of the ozone layer[148] - none could be solved without a stabilized population.[149] The reason was simple enough: "Humanity cannot now be supported on income - that is, renewable resources. Civilization endures only by using up a one-time bonanza of 'capital' - especially deep agricultural soils, Ice Age ground water and 'biodiversity' (populations and species of other organisms that are working parts of life-support systems). ... We are squandering our inheritance and calling it 'growth.'"[150]

If these arguments impressed us as reasonable, they were rejected by traditional American capitalists. President Reagan distinguished himself by opposing all of them through his eight-year reign.[151] In Texas where the environment "is viewed mostly as a place to drill or hunt,"[152] a great many would no doubt have agreed "environmentalists are almost always hostile to freedom, individual rights and capitalism." It was the last named "that frees man from man, the system that encourages man ... to preserve his values ... capitalism."[153]

Undeterred by objections from these rugged individualists, André Gorz had the courage to say simply but graphically that other scholars implied: "We know *our* world is ending; that if we go on as before, the oceans and rivers will be sterile, the soil infertile, the air unbreathable in the cities...."[154]

Once, however, scientists realized the world's natural resources were sharply limited, and human reproduction was rampant, the zero growth rate concept became the generally accepted solution.[155]

As far as the exponents of free enterprise capitalism are concerned, scientists might just as well have advocated public acceptance of Marx's

Das Kapital. This is because free, unplanned, wildcatting development is largely responsible for our ecological plight today. That responsibility, of course, must be shared with the Society for Human Procreation Unlimited.

When Aleksandr Solzhenitsyn took the bold step of advocating zero-population growth, he attacked those who believed in the magic apple, or that a dozen worms can keep nibbling it forever without diminishing it. A civilization greedy for perpetual material progress has now choked and is on its last legs. Unless we relinquish the specious idea of continual economic progress, there will be catastrophic disaster by the middle of the next century. The biosphere is apt to become unfit even in our own life time. Even if future prospecting uncovers material resources two or three times as big as we imagined, even if agriculture doubles production and man succeeds in harnessing nuclear energy which is also safe to dispose of, we are sure to run into disaster on one of two counts. Either we will exhaust our resources or destroy our environment. Thus, we will have paid the penalty for having squandered our raw materials, destroyed our fertile soil and contaminated our large cities with waste belts around our industrial centers.[156] Both the super powers, Soviet Russia and the United States, are equally guilty because both countries accepted the same false gods, i.e., bigness and growth.[157]

While noteworthy how many scholars agreed with the zero growth option,[158] we were attracted by those exponents of it who also pointed out this present age of bigness and growth failed to procure happiness for the masses. Since this was explicitly promised by the idea of progress, it must be considered as a very significant social and economic failure.[159] Since a higher GNP (gross national product) does not automatically result in an increase in social well-being, it thus should not be used as a measuring rod for assessing economic welfare. Some economists and ecologists suggest that a stationary economy may well be best for not only man's environment but for the quality of life in the long run. Human values thus tend to persist over purely material ones, or those placed upon things or objects rather than on man himself.[160]

Most intriguing, however, are those, like Robert L. Heilbroner, who predict that, within the next three to four generations, international capitalism will have entered the danger zone of climatic change, thereby launching a post-industrial society.[161] Because of the combustible combination of over-population, dwindling resources, inequities of rewards between advanced nations and the Third World, and the availability of "obliterative" firepower,[162] nature will present us with a conscious choice for change or final disaster. One need only mention a few possibilities here, such as industrial asphyxiation, large-scale urban temperature inversions, massive crop failures, critical resources shortages and, of course, wars.[163]

Also compelling great interest is the logic of André Gorz who dared criticize the boldest concept modern political economy would come up with, and that was the "zero growth" option; such criticism was on the grounds that it did not go far enough.[164] He, of course, agrees that it was "the ideological and social bankruptcy of the market based production" which eventuated in the current "crisis of the capitalist lifestyle."[165] But merely to go from a system which squandered critical resources for immediate profit to one which promised merely to refrain from those excesses was not enough. "The point is not to refrain from consuming more and more, but to consume less and less - there is no other way of conserving the available resources for future generations."[166]

Such critics offer radically different and tantalizing visions of this future post-industrial society, but here we only have time to point out two glimpses. Gorz argues that the "only way to live better is to produce less, to consume less, to work less, to live differently."[167] Heilbroner amplifies this sort of perspective. The new "societal view of production and consumption must stress parsimonious, not prodigal, attitudes. Resource-consuming and heat-generating processes must be regarded as necessary evils ... to be relegated to as small a portion of economic life as possible. This implies a sweeping reorganization of production ... that would seem to imply the end of the giant factory, the huge office, perhaps of the urban complex."[168]

There is little doubt that, as society is presently constituted, educated, propagandized and governed, such revolutionary postulates are unpalatable and, therefore, rejected outright. As Marx observed, the last or present form of social order regards all its historical predecessors as necessary stages leading to its own establishment, is generally incapable of self-criticism, and certainly unable to envision itself as socially significant only in the fact that it leads in time to another and different social order.[169] Whatever else one could say in the defense of historical Christianity and Western industrial capitalism, one would have to admit they certainly fall into this category both of attempting to idolize and perpetuate themselves forever. Both fail to grasp one of the oldest and wisest concepts in the world: "And this too shall pass away."

Using historical perspective, we perceive how we arrived at our present advantage point from which to make an educated guess. As critics correctly pointed out, Marx was wrong when concluding that the working classes would rise above selfish nationalism to achieve international brotherhood.[170] Curiously, Big Business succeeded in a world outlook where workers failed because they transcended nationalism, scorning loyalty to their workers and place of national origin, and subordinated everything to concepts of growth and profit.[171] Thus, they had absolutely no vision of what Buckminster Fuller called spaceship earth. But, as one of his most prominent admirers interpreted it: "The most rational way of considering the whole human race today is to see it as the ship's crew of a single spaceship on which all of us, with a remarkable combination of security and vulnerability, are making a pilgrimage through infinity."[172] It is precisely because both international capitalism and socialism failed to grasp that simple concept that we may say it will be the opportunity of post-industrial society to do so.

For those who can afford to linger long enough to contemplate the social values of that post-industrial society, Heilbroner explains how it completes our full circle, from primitive values, to their extinction and, finally, revival. "It is therefore possible," he concluded, "that a post-industrial society would also turn in the direction of many pre-industrial societies - toward the exploration of inner states of experience rather than the outer world of fact and material accomplishment. Tradition and ritual ... would probably once again assert their ancient claims as the guides to and solace for life. The struggle for individual achievement, especially for materials ends, is likely to give way to the acceptance of communally organized and ordained roles."[173]

In the short run - as one approaches the year 2,000 - there exists another probability, one where the cult of the true believer will peak sharply. Remember that his is the only Western group which characteristically thrives amid social disorganization and individual alienation. This probability involves the revival of the "old and absurd idea of the world dying in a single day." When, as likely, "the earth becomes a model not of permanence but of sudden, unexpected, and devastating change [predictable climatic changes], the number of people seeking an explanation in obscure Scripture ... will certainly increase. The chance confluence of this turmoil with the approaching millennium will bring out the low-budget prophets on truly record numbers."[174] Thus, we "are probably in for a siege of apocalytic and fanatical creeds."[175] Finally, it is imperative to realize that this segment of Christian theology is on the same philosophical level as that of The Ghost dances of the Plains Indians in 1890 (see vol. I, Chapter IX CULTURE CLASH, ft. 137).

And so, we have come full circle, exiting by the same door as in we went. If one assumes a religious posture, it is possible to believe the primitive was right. The gods may and do punish those who boast of their conquests while their feet are still upon the necks of the conquered.[176] Both exponents of Christianity and the idea of progress displayed pride and arrogance at their moments of triumph from the sixteenth to the twentieth century. Could this be the crime, the sin, the hubris for which Heaven itself decreed that pagan ideas and attitudes would survive the demise of their many cultures at the hands of the West?

The lessons of archaeology, of anthropology, of history all warn against the folly of boasting about power and immortality, whether of the civilization itself, or its ideology, or both. But none put it more aptly than Percy Bysshe Shelley:

> *I met a traveller from an antique land*
> *Who said:*
> *Two vast and trunkless legs of stone*
> *Stand in the desert...Near them, on the*
> *sand,*

Half sunk, a shattered visage lies, whose
frown,
And wrinkled lip, and sneer of cold
command,
Tell that its sculptor well those passions
read
Which yet survive, stamped on these
lifeless things,
The hand that mocked them, and the heart
that fed:
And on the pedestal these words appear:
"My name is Ozymandias, king of kings:
Look on my works, ye Mighty, and
despair!"
Nothing beside remains. Round the decay
Of that colossal wreck, boundless and
bare
The lone and level sands stretch far
away.[177]

Footnotes

1   Bill McKibben, *The End of Nature* (New York, Random House, 1989), 151, 154.

2   Cyril C. Caldwell, *Henry Ford*. Illustrated by Ed Ashe (New York, Julian Messner Inc., 1947), 164-165.

3   The great contrast between the primitive attitude and that of the West toward nature and technology has been best captured by Barry Commoner: "Among primitive people, a person is seen as a dependent part of nature, a frail reed in a harsh world governed by natural laws that must be obeyed if he is to survive. Pressed by this need, primitive peoples can achieve a remarkable knowledge of their environment. ...All this [technology] leads us to believe that we have made our own environment and no longer depend on the one provided by nature. ...we have become enticed into a nearly fatal illusion: that through our machines we have at last escaped from dependence on the natural environment." *The Closing Circle. Nature, Man and Technology* (New York, Alfred A. Knopf, 1971), 15. If, however, the reader wishes to know about primitive exceptions from the rule we refer him to the following: René Dubos, "Franciscan Conservatism versus Benedictine Stewartship," 114-136 in *Ecology and Religion in History*, edited by David and Eileen Spring (New York, Harper Torchback, Harper and Row, 1974).

4   *The Anatomy of Revolution* (New York, Prentice-Hall, 1952), 45, 49-50.

5   Foreword to *Tönnies, Community and Society (Gemeinschaft and Gesellschaft)*. Translated and edited by Charles P. Loomis (East Lansing, the Michigan State University Press, 1957), x.

6   Despite the extension of the political franchise which slows down "the always widening hiatus between the wealth monopoly of the narrow and real Gesellschaft and the poverty of the people, but it cannot change the essential character of the hiatus. Indeed, it deepens it, spreading and strengthening the consciousness of the 'social question.'" *Ibid.*, 259.

7   *The Philosophy of Money*. Translated by Tom Bottomore and David Frisby (London, Routledge and Kegan Paul, 1978), 297-298, 443-444.

8   *Ibid.*, 484.

9   *Ibid.*, 482.

10   Wachtel, *Poverty of Affluence*, 70. Orders, decisions and plans that are unethical are carried out by underlings "because they feel they have no choice; they feel powerless to disobey, regardless of the intent of the order." Simon and Eitzen, *Elite Deviance*, 236-237.

11   Wachtel, *Poverty of Affluence*, 166-167.

12   Peter and Brigitte Berger, Hansfried Kellner, *The Homeless Mind. Modernization and Consciousness* (New York, Vintage Books, a Division of Random House, 1974), 195-

196.

13   *Escape from Freedom,* (New York, Farrar and Rinehart, 1941), 240, 253. As a result, concluded Fromm, the most pressing need of this pathetic individual is to find somebody to whom he can surrender, as quickly as possible, that precious gift of freedom which frightens hell out of him. *Ibid.,* 151-512.

14   Kathleen Agena, "The Return of Enchantment," 67-80 in The New York *Times* Magazine, November 27, 1983, 76. My own first brush with the magic of the computer occurred the night of the presidential elections of 1952. Four years previously, I sat up virtually all night waiting for the final Truman-Dewey results. Consequently, when invited to a friend's house to watch the 1952 returns, on the race between Eisenhower and Stevenson, I was in no hurry to get there. When I arrived, he greeted me at the door at about 9:30 p.m. with the startling news that the computer conceded the election to the former. At that time about five to eight percent of the total vote was in. I was immediately shaken but did not abandon ship until hours later. The thing that dazzled me so was that the predicted percentage victory ultimately materialized, right on the mark so to speak.

15   Agena, "The Return of Enchantment," *loc. cit.,* 68, 76, 78-80.

16   *The Future as History* (New York, Harper & Brothers, 1960), 169.

17   "The Crisis of Western Societies," 17-28 in *Telos. A Quarterly Journal of Radical Thought,* No. 53, Fall, 1982.

18   Tom Schactman, *Decade of Shocks: Dallas to Watergate, 1963-1974* (New York, Poseidon Press, 1974), 289.

19   Jack Beatty, Washington Post-Los Angeles Times, "Secular culture too weak even to laugh off the likes of Pat Robertson," in the Kansas City *Times,* January 29, 1988, A-11.

20   McKibben, *The End of Nature,* 79.

21   *The True Believer, Thoughts on the Nature of Mass Movements* (New York, Harper & Brothers, 1951), 129.

22   *Ibid.,* xi.

23   Angus Hall, *Strange Cults* (Garden City, New York, Doubleday, 1976), 142. "... the function of the cult is to assuage individual suffering from common human viscissitudes. Limited in power as each discovers himself to be, group-adherence promises omnipotence; religion is an attempt to overcome and lack of equipment to deal with a threatening situation alone." La Barre, *Ghost Dance,* Introduction, 14.

24   *The True Believer,* 12.

25   *Ibid.,* 80-81.

26   Willa Appel, *Cults in America. Programmed for Paradise* (New York, Holt,

Rinehart and Winston, 1983), 38.

27   *American Now. The Anthropology of a Changing Culture* (New York, Simon and Schuster, 1981), 173.

28   *Ibid.*, 150. Most Hindus, for example, are less interested in achieving transcendental bliss than in ample rains, concern for a sick child or for their cow to deliver a healthy calf. *Ibid.*, 151.

29   Douglas W. Johnson, "Trends and Issues Shaping the Religious Future," 93-110 in Jackson W. Carroll, Douglas W. Johnson, Martin E. Marty, *Religion in America, 1950 to the Present* (New York, Harper & Row, 1979), 98.

30   Otto Friedrich, "New Age Harmonies," 62-72 in *Time*, December 7, 1987, 69.

31   Allan Dundes, professor of anthropology and folklore at the University of California at Berkeley, concluded: "A lot of it is a cop-out, an escape from reality, an anti-intellectual movement defying reality." Friedrich, "New Age Harmonies," in *ibid.*, 72.

32   *Ibid.*, 64.

33   *Ibid.*, 65.

34   Richard Blow, United Features Syndicate (Reprint from the *New Republic*, "New Age Gung-ho but vague," in the Kansas City *Star*, January 24, 1988, H-3. In Shirley's forthcoming book, *Going Within*, she speaks of "techniques of meditation, visualization, color therapy, sound therapy, how to work with crystals, how to work with colored jewelry...." Friedrich, "New Age Harmonies," *loc. cit.*, 72.

35   Asian religions emphasized inner experience as contrasted with external deeds, harmony with nature as opposed to its exploitation and intense personal relations with one's guru rather than our impersonal ones with minister or priest. As Berkeley sociologist, Robert Bellah, put it, the awakening marks the acceptance of "Asian spirituality" as an antidote for the Western "Utilitarian individualism" of Jeremy Bentham and other nineteenth century thinkers. Harris, *America Now*, 143-144. See also George Reed, "Astronomy & Astrology. East vs. West," 90-95 in *Astronomy*, vol. 14, No. 1, January 1986, 95.

36   "Christianity is universally rejected by those aligned with the New Age." Robert J.L. Burrows, "Americans Get Religion in a New Age," 17-23 in *Christianity Today*, May 16, 1986, vol. 30, No. 8, 22. Asian religions generally stress a belief in reincarnation. Any one who believes he is periodically revived to live again has no need of the Christ to resurrect him. Twenty-three percent of Americans affirm they believe in reincarnation whereas three decades ago it was unknown, as well as unpronouncable. *Ibid.*, 17.

37   Marvin Henry Harper, *Gurus, Swamis, & Avataras, Spiritual Masters & Their American Disciples* (Philadelphia, Pa., the West-minster Press, 1972), 242.

38   *Ibid.*, 242.

39   Friedrich, "New Age Harmonies," *loc. cit.*, 62.

40   *America Now*, 149.

41   Richard Blow, "New Age Gung-ho but vague," *loc. cit.*

42   Harris, *America Now*, 147.

43   *Ibid.*, 157.

44   The Washington Post, "Truth about crystals is cloudy: Rocks of magic force - or farce?" in the Kansas City *Times*, November 26, 1987, I-8.

45   *Don't Fall Off the Mountain* (New York, W.W. Norton, 1970), 126-127.

46   *You Can Get There From Here* (New York, W.W. Norton, 1975), 199-200.

47   *Don't Fall Off the Mountain*, 125.

48   *Ibid.*, 187.

49   *Ibid.*, 180-181.

50   *Ibid.*, 128.

51   Jeff Rovib, "Shirley!" 109-151 in *Ladies' Home Journal*, vol. 102, No. 8, August 1985, 150-151.

52   In *Don't Fall Off the Mountain*, 224.

53   "... we are all God ...we have the attributes of God." Rodney Clapp, "Cults: A Reality that has Staggered Our Imaginations," 50, 56 in *Christianity Today*, vol. 26, No. 1, January 1, 1982, 56. Shirley often talks with her "higher self" whom she sees as at one with God. Adrianna Stassinopoulos, "Shirley MacLaine," 28-41 in *Ladies' Home Journal*, vol. 101, No. 5, May 1984, 41. By recognizing that you are God, "you can create your own reality." Richard Blow, "New Age movement is gung-ho but vague," *loc. cit.*

54   "Shirley MacLaine Talks About Spirit vs. Action," in *Ms.*, vol. 14, No. 6, December 1985, 100.

55   Charles Leerhsen with Janet Huck, "Out There with Shirley," in *Newsweek*, October 21, 1985, 78.

56   Friedrich, "New Age Harmonies," *loc. cit.*, 63-64.

57   Peter Turnbull, Scripps Howard News Service, "'Communion' with other Worlds," in the Kansas City *Star*, February 22, 1988, C-4.

58   *History of the Idea of Progress* (New York, Basic Books, 1980), 352-355.

59   "Millenarian activity is a classic response when people feel frustrated and confused, when they face changes that violate cherished aspirations." Appel, *Cults in America*, 8; also 17, 166.

60   William Robertson, Knight-Ridder Newspapers, "Passion and the Preachers," in the Kansas City *Star*, March 6, 1988, K-1.

61   Billy Graham, Tribune Media Services in the Kansas City *Star*, March 14, 1988, C-5.

62   Lowell D. Streiker, *The Gospel Time Bomb. Ultrafundamentalism and the Future of America* (Buffalo, New York, Prometheus Books, 1984), 92.

63   Streiker, *Gospel Time Bomb*, 79. The Bible is the only book anyone needs to know, and any secular learning or science not based on the Scriptures is worthless. *Ibid.*, 192.

64   "... nothing has ever been more insupportable for man than freedom. ... There are three powers on earth ... able to conquer and to hold captive forever the conscience of these important rebels for their happiness - those powers are miracle, mystery and authority." Fydor Dostoevsky, *The Brothers Karamazov. A Novel in four parts*. Translation by Constance Garnett, revised, with an introduction by Avrahm Yarmolinsky (New York, The Heritage Press, 1961), 191.

65   Alcohol, tobacco, premarital sex and sometimes even dancing, were the chief targets of the attack. Joe Bell, "Are Teens *Really* turning to Religion?" 234-235 plus in *Seventeen*, March 1985, 268.

66   Haynes Johnson, The Washington Post, "Is this nation in decline - again?" in the Kansas City *Star*, March 6, 1988, K-5; Donald Kaul, Tribune Media News, "Anyone reminded a bit of a fallen-away tent preacher in 'Grapes of Wrath?", in the Kansas City *Times*, February 27, 1988, A-23; Ellen Goodman, Washington Post Writers Group "Two sets of answers to question posed by Swaggart: 'Why? Why?'" in the Kansas City *Star*, March 1, 1988, A-11; John Welter, Carroboro, N.C., "Swaggart demise inspires a little light verse," in the Kansas City *Star*, March 3, 1988, A-10; Cal Thomas, Los Angeles Times Syndication, "Forgiveness is one thing," in the Kansas City *Times*, March 4, 1988, A-11; C.W. Gusewelle, "Pure purging tears, or those of a crocodile?" in the Kansas City *Star*, February 26, 1988, A-2.

67   Fred J. Cook, *The Nightmare Decade. The Life and Times of Senator Joe McCarthy* (New York, Random House, 1971), 68, 243; John G. Adams, *Without Precedent. The Story of the Death of McCarthyism* (New York, W.W. Norton, 1983), 92-93; Richard M. Fried, *Men Against McCarthy* (New York, Columbia University Press, 1976), 5; Jack Anderson and Ronald W. May, *McCarthy. The Man, the Senator, the 'Ism.'* (Boston, Beacon Press, 1952), 192-193.

68   The Admission came from a Christian historian, K.S. Latourette, See Hofer, *True Believer*, 106.

69   Harris, *America Now*, 181.

70   Joel Carpenter, "Geared to the Times, but Anchored to the Rock," 44-47 in *Christianity Today*, November 8, 1985, 47.

71   *Ibid.*, 44, 46.

72   *The Future as History* (New York, Harper & Brothers, 1960), 180.

73   *Ibid.,* 176.

74   *Ibid.,* 94.

75   *Ibid.,* 185.

76   A typical but fair account was that of William D. Dinges, "The Vatican Report on Sects, Cults and New Religious Movements," in *America,* vol. 155, No. 7, September 27, 1986, 145-147, 154. There was a vast new market among the psychologically deprived - the products of divorce, disruption in the labor market, alienating mobility - or all the wholesale confusion and the aimless drifting one currently sees in society. Strieker, *Gospel Time Bomb,* 176, 180. See also Harris, *America Now,* 157-158.

77   *True Believer,* 14.

78   *Gospel Time Bomb,* 86.

79   One need not uproot themselves from home, job or family in order to participate in the healing and soothing powers of a caring and supportive fellowship. Harris, *America Now,* 158. This has great appeal to those who are weak, neglected and isolated. *Ibid.,* 156.

80   Jack Beatty, Washington Post-Los Angeles Times, "Secular culture too weak to laugh off the likes of Pat Robertson," in the Kansas City *Times,* January 29, 1988, A-11.

81   Harris *America Now,* 159.

82   *Ibid.,* 161.

83   *Ibid.,* 159.

84   *Ibid.,* 164.

85   "Modern Fundamentalism," 133-135 in *America,* vol. 155, No. 7, September 27, 1986, 135.

86   Harris, *America Now,* 172.

87   Douglas W. Johnson, "Trends and Issues Shaping the Religious Future," 93-110 in *Religion in America. 1950 to the Present,* 99. Many of these youths had been involved in the protest movements of the Sixties. *Ibid.,* 99. The same type of individual was involved in the origin of the New Age movement in California. Richard Blow "Gung-ho but vague," in the Kansas City, *Star,* January 24, 1988, H-3.

88   Joe Bell, "Are Teens *Really* Turning to Religion?" *loc. cit.,* 268.

89   Harper, *Gurus, Swamis,* 245.

90   Philosophy in a New Key (Cambridge, Harvard University Press, 1957), 226.

91   "Our whole life is startlingly moral. There is never an instant's truce between virtue and vice. Goodness is the only investment that never fails. ...Who knows what sort of life would result if we attained to purity? ... What avails it that you are Christian, if you are not purer than the heathen, if you deny yourself no more, if you are not more religious?" *Walden*. Edited and with an Introduction and Notes by Sherman Paul. Riverside Edition (New York, Houghton-Mifflin, 1957), 150-152.

92   Maxine Abrams, "Even kids are victims of stress," in the Kansas City *Star*, March 7, 1988, C-1. "There are 2 million children in this country younger than 12, and do you know what worries them most? They wonder whether a nuclear war may keep them from turning into teen-agers. They don't talk about it a lot, but in a recent poll 44 percent of them listed it as their No. 1 concern." Erma Bombeck, Universal Press Syndicate, "Try peace; kids deserve a future, too," in the Kansas City *Star*, April 15, 1988, D-3.

93   "Churches Respond to Teen Suicide," 436-439 in *Christian Century*, vol. 103, No. 15, April 30, 1986, 438.

94   "Youth Suicide," 39 in the *New York*, vol. 19, No. 22, June 2, 1986, 39.

95   Charlotte Ross was the author of the quotation. *Ibid.*

96   Joe Bell "Are Teens *Really* Turning to Religion?" *loc. cit.*, 268.

97   Harper, *Gurus, Swamis*, 246-247; Douglas W. Johnson, "Trends and Issues Shaping the Religious Future," *loc. cit.*, 98-99.

98   Bell, "Are Teens *Really* Turning to Religion?" *loc. cit.*, 270.

99   *Ibid.*, 268.

100   "Devotions," XVII, in *The Complete Poetry and Selected Prose of John Donne*. With an Introduction by Robert S. Hillyer (New York, Macmillan, 1946), 331-332.

101   *The Trinity and the Religious Experience of Man. Icon-Person-Mystery* (New York, Orbis Books, 1973), 28.

102   *The Closing Circle. Nature, Man, and Technology* (New York, A. Knopf, 1971), 33-46.

103   "The spirit is truly scientific, in the modern and strictest sense of the word. There is no superstition.... Instead, there is close, even minute observation of symptoms and their sequences, acute remarks on remedies, and recording ... of atmospheric phenomena, which preceeded or accompanied certain 'epidemics.'" General Introduction in *Hippocrates*. With an English Translation by W.H.S. Jones, 4 vols., I (Cambridge, Harvard University Press, 1948), xv. "Religious dogmas do not discover new knowledge for us, whereas scientific hypotheses do. The reason is that dogma must be believed unquestioned, since it insists it is ultimate knowledge itself; on the contrary, if dogma generates no new knowledge, it is not even good hypothesis! But scientific hypotheses must be reality tested.... ... wrongly ... phrased questions (absolutes, angelic spirits ...) get no answers at all from nature." La Barre, Introduction to *The Ghost Dance*, 23-24.

104   Introduction to *The Ghost Dance*, 24-25.

105   Dr. Norman F. Hall and Lucia K.B. Hall, "Is the War-between Science and Religion over?" 26-28, 32 in *The Humanist*, vol. 46, No. 3, May-June 1986, 26.

106   *Ibid.*, 27.

107   *Ibid.*, 27-28. "... extinction is the environment's norm: 99 percent of the creatures ever known to have come into existence have vanished. Nature doesn't care if the globe is populated by trilobites or thunder lizards or people or six-eyed telepathic slugs. ...Should man sour the environmental conditions now slanted in our favor, creatures will rise up in our stead that thrive on murky greenhouse air, or dine on compounds human metabolisms find toxic. The full measure of the ecosystems toughness is how little it needs us." Gregg Easterbrook, "Special Report. Cleaning Up," 26-42 in *Newsweek*, vol. 114, No. 4, July 24, 1989, 27.

108   David J. Darling, "Deep Time: The Fate of the Universe," 6-13 in *Astronomy*, vol. 14, No. 1, January 1986, 8-11. "Even astronomy's best model for the universe is linear. It began some 15 billion years ago with the Big Bang and is proceeding toward a cold, motionless end." George Reed, "Astronomy & Astrology. East vs. West," in *Astronomy*, vol. 14, No. 1, January 1986, 95.

109   *Structural Anthropology*, 336.

110   *The Living Sea* (New York, Harper & Row, 1963), 305-306; "Cousteau's Plea for the Mediterranean," 53 in *World Press Review*, vol. 34, No. 6, June 1987, 53.

111   *The Living Sea*, 312.

112   *Ibid.*, 311-312.

113   *Ibid.*, 306-307. Other scientists also postulate 100 billions of human beings on the earth planet by 2075. André Gorz, *Ecology as Politics* (Boston, South End Press, 1980), 93.

114   *Living Sea*, 312.

115   Timothy A. Murray, "A Conversation with Jacques Cousteau. 'We Face a Catastrophe' If the Oceans are not Cleaned Up," in *U.S. News and World Report*, vol. 98, No. 24, June 24, 1985, 68.

116   *Ibid.*

117   "Ethics and Ecology," 16-42 in *Philosophy and the Environmental Crisis* (Athens, University of Georgia Press, 1974), 16. "We have viewed nature as infinite, atomistically isolated, and capable of an infinitely extended range of transformations." Pete A.Y. Gunter, "The Big Thicket: A Case Study in Attitudes Toward the Environment," 117-137 in *ibid.*, 134.

118   "The Religious Background of the Present Environmental Crisis," 137-149 in *Ecology and Religion in History*, edited by David and Eileen Spring. Harper Torchback

(New York, Harper & Row, 1974), 141, 147.

119   Susan Q. Stranahan, "50 Years of Environment. The Nation Tries to Unfoul Its Nest," 29-33 in *National Wildlife*, vol. 26, No. 3, April-May 1986, 30. Garrett Hardin called this mood the worship of the Technological Imperative: "Whatever we can invent we are required to use." *Exploring New Ethics for Survival, The Voyage of Spaceship Beagle* (New York, Viking Press, 1972), 213.

120   The issue that the Sierra Club could not get the public excited about in the Seventies, toxic waste, has become the hottest environmental issue of the Eighties. Various groups have coalesced around such issues as ground-water contamination, waste dumps and, most recently, plans to incinerate garbage.... "It's the threat of something in their own backyard that gets people going." Seth Zukerman, "Environmentalism Turns 16," 368-370 in *The Nation*, vol. 243, No. 12, October 18, 1986, 369. See also Jan Knippers Black, "Greenpeace: The Ecological Warriors," 26-29 in *USA Today*, vol. 115, No. 2498, 28-29; Peter Dykstra, "Institutions. Greenpeace," 44-45 in *Environment*, vol. 28, No. 6, July-August, 1986, 44-45.

121   *The Closing Circle*, 21.

122   "The Religious Background of the Present Environmental Crisis," *loc. cit.*, 147.

123   Interview with Lévi-Strauss in the New York *Times*, December 31, 1969 from The Introduction, ft. 2 in *Ecology and Religion in History*.

124   *George Perkins Marsh, Man and Nature*, edited by David Lowenthal (Cambridge, The Belknap Press of Harvard University), 1965, ix-xx.

125   Lewis W. Moncrief, "The Cultural Basis for Our Environmental Crisis," 76-90 in *Ecology and Religion in History*, edited by David and Eileen Spring. Harper Torchback (New York, Harper & Row, 1974), 87. The belief that technology could solve most problems, and that man's intellectual and social capacity could solve the remainder, was the essence of the arrogance of humanism. Oscar Wilde represented a typical instance when he postulated two false propositions: 1) the world is immensely rich and suffers chiefly from maldistribution and 2) it is a simple matter to arrange that all unpleasant work be done by machinery. David Ehrenfeld, *The Arrogance of Humanism* (New York, Oxford University Press, 1978), 16-18.

126   "The Environmental Results of Technology," 69-78 in *Philosophy and the Environmental Crisis*, 71.

127   Lester Brown *et al*, "Report on Reports." *State of the World, 1984, 1985 and 1986 editions ... Progress Toward Sustainable Society*, 25-28 in *Environment*, vol. 28, No. 2, March 1986, 26.

128   Laura Scott, of the Editorial Staff, "People flood the earth," in the Kansas City *Star*, May 27, 1990, J-1.

129   Lester Brown, "Report on Reports," *loc. cit.*, 26.

130   André Gorz, *Ecology as Politics* (Boston, South End Press, 1981), 92.

131   Gorz, *Ecology as Politics*, 64. Recently, each year sees the disappearance of forty to fifty million acres of tropical forests. This is an area the size of Washington state. Forests absorb carbon dioxide, the source of the warming trend. Phillip Shabecoff, The New York Times, "Tropical forest loss is worsening," in the Kansas City *Star*, June 8, 1990, A-1, 4.

132   Brown, "Report on Reports," *loc. cit.*, 26.

133   Gorz, *Ecology as Politics*, 194.

134   "Acid rain involves the fewest uncertainties, since cause and cure are well known. Antiquated coal-fired power plants are the primary source of sulfur dioxide, the chief acid-rain precursor. Just 50 generating stations, most located in the Midwest, account for full half of U.S. sulfur pollution." Gregg Easterbrook, "Special Report. Cleaning Up," *loc. cit.*, 33. Considerable evidence from Canada and Northern Europe suggests waters rapidly improve as sulfur content is lowered. This is not true of some fish populations. J. M. Gunn and W. Keller, "Biological Recovery of an acid lake after reductions in industrial emissions of sulfur," 431-432 in *Nature*, vol. 435, May 31, 1990.

135   Dixie Lee Ray with Lou Guzzo, *Trashing the Planet. How Science Can Help Us Deal with Acid Rain, Depletion of the Ozone, and Nuclear Waste....* (Washington, D.C., Regnery, 1990), 59-61. See also "Special Report: Part 4. Acid Rain: No Harm Done?," 18-19 in *Consumers' Research*, vol. 73, March 1990.

136   "Most knowledgeable scientists agree that about half of all the atmospheric sulfur worldwide comes from natural causes, including volcanic eruptions. We also know that rainwater is naturally acidic...." Ray, *Trashing the Planet*, 66. "Many lakes, however, are acidic from natural causes. In Florida, for example, 22% of the lakes are acidic, despite the fact there is little sulphur emission in that area." "Acid Rain: No Harm Done?," *loc. cit.*

137   Tanya Barrientos, Knight-Ridder Newspapers, "Marshland is dying at the hands of humans," in the Kansas City *Star*, June 13, 1990, A-1.

138   Brown, "Report on Reports," *loc. cit.*, 26. Since the earth has clearly warmed up during the Eighties, the greenhouse theory is the most popular hypothesis used to explain that fact. It predicts gasses emitted by fossil fuels, like coal, gas and oil, will warm up the earth's atmosphere. These gasses, such as carbon dioxide, act as if they were greenhouse windows. They let in the light but contain the heat. Experts on climate predict a global warming of a few degrees could alter rainfall patterns, melt glaciers and flood coastal cities. A mere five degrees of temperature separates us from an ice age. Glenna Chui, Knight-Ridder Newspapers, "The world is warmer, but the trend is still uncertain," in the Kansas City *Star*, March 29, 1988, Tech-2.

139   McKibben, *End of Nature*, 99.

140   *Ibid.*, 58. See also Easterbrook, "Special Report, Clean Up," *loc. cit.*, 42.

141   The Washington Post, Washington, "International study shows surprising loss in ozone layer," in the Kansas City *Times*, March 16, 1988, A-9.

142   The New York Times, "Ozone hole reopens above Antartica," in the Kansas City *Star*, October 12, 1990, A-3.

143   Associated Press, London, "Ozone deterioration worsening, studies show at London session," in *ibid.*, June 21, 1990, A-7.

144   Mustafe Tolba, New Perspectives Quarterly, "World peace and stability depend now on restoring our balance with nature," in *ibid.*, April 2, 1990, B-7.

145   Scientists are not sure whether this represents a natural and periodic pattern, or the result of "a greenhouse effect caused by a buildup of pollutants." The Washington Post, Washington, "Coral reefs are dying, and scientists cite warmer seas," in *ibid.*, October 12, 1990, A-5.

146   Ironically, however, "less than twenty percent of the world's population probably live in a way which could be called truly sustainable." Henry Hobhouse, *Forces of Change. An Unorthodox View of History* (New York, Arcadia Publications. Little, Brown and Co., 1989), 7. See also *ibid.*, 234-235.

147   Paul R. and Anne H. Erlich, *The Population Explosion* (New York, Simon and Schuster, 1990), 161-163. Dave Foreman, chief lobbiest for the Wilderness Society, came to the conclusion "that the industrial empire was a cancer on the earth." McKibben, *End of Nature*, 179. "If industrial civilization is ending nature, it is not utter silliness to talk about ending - or, at least, transforming industrial civilization." McKibben, *End of Nature*, 186.

148   Paul R. and Anne H. Erlich, Washington Post-Los Angeles Times News Services, "Population expansion fuels every human problem on the planet," in the Kansas City *Star*, April 15, 1990, C-7.

149   *Ibid.* See also McKibben, *End of Nature*, 144, 181, 191.

150   Paul R. and Anne H. Erlich, "Population expansion fuels every human problem on the planet," *loc. cit.*

151   Fran Smith, Knight-Ridder Newspapers, "Author still stressed that fewer is better," in the Kansas City *Star*, April 12, 1990, F-8. Rather than being part of a conspiracy to despoil the land, Reagan is thought by some to be part of a generational problem. When he was growing up, "nature was the enemy, industrialization the ally. Nature spread disease and spoiled food, savaged the countryside with floods and dust bowls. Pesticides, pharmaceuticals, dams, and similar enterprises held out the hope of a more civilized existence. By the time the postwar generation came along nature's excesses had been tamed, replaced by industrial excess. Paved acreage was expanding resolutely, making nature seem the aggrieved party; an expanding body of information about synthetic substances suggested civilization conferred mixed blessings." Easterbrook, "Special Report, Cleaning Up," *loc. cit.*, 29.

152   Katie Sherrod, Fort Worth Star-Telegram, "Texas unsurprisingly among least prepared for spill," in the Kansas City *Star*, June 15, 1990, C-9.

153   Roger Fusselman, President, Ayn Rand Society, Kansas City chapter, "No Holiday

for man," in *ibid.*, May 5, 1990, C-8.

154   *Ecology as Politics*, 12. George Woodwell, Woods Hole marine biologist, declared there was "no question we have reached the end of the age of fossil fuel." The choice of doing nothing is not a choice. It leads to disaster. McKibben, *End of Nature*, 146.

155   Robert G. Burton, "A Philosopher Looks at the Population Bomb," 105-116 in *Philosophy and the Environmental Crisis*, edited by Blackstone, 111. See also Wilbur R. Jacobs, "Indians as Ecologists ... in American Frontier History," 46-64 in *American Indian Environments. Ecological Issues in Native American History*, edited by Christopher Vecsey and Robert W. Venables (Syracuse, Syracuse University Press, 1980), 60.

156   *Letter to the Soviet Leaders.* Translated from the Russian by Hilary Sternberg (New York, Harper & Row, 1975), 21-26.

157   *Ibid.*, 369-370.

158   The Nobel physics laureate Denis Gabor reflected the changed attitude of scientists. Few people dared, he observed sadly, face the obvious fact that exponential growth cannot be continued indefinitely. "Growth in my time, O Lord," seems to be their plaintive but futile cry. Wachtel, *Poverty of Affluence*, 50.

159   Nicholas Rescher, "The Environmental Crisis and the Quality of Life," 90-104 in *Philosophy and the Environmental Crisis*, edited by Blackstone, 93-95, 100.

160   William T. Blackstone, "Ethics and Ecology," 16-42 in *ibid.*, 37-40.

161   *An Inquiry into the Human Prospect.* (New York, W. W. Norton, 1974), 128-129. "Some experts ... argue that the climate can suddenly - within a century or less - flip into an entirely different state. Indeed, they say that evidence recently drawn from cores of ancient polar ice and ocean sediments show that past climates have already done just that." And they follow with the judicious philosophy of Cousteau: "Until they better understand the changeable arms and gears of the climate machine, scientists worry that they can barely guess the ultimate consequences of human influences." New York Times News Services, New York, "Don't fool around with Mother Nature," in the Kansas City *Star*, March 27, 1988, I-3.

162   Heilbroner, *Inquiry into the Human Prospect*, 127.

163   *Ibid.*, 132-133. Christopher Lasch argues much in the same way. "Neither the right nor the left has come to terms with an increasingly obvious problem: 'the earth's finite resources will not support an indefinite expansion of industrial civilization.' Given the present rate of population growth, he argues, an environmental disaster would be created if the Western standard of living were successfully exported to the poorer nations of the world. Moreover, the advanced countries have neither the will today nor the resources to assume such an immense program of development. They cannot even address their own problems of poverty. In the United States, the richest country in the world, Mr. Lasch writes, 'a growing proletariat faces a grim future, and even the middle class has seen its standard of living begin to decline.'" William Julius Wilson, "Where has Progress Got Us? *The True and Only Heaven*. Progress and Its Critics," 9, 28 in the New York *Times* Book Review, January 27, 1991. See also Louis Menand, "Man of the People, The True

and Only Heaven. Progress and Its Critics," 39-44 in *The New York Book Review of Books*, vol. 38, No. 7, April 11, 1991, 41.

164   *Ecology as Politics*, 13.

165   *Ibid.*, 64-65.

166   *Ibid.*, 13.

167   *Ibid.*, 64-65.

168   *Inquiry into the Human Prospect*, 139. Precisely because both land and natural resources are sharply limited, and technology has been unhorsed as omnipotent, it is inevitable that population control - not merely birth control - be adopted. The stabilizing factor here would be 2.2 children to a mother and, ideally, only one daughter born to her. The best system for this would be a mutually agreed upon social coercion. Birth control, on the contrary, is merely one where every woman or married couple decided on how many children they want. Red China is currently practicing population control. Hardin, *Exploring New Ethics for Survival*, 205-207.

169   Marx made these observations in a posthumously published book, entitled *A Contribution to the Critique of Political Economy*. *Lévi-Strauss, Structural Anthropology*, 337.

170   Col. Harry Summers, Los Angeles Times Syndicate, "U.S. has troubles alright, but Soviets have worse," in the Kansas City *Times*, March 17, 1988, A-13.

171   Charles Levison, secretary general of the International Chemical Federation, declared: "Products *Made in Japan* were in fact made by Japanese subsidiaries of U.S. companies. The invasion of the American market was being directed from New York via Tokyo. The enemy of American workers was neither the Japanese worker nor even the Japanese government; it was U.S. capital itself, which was American only in origin and name." Gorz, *Ecology as Politics*, 115. The new imperialism differs from the old in that, under its egis, all so-called national firms in colonial areas are in reality "watchdogs for capitalism in general and simply keeping anyone from harming the profit economy." *Ibid.*, 127.

172   Barbara Ward, *Spaceship Earth* (New York, Columbia University Press, 1966), 15.

173   *Inquiry into the Human Prospect*, 140.

174   McKibben, *End of Nature*, 147.

175   *Ibid.*, 80.

176   See vol. I, Chapter VII. RITUAL: WAR footnotes 99, 100. Furthermore, the very hubris of blood-letting of a foe demanded ritual penance before the victor could resume normal and worldly chores. *Ibid.*, footnotes 101-105.

177   *The Poems of Percy Bysshe Shelley*. Selected, Edited, and Introduced by Stephen

Spender (New York, The Heritage Press, 1974), 255. I added this final paragraph at the advice and request of my proofreader, Betty Dusing.

BIBLIOGRAPHY

Books

Abramovitch, Raphael R., *The Soviet Revolution, 1917-1919*. Introduction by Sidney Hook (New York, International University Press, 1962).

Adams, Brooks, *The Law of Civilization and Decay. An Essay on History* (New York, Macmillan, 1896).

Adams, Henry, *The Education of Henry Adams. An Autobiography*, edited by Henry Cabot Lodge (New York, Houghton Mifflin, 1924).

Adams, James Ring, *The Big Fix. Inside the S & L Scandal. How an Unholy Alliance of Politics and Money Destroyed America's Banking System* (New York, John Wiley & Son, 1990).

Adams, John G., *Without Precedent. The Story of the Death of McCarthyism* (New York, W. W. Norton, 1983).

Albanese, Catherine L., *America. Religions and Religion* (Belmont, California, Wadsworth Publishing Company, 1981).

Anderson, Andy, *Hungary '56* (London, Solidarity Press, 1976).

Anderson, Jack and May, Ronald W., *McCarthy. The Man, the Senator, the 'Ism'* (Boston, Beacon Press, 1952).

Anouilh, Jean, *Becket; or the Honor of God,* translated by Lucienne Hill (New York, Cowan-McCann, 1960).

The Anti-Stalin Campaign and International Communism. A Selection of Documents. Edited by the Russian Institute, Columbia University (New York, Columbia University Press, 1956).

296

Appel, Willa, *Cults in America. Programmed for Paradise* (New York, Holt, Rinehart and Winston, 1983).

Aristotle's Metaphysics. Translated with Commentaries and Glossary by Hippocrates G. Apostle (Bloomington, Indiana, University of Indiana Press, 1966).

Arrowood, Charles Flinn, *Thomas Jefferson and Education in a Republic* (New York, McGraw-Hill Book Company, 1930).

Aquinas, Thomas, *Summa Theologie* in 60 vols. Latin text and English translation, Introduction, Notes, Appendices and Glossaries. *Existence and Nature of God* (New York, Blackfriars and McGraw-Hill, 1964), II.

Barr, Alfred, Jr., *Masters of Modern Art.* The Museum of Modern Art (Garden City, New York, Doubleday, 1958).

Barr, Alfred, Jr., and Liberman, William S., *Philosophy of the Arts* (Cambridge, Harvard University Press, 1950).

Barth, Karl, *Credo. A Presentation of the Chief Problems of Dogmatics with Reference to the Apostle's Creed,* translated by J. Strathern McNab (New York, Scribner's, 1936).

The Doctrine of the Word of God. Prolegomena to Church Dogmatics, being vol. I, Part I, translated by G. T. Thomson (Edinburgh, Scotland, T. and T. Clark, 1936).

The Knowledge of God and the Service of God According to the Teaching of the Reformation, translated by J. L. M. Haire and Ian Henderson (London, Hodder and Staughton, 1938).

Beard, Charles A., *The Economic Basis of Politics* (New York, Alfred A. Knopf, 1934).

Bell, Clive, *Art* (New York, Frederick A. Stokes, no date).

Since Cézanne (Freeport, New York, Books for Libraries Press, reprinted 1969).

Berenson, Bernard, *Aesthetics and History* (Garden City, New York, Doubleday, 1948).

Berger, Peter L., *The Sacred Canopy. Elements of a Sociological Theory of Religion* (Garden City, New York, Doubleday, 1967).

Berger, Peter, and Brigitte, Hansfried Kellner, *The Homeless Mind. Modernization and Consciousness* (New York, Vintage Books, a Division of Random House, 1974).

Berle, Alfred A., Jr., *The Twentieth Century Capitalist Revolution* (New York, Harcourt Brace, 1954).

Best, Harry, *The Soviet Experiment* (New York, Richard R. Smith, 1941).

Bloom, Allan, *The Closing of the American Mind* (New York, Simon and Schuster, 1987).

Brandeis, Louis, *Other People's Money and How They Use It.* Edited and with an Introduction and Notes by Richard M. Abrams (New York, Harper Torchback, Harper and Row, 1967).

Brinton, Crane, *The Anatomy of Revolution* (New York, Prentice-Hall, 1952).

Brinton, Maurice, *The Bolsheviks & Worker's Control, 1917-1921. The State and Counter-Revolution* (London, Solidarity Press, 1970).

Brown, Anthony Cave, *"C." The Secret Life of Sir Stewart Graham Menzies, Spymaster to Winston Churchill* (New York, Macmillan, 1987).

Bultmann, Rudolph, *Jesus Christ and Mythology* (New York, Scribner's, 1958).

Form Criticism. A New Method of New Testament Research, Including a Study of the Synoptic Gospels and Primitive Christianity in the Light of Gospel Research, by Karl Knudson, translated by Frederick C. Grant (Chicago and New York, Willett, Clark, 1934).

Theology of the New Testament (New York, Scribner's, 1951), I.

Burawoy, Michael, *Manufacturing Consent. Changes in the Labor Process under Monopoly Capitalism* (Chicago, University of Chicago Press, 1979).

Burke, Edmund, *Reflections on the French Revolution ...* with an Introduction by Russell Kirk (New Rochelle, New York, Arlington House, no date).

Bury, J. B., *The Idea of Progress. An Inquiry into Its Origin and Growth* (New York, Dover Publications, 1932).

Butterfield, Herbert, *Christianity and History* (New York, Scribner's, 1950).

Caldwell, Cyril C., *Henry Ford.* Illustrated by Ed Ashe (New York, Julian Messner Inc., 1947).

Carr, Edward Hallett, *The New Society* (Boston, Beacon Press, 1951).

The Soviet Impact on the Western World (New York, Macmillan, 1947).

298

Carter, Paul A., *The Decline and Revival of the Social Gospel. Social and Political Liberalism in American Protestant Churches, 1920-1940* (Ithaca, New York, Cornell University Press, 1954).

Chamberlin, William Henry, *The Russian Enigma. An Interpretation* (New York, Charles Scribner's, 1943).

The Russian Revolution, 1917-1921 in 2 vols. (New York, Macmillan, 1935), I.

Cochran, Charles Norris, *Christianity and Classical Culture. A Study of Thought and Action from Augustus to Augustine* (New York, Oxford Press, 1944).

Cohn-Bendit, Daniel and Gabriel, *Obsolete Communism. The Left-Wing Alternative* (New York, McGraw-Hill, 1968).

Collingwood, H. G., *The Principles of Art* (Oxford, Clarendon Press, 1955).

Commoner, Barry, *The Closing Circle. Nature, Man and Technology* (New York, Alfred Knopf, 1971).

Cook, Fred J., *The Nightmare Decade. The Life and Times of Senator Joe McCarthy* (New York, Random House, 1971).

Cousteau, Jacques, *The Living Sea* (New York, Harper & Row, 1963).

Cowell, F. R., *Cicero and the Roman Republic* (Baltimore, Penguin Books, 1964).

Cullman, Oscar, *Christ and Time. The Primitive Christian Conception of Time and History*. Revised edition. Translated from the German by Floyd V. Filson (Philadelphia, Westminster Press, 1964).

Cute, David, *The Great Fear. The Anti-Communist Purge under Truman and Eisenhower* (New York, Simon and Schuster, 1978).

Davis, Charles, *A Question of Conscience* (New York, Harper and Row, 1967).

de Camp, L. Sprague, *The Great Monkey Trial* (Garden City, New York, Doubleday, 1968).

de Tocqueville, Alexis, *Democracy in America*. Translated by Henry Reeve. With an Introduction Written Especially for This Heirloom Edition by Erik von Kuehnelt-Leddihn (New Rochelle, New York, Arlington House, no date), I, II.

Deutscher, Isaac, *Ironies of History. Essays on Contemporary Communism* (NewYork, Oxford University Press, 1966).

Dewey, John, *Art as Experience* (New York, Minton, Balch, 1934).

Djilas, Milovan, *The New Class. An Analysis of the Communist System* (New York, Frederick Praeger, 1957).

Donne, John, *The Complete Poetry and Selected Prose of John Donne.* With an Introduction by Robert S. Hillyer (New York, Macmillan, 1946).

Donovan, Timothy Paul, Henry Adams and Brooks Adams, *The Education of American Historians* (Norman, University of Oklahoma Press, 1961).

Dorfman, Joseph, *Thorstein Veblen and His America.* With New Reprints of Economics Classics (New York, August M. Kelley, 1961).

Dostoevsky, Fydor, *The Brothers Karamozov. A Novel in four parts.* Translation by Constance Garnett, revised with an introduction by Avrahm Yarmolinsky (New York, The Heritage Press, 1961).

Drucker, Peter, *Adventures of a Bystander* (New York, Harper and Row, 1979).

America's Next Twenty Years (New York, Harper and Brothers, 1955).

The End of Economic Man; a Study of the New Totalitarianism with an introduction by H. N. Brailsford (New York, John Day Co., 1939).

The Future of Industrial Man (New York, John Day Company, 1942).

Edwards, Richard C. *et al, The Capitalist System. A Radical Analysis of American Society.* Written and Edited by Richard C. Edwards *et al* (Englewood Cliffs, New Jersey, Prentice-Hall, 1972).

Ehrenfeld, David, *The Arrogance of Humanism* (New York, Oxford Press, 1978).

Eliade, Mircea, *Myth and Reality.* Planned and edited by Ruth Nanda Anshen (New York, Harper and Row, 1963).

Ellis, Albert, *The Origins and Development of the Incest Taboo* (New York, Lyle Stuart, Inc., 1963).

Erasmus, *The Praise of Folly.* With a Short Life of the Author by Hendrik van Loon .... Published for the Classics Club (New York, Walter Black, 1942).

Erlich, Paul R. and Anne E., *The Population Explosion* (New York, Simon and Schuster, 1990).

Evans-Pritchard, E. E., *The Nuer: a Description of the Modes of Livelihood and Political Institutions of a Nilotic Peoples* (Oxford, England,

Clarendon Press, 1940).

Ewen, Stuart, *Captains of Consciousness. Advertising and the Social Roots of the Consumer Culture* (New York, McGraw-Hill, 1976).

Fischer, Harold H., *The Communist Revolution. An Outline of Strategy and Tactics*. The Hoover Institute and Library on War, Revolution and Peace (Stanford, California, Stanford University Press, 1955).

Fitzgerald, F. Scott, *The Great Gatsby* (New York, Charles Scribner's Sons, 1925, 1953).

Ford, Henry, *Moving Forward* (Garden City, New York, Doubleday, Doran, 1930).

Frazer, Sir James George, *The Magic Art and the Evolution of Kings* in 2 vols. (New York, Macmillan, 1935), II.

Freud, Sigmund, *Totem and Taboo. Some Points of Agreement between the Mental Lives of Savages and Neurotics* (New York, W. W. Norton, 1950).

Fried, Richard M., *Men Against McCarthy* (New York, Columbia University Press, 1976).

Friedell, Egon, *A Cultural History of the Modern Age, 3 vols. The Crisis of the European Soul from the Black Death to the World War. Renaissance and Reformation, from the Black Death to the Thirty Years War* (New York, Alfred A. Knopf, 1930), I.

Fromm, Eric, *Escape from Freedom* (New York, Farrar & Rinehart, 1941, 1947).

Fry, Roger, *Vision and Design* (New York, Brentano's, no date).

Galbraith, John Kenneth, *American Capitalism, the Concept of Countervailing Power* (Boston, Houghton Mifflin, 1952).

Gilson, Étienne, *Being and Some Philosophers* (Toronto, Canada, Pontifical Institute of Medieval Studies, 1949).

God and Philosophy (New Haven, Yale University Press, 1946).

Gorz, André, *Ecology as Politics* (Boston, South End Press, 1980).

Gouldner, Alvin W., *The Coming Crisis of Western Sociology* (New York, Basic Books, 1970).

Grant, R. M., *Gnosticism and Early Christianity* (New York, Columbia University Press, 1959).

Guérin, Daniel, *Anarchism. From Theory to Practice*. Introduction by Noam Chomsky. Translated by Mary Klopper (New York, Monthly Review Press, 1970).

Guthrie, A. B., Jr., *Fair Land, Fair Land* (Boston, Houghton Mifflin, 1982).

Hall, Angus, *Strange Cults* (Garden City, New York, Doubleday, 1976).

Hardin, Garrett, *Exploring New Ethics for Survival. The Voyage of the Spaceship Beagle* (New York, Viking Press, 1972).

Harnack, Adolph, *What Is Christianity?* Sixteen Lectures delivered in the University of Berlin during the Winter Term 1899-1900. Translated into English by Thomas B. Saunders (New York, G. P. Putnam's, 1901).

Harper, Marvin Henry, *Gurus, Swamis, & Avataras. Spiritual Masters & Their American Disciples* (Philadelphia, Pennsylvania, The Westminster Press, 1972).

Harris, Marvin, *America Now. The Anthropology of a Changing Culture* (New York, Simon and Schuster, 1981).

Heard, Gerald, *Is God in History? An Inquiry into Human and Prehuman History in Terms of the Creation, Fall and Redemption* (New York, Harper, 1950).

Heilbroner, Robert L., *An Inquiry into the Human Prospect* (New York, W. W. Norton, 1974).

The Future as History (New York, Harper & Brothers, 1960).

Higginbotham, John, *Cicero on Moral Obligation*. A New translation of Cicero's 'De officis' with Introduction and Notes (Berkeley, University of California Press, 1967).

Hippocrates. With an English Translation by W. H. S. Jones, 4 vols. (Cambridge, Harvard University Press, 1948), I.

Hobhouse, Henry, *Forces of Change. An Unorthodox View of History* (New York, Arcadia Publications, Little Brown and Co., 1989).

Hobson, John, *Imperialism. A Study* (London, George Allan & Unwin, first publication 1902, fifth impression 1954).

Hoffer, Eric, *The True Believer. Thoughts on the Nature of the Mass Movements* (New York, Harper & Brothers, 1951).

Hopkins, Charles Howard, *The Rise of the Social Gospel in American Protestantism, 1865-1915* (New Haven, Yale University Press, 1940).

Hospers, John, *Meaning and Truth in the Arts* (Chapel Hill, University of North Carolina Press, 1946).

Hudson, G. F., *Fifty Years of Communism, Theory and Practice, 1917-1967* (New York, Basic Books, 1968).

Hulme, T. E., *Speculations. Essays on Humanism and the Philosophy of Art.* A Harvest Book (New York, Harcourt-Brace and Co., first published, 1942).

I'll Take My Stand. The South and the Agrarian Tradition. By Twelve Southerners (New York, Harper & Row, 1930).

The Inquisition. A Political and Military Study of Its Establishment. 2nd edition. With a Preface by Hilaire Belloc (Port Washington, New York, Kennikat Press, 1968).

Jaeger, Werner, *Aristotle. Fundamentals of the History of His Development.* Translated by Richard Robinson (London, Oxford University Press, 1948).

Johnson, Woodbridge O., *Other Christs. The Coming Christology* (New York, Pageant Press, 1971).

Keynes, John Maynard, *The General Theory of Employment Interest and Money* (New York, Harcourt, Brace, 1936).

Kleppner, Paul, *The Third Electoral System, 1853-1892. Parties, Voters and Political Cultures* (Chapel Hill, University of North Carolina Press, 1979).

Koestler, Arthur, *Arrow in the Blue. An Autobiography* (New York, Macmillan, 1952).

Koestler, Arthur, *et al, The God That Failed* (New York, Harper & Brothers, 1949).

La Barre, Weston, *Ghost Dance. Origins of Religion* (Garden City, New York, Doubleday, 1970).

Langer, Suzanne K., *Philosophy in a New Key* (Cambridge, Harvard University Press, 1957).

Laski, Harold J., *The Communist Manifesto. An Introduction.* Together with the Original Text and Prefaces by Karl Marx and Friedrich Engels. Foreword for the American Edition by T. B. Bottomore (New York, Pantheon Books, Random House, 1967).

Lévi-Strauss, Claude, *Structural Anthropology,* translated from the French by Claire Jacobson and Brooke Grundfest Schoef (New York, Basic Books, 1963).

Lippman, Walter, *Drift and Mastery. An Attempt to Diagnose the Current Unrest* (New York, Mitchell Kennerley, 1914).

Luce, Henry R., *The American Century.* With comments by John Chamberlain, Quincy Howe *et al* (New York, Farrar & Rinehart, 1941).

Luxemburg, Rosa, *The Russian Revolution and Leninism or Marxism?* (Ann Arbor, University of Michigan Press, 1976).

McGiffert, Arthur Cushman, *A History of Christian Thought, From Jesus to John of Damascus* (New York, Scribner's Sons, 1932), I.

McKibben, Bill, *The End of Nature* (New York, Random House, 1989).

MacLaine, Shirley, *Don't Fall Off the Mountain* (New York, W. W. Norton, 1970).

You Can Get There From Here (New York, W. W. Norton, 1975).

McMullen, Roy, *Art, Affluence and Alienation. The Fine Arts Today* (New York, Prager, 1968).

Marsh, George Perkins, *George Perkins Marsh, Man and Nature,* edited by David Lowenthal (Cambridge, The Belknap Press of Harvard University, 1965).

Mead, Margaret, *Soviet Attitudes Toward Authority. An Interdisciplinary Approach to Problems of Soviet Character.* (The Rand Series. New York, McGraw-Hill, 1951).

Cooperation and Competition Among Primitive Peoples. Edited by Margaret Mead (New York, McGraw-Hill, 1937).

Melman, Seymour, *Pentagon Capitalism. The Political Economy of War* (New York, McGraw-Hill, 1970).

Monter, William E., *Calvin's Geneva in New Dimensions in History. Historical Cities series.* Edited by Norman F. Cantor (New York, John Wiley and Sons, 1967).

Morais, Herbert M., *Deism in Eighteenth Century America* (New York, Columbia University Press, 1934).

Mumford, Lewis, *Art and Technics* (New York, Columbia University Press, 1952).

Nader, Ralph, *Unsafe at Any Speed. The Designed-in Dangers of the American Automobile* (New York, Grossman Publishing, 1965).

Naisbitt, John, *Megatrends. Ten New Directions Transforming Our Lives*

(New York, Warner Books, 1982).

Nearing, Scott, and Freeman, Joseph, *Dollar Diplomacy. A Study in American Diplomacy* (New York, Modern Reader Paperbacks, reprint, 1966).

Niebuhr, Reinhold, *Beyond Tragedy. Essays on Christian Interpretation* (New York, Scribner's, 1937).

Leaves from the Notebook of a Tamed Cynic (Hamden, Connecticut, The Shoestring Press, 1956).

The Nature and Destiny of Man. A Christian Interpretation, Human Nature. Gifford Lectures (New York, Scribner's, 1941), I.

The Nature and Destiny of Man, a Christian Interpretation, Human Destiny. Gifford Lectures (New York, Scribner's, 1943), II.

Reflections on the End of an Era (New York, Scribner's, 1934).

Niebuhr, Richard, *The Meaning of Revelation* (New York, Macmillan, 1941).

Nietzsche, Friedrich, *The Use and Abuse of History,* translated by Adrian Collins (New York, Liberal Arts Press, 1949).

Nisbet, Robert A., *History of the Idea of Progress* (New York, Basic Books, 1980).

Social Change and History. Aspects of the Western Theory of Development (New York, Oxford University Press, 1969).

Northrop, F. S. C., *The Meeting of East and West. An Inquiry Concerning World Understanding* (New York, Macmillan, 1946).

Panikkar, Raimundo, *The Trinity and the Religious Experience of Man. Icon-Person-Mystery* (New York, Obis Books, 1973).

Pares, Sir Bernard, *The Fall of the Russian Monarchy. A Study of the Evidence* (New York, Vintage Books, Random House, 1939).

Parker, DeWitt H., *The Analysis of Art* (New Haven, Yale University Press, 1926).

The Pentagon Papers as published by the New York *Times*. Based on investigative reporting by Neil Sheehan (New York, Bantam Books, 1971).

Pivan, Frances Fox, and Cloward, Richard A., *The New Class War. Reagan's Attack on the Welfare State and Its Consequences* (New York, Pantheon Books, 1982).

Podrabinek, Alexander, *Punitive Medicine.* Foreword by Alexander Ginzburg (Ann Arbor, Michigan, Karoma Publishing, 1980).

Polayni, Karl, *The Great Transformation* (New York, Farrar & Rinehart, 1944).

The Political Writings of Thomas Jefferson with an Introduction by Edward Dumbauld (New York, Liberal Arts Press, 1956).

Previté-Orton, C. W., *The Shorter Cambridge Medieval History* in 2 vols. *The Later Roman Empire to the Twelfth Century* (Cambridge, England, The University Press, 1952),I, II.

Rabinovitch, Alexander, *Prelude to Revolution. The Petrograd Bolsheviks and the July 1917 Uprising* (Bloomington, University of Indiana Press, 1968).

Raglan, Fitzroy, Lord, *The Hero. A Study in Tradition, Myth and Drama* (London, Methuen, first published in 1936).

Ray, Dixie Lee with Guzzo, Lou, *Trashing the Planet. How Science Can Help Us Deal with Acid Rain, Depletion of the Ozone, and Nuclear Waste....*(Washington, D. C., Regnery, 1990).

Read, Herbert, *Icon and Idea. The Function of Art in Development of Human Consciousness* (Cambridge, University of Harvard Press, first published in 1955).

Redfield, Robert, *The Folk Culture of Yucatan* (Chicago, University of Chicago Press, 1942).

Reed, John, *Ten Days That Shook the World* (New York, Penguin Books, 1977).

Reuther, Walter P., *Selected Papers,* edited and with an Introduction by Henry M. Christman (New York, Macmillan, 1961).

Richards, I. A., *The Foundations of Aesthetics* (New York, Lear Publishers, 1925).

Riesman, David, *The Lonely Crowd. A Study of the Changing American Character.* Abridged edition with a 1969 preface (New Haven, Yale University Press, 1973).

Robinson, James Harvey, *Readings in European History. A Collection of Extracts from the Sources,* 2 vols. (New York, Ginn and Company, 1904), I.

Rostovtzeff, M., *Rome,* translated from the Russian by J. D. Duff, edited by E. J. Bickerman. Galaxy edition (New York, Oxford University Press, reprint 1967).

The Social and Economic History of the Roman Empire, 2 vols. (Oxford, England, Clarendon University Press, 1963), I.

Rowland, Benjamin, Jr., *Art in East and West. An Introduction through Comparisons* (Cambridge, Harvard University Press, 1954).

Rubáiyát of Omar Kháyyam. Translated into English Quatrains by Edward Fitzgerald. Edited with an Introduction by Louis Untermeyer (New York, Random House, 1947).

Rubin, Lilian Breslow, *Worlds of Pain. Life in the Working-Class Family* (New York, Basic Books, 1976).

Runes, Dagobert D., *The Soviet Impact on Society. A Recollection.* With a Foreword by Harry Elmer Barnes (New York, Philosophical Library, 1953).

Roman Civilization. Selected Readings. Edited with an Introduction and Notes by Naphtali Lewis and Meyer Reinhold, *The Republic* (New York, Columbia University Press, 1951), I.

Salisbury, Harrison E., *A Journey for Our Times. A Memoir* (New York, A. Cornelia and Michael Bessie Book, Harper and Row, 1983).

Santayana, George, *The Life of Reason or the Phases of Human Progress* in 5 vols. (New York, Charles Scibner's Sons, 1922), I.

Schactman, Tom, *Decade of Shocks: Dallas to Watergate, 1963-1974* (New York, Poseidon Press, 1974).

Schweitzer, Albert, *The Quest for the Historical Jesus. A Critical Study of Its Progress from Reimarus to Wrede* (New York, Macmillan, 1948).

Sennett, Richard, and Cobb, Jonathan, *The Hidden Injuries of Class* (New York, Alfred A. Knopf, 1972).

Shelley, Percy Bysshe, *The Poems of Percy Bysshe Shelley.* Selected, Edited and Introduced by Stephen Spender (New York, The Heritage Press, 1974).

Simmel, George, *The Philosophy of Money.* Translated by Tom Bottomore and David Frisby (London, Routledge and Kegan Paul, 1978).

Simon, David R., and Eitzen, D. Stanley, *Elite Deviance,* 2nd edition (Boston, Allyn and Bacon, 1986).

Sinclair, Upton, *The Jungle.* (New York, Doubleday, 1906).

Smith, Wilfred Cantwell, *Belief and History* (Charlottesville, University Press of Virginia, 1977).

Meaning and End of Religion. A New Approach to the Religious Traditions of Mankind (New York, Macmillan, 1963).

Solzhenitsyn, Aleksandr I., *The Gulag Archipelago, 1918-1956. An Experiment in Literary Investigation.* Translated from the Russian by Thomas P. Whitney (New York, Harper and Row, 1975), Parts III-IV.

Letter to the Soviet Leaders. Translated from the Russian by Hilary Sternberg (New York, Harper & Row, 1974-1975).

The Soviet Economy. A Book of Readings, edited by Morris Burnstein and R. Fusfeld (Homewood, Illinois, Richard D. Irwin, Inc., 1970).

Spencer, Robert F., *The North Alaskan Eskimo. A Study in Ecology and Society* (Washington, D. C., Bureau of Ethnology, Smithsonian Institute, 1959). Republished in 1969.

Stearns, Raymond P., *Pageant of Europe. Scources and Selections from the Renaissance to the Present Day* (New York, Harcourt, Brace, 1947).

Steffens, Lincoln, *The Autobiography of* (New York, Literary Guild, 1931).

Streiker, Lowell D., *The Gospel Time Bomb. Ultrafundamentalism and the Future of America* (Buffalo, New York, Prometheus Books, 1984).

Tawney, R. H., *Religion and the Rise of Capitalism. A Historical Study* (New York, Harcourt, Brace, 1926).

Taylor, Frederick Winslow, *The Principles of Scientific Management* (New York, Harper & Brothers, 1915).

Thompson, James Westfall, *A History of Historical Writing,* 2 vols. (New York, Macmillan, 1950), I.

Thomte, Reidar, *Kierkegaard's Philosophy of Religion* (Princeton, New Jersey, Princeton University Press, 1949).

Thoreau, Henry David, *Walden.* Edited and with an Introduction and Notes by Sherman Paul. Riverside Edition (New York, Houghton Mifflin, 1957).

Thucydides, *History of the Peloponnesian War,* translated by Richard Crawley, Everyman's Library, edited by Ernest Rhys No. 455 (London, J. M. Dent, 1945).

The Complete Writings of Thucydides: *The Peloponnesian War.* The unabridged Crawley translation with an introduction by John H. Finley, Jr. (New York, The Modern Library, Random House, 1951).

Tillich, Paul, *A History of Christian Thought* (New York and Evanston,

Harper and Row, 1968).

The Interpretation of History, translated by N. A. Rasetzki and Elsa L. Talney (New York, Scribner's, 1936).

Systematic Theology. Life and the Spirit History and the Kingdom of God (Chicago, University of Chicago Press, 1963), III.

Tönnies, Ferdinand, *Community and Society (Gemeinschaft and Gesellschaft).* Translated and edited by Charles P. Loomis (East Lansing, Michigan State University Press, 1957).

Toynbee, Arnold, *Civilization on Trial* (New York, Oxford University Press, 1948).

A Study of History, 12 vols. (London, Oxford University Press, 1939), VI.

Trotsky, Leon, *The History of the Russian Revolution,* 3 vols. Translated from the Russian by Max Eastman (Ann Arbor, University of Michigan Press, 1932), III.

Tuchman, Barbara, *The March of Folly. From Troy to Vietnam* (New York, Alfred A. Knopf, 1984).

Urban, C. Stanley, *Slavocracy and Empire: New Orleans and the Attempted Expansion of Slavery, 1845-1861* (1976), edited by Robert W. Wadsworth, 352 pp. (Revision of a Ph.D. dissertation, 1943, entitled *The Idea of Progress and Southern Imperialism, 1845-1861).* Both volumes are available at Northwestern University Library in Evanston, Illinois.

Veblen, Thorstein, *The Engineers and the Price System* (New York, Viking Press, 1921, 1940).

The Place of Science in Modern Civilization and Other Essays (New York, Russell and Russell, 1961).

The Theory of Business Enterprise (New York, Charles Scribner's Sons, 1935).

The Theory of the Leisure Class. An Economic Study of Institutions (New York, Modern Library, Random House, 1934).

Vidal, Gore, *Empire. A Novel* (New York, Random House, 1987).

Voline, *The Unknown Revolution, 1917-1921.* Foreword by Rudolph Rocker (New York, Free Life Editions, 1975).

Wachtel, Paul L., *The Poverty of Affluence. A Psychological Portrait of the American Way of Life* (New York, Free Press, Macmillan, 1983).

Walsh, James J., *The Thirteenth Greatest of Centuries* (New York, Catholic Summer School Press, 1913).

Wambaugh, Joseph, *The Glitter Dome* (New York, William Morrow, 1981).

Ward, Barbara, *Spaceship Earth* (New York, Columbia University Press, 1966).

Weber, Max, *Essays in Sociology*. Translated, edited, and with an introduction by H. H. Gerth and C. Wright Mills (New York, Oxford University Press, 1953).

Selections from His Works, with an introduction by S. M. Miller (New York, Thomas Y. Crowell, 1968).

The Sociology of Religion, translated by Ephraim Fischoff. Introduction by Talcott Parsons (Boston, Beacon Press, 1963).

Weitz, Morris, *Philosophy of the Arts* (Cambridge, University of Harvard Press, 1950).

Wilson, James Q., *The 1988 Election* (Lexington, Massachusetts, D. C. Heath, 1989).

Wittner, Lawrence S., *Cold War America. From Hiroshima to Watergate* (New York, Praeger Publishing, 1974).

Wu, K. C., *The Chinese Heritage* (New York, Crown Publishers, Inc., 1982).

Zeitlin, Maurice, *Classes, Class Conflict, and the State. Empirical Studies in Class Analysis* (Cambridge, Massachusetts, Winthrop Publications, Inc., 1980).

Capitalism and Imperialism. An Introduction to Neo-Marxian Concepts (Chicago, Markham Publishing, 1972).

Articles

Abouhalkah, Yael T., of the Editorial Staff, "Federal officials can't be trusted on radiation," in The Kansas City *Star*, July 29, 1990, J-1.

"U. S. has spent 17 years not prepared for this moment," in The Kansas City *Star*, August 6, 1990, B-7.

"When it comes to taxes, Americans aren't so bright," in The Kansas City *Star*, December 6, 1987, K-1.

Abrams, Maxine, "Even kids are victims of stress," The Kansas City *Star*, March 7, 1988, C-1.

Adams, Brooks, "Brooks Adams, America's Economic Supremacy," with a new evaluation by Marquis W. Childs, 4-5 in *Book Review Digest,* 1947, edited by Mertice M. James and Dorothy Brown (New York, H. W. Wilson, 1948).

Adams, Elaine, Metropolitan Star, "Overworked, taken for granted, priests near point of exhaustion," in The Kansas City *Times,* February 17, 1990, E-8.

Adams, Gordon, "The Department of Defense and the Military-Industrial Establishment: The Politics of the Iron Triangle," 320-334 in *Criticial Studies in Organization and Bureaucracy,* edited by Frank Fischer and Carmen Sirianni (Philadelphia, Temple University Press, 1984).

Agena, Kathleen, "The Return of Enchantment," 67-80 in the New York *Times* Magazine, November 27, 1983.

Apple, R. W., Jr., The New York Times, Washington, "Germany-NATO issue to steal summit spotlight," in The Kansas City *Star,* May 28, 1990, A-8.

Armas, José, Albuquerque, New Mexico, "Poindexter fiasco cost U.S. $100 million," in The Kansas City *Star,* June 29, 1990, C-11.

Balz, Dan, Washington Post Writer, "If Happy Days are Here, Why Aren't Conservatives Singing," in the Washington *Post* Weekly Edition, June 4-10, 1990, 14.

Baran, Paul and Sweezy, Paul, "The Multinational Corporation and Modern Imperialism," 435-442 in *The Capitalist System. A Radical Analysis of American Society.* Written and edited by Richard C. Edwards *et al* (Englewood Cliffs, New Jersey, Prentice-Hall, 1972).

Barrientos, Tanya, Knight-Ridder Newspapers, "Marshland is dying at the hands of humans," in The Kansas City *Star,* June 13, 1990, A-1.

Barry, Dave, Knight-Ridder Newspapers, "They probably hate us in Kazoot, too," in The Kansas City *Star,* August 28, 1990, E-4.

Barta, Carolyn, Dallas Morning News, "American politics becoming dangerously close to brain dead," in The Kansas City *Star,* April 1, 1990, K-4.

Baxendale, Michael, Chairman, Veterans Affairs, Vietnam Veterans of America, No. 317, Kansas City, "Veterans neglected," in The Kansas City *Times,* December 28, 1987, S-16.

Beaber, Rex Julian, Los Angeles Times-Washington Post News Service, "Computer age brings spectre of unemployment," in The Kansas City *Times,* August 15, 1983, A-12.

Beatty, Jack, Washington Post-Los Angeles Times, "Secular culture too weak even to laugh off the likes of Pat Robertson," in The Kansas City *Times,* January 29, 1988, A-11.

Beaumont, Peter, London Observer Service, "Fewer priests serving Britain's Catholics," in The Kansas City *Times,* March 3, 1990, E-11.

Beck, Joan, Chicago Tribune, "Veterans won't easily let grievance go," in The Kansas City *Star,* September 8, 1987, A-8.

Bekkers, W. M., "Mercy and the Sacrament of Penance," 228-232 in *The Catholic World,* vol. 203, July, 1966.

Bell, Herbert C. F., "The Place of History in Catholic Education," 413-426 in *The Catholic Historical Review,* vol. 23, No. 4 (1938).

Bell, Joe, "Are Teens *Really* turning to Religion?," 234-235 plus in *Seventeen,* March, 1985.

Belloc, Hilaire, "Preface," xxix-xli, in Hoffman Nickerson, *The Inquisition. A Political and Military Study of Its Establishment,* 2nd edition (Port Washington, New York, Kennikat Press, 1968).

Bendix, Richard, "The Protestant Ethic Revisited," 299-310 in Reinhard Bendix and Roth Gutenther, *Scholarship and Partisanship: Essays on Max Weber* (Berkeley, University of California Press, 1971).

Bennett, Scott, Dallas Morning News, Dallas, "Morning in America is over; here comes the night," in The Kansas City *Star,* July 27, 1990, C-11.

Beregov, N., The Washington Post, "Soviets may be trying to reform, but they have no plan to follow," in The Kansas City *Star,* April 26, 1987, K-2.

Bialer, Seweryn, and Afferica, Joan, "The Genesis of Gorbachev's World," 605-644 in *Foreign Affairs,* vol. 64, No. 3, 1985.

Black, Jan Knippers, "Greenpeace: The Ecological Warriors," 26-29 in *USA Today,* vol. 115, No. 2498, November 1986.

Blackstone, William T., "Ethics and Ecology," 16-42 in *Philosophy and the Environmental Crisis,* edited by W. T. Blackstone (Athens, University of Georgia Press, 1974).

Blow, Richard, United Features Syndicate (Reprint from the *New Republic)* "New Age Gung-ho but vague," in The Kansas City *Star,* January 24, 1988, H-3.

Bombeck, Erma, Universal Press Syndicate, "Try peace; kids deserve a future, too," in The Kansas City *Star,* April 15, 1988, D-3.

312

Borosage, Robert, "Making of the National Security State," 3-63 in *Pentagon Watchers, Student Report on the National Security State,* edited by Leonard S. Rodberg and Derek Shearer (Garden City, New York, Anchor Books Doubleday, 1970).

Brandt, Allan M., "Racism and Research; The Case of the Tuskegee Syphilis Study," 186-195 in *The Social World,* edited by Jan Robertson (New York, Worth Publishing Company, 1981).

Broder, David S., Washington Post Writers Group, Washington, "Additional restrictions on the president won't help," in The Kansas City *Times,* June 17, 1987, A-15.

"Brock treatment another symptom of ailing White House," in The Kansas City *Star,* January 19, 1987, A-9.

"Encouraging words from youth group," in The Kansas City *Star,* July 3, 1990, B-9.

"Flag flap signals loss of purpose," in The Kansas City *Star,* June 18, 1990, B-5.

"New Generation wrestling with altered world order," in The Kansas City *Star,* May 2, 1990, C-9.

"Reagan approach is to substitute symbols for substance," in The Kansas City *Times,* February 13, 1984, A-11.

"Reagan team has strange concept of the 'public interest'," in The Kansas City *Times,* December 5, 1983, A-10.

Brown, Lester, *et al,* "Report on Reports." *State of the World, 1984, 1985 and 1986 editions... Progress Towards Sustainable Society,* 25-28 in *Environment,* vol. 28, No. 2, March 1986.

Buckley, William F., "Disheartening news of German unification front," in The Kansas City *Star,* June 11, 1990, C-11.

"The Non-Latin Mass," 167-169 in *Commonweal,* vol. 87, No. 6, November 10, 1967.

Burkitt, F. C., "Pagan Philosophy and the Christian Church," 450-475 in *The Cambridge Ancient History,* vol. XII. *The Imperial Crisis and Recovery, A. D. 193-324.* Edited by S. A. Cook *et al* (Cambridge, England, University of Cambridge Press, 1961).

Burrows, Robert J. L., "Americans Get Religion in a New Age," 17-23 in *Christianity Today,* May 16, 1986, vol. 30, no. 8.

Burton, Robert G., "A Philosopher Looks at the Population Bomb," 105-116 in *Philosophy and the Environmental Crisis,* edited by W. T.

Blackstone (Athens, University of Georgia Press, 1974).

Buursma, Bruce, Chicago Tribune, "TV Evangelists espouse prosperity philosophy," in The Kansas City *Times,* April 17, 1987, A-12.

Callahan, Daniel, "Pie in the Sky Theology," 40-44 in *Commonweal,* vol. 88, No. 1, March 22, 1968.

Capon, John, London, "Liberal Bishop's Appointment Causes a Stir in England, 74, in *Christianity Today,* September 7, 1984.

Carpenter, Joel, "Geared to the times, but Anchored to the Rock," 44-47 in *Christianity Today,* November 8, 1985.

Castoriadis, Cornelius, "The Crisis of Western Societies," 17-28 in *Telos. A Quarterly Journal of Radical Thought,* No. 53, Fall, 1982.

Chapman, Janet G., "Consumption in the Soviet Union," 323-334 in *The Soviet Economy. A Book of Readings,* edited by Morris Burnstein and Daniel R. Fusfeld (Homewood, Illinois, Richard D. Irwin, Inc., 1970).

Cheyney, Edward P., "Law in History," 231-248 in *The American Historical Review,* vol. 29, No. 2, January, 1924.

Christy, Marian, The Boston Globe, "Brinkley has the last laugh," in The Kansas City *Star,* January 25, 1990, D-1.

Chui, Glenna, Knight-Ridder Newspapers, "The world is warmer, but the trend is still uncertain," in The Kansas City *Star,* March 29, 1988, Tech-2.

Clapp, Rodney, "Cults: a Reality that has staggered Our Imaginations," 50-56 in *Christianity Today,* vol. 26, No. 1, January, 1982.

Cockburn, Alexander, Los Angeles Times, "The harsh discipline of capitalism," in The Kansas City *Star,* June 24, 1990, J-5.

Coelho, Tony, "The Foreign Greening of America. Outsiders Banking Moves Threaten Our Ability to Compete," in the Los Angeles *Times,* March 26, 1987, Part II, 5.

Cohen, Stephen F., "Gorbachev's reforms would alter the very shape of Stalin's system," in The Kansas City *Star,* March 28, 1987, K-3.

"Sovieticus," 511 in *The Nation,* vol. 234, No. 16, November 15, 1986.

Collins, Thomas, Newsday, "Iran-contra; The press meekly trips away," in The Kansas City *Star,* May 9, 1990, C-9.

Conine, Ernest, Los Angeles Times, "Buy American sounds good," in The

314

Kansas City *Star,* August 16, 1987, K-3.

"Court hands corporate managers another big stick," in The Kansas City *Star,* February 29, 1984, A-13.

"Gorbachev's reform efforts face some very tough tests," in The Kansas City *Times,* April 3, 1987, A-12.

Conrad, Peter, "The Discovery of Hyperkenesis: Notes on the Medicalization of Deviant Behavior," 12-21 in *Social Problems,* vol. 23, No. 1, October, 1975.

Cooper, May H., Congressional Quarterly, Washington, "High tech and permanent unemployment," in The Kansas City *Times,* August 2, 1983, A-9.

Cooperstein, Bruce, and Pearl, Art, Knight-Ridder Newspapers, "It is in society," in The Kansas City *Times,* September 19, 1983, A-9.

Cornell, George W., AP Religion Writer, "Homosexuals see 'domino effect' after tougher Catholic stance," in The Kansas City *Times,* May 2, 1987, E-8.

"Cousteau's Plea for the Mediterranean," 53 in *World Press Review,* vol. 34, No. 6, June, 1987.

Crumpley, Charles R. T., Staff Writer, "In a strange market, bad news can be good," in The Kansas City *Star,* July 21, 1990, A-1, 16.

Curran, Charles E., "On dissent in the Church," 461-470 in *Commonweal,* vol. 113, No. 15, September 12, 1986.

Curtis, Charlotte, New York Times News Service, New York, "Effects of poverty in America aren't as well hidden as they were 25 years ago," in The Kansas City *Times,* November 25, 1983, A-15.

Daly, Mary, "The Woman Intellectual and the Church. A Commonweal Symposium,"446-458 in *Commonweal,* vol. 85, No. 16, January 26, 1967.

Darling, David J., Deep Time: the Fate of the Universe," 6-13 in *Astronomy,* vol. 14, No. 1, January, 1986.

Davis, Jim, Business Staff, "Ethics, scandal tied, writer says," in The Kansas City *Times,* September 23, 1987, D-1.

Davis, Kenneth S., Los Angeles Times, "Public values security over truth," in The Kansas City *Star,* August 27, 1987, M-3.

Denton, Tommy, Fort Worth Star-Telegram, "Freedom kept alive and well by its exercise," in The Kansas City *Star,* June 27, 1990, C-11.

Dickinson, Brian, Providence Journal, "No haven from strains of society," in The Kansas City *Star,* February 6, 1990, C-1.

Dinges, William D., "The Vatican Report on Sects, Cults and New Religious movements," in *America,* vol. 155, No. 7, September 27, 1986.

Dixon, Paul Rand, "Statement of Chairman Paul Rand Dixon," 179-191 in *The Nader Report on the Federal Trade Commission* by Edward F. Cox *et al* (New York, Richard W. Baron, 1969).

Dobbs, Michael, The Washington Post, Moscow, "Gorbachev prevailing in party, failing in economic crisis," The Kansas City *Star,* July 15, 1990. A-14.

"Strained Soviet party wrenched again," The Kansas City *Star,* July 4, 1990, A-1.

"Yeltsin leads defectors who demand share of assets," The Kansas City *Star,* July 13, 1990, A-1.

Drake, Stillman, "Galileo. A Bibliographical Sketch," 52-66 in *Galileo. Man of Science,* edited by Ernam McMullin (New York, Basic Books, 1967).

Dubos, René, "Franciscan Conservatism versus Benedictine Stewartship," 114-136 in *Ecology and Religion in History,* edited by David and Eileen Spring (New York, Harper Torchback, Harper and Row, 1974).

Du Brow, Rick, Los Angeles Times, "Up next; big changes for big newscasters," in The Kansas City *Star,* August 30, 1990, D-1, 4.

Dunning, Brian, a Special Correspondent, "Truth is hidden under history," in The Kansas City *Star,* April 1, 1990, K-1.

Dvorak, John A., Missouri Notebook. "Eagleton offers harsh advice for liberalism's troubled times," in The Kansas City *Times,* December 13, 1986, B-3.

Dykstra, Peter, "Institutions Greenpeace," 44-45 in *Environment,* vol. 28, No. 6, July-August, 1986.

Eagar, Harry, Contributing Reviewer, "Seeds of change were planted long ago, historian contends," in The Kansas City *Star,* May 6, 1990, I-9.

Easterbrook, Gregg, "Special Report. Cleaning Up," 26-42 in *Newsweek,* vol. 114, No. 4, July 24, 1989.

Edwards, Richard C., "The Logic of Capitalist Expansion," 98-106 in *The Capitalist System. A Radical Analysis of American Society.* Written and edited by Richard C. Edwards *et al* (Englewood Cliffs, New

Jersey, Prentice-Hall, 1972).

Ehrenriech, Barbara and Stallard, Karlin, "The Nouveau Poor," 217-223 in *MS.,* July-August, 1982.

Evans, David, The Chicago Tribune, "Sadaam to the rescue," in The Kansas City *Star,* September 4, 1990, B-5.

Fagan, Richard R., "The United States and Chile. Roots and Branches," 297-313 in *Foreign Affairs. An American Quarterly Review,* January, 1975.

Fain, Jim, New York Times News Service, "Nation split by shift in tax burden from wealthy to middle class," in The Kansas City *Star,* September 11, 1990, B-5.

Falin, Valentin, chief of the internal affairs of the communist party central committee, New Perspectives Quarterly, Washington, "New treaty, not Nato, needed to end German impasse," in The Kansas City *Star,* June 11, 1990, B-5.

Fehr, Stephen C., Washington Correspondent, "Bond-Woods race among the costliest," in The Kansas City *Times,* February 13, 1987, C-7.

Feldstein, Martin and Kathleen, Los Angeles Times-Washington Post News Service, "Bitter medicine in store for U. S. consumers," in The Kansas City *Times,* March 6, 1987, A-11.

Fischer, Louis, 196-228 in *The God That Failed,* by Arthur Koestler *et al* (New York, Harper & Brothers, 1949).

Flahiff, George B., "A Catholic Looks at History," 1-15 in *The Catholic Historical Review,* vol. 27, No. 1, 1941.

Flanagan, James, "Competition will change U. S. education in the 90s," in The Kansas City *Times,* January 29, 1990, A-6.

"The dollar is losing its muscle," in The Kansas City *Star,* August 13, 1990, A-9.

"Lean economic times await U. S. consumers," in The Kansas City *Times,* November 30, 1987, A-9.

"Oil is only 1 factor in Gulf mess," in The Kansas City *Star,* August 27, 1990, A-11.

"S & L mess just keeps growing," in The Kansas City *Star,* April 9, 1990, A-7.

Foran, Katherine, "Few are neutral on Oral Roberts," in The Kansas City *Times,* March 28, 1987, A-1, 14.

Frankel, Glenn, The Washington Post, London, "Is history on Hussein's side?," in The Kansas City *Star*, September 4, 1990, A-1, 8.

Friedman, Thomas L., "Why defend Saudi Arabia," in The Kansas City *Star*, August 12, 1990, A-1, 13.

Friedrich, Otto, "New Age Harmonies," 62-72 in *Time*, December 7, 1987.

Fritchey, Clayton, Newsday, "Shorter work week," in The Kansas City *Star*, July 18, 1983, A-7.

Fusselman, Roger, President, Ayn Rand Society, Kansas City chapter, "No holiday for man," in The Kansas City *Star*, May 5, 1990, C-8.

Gaines, Sally, Chicago Tribune, "Business schools re-evaluating offerings to students," in The Kansas City *Star*, May 24, 1987, F-1.

Galbraith, John Kenneth, Los Angeles Times-Washington Post News Service, Cambridge, Massachusetts, "Economic truth surrenders to politics," in The Kansas City *Star*, December 15, 1983, A-15.

Gallup, George, Jr. and Castelli, Jim, The Gallop Organization in The Kansas City *Star*, June 9, 1990, F-11.

Garron, Barry, "Television in the Role of Religion," in The Kansas City *Star*, May 14, 1987, C-1.

Gay, Lance, Scripps Howard News Service, "Time to worry when important folks say it can't happen," in The Kansas City *Star*, October 21, 1987, A-19.

Gide, André, 165-195 in *The God That Failed*, by Arthur Koestler *et al* (New York, Harper & Brothers, 1949).

Goldman, Marshall and Reddaway, Peter, "Report Cites Growth in Soviet Economy," in The Kansas City *Times*, March 28, 1987, A-1, 18.

Goodman, Ellen, Washington Post Writers Group, "Two sets of answers to question posed by Swaggart: Why? Why?," in The Kansas City *Star*, March 1, 1988, A-11.

"War story intrudes on chronicle of change," in The Kansas City *Star*, August 13, 1990, B-5.

Gordon, David M., Special to the Washington Post, Washington, "Average citizens losing key fights to affluent class," in The Kansas City *Star*, November 9, 1986, K-1.

Gough, Ian and Steinberg, Anne, "The Welfare State and Crisis," 141-171 in *Political Power and Social Theory*, 2 vols., edited by Maurice Zeitlin (New York, Jai Press, 1980-1981), II.

Gouldner, Alvin W., "Stalinism: a Study of Internal Colonialism," 209-259 in *Political Power and Social Theory. A Research Annual* in 3 vols., edited by Maurice Zeitlin (Greenwich, Connecticut, Jai Press, 1981), I.

Gracey, Harry L., "Learning the Student Role: Kindergarten as Academic Boot Camp," 215-226 in *Readings in Introductory Sociology,* 3rd edition (New York, Macmillan, 1977).

Graham, Billy, Tribune Media Services, no title to article, in The Kansas City *Star,* March 14, 1988, C-5.

Grinnel, George Bird, "The Cheyenne Indians," 139-148 in *The Golden Age of American Anthropology,* selected with introduction and notes by Margaret Mead and Ruth Bunzel (New York, George Braziller, 1960).

Gray, Helen T., Religion Editor, "Christ's first coming was joy, but his return is fulfillment," in The Kansas City *Times,* December 16, 1989, F-1, 3.

"Married priests await call from their church," in The Kansas City *Star,* March 17, 1990, E-10.

"Questions of theology costs Baptist missionary his job," in The Kansas City *Times,* September 5, 1988, B-3.

"Southern Baptists prepare for faceoff," in The Kansas City *Star,* May 19, 1990, E-11.

Greider, William, "The Education of David Stockman," 27-54 in *The Atlantic,* vol. 248, No. 6, December, 1981.

Gunn, J. M. and Keller, W., "Biological Recovery of an Acid Lake after Reductions in Industrial Emissions of Sulphur," 431-432 in *Nature,* vol. 435, May 31, 1990.

Gunter, Pete A. Y., "The Big Thicket: a Case Study in Attitudes Toward the Environment," 117-137 in *Philosophy and the Environmental Crisis,* edited by W. T. Blackstone (Athens, University of Georgia Press, 1974).

Gusewelle, C. W., "Pure purging tears, or those of a crocodile?," in The Kansas City *Star,* February 26, 1988, A-2.

"And the meek shall inherit the pink slip," in The Kansas City *Star,* July 21, 1990, D-1.

Haley, Jean, of the Editorial Staff, "So many of the young at risk," in The Kansas City *Star,* May 13, 1990, I-1, 4.

Hall, Norman F. and Lucia K. B., "Is the War between Science and Religion

Over?," 26-28 in *The Humanist,* vol. 46, No. 3, May-June, 1986.

Hall, Virginia, "Bush stuck without ifs, ands and buts," in The Kansas City *Star,* July 3, 1990, B-7.

Hampton, Jim, Knight-Ridder Newspapers, "Ruthless system of censorship feeds Soviet people's paranoia," in The Kansas City *Times,* September 15, 1983, A-15.

Harrington, Michael, Los Angeles Times News Service, "Tax inequality haunts U. S.," in The Kansas City *Times,* January 25, 1988, A-7.

Hartshorne, Charles, "The Environmental Results of Technology," 69-78 in *Philosophy and the Environmental Crisis,* edited by W. T. Blackstone (Athens, University of Georgia Press, 1974).

Hauptmann, Emily, "When Politics Makes Choices Disappear: Marcel Ophuls' France and Rational Choice Theories America." Paper read in March, 1990, at the Western Political Science Association in Newport Beach, California.

Heaster, Jerry, "Why no outrage on S & Ls?," in The Kansas City *Star,* April 11, 1990, B-1.

"Iacocca didn't take apology far enough," in the Kansas City *Star,* July 6, 1987, H-6.

Hirsch, E. D., Jr., "Cultural Illiteracy," in The Kansas City *Star,* July 8, 1987, A-15.

Hoagland, Jim, Washington Post Writers Group, Washington, "Nobody is following," The Kansas City *Star,* May 28, 1990, B-5.

"U. S. all but invited Saddam to go ahead and take Kuwait," in The Kansas City *Star,* September 15, 1990, C-9.

Hoffman, Ross J. S., "Catholicism and Historismus," 401-410 in *The Catholic Historical Review,* vol. 24, New Series, 1939.

Hood, Rich, "Tactics say voters ardor for democracy," The Kansas *Star,* May 13, 1990, B-2.

Hook, Sidney, "Introduction," to Raphael R. Abramovitch, *The Soviet Revolution, 1917-1919* (New York, International University Press, 1962).

Hyer, Marjorie, "U. S. bishops reject Vatican paper defining their ties to Rome," in The Kansas City *Times,* November 17, 1988, A-15.

"Baptist group blocking U. S. pamphlet on AIDS," in The Kansas *Times,* October 1, 1988, E-9.

320

Iacocca, Lee, Guest Columnist, "Tactics of takeover artists, arbitragers hurt U.S. business," in The Kansas City *Times,* January 29, 1987, C-1, 3.

Jacobs, Wilbur R., "Indians as Ecologists ... in American Frontier History," 46-64 in *American Indian Environments. Ecological Issues in Native American History,* edited by Christopher Vecsey and Robert W. Venables (Syracuse, Syracuse University Press, 1980).

Johnson, Douglas W., "Trends and Issues Shaping the Religious Future," 93-110 in Jackson W. Carroll, Douglas W. Johnson, Martin E. Marty, *Religion in America, 1950 to the Present* (New York, Harper & Row, 1979).

Johnson, Haynes, Washington Post, Knoxville, Tennessee, "Best and brightest of college set know exactly what they want in life," in The Kansas City *Star,* April 23, 1987, A-15.

"Everything to excess in this land of plenty," in The Kansas City *Times,* May 8, 1987, A-15.

"Is this nation in decline - again," in The Kansas City *Star,* March 6, 1988, K-5.

"'Teflon Years' closely resemble '20s," in The Kansas City *Times,* March 20, 1987, A-17.

"Televangelical drama more like 'Dynasty' or 'Dallas' than any biblical tale," in The Kansas City *Star,* March 27, 1987, A-15.

"That isn't smoke, that's fire," in The Kansas City *Times,* May 22, 1987, A-16.

Kaiser, Robert G., Washington, "Reagan's '84 prospects tied to economy," in The Kansas City *Star,* October 23, 1983, F-1.

Kaul, Donald, Tribune Media News, "Anyone reminded a bit of a fallen-away tent preacher in 'Grapes of Wrath?'," in The Kansas City *Times,* February 27, 1988, A-23.

"The buck never stops where the bucks flow," in The Kansas City *Times,* July 9, 1987, A-15.

"Circumstantial opinions about absolute matters," in The Kansas City *Star,* July 7, 1990, C-9.

"Environment in bad enough shape without military aid," in The Kansas City *Star,* July 14, 1990, C-11.

"A great and roaring example of incompetence at every level," in The Kansas City *Times,* June 18, 1987, A-17.

"Let's save Detroit," in The Kansas City *Star*, August 13, 1987, A-15.

"One last hurrah for American gunboat diplomacy," in The Kansas City *Star*, August 30, 1990, C-9.

"River of patriots bilge let loose," in The Kansas City *Star*, June 18, 1990, C-11.

"Russians must think this Iran-contra thing is some kind of trick," in The Kansas City *Times*, May 16, 1987, A-13.

"Shiny statements of principle aside," in The Kansas City *Star*, August 13, 1990, B-7.

"Titanic metaphor resurfaces," in The Kansas City *Times*, November 28, 1987, A-21.

"Tragic victory of Chamorro," in The Kansas City *Star*, March 1, 1990, C-19.

"Whole evangelical nightmare is a secular humanist's dream come true," in The Kansas City *Times*, March 28, 1987, A-19.

"With friends like this, who needs muggers?," in The Kansas City *Star*, September 10, 1990, B-7.

Keller, Bill, The New York Times, Washington, "Soviet union today likened to Germany after WW I," in The Kansas City *Star*, May 31, 1990, A-14.

"Walkout may undo the gains Gorbachev won at congress," The Kansas City *Star*, July 13, 1990, A-1.

The New York Times, "Soviet calls proposals the way to safe future," in The Kansas City *Star*, July 7, 1990, A-14.

Kennedy, Paul, "The (Relative) Decline of America," 29-38 in *The Atlantic*, vol. 260, No. 2, August, 1987.

Kent, Rev. W. H., "Catholic Truth and Historical Truth," 275-293 in *The Catholic Historical Review*, vol. 6, Old Series, 1920.

Kilpatrick, James J., Universal Press, Washington, "Another devastating report on deterioration of U. S. schools," in The Kansas City *Times*, September 18, 1987, A-14.

"Eggs Bentson may bring action," in The Kansas City *Times*, February 13, 1987, A-11.

"Harvard gets a sample of education," in The Kansas City *Star*, October 28, 1986, A-17.

"Miserable performance on deficit reduction," in The Kansas City *Times*, November 30, 1987, A-11.

"Senators agree on one point: something has to be done to curb campaign spending," in The Kansas City *Star*, March 27, 1987, A-15.

"U. S. Security & Latin America," 29-40 in *Commentary*, vol. 71, No. 1, January, 1981.

Koppel, Ted, "New Global Marketplace," PBS program, June 11, 1990.

Lasch, Robert, "The Origins of American Postwar Foreign Policy," 34-37 in *America Since World War II. Historical Interpretations*, edited by Jean Christie and Leonard Dinnetstein (New York, Praeger Publishing, 1976).

Lee, Gary, The Washington Post, Moscow, "Others follow Yeltsin out of party," The Kansas City *Star*, July 14, 1990, A-20.

Leerhsen, Charles with Huck, Janet, "Out There with Shirley," *Newsweek*, October 21, 1985.

Leubsdorf, Carl P., Dallas Morning News, "Public support for Persian Gulf action could erode," in The Kansas City *Star*, August 31, 1990, C-9.

Levinson, Marc, Journal of Commerce, "Queasy economy," in The Kansas City *Star*, July 25, 1990, C-9.

Lévi-Strauss interview in the New York *Times*, December 31, 1969, from The Introduction in *Ecology and Religion in History*, edited by David and Eileen Spring. Harper Torchback (New York, Harper & Row, 1974).

Lewis, Anthony, New York Times News Services, Boston, "Best argument for Reagan defense was made in 1977," in The Kansas City *Times*, May 25, 1987, A-23.

"Cold war years did terrible damage to real sources of U. S. security," in The Kansas City *Star*, July 16, 1990, B-5.

"Grotesque disparity in party resources," in The Kansas City *Times*, November 4, 1987, A-7.

"Institutions that worked in Watergate failed in Iran-contra," in The Kansas City *Star*, May 14, 1990, B-7.

"Lessons from Argentina on conduct of American foreign policy," in The Kansas City *Times*, January 27, 1984, A-13.

"Reagan folly led the way to imminent war in the desert," in The Kansas City *Star*, October 8, 1990, B-7.

"Something like divine right," in The Kansas City *Times,* May 11, 1987, A-9.

"Time for hard questions on El Salvador," in The Kansas City *Star,* April 29, 1990, J-3.

"U. S. paying dearly for president's cheerfulness," in The Kansas City *Times,* February 21, 1984, A-11.

"Whole host of problems plague us," in The Kansas City *Star,* February, 1980, I-5.

Lewis, Claude, Philadelphia Inquirer, "Persistent, inflammatory issues shaping U. S. future," in The Kansas City *Star,* June 15, 1990, C-9.

Lewis, Flora, Cairo. New York Times News Service, "Fundamentalism thrives in three religions: fills vacuum in world of ideas," in The Kansas City *Star,* December 29, 1986, A-9.

"Missouri journalism students belie image," in The Kansas City *Times,* November 15, 1987, A-15.

"Money the measure of prestige," in The Kansas City *Star,* April 26, 1987, K-5.

Lipset, Seymour Martin, "Introduction," 5-29 in Robert Michels, *Political Parties. A Sociological Study of the Oligarchical Tendencies of Modern Democracy.* Translated by Eden and Cedar Paul (New York, Free Press, Collier-Macmillan, 1962).

Lobos, Ignacio, Staff Writer, "Wealth's importance diminished, poll says" in The Kansas City *Star,* April 14, 1987, A-3.

Lokeman, Rhonda Chriss, from the Dallas Times Herald, "Blacks suffer legal injustice," in The Kansas City *Star,* June 10, 1990, J-1, 4.

"Salvador getting away with murder," in The Kansas City *Star,* August 20, 1990, B-5.

Luedtke, Kurt, Los Angeles Times-Washington Post News Service, "A right to speak, but no one listens," in The Kansas City *Star,* January 18, 1987, K-2.

McClanahan, E. Thomas, of the Editorial Staff, "Deficit politics as usual," in The Kansas City *Star,* October 3, 1990, C-7.

"Savings and loan, they need more help than Congress is giving," in The Kansas City *Star,* September 23, 1990, K-1, 4.

McCormick, Richard A., "The Search for Truth in the Catholic Context," 276-281 in *America,* vol. 155, No. 13, November 8, 1986.

MacEwan, Arthur, "Capitalist Expansion, Ideology and Intervention," 409-420 in *The Capitalist System. A Radical Analysis of American Society*. Written and edited by Richard C. Edwards *et al* (Englewood Cliffs, New Jersey, Prentice-Hall, 1972).

Magdoff, Henry, "Militarism and Imperialism," 421-426 in *The Capitalist System, A Radical Analysis of American Society*. Written and edited by Richard C. Edwards *et al* (Englewood Cliffs, New Jersey, Prentice-Hall, 1972).

Mannion, J. B., "The Pope and Mr. Dooley on Jazz Masses," 416-417 in *Commonweal*, vol. 85, January 20, 1967.

Márquez, Gabriel García, "The Death of Salvadore Allende," translated by Gregory Rabass," 46-55 in *Harper's*, vol. 248, No. 1486, March, 1974.

Marshall, Eliot. "Gore Investigates Radiation Clinic," 423-424 in *Science*, vol. 214, October 23, 1981.

Marty, Martin E., "Modern Fundamentalism," 133-135 in *America*, vol. 155, No. 7, September 27, 1986.

Mearsheimer, John J., "Why We Will Soon Miss the Cold War," 35-50 in *The Atlantic*, vol. 266, No. 2, August, 1990.

Meisler, Stanley, and Jackson, Robert L., Los Angeles Times, "Poindexter found guilty," in The Kansas City *Star*, April 8, 1990, A-1.

Menand, Louis, "Man of the People, The True and Only Heaven. Progress and Its Critics," 39-44 in *The New York Book Review of Books*, vol. 38, No. 7, April 11, 1991.

Merton, Robert K., "Puritanism, Pietism, and Science," 574-606 in *Social Theory and Social Structure*. Revised and enlarged (Glencoe, Illinois, Free Press, 1961).

Michels, Robert, "Democracy and the Iron Law of Oligarchy," 342-356 in *Political Parties. A Sociological Study of the Oligarchical Tendencies of Modern Democracy*. Translated by Eden and Cedar Paul. Introduction by Seymour Martin Lipset (New York, Collier-Macmillan, 1962).

Mitgang, Lee, AP Education Writer, "People are wrong to think students aren't concerned," in The Kansas City *Star*, September 2, 1987, A-17.

Mohr, Charles, New York Times News Service, Washington, "Great Plains rebels don't like Pentagon ways," in The Kansas City *Times*, October 14, 1983, A-21.

Moncrief, Lewis W., "The Cultural Basis for Our Environmental Crisis," 76-90 in *Ecology and Religion in History,* edited by David and Eileen Spring, Harper Torchback (New York, Harper & Row, 1974).

Montgomery, Rick, Ruess, Michelle, and Hughes, Terry, "Opinions differ in K. C. on Vatican moves against U. S. clerics, liberal stance," in The Kansas City *Star,* November 16, 1986, A-10.

Morris, David, St. Paul Pioneer Press, "Beneficiaries of thrift crisis should pay the bailout bill," in The Kansas City *Star,* August 16, 1990, C-11.

Moseley, Fay, Chicago Tribune, Glasgow, Scotland, "Scots have an edge in high tech," in The Kansas City *Times,* January 6, 1984, A-11.

Murray, Timothy A., "A Conversation with Jacques Cousteau. 'We face a Catastrophe' If the Oceans are not Cleaned Up," 68 in *U. S. News and World Report,* vol. 98, No. 24, June, 1985.

Nanton, Dick K., Los Angeles Times News Services, "U. S. boosts Japan's rising arrogance," in The Kansas City *Times,* April 29, 1987, A-11.

Neikirk, William R., Chicago Tribune, Washington "'Competitiveness' a meaningless word," in The Kansas City *Star,* August 6, 1987, B-6.

"World affairs weaken U. S. economic policy," in The Kansas City *Star,* February 16, 1988, A-5.

Nelson, Lars Eric, New York Daily News, Washington, "Nation's capital isn't blue-collar town," in The Kansas City *Times,* January 10, 1984, A-9.

"Saudis come out ahead any way you look at it," in The Kansas City *Star,* September 12, 1990, C-11.

Neumeyer, Kathleen, "Finding God in the 90s," in The Kansas City *Star,* October 1, 1989, H-1.

Newron, Verne W., "The Real Cause of Revolution," in The Kansas City *Star,* October 9, 1983, H-4.

Nugent, Tom, "A birthday, but not a quiet one," in The Kansas City *Star,* November 5, 1989, E-1.

Nyham, David, Boston Globe, "Hooked on Iran-contra scandal," in The Kansas City *Times,* September 2, 1987, A-8.

"Japanese investors buying a lot more," in The Kansas City *Star,* April 14, 1987, A-9.

O'Brien, John A., "Crisis in the Catholic Church," 1233-1234 in *Christian*

Century, vol. 88, October 20, 1971.

O'Neill, Tip, with William Novak, "Friendship not leadership," first of five articles in The Kansas City *Star,* September 13, 1987, A-1, 16.

Oreskes, Michael, New York Times News Service, "Alienation a threat to political system," from the Times Mirror Center for the People and the Press in The Kansas City *Star,* September 23, 1990, K-4.

Ortega y Gasset, "The Dehumanization of Art," 411-419 in *A Modern Book of Esthetics.* An Anthology, 3rd edition (New York, Holt, Rinehart and Winston, 1960).

O'Shea, Kevin, "Is Resurrection Theology Outdated," 7-11 in *The Catholic World,* vol. 209, No.1, April, 1969.

Page, Clarence, Tribune Media News Services, "Dubious Drug War," The Kansas City *Star,* May 4, 1990, C-15.

Pastur, Robert, 4-6 in "Letters from Readers. U. S. Security & Latin America," in *Commentary,* 4-20, vol. 71, No. 4, April, 1981.

Paul, Sherman, "Introduction," to Henry David Thoreau, *Walden.* Edited with an Introduction and Notes by Sherman Paul (Boston, Houghton-Mifflin, 1957).

Pendleton, Elmer D., Special Correspondent, "Iraq threat must be contained," in The Kansas City *Star,* August 19, 1990, J-1, 4.

Phillips, Kevin, Los Angeles Times-Washington Post News Service, "Economic boom of 1983-1988 may yet go bust," in The Kansas City *Star,* January 24, 1988, H-3.

"U. S. is over-committed to the world," in The Kansas City *Star,* July 5, 1987, C-1, 6.

"Worst of Vietnam, Iran crisis combines," in The Kansas City *Star,* August 27, 1990, B-5.

Pickel, Helmut, Nurnberger Nachrichten (Reprinted from the *German Tribune*), "Saber-rattling is too dangerous to be indulged," in The Kansas City *Star,* July 5, 1987, A-1.

Pike, Otis, Newhouse News Services, Washington, "Iran-contra report teaches nothing new," in The Kansas City *Star,* November 23, 1987, A-9.

Pluckhahn, Labor Writer, "Jobless begin to cope as the work place changes," in The Kansas City *Star,* September 18, 1983, K-1.

Portal, Roger, "Preface" to Marc Ferro, *The Russian Revolution of February*

1917. Translated by J. L. Richards (Englewood Cliffs, New Jersey, Prentice-Hall, 1972).

Praisewater, Eldon D., Chairman, National Association of Atomic Veterans, Missouri Chapter, "First-hand knowledge," The Kansas City *Star,* October 31, 1983, A-10.

Rather, Dan, "The Ford Escort Story," CBS TV broadcast, January 10, 1984.

Reed, George, "Astronomy & Astrology. East vs West," 90-95 in *Astronomy,* vol. 14, No. 1, January 1986.

Reeves, Richard, "Beware the falling superdollar," in The Kansas City *Times,* January 26, 1987, A-7.

"'Business is business' mentality reigns," in The Kansas City *Times,* March 1, 1984, A-11.

"Europeans doing some trail-blazing on jobs," in The Kansas City *Times,* September 2, 1983, A-15.

"Journalism has suddenly become another business without value," in The Kansas City *Star,* June 30, 1987, A-6.

"Ongoing S & L debacle demonstrates bankruptcy of American government," in The Kansas City *Star,* April 19, 1990, C-7.

"Patriotic paranoia grows in the dark," in The Kansas City *Times,* August 1, 1987, A-23.

"President Bush is a liar, but that's no surprise," in The Kansas City *Star,* July 2, 1990, B-7.

"Recovering from Reagan revolution will be painful," in The Kansas City *Times,* November 25, 1987, A-11.

"Remember when we could successfully compete," in the Norwich Connecticut *Bulletin,* July 29, 1987, A-7.

"U. S. suddenly out of step in world of new realities," in The Kansas City *Times,* April 19, 1987, A-15.

"What's news any day depends on what else is news," in The Kansas City *Star,* August 15, 1990, C-13.

Reich, Michael and Finkelhor, "Up Against the American Myth," 393-406 in *The Capitalist System. A Radical Analysis of American Society.* Written and edited by Richard C. Edwards *et al* (Englewood Cliffs, New Jersey, Prentice-Hall, 1972).

328

Reidy, Chris, Orlando Sentinel, Washington, "Foreign money pays for America's standard of living," in The Kansas City *Star,* December 6, 1987, K-3.

Rescher, Nicholas, "The Environmental Crisis and the Quality of Life," 90-104 in *Philosophy and the Environmental Crisis* edited by W. T. Blackstone (Athens, University of Georgia Press, 1974).

Reston, James, New York Times News Service, Washington, "Now Congress is Angry," in The Kansas City *Star,* June 11, 1987, A-21.

"Oliver North is not on trial," in The Kansas City *Star,* July 14, 1987, A-9.

Rivlin, Alice M., The Washington Post, Washington, "A new world order presents Americans with new challenges," in The Kansas City *Star,* April 15, 1990, I-4.

Roberts, Paul Craig, Scripps Howard News Services, "How did S & L bill mount up?," in The Kansas City *Star,* May 31, 1990, C-7.

Robertson, William, Knight-Ridder Newspapers, "Passion and the Preachers," in The Kansas City *Star,* March 6, 1988, K-1.

Roche, Douglas J., "The Catholic Revolution," 33-36 in *The Catholic World,* vol. 280, No. 1, October, 1968.

Roessner, Barbara T., The Hartford Courant, in The Kansas City *Star,* May 25, 1990, C-9.

Rosenberg, Howard L., "Informed Consent," 31-44 in *Mother Jones,* September-October, 1981.

Rosenthal, A. M., New York Times News Service, "Warm moment in history chilled by Gorbachev's threat on immigration," in the Kansas City *Star,* June 8, 1990, C-9.

Rovib, Jeff, "Shirley!," 109-151 in *Ladies Home Journal,* vol. 102, No. 8, August, 1985).

Rowan, Carl T., North American Syndicate, Washington, "Chuckholes on Reagan road to greatness," in The Kansas City *Times,* April 17, 1987, A-13.

News America, Washington, "Education budget may be bigger than Iran mistake," in The Kansas City *Star,* January 19, 1987, A-9.

Royko, Mike, Tribune Media News Service, "It's horrible to think what might happen," in The Kansas City *Star,* October 29, 1987, A-19.

"To get job age has no privileges," in The Kansas City *Star,* July 20, 1990, C-11.

Rubin, Trudy, "New world order easier said than achieved," in The Kansas City *Star*, September 17, 1990, B-7.

Rutberg, Sidney, Fairchild News Services, "Bargains like this are few indeed," in The Kansas City *Star*, January 20, 1987, A-4.

Safire, William, New York Times News Services, Washington, "President should retire when he is ahead," in The Kansas City *Star*, October 4, 1983, A-10.

Sagan, Carl, interview of George Kistiakowsky, "Confessions of a Weaponeer," September 8, 1987, PBS.

Sage, Wayne, "Crime and Clockwork Lemon, 16-23 in *Human Behavior*, vol. 3, No. 9, September, 1974.

Schrembs, Joseph, "The Catholic Philosophy of History, in *The Catholic Philosophy of History*, III. Papers of the American Catholic Historical Association, edited by Peter Guilday (New York, 1936).

Schwarz, John C., "Celibacy: the foundations have shifted," 254-257 in *Catholic World Journal*, vol. 212, Fall, 1971.

Scobie, W. I., "Mini-Mass," 317-318 in *National Review*, vol. 25, March 16, 1973.

Scott, Laura, of the Editorial Staff, "People flood the earth," in The Kansas City *Star*, May 27, 1990, J-1.

Selikoff, D. I. J., "Asbestos," 2-7 in *Environment*, vol. 11, No. 2, March, 1969.

Sentell, Will, Jefferson City Correspondent, Mobile, Alabama, "A dozen governors give education reforms bad marks," in The Kansas City *Star*, July 29, 1990, A-5.

Shabecoff, Phillip, The New York Times, "Tropical forest loss is worsening," in The Kansas City *Star*, June 8, 1990, A-1, 4.

Shanan, Rt. Rev. Thomas J., "The Study of Church History," 303-332 in *The Catholic Historical Review*, II, No. 3, New Series, 1922.

Shanley, Rev. Albert J., "Catholicism and the Writing of History," in *Studies in Sacred Theology*, 61 vols. (Washington, D. C., The Catholic University of America, 1941), vol. 12, 6.

Shannon, William V., Boston Globe, "A certain extravagance of objectives," in The Kansas City *Times*, May 28, 1987, A-15.

"Reagan offense basically same as Nixon's," in The Kansas City *Star*, February 19, 1987, A-14.

"Thatcher has her doubts about Reagan," in The Kansas City *Star*, June 11, 1987, A-20.

Sherrod, Katie, Fort Worth Star Telegram, "Texas unsurprisingly among last prepared for spill," in The Kansas City *Star*, June 15, 1990, C-9.

Shulman, Marshall D., "Beyond the Containment Policy," 665-673 in *Soviet Society. A Book of Readings*, edited by Alex Inkeles and Kant Geiger (Boston, Houghton Mifflin, 1961).

Shuster, George, "History: A Barrier or a Blessing," 185-190 in *The Catholic Historical Review*, vol. 22, No. 2, New Series, 1936.

Siegfried, Francis J., "Historical Criticism and Philosophy," 75-83 in *The Catholic Historical Review*, vol. 5, New Series, 1925.

Sims, David E., "Spoon-Feeding the Military - How New Weapons Came to Be," 225-265 in *Pentagon Watchers. Student Report on the National Security State*, edited by Leonard Rodberg and Derek Shearer (Garden City, New York, Anchor Books, Doubleday, 1970).

Sitkoff, Harvard, "Years of the Locust. Interpretations of the Truman Presidency Since 1945," 75-112 in *The Truman Period as a Research Field. A Reappraisal*, 1972, edited by Richard S. Kirkendall (Columbia, University of Missouri Press, 1974).

Smith, Fran, Knight-Ridder Newspapers, "Author still stressed that fewer is better," in The Kansas City *Star*, April 12, 1990, F-8.

Smith, Randall D., "Who'll pay for the S & L mess?," in The Kansas City *Star*, June 28, 1990, B-1.

Sobran, Joseph, Universal Press, Washington, "Melodrama in the desert," in The Kansas City *Star*, August 20, 1990, B-7.

"Our 'warrior pundits' assume events can be controlled," in The Kansas City *Star*, September 3, 1990, B-5.

"Turns out there is only one lesson in the sum total of history," in The Kansas City *Star*, August 27, 1990, B-7.

Sorokin, Pitirim, Foreword to *Tönnies, Community and Society (Gemeinschaft and Gesellschaft)*. Translated and edited by Charles P. Loomis (East Lansing, the Michigan State University Press, 1957).

Spender, Stephen, 229-273 in *The God That Failed*, edited by Arthur Koestler *et al* (New York, Harper, 1949).

Stassinopoulos, Adrianna, "Shirley MacLaine," 28-41 in *Ladies Home Journal*, vol. 101, No. 5, May, 1984.

Steel, Ronald, United Features Syndicate (Reprinted from the *New Republic*). "U. S. has a troubling naivete about how the world works," in The Kansas City *Star*, February 22, 1987, K-3.

Steinem, Gloria, "Shirley MacLaine Talks About Spirit vs. Action," 100 in *Ms.*, vol. 14, No. 6, December, 1985.

Steinfels, Peter, the New York Times, "Big religious battles of today are waged inside denominations," in The Kansas City *Times*, February 24, 1990, E-8.

Stranahan, Susan Q., "50 Years of Environment. The Nation Tries to Unfoul Its Nest," 29-33 in *National Wildlife*, vol. 26, No. 3, April-May, 1986.

Strong, James, Chicago Tribune, "Reagan stance on PATCO hurt all labor," in The Kansas City *Star*, January 29, 1984, E-5, 7.

Summers, Harry, Col., Los Angeles Times Syndicate, "Hussein's colossal miscalculation," in The Kansas City *Star*, August 15, 1990, C-11.

"Let Saddam Hussein's actions be a lesson to us," in The Kansas City *Star*, August 8, 1990, C-9.

"U. S. has troubles alright, but Soviets have worse," in The Kansas City *Times*, March 17, 1988, A-13.

"Wrong questions, wrong answers," in The Kansas City *Times*, July 15, 1987, A-19.

Takaki, Ronald, Newsday, "Economic disparity breeds contempt," in The Kansas City *Star*, July 8, 1990, J-1, 4.

Tapscott, Kansas Correspondent, "Pinch on welfare mothers in states," in The Kansas City *Times*, January 24, 1984, A-1.

Thibodeau, Ralph, "Fiasco in Church Music," 73-78 in *Commonweal*, vol. 84, No. 3, April, 1966.

Thomas, Cal, Los Angeles Times Syndication, "Forgiveness is one thing," in The Kansas City *Times*, March 4, 1988, A-11.

Thompson, Bill, Fort Worth Star Telegram. "Trouble in the world didn't end with culmination of the Cold War," in The Kansas City *Star*, August 9, 1990, C-7.

Thompson, Jake, Washington Correspondent, Washington, "New national issues and easy times for the GOP," in The Kansas City *Star*, July 8, 1990, A-1, 8.

Thompson, Roger, Congressional Quarterly, "Illiteracy takes toll in lives and dollars," in The Kansas City *Star*, July 18, 1983, A-15.

Thurlow, Lester C., Dean of MIT's Alfred P. Sloan School of Management, "Economic mythology underlies budget fiasco," in The Kansas City *Star*, October 14, 1990, L-1, 4.

Tolba, Mustafe, New Perspectives Quarterly, "World peace and stability depend now on restoring our balance with nature," in The Kansas City *Star*, April 2, 1990, B-7.

Toynbee, Arnold, "The Religious Background of the Present Environmental Crisis," 137-149 in *Ecology and Religion in History*, edited by David and Eileen Spring. Harper Torchback (New York, Harper & Row, 1974).

"Russia and Western Civilization," 643-648 in *Soviet Society. A Book of Readings*, edited by Alex Inkeles and Kent Geiger (Boston, Houghton Mifflin, 1961).

Turnbull, Peter, Scripps Howard News Service, "'Communion' with other worlds," in The Kansas City *Star*, February 22, 1988, C-4.

Urban, C. Stanley, "Veblen's Analysis of American Capitalism," 9 pp., Park College, May 4, 1970.

Unger, Robert, National Correspondent, "Has U. S. lost jobs? Depends on point of view," in The Kansas City *Star*, April 28, 1990, A-16.

"A war wouldn't bolster business in U. S. this time, economists say," in The Kansas City *Star*, August 27, 1990,   A-1.

Uelmen, Gerald, Los Angeles Times News Services, "Rush to Injustice," in The Kansas City *Star*, May 29, 1990, B-5.

Vogel, David, Washington Post-Los Angeles Times News Service, "Changing family situations in America" in The Kansas City *Star*, January 16, 1987, A-11.

"Trade deficit only starting point in making U. S. competitive again," in The Kansas City *Star*, May 3, 1987, M-2.

Wallerstein, Immanuel, "The Rise and Future Demise of the World Capitalist System.   Concepts for Comparative Analysis," 387-415 in *Comparative Studies in Society and History*, vol. 16, 1974.

Warburg, James J., "Onset of the Cold War," 958-966 in *Shaping of American Diplomacy*, edited by William Appleman Williams (Chicago, Rand McNally, 1965).

Waters, Sister Annette, "The 'Double Bind' in Religious Life Today," 22-26 in *The Catholic World*, vol. 210, No. 1, 255, October, 1969.

Wehr, Elizabeth, Congressional Quarterly, Inc., Washington, "No dire predictions from the seers - yet," in The Kansas City *Star*, July 29, 1987, K-3.

Weinberger, Casper W., New Perspective Quarterly, "All combat criteria met," in The Kansas City *Star*, August 10, 1990, C-7.

Weisskopf, Thomas E., "Capitalism and Inequality," 125-133 in *The Capitalist System*, edited by Richard C. Edwards *et al* (Englewood Cliffs, New Jersey, Prentice-Hall, 1972).

"United States Foreign Private Investment: An Empirical Survey," 426-434 in *The Capitalist System. A Radical Analysis of American Society.* Written and edited by Richard C. Edwards *et al* (Englewood Cliffs, New Jersey, Prentice-Hall, 1972).

Welter, John, Carroboro, N.C., "Swaggart demise inspires a little light verse," in The Kansas City *Star*, March 3, 1988, A-10.

Wenske, Paul, "PTL backers not at ease with Falwell," in The Kansas City *Times*, March 28, 1987, A-1, 16.

Wesson, Robert, "Grim lessons from airliner massacre," in The Kansas City *Star*, September 25, 1983, E-4.

White, Lynn, Jr., "Christian Myth and Christian History," 145-158 in *Journal of the History of Ideas*, vol. 3, No. 2, 1942.

Wicker, Tom, New York Times News Services, New York, "America's standard of living is falling (yes, falling)," in The Kansas City *Times*, August 18, 1987, A-9.

"Are big deficits part of Reagan plot?," in The Kansas City *Times*, February 8, 1984, A-17.

"Political consultants are no asset," in The Kansas City *Star*, November 23, 1986, C-5.

"President's Domestic Policy Council says 'let them eat cake'," in The Kansas City *Star*, July 27, 1990, C-9.

"President's polls reinforce lesson often ignored by Democrats," in The Kansas City *Star*, January 24, 1990, A-7.

"Vets of atomic blasts still paying for service to nation," in The Kansas City *Times*, September 1, 1983, A-19.

Wikle, Gretel, The Associated Press, "Church survives budget cutting," in The Kansas City *Star*, March 17, 1990, E-11.

Wilde, Margaret, "Jeanne Kirkpatrick; Utilitarianism as U. S. Foreign

Policy," 226-229 in *Christian Century,* vol. 97,   No. 7.

Will, George, Washington, "Poor George began tumbling down hill at his inauguration," in The Kansas City *Times,* January 22, 1990, A-9.

Willems, Boniface A., "The Death of God Phenomenon," 17-19 in *The Catholic World,* vol. 204, No. 1, October, 1966.

Williams, Diana, Staff Writer, "Abortion opponents celebrate anniversary of Webster decision," The Kansas City *Star,* July 4, 1990, C-6.

Williams, William Appleman, "The Legend of Isolation," 657-663 in *The Shaping of American Diplomacy,* edited by W. A. Williams (Chicago, Rand McNally, 1956).

Wilson, William Julius, "Where Has Progress Got Us? *The True and Only Heaven.* Progress and Its Critics," 9, 28 in The New York *Times* Book Review, January 27, 1991.

Wirth, Louis, "Preface," to Karl Mannheim, xiii-xxxi in *Ideology and Utopia. An Introduction to the Sociology of Knowledge* (New York, Harcourt-Brace, 1940).

Wolfe, Bertram D., "The Durability of Soviet Totalitarianism," 648-659 in *Soviet Society. A Book of Readings,* edited by Alex Inkeles and Kent Geiger (Boston, Houghton Mifflin, 1961).

Woo, William F., St. Louis Post Dispatch, "It's galling to watch erosion of (morality)," in The Kansas City *Times,* August 5, 1987, A-13.

Wright, Guy, San Francisco Examiner, "Buying American is becoming harder," in The Kansas City *Star,* March 26, 1987, A-11.

Yardley, Jonathan, Washington Post, "Civil rights, civil wrongs," in The Kansas City *Times,* March 25, 1987, A-13.

"If these are happy times, why do Americans seem to hate each other so much?," in The Kansas City *Star,* June 24, 1990, J-4.

"Schools undue by 'process' sophistry," in The Kansas City *Times,* September 9, 1987, A-17.

Zeitlin, Maurice, "Who Owns America? The Same Old Gang," 167-172 in *The Social World,* edited by Ian Robertson (New York, Worth Publishers, 1981).

Zola, Irving Kenneth, "Medicine as an Institution of Social Control," 511-526 in *The Sociology of Health and Illness,* edited by Peter Conrad and Rochelle Kern (New York, St. Martin's Press, 1981).

Zukerman, Seth, "Environmentalism Turns 16," 368-370 in *The Nation,* vol. 243, No. 12, October 18, 1986.

Unsigned Articles in Magazines and Periodicals

"All Things Considered. The Emerging Nun," 104 in *Commonweal*, vol. 82, No. 4, April 16, 1965.

"The Asbestos Hits the Fan," 26-27 in *Maclean's*, April 14, 1980.

"A big break for Ollie; Will a court ruling mean that North goes free," 30 in *Time*, vol. 136, No. 5, July 30, 1990.

"Blessed be the Name of Ford," 29-30 in *Maclean's*, March 24, 1980.

"Celibacy, No!," 49 in *Time*, vol. 95, January 19, 1970.

"Chevrolet's Failing Engine Mounts," 118-121 in *Consumer Reports*, vol. 37, No. 2, February, 1972.

"Choosing Anglican Bishops," 460 in *The Christian Century*, May 13, 1987.

"Church unmilitant," 17-18 in London, *The Economist*, (London) April 1, 1990.

"Churches Respond to Teen Suicide," 436-439 in *Christian Century*, vol. 103, No. 15, April 20, 1986.

"Comments and Ratings. Subcompact Cars," 274-275 in *Consumer Reports*, vol. 38, No. 4, April, 1973.

"The Cool Generation and the Church. A Commonweal Symposium," 11-23 in *Commonweal*, vol. 87, No. 1, October 6, 1967.

"Conscience and Orthodoxy," 53-55 in *Commonweal*, vol. 84, No. 1, March 25, 1966.

"Dateline Washington," 4 in *Consumers' Research*, vol. 64, No. 3, March, 1981.

"A Dead Stop in the Ford Pinto Trial," 65-66 in *Newsweek*, February 25, 1980.

"Deadly Legacy: Dioxin and the Vietnam Veteran," 15-19 in *The Bulletin of the Atomic Scientists*, vol. 35, No. 5, May, 1979.

"Durham: The Saga Continues," London Letter, 437, in *The Christian Century*, May 1, 1985.

"Faulty Engine Mounts and Faulty Recall Program," 83-84 in *The Consumer Reports*, vol. 38, No. 2, February, 1973.

"A Grim Legacy from World War II," 31 in *Business Week*, September 29, 1975.

"The Little Cars," 8-17 in *Consumer Reports*, vol. 36, No. 1, January, 1971.

"Liturgy and headlines," 79 in *America*, vol. 116, January 21, 1967.

"A Local D.A. Charges the Pinto with Murder," 36-38 in *People*, February 4, 1980.

"The Making of a Monster," 29-32 in *Newsweek*, vol. 116, No. 8, August 20, 1990.

"A Mistake in San Diego, 416 in *America*, vol. 161, December 8, 1989.

"Out of the Backwaters? The Problem of Catholic University," 39-41 in *Commonweal*, vol. 86, No. 1, March 24, 1967.

"Overview," 2-4 in *Environment*, vol. 21, No. 5, June, 1979.

"A papal decree on church ritual," 16 in *U. S. News and World Report*, vol. 66, May 12, 1969.

"Pinto Precedent," 356-357 in *The Nation*, March 29, 1980.

"The Pope Gets Tough," 67-68 in *U. S. News and World Report*, vol. 101, No. 20, November 17, 1986.

"Racism and Research: The Case of the Tuskogee Syphilis Study," 186-195 in *The Social World*, edited by Jan Robertson (New York, Worth Publishing Company, 1981).

"Restive Nuns: Steady Loss Among Sisters," 66-68 in *Time*, vol. 89, January 13, 1967.

"Rules Roundup," 111 in *Motor Trend*, vol. 33, No. 11, November 11, 1981.

"Safety Clothing," 51-52 in *Scientific American*, July, 1945.

"Special Report: Part 4. Acid Rain: No Harm Done?," 18-19 in *Consumers' Research*, vol. 73, March, 1990.

"Where is My Country?," 20 in *Time*, vol. 115, No. 8, February 25, 1980.

"Why Priests Marry?," 105-110 in *Reader's Digest*, vol. 95, December, 1969. (Condensed from the *Christian Herald*).

"Wrongful Death," 9-10 in *Progressive*, vol. 44, No. 11, November 10, 1980.

"Youth Suicide," 39 in *New York*, vol. 19, No. 22, June 2, 1986.

Unsigned Articles in Newspapers

"Abortion showdown set in Louisiana," The Associated Press, Baton Rouge, Louisiana, in The Kansas City *Star*, June 28, 1990, A-6.

"Actions subverted the Constitution's check on executive branch," The Associated Press, Washington, in The Kansas City *Times*, October 19, 1987, A-8.

"America has come full circle on energy," The Economist (London), Washington, in The Kansas City *Star*, August 19, 1990, J-4.

"Apathy, acceptance permeated 1988 election, panel says," The Associated Press, Washington, in The Kansas City *Star*, May 6, 1990, A-4.

"Audit finds huge profit on tools for military," the Knight Ridder Newspapers, Washington, in The Kansas City *Star*, November 2, 1983, A-1.

"Baby Boomer Madness: amid success there is happiness?," Los Angeles Times, Washington, in The Kansas City *Times*, November 27, 1986, K-2.

"Baptist schism may be the answer to internal fight, scholar says," The Washington *Post*, in The Kansas City *Times*, April 4, 1987, C-17.

"Better business bureau to rule on complaints of faulty GM cars," the Associated Press, Washington, in The Kansas City *Star*, November 17, 1983, C-2.

"A camp-meeting preacher in the big time," from the Star's Wire Service, in The Kansas City *Star*, March 27, 1987, A-6.

"Can the Pope command his flock in America?," from the Economist (London), in The Kansas City *Star*, April 29, 1984, D-1, 4.

"Catholics appealing for reforms," The New York Times, Chicago, in The Kansas City *Times*, February 28, 1990, A-3.

"Chrysler gets $1.5 million safety fine," by the Associated Press, in The Kansas City *Star*, July 6, 1987, A-6.

"Coral reefs are dying, and scientists cite warmer seas," The Washington *Post*, Washington, in The Kansas City *Star*, October 12, 1990, A-5.

"Court finds Ford guilty in fiery crash," Corpus Christi, Texas, in The Kansas City *Times*, November 23, 1983, A-4.

"Crash victim's family awarded $1.1 million," Los Angeles, in The Kansas City *Times*, December 24, 1983, A-4.

"Debt level threatens U. S. Status," by the Associated Press, Washington, in The Kansas City *Star*, August 10, 1987, A-1.

"Dollar resumes fall," New York *Times*, Washington, in The Kansas City *Times*, November 11, 1987, A-1, 21.

"Dollar's nose dive betters market," New York *Times*, Washington, in The Kansas City *Times*, December 1, 1987, A-1.

"Don't fool around with Mother Nature," New York *Times* News Services, New York, in The Kansas City *Star*, March 27, 1988, I-3.

"Dow declines in heavy trading," from the Times Staff and Associated Press, in The Kansas City *Times*, November 5, 1987, E-3.

"Dow near crash level," by the Associated Press, New York, in The Kansas City *Times*, December 5, 1987, B-1.

"Dow sinks 108.36 in frantic 'blowout'," Los Angeles Times, New York, in The Kansas City *Times*, October 17, 1987, A-1.

"Drug ring broken on Wall Street," from the Times News Services, New York, in The Kansas City *Times*, April 17, 1987, A-1.

"Economists predict number of jobs will decline in '88," The Associated Press, New York, in The Kansas City *Times*, December 30, 1987, D-1.

"Effects of Agent Orange acknowledged," Washington Post, Washington, in The Kansas City *Star*, May 19, 1990, A-7.

"Figures to reinforce U. S. slide into debt," the Associated Press, Washington, in The Kansas City *Star*, June 22, 1987, B-7.

"Ford to build plant in Mexico to make autos for export," the Times News Service, Mexico City, in The Kansas City *Times*, January 14, 1984, F-1.

"A frown is visible on America's face," from the Economist (London), in The Kansas City *Star*, September 27, 1987, H-1.

"German pledge aid in crisis," The Associated Press, Ludwigshafen, West Germany, in The Kansas City *Star*, September 16, 1990, A-1, 10.

"GM was aware brakes were flawed, documents indicate," from the Times News Service, Washington, in The Kansas City *Times*, October 21, 1983, A-1.

"GNP grows weak," The Associated Press, in The Kansas City *Star*, March 18, 1987, A-17.

"Gorbachev hints he may quit party post," The Washington Post, Moscow, in The Kansas City *Star*, June 21, 1990, A-6.

"Gorbachev suggest reforming the union," The Associated Press, Moscow, in The Kansas City *Star*, June 13, 1990, A-1.

"Iacocca says Chrysler sorry," New York Times News Service, Highland Park, Michigan, in The Kansas City *Times*, July 3, 1987, A-1.

"International study shows surprising loss in ozone layer," The Washington Post, Washington, in The Kansas City *Times*, March 16, 1988, A-9.

"Kerner report revisited," The Washington Post, Racine, Wisconsin, in The Kansas City *Times*, March 1, 1988, A-1, 4.

"Levine gets two years," The Associated Press, White Plains, New York, in The Kansas City *Times*, February 21, 1987, E-10.

"Lying low or falling down may be the best Japan can do," The Economist (London), in The Kansas City *Star*, September 11, 1990, B-7.

"Manville Files Suit," New York *Times*, November 17, 1983, D-4.

"Manville Suite Asks U. S. to Pay Asbestos Claims," New York *Times*, July 20, 1983, D-1, 2.

"Meese saw Wedtech report before investing, memo says," The Associated Press, Washington, in The Kansas City *Star*, September 29, 1987, A-1, 2.

"Minimum wage puts family of four below poverty line," Consumer Reports, in The Kansas City *Star*, November 4, 1986, A-8.

"Mission impossible in the Persian Gulf," editorial in The Kansas City *Star*, June 23, 1987, A-14.

"Modern Baptists set separate agenda," The Associated Press, New York, in The Kansas City *Times*, September 17, 1988, E-8.

"New arrests stun Wall Street," the Star's Wire Services, in The Kansas City *Star*, February 13, 1987, A-9.

"New stats highlight decline in U. S. education," The Associated Press, Washington, in The Kansas City *Star*, January 5, 1984, A-1.

"O'Connor the real issue," in The New York *Times*, February 1, 1990, A-1.

"Oil prices pose two threats," Los Angeles, Washington, in The Kansas City *Star*, September 23, 1990, A-17.

"One thing is sure: America's feast is coming to an end," The Economist (London), in The Kansas City *Times*, December 29, 1987, A-7.

"Outrage of the Week," in The Kansas City *Star*, December 20, 1983, A-11.

340

"Ozone deterioration worsening, studies show at London session," Associated Press, London, in The Kansas City *Star*, June 21, 1990, A-7.

"Ozone hole reopens above Antarctica," The New York Times, in The Kansas City *Star*, October 12, 1990, A-3.

"Paint them a little shinier," Editorial in The Kansas City *Star*, July 9, 1990, B-6.

"Party picks Gorbachev ally," The Washington Post, Moscow, in The Kansas City *Star*, July 12, 1990, A-3.

"Pentagon and Contractors Said to Agree to Understate Cost of Weapons," Washington, in the New York *Times*, July 30, 1987, A-16.

"Plant closings are ominous," the New York Times, in The Kansas City *Times*, December 28, 1983, A-12.

"Polls finds distrust of TV evangelicals," New York Times, in The Kansas City *Times*, March 31, 1987, A-6.

"Pope urges Catholics to return to church," in The Kansas City *Times*, November 27, 1986, C-15.

"Poverty report faults economy," Associated Press, Washington, in The Kansas City *Times*, December 22, 1986, A-3.

"President's budget will control future debate, agenda," Washington Post Writers Group, Washington, in The Kansas City *Times*, January 12, 1987, A-9.

"PTL success led to excess and disgrace," in The Kansas City *Times*, May 30, 1987, A-1.

"Public Pays for Pentagon profligacy," United Features, Washington, in The Kansas City *Times*, September 17, 1983, A-15.

"Reagan's popularity slides, survey says," New York Times News Service, in The Kansas City *Times*, December 1, 1987, A-3.

"Religious intolerance of powerful TV preachers cannot be tolerated," Los Angeles Times News Service, in The Kansas City *Times*, March 20, 1987, A-17.

"Report Cites Growth in Soviet Economy," Los Angeles Times, in The Kansas City *Times*, March 28, 1987, A-1, 18.

"Report criticizes colleges for decline in the humanities," Times News Services, Washington, in The Kansas City *Times*, November 26, 1984, A-1.

"Republicans spent more," Washington, in The Kansas City *Times*, February 16, 1987, B-8.

"The rich get richer in the U.S.," the Star's News Service, Washington, in The Kansas City *Star*, July 24, 1990, A-1, 8.

"Rising interest swallows Reagan budget cutbacks," New York Times News Service, Washington, in The Kansas City *Star*, February 5, 1984, A-1.

"Roberts asks for 'overflow'," The Associated Press, in The Kansas City *Times*, April 1, 1987, A-4.

"Roberts' vigil reaching conclusion," The Associated Press, in The Kansas City *Star*, March 31, 1987, A-2.

"Salvadoran evidence vanishes in death of priests, 2 women," New York Times, San Salvador, in The Kansas City *Star*, May 7, 1990, A-8.

"Some confusion between president, supporters on nature of Reaganomics,"United Features, in The Kansas City *Times*, November 3, 1987, A-9.

"Southern Baptists choose fundamentalist president," The Associated Press, New Orleans, in The Kansas City *Star*, June 13, 1990, A-4.

"Standard of living is suffering, according to a professor's report," The Baltimore *Sun*, Washington, in The Kansas City *Star*, May 14, 1990, A-7.

"Steel's woes deepen with job cutback," Editorial in The Kansas City *Star*, December 29, 1983, A-10.

"Stocks take a 53.71-point fall," New York Times, New York, in The Kansas City *Star*, June 19, 1990, D-1.

"Study links cancer, Vietnam duty," The New York Times News Service, Washington, in The Kansas City *Times*, September 4, 1987, B-9.

"Study says deficits, foreign debt will be longer," New York Times, Washington, in The Kansas City *Times*, November 6, 1987, C-1.

"Tax increase will be needed in thrift bailout," The Associated Press, Washington, in The Kansas City *Star*, April 19, 1990, A-7.

"Terrible Tuesday examined," The Associated Press, New York, in The Kansas City *Times*, November 21, 1987, A-1, 15.

"Truth about crystals is cloudy: rocks of magic force - or farce?," The Washington Post, in The Kansas City *Times*, November 26, 1987, I-8.

"Turmoil dividing Ministers," the Times News Service, in The Kansas City *Times*, March 26, 1987, A-1.

"U. S. blocked study, says House panel," The New York Times, Washington, in The Kansas City *Star*, August 10, 1990, A-1.

"U. S. deficits blamed for trade lag," The Associated Press, New York, in The Kansas City *Star*, January 23, 1987, A-13.

"U. S. economy at stake in mounting deficit crisis," in The Kansas City *Star*, December 22, 1983, A-23.

"U. S. economy feels foreign influence," Cunniff, Associated Press, New York, in The Kansas City *Star*, June 23, 1987, A-5.

"U. S. Fights Manville Suit," New York *Times*, September 17, 1983, A-34.

"U. S. maintains largest debt," The Associated Press, Washington, in The Kansas City *Star*, March 17, 1987, A-1.

"VA fined for destroying papers," The Associated Press, San Francisco, in The Kansas City *Times*, January 9, 1987, A-4.

"Veterans health study hits snag," The New York Times News Service, Washington, in The Kansas City *Times*, September 1, 1987, A-1.

"Wages low in most new jobs," The Associated Press, Washington, in The Kansas City *Times*, December 10, 1986, D-1.

"Wall street can never be the same again," The New York Times, New York, in The Kansas City *Times*, October 26, 1987, A-1.

"Wall street trader enters guilty plea," The Associated Press, New York, in The Kansas City *Star*, April 23, 1987, A-1.

"Why should Americans mind if dollar drops?," The Washington Post, Washington, in The Kansas City *Times*, January 22, 1987, A-1.

"Worldwide panic travels like lightning," Los Angeles Times, in The Kansas City *Times*, October 27, 1987, A-1, 12.

"Young Americans don't care about public affairs, study says," Los Angeles Times, Washington, in The Kansas City *Star*, June 28, 1990, A-1, 11.

"92 million in PTL funds is missing," Washington Post, in The Kansas City *Times*, May 16, 1987, A-1.

"700 banks may fail, budget office warns," The Associated Press, in The Kansas City *Star*, September 13, 1990, B-1.

Encyclopedias

Art and Mankind. Larousse Encyclopedia of Modern Art from 1800 to the Present Day, edited by René Huyghe (New York, Prometheus Press, 1961).

Encyclopedia Britannica, 30 vols. (Chicago, Encyclopedia Britannica, University of Chicago Press, 1975), V.

Encyclopedia of World Art (New York, McGraw-Hill, 1963), VIII.

McGraw-Hill Dictionary of Art, edited by Bernard Myers (New York, McGraw-Hill, 1969).

New Catholic Encyclopedia (New York, McGraw-Hill, 1967), volumes 7, 13, 14 and 15.

Treasury of Art. Masterpieces from the Renaissance to the Present Day, edited by Thomas Craven (New York, Simon and Schuster, 1912).

Documents

"The Demands of the Workers, Peasants, and Soldiers in the Russian Revolution," 112-136 in Marc Ferro, *The Russian Revolution of February 1917.* Translated by J. L. Richards (Englewood Cliffs, New Jersey, Prentice-Hall, 1972).

"Elements of a Medieval World View. Philosophy of History," 143-147 in *Ideas and Institutions in European History, 800-1715,* edited by Thomas C. Mendenhall *et al* (New York, Holt, Rinehart and Winston, 1948), II.

Jefferson, Thomas, "First Inaugural Address," 426-428 in *The People Shall Judge. Readings in the Formation of American Policy.* Selected and Edited by the Staff, Social Sciences I (Chicago, University of Chicago Press, 1967), I.

Mahan, Alfred, Admiral, "The Influence of Sea Power in History," 260-265 in *The People Shall Judge. Readings in the Formation of American Policy.* Selected and Edited by the Staff, Social Sciences I (Chicago, University of Chicago, 1967), II.

"The Monroe Doctrine," 235-237 in *Documents of American History* in 2 vols., edited by Henry Steele Commager (New York, Appleton-Century-Crofts, 1963), I.

Syllabus of Errors, 854-856 in *New Catholic Encyclopedia* (New York, McGraw-Hill, 1967, XIII.

Testimony of Dean Acheson, Assistant Secretary of State, before the

Hearings on Post-War Economic Policy and Planning, Select Sub-Committee on Post-War Economic Policy and Planning, House, 78th Congress, 2nd session, 1944, in *The Pentagon Watchers. Students Report on the National Security State*, edited by Leonard S. Rodberg and Derek Shearer (Garden City, New York, 1970).

"USSR Art," PBS program, June 4, 1990.

Letters and Postcards

Dillenberger, John, Harvard Divinity School, to Urban, C. Stanley, Arlington, Massachusetts, June 29, 1956.

Hanovers, 606 N. 1st, Burlington, KS 66839. To C. Stanley Urban - "Planned Parenthood Abortion Holocaust signer." Postcard with illegible date. Circa 1987.

AUTHOR INDEX

Specific Citation in Text or in Explanatory Footnote

A

Abouhalkah, Yael T., 199,244-245

Abramovitch, Raphael R., 82

Acheson, Dean, 166, 168

Adams, Brooks, 53, 189-190, 201

Adams, Henry, 53, 189, 201

Agar, Herbert, 167, 188

Agena, Kathleen, 251

Albanese, Catherine, 65

Anouilh, Jean, 184

Appel, Willa, 284

Aquinas, Thomas, Saint, 23, 57

Aristotle, 3

Augustine, Saint, 25-26

B

Bakker, Jimmy, 46, 260, 262-263

Barry, Dave, 199-200

Barth, Karl, 30

Baxendale, Michael, 153-154

Beard, Charles, 126, 134

Bekkers, W. M., 75

Bell, Joe, 285

Belloc, Hilaire, 107-108, 133

Bendix, Reinhard, 69

Berenson, Bernard, 6

Berger, Peter L., 11, 40, 51, 60, 251

Bergson, Henri, 5

Blackstone, William T., 270

Bloom, Allen, 126, 142-145

Blow, Richard, 284, 286

Bluestone, Barry, 234

Bombeck, Erma, 287

Borsage, Robert, 170

Bosworth, Barry, 220

Brandeis, Louis, 215-216

Brighton, Louis, 31

Brinkley, David, 146

Brinton, Crane, Foreword, vii, 250

Broder, David S., 112, 147, 157, 233, 243-244

Brown, Anthony Cave, 160-161

Buckley, William F., 75, 100

Buffon, 7

Burawoy, Michael, 163

Burnstein, Morris, 109

Buursma, Bruce, 71

C

Carr, Edward H., 94, 235

Carter, Paul A., 73

Castoriadis, Cornelius, 252

Chamberlain, John, 192

Chamberlin, William H., 88, 104-105, 107

Chapman, Janet, 109

Cheyney, Edward P., 54

Childs, Marquis, 201

Chui, Glenna, 290

Cicero, 25

Cobb, Jonathan, 235

Cockburn, Alexander, 163

Commoner, Barry, 267, 271, 281

Conine, Ernest, 110, 214, 235

Constantine, Emperor, 45

Constantine II, 25

Cooperstein, Bruce, 235

Cousteau, Jacques, 268-270

Croly, Herbert, 54

Cullman, Oscar, 30-31

Cute, David, 170., 193

D

Daly, Mary, 59

Darwin, Charles, 23-24

Davis, Charles, 60

Davis, Kenneth S., 196

de Camp, L. Sprague, 70-71

de Tocqueville, Alexis, 125-126, 145, 172, 231

Deutscher, Isaac, 108

Dewey, John, 7

Djilas, Milovan, 84-85, 92, 105-106

Dobbs, Michael, 110-111

Donne, John, 267

Dostoevsky, Fydor, 260, 285

Drucker, Peter, 123, 180, 205

Du Brow, Rick, 161

Dunning, Brian, 198

Dvorak, John A., 237

E

Eagar, Harry, 112

Easterbrook, Greg, 288, 290-291

Edwards, Richard C., 193

Ehrenfeld, David, 289

Eitzen, D. Stanley, 281

Eliade, Mircea, 30, 39, 106

Ellis, Albert, 27

Ellis, Mark, 253

Erasmus, Desiderius, 40

Erlich, Paul R. and Anne H., 291

Evans, David, 199

Evans-Pritchard, E. E., 97

Ewen, Stuart, 170

F

Fagan, Richard R., 176

Falin, Valentin, 111

Falwell, Jerry, 46, 262

Ferre, Nels, 255

Finn, Chester E., 159

Fitzgerald, F. Scott, 150, 230

Flanagan, James, 242

Ford, Henry, 88, 106, 248

Frazer, James George, Sir, 39

Freud, Sigmund, 3

Friedman, Milton, 225

Friedman, Thomas C., 199

Friedrich, Otto, 283

Fromm, Eric, 127-128, 251

Fry, Roger, 7

Fuller, Buckminster, 278

Fusfeld, Daniel R., 109

G

Galbraith, John K., 206

Gallup, George, Jr., 71

Garron, Barry, 71

Gephardt, Richard H., 216

Gide, André, 94, 109

Gilson, Étienne, 22

Goodman, Ellen, 199

Gorz, André, 275, 277, 293

Graham, Billy, 259, 261

Griffin, Kelley, 159

Guérin, Daniel, 106

Gunter, Pete A. Y., 288

Gusewelle, C. W., 236

Guthrie, A. B., 97

H

Haley, Jean, 162

Hampton, Jim, 104

Hardin, Garrett, 289, 293

Harrington, Michael, 244

Harris, Marvin, 254-255, 283, 286

Harrison, Bennett, 234

Hartshorne, Charles, 272

Hauptmann, Emily, 157-158

Heard, Gerald, 33

Heilbroner, Robert L., 228, 251-252, 261, 276-278

Hippocrates, 267, 287

Hirsch, Seymour, 184

Hoagland, Jim, 111, 200

Hobhouse, Henry, 291

Hobson, John, 165

Hoffer, Eric, 253, 262

Hollings, Ernest F., 220

Hood, Rich, 157

Howe, Quincy, 192

Hubbard, L. Ron, 255

I

Iacocca, Lee, 216

J

Jackson, Robert L., 197

Jaeger, Werner, 11

Jefferson, Thomas, 116, 142

Jenkins, David, Bishop, 20, 49, 73

John XXIII, Pope, 57, 62

Johnson, Haynes, 71, 197

Johnson, Woodbridge O., 21-22

K

Kaul, Donald, 152, 156, 183, 186, 195, 200

Keller, Bill, 110-111

Kennedy, Paul, 185

Keynes, John Maynard, 55, 226

Kháyyam, Omar, 247

Khruschev, Nikita S., 89-90

Kilpatrick, James J., 159, 161, 241

Kinsley, Michael, 220

Kirkpatrick, Jeanne, 176-177

Kleppner, Paul, 42

Koestler, Arthur, 84, 109

Koop, C. Everett, 48

L

La Barre, Weston, 244, 282, 287

Langer, Suzanne K., 264

Lasch, Christopher, 190, 292

Lee, Gary, 111

Lenin, Vladimir Ill'ich, 86-88, 99

Leo XIII, Pope, 22, 63

Leubsdorf, Carl P., 198-200

Lévi-Strauss, Claude, 268, 271

Lewis, Anthony, 156, 162-163, 177, 185, 195-197

Lewis, Flora, 159-160

Linton, Ralph, 66

Lippman, Walter, 54

Lipset, Seymour M., 80, 125

Lobos, Ignacio, 245

Locke, John, 41, 44

Lokeman, Rhonda C., 195

Lolley, Randall, Rev., 49

Luce, Henry, 167, 188, 217

Luke, 18

Luxemburg, Rosa, 89

M

McClanahan, E. Thomas, 241

McConnel, James V., 128

McGiffert, Arthur C., 108

McKenna, Richard, 54

McKibben, Bill, 292

MacLaine, Shirley, 256-258, 268

Maguire, Daniel, 62

Mahan, Alfred, Admiral, 190

Mannheim, Karl, 115

Marsh, George Perkins, 272

Marshall, Elliot E., 152

Marty, Martin E., 263

Marx, Karl, 88, 206, 277-278

Matthew, 18

Mead, Margaret, 90-92

Meisler, Stanley, 197

Melman, Seymour, 175

Menand, Louis, 292-293

Merton, Robert K., 41-44, 49-52

Michels, Robert, 80

Mitgang, Lee, 159

Moberg, Vilhelm, 38

Mohr, Charles, 154

Monod, Jacques, 268

Monter, E. William, 108

Morais, Herbert M., 11

Morris, David, 242

Moseley, Fay, 233

Moyers, Bill, 49

Moynihan, Daniel, 218, 220

Mumford, Lewis, 6

Myrdal, Gunnar, 192

N

Nader, Ralph, 134, 154, 159

Naisbitt, John, 235

Neikirk, William R., 241

Nelson, Lars Erik, 236, 238

Niebuhr, Reinhold, 44, 50

Nietsche, Friedrick, 29

Nisbet, Robert A., 25-26, 115-117, 141, 258

Northrop, F. S. C., 8, 42, 44, 51-52, 70

O

O'Brien, John A., 76

Oreskes, Michael, 140

Ortega y Gasset, José, 6

P

Panikkar, Raimundo, 21, 34, 267

Pares, Bernard, Sir, 81

Pearl, Art, 235

Pericles, 25

Phillips, Kevin, 199, 240

Pike, Otis, 197

Pius IX, Pope, 52

Pluckham, Charles, 234

Polanyi, Karl, 171

Porter, Michael E., 238

Praisewater, Eldon D., 153

R

Rabinowitch, Alexander, 103

Raglan, Fitzroy, Lord, 18, 29

Ravitch, Diane, 159

Ray, Dixie Lee, 290

Redfield, Robert, 144

Reed, George, 288

Reed, John, 105

Reeves, Richard, 114, 183, 196-197, 214, 217, 233, 242

Reidy, Chris, 239

Reston, James, 182, 196

Reuther, Walter, 233

Riesman, David, 127-128

Roberts, Oral, 45

Robertson, Pat, 258-259, 262-263

Roosevelt, Teddy, 55, 189-190

Rosenthal, A. M., 100

Rostovtzeff, M., 26

Roth, Gutenther, 69

Rothenburg, Michael, 265

Rowan, Carl T., 243

Rowland, Benjamin, Jr., 13

Royko, Mike, 236

Rubin, Lilian B., 211, 235

S

Salisbury, Harrison E., 146

Santayana, George, 143,

Sentell, Will, 158

Schwarz, John C., 76

Schweitzer, Albert, 18

Selikoff, D. I. J., 131

Sennett, Richard, 235

Shabecoff, Phillip, 290

Shelley, Percy Bysshe, 279-280

Shulman, Marshall, 108

Simmel, George, 250

Simon, David R., 281

Sims, David E., 208

Sinclair, Upton, 118-119

Smith, Randall D., 158

Smith, Wilfred Cantwell, 27

Sobran, Joseph, 199-200

Solzhenitsyn, Aleksandr, 109, 276

Soper, Edmund D., 255

Sorokin, Pitirim, 250

Spender, Stephen, 104

Spivak, John, 192

Stassinopoulos, Adrianna, 284

Steel, Ronald, 180-181

Steffens, Lincoln, 184, 197, 203-204

Steinem, Gloria, 257

Stockman, David, 226-227

Streiker, Lowell D., 262, 285-286

Strieber, Whitley, 258

Summers, Harry, Colonel, 183, 200

Swaggart, Jimmy, 46, 260

T

Takaki, Ronald, 162

Tapscott, Richard, 244

Tawney, R. H., 41-42

Taylor, Frederick W., 87, 106

Tertullian, 25

Thibodeau, Ralph, 75

Thompson, Jake, 161-162

Thompson, James Westfall, 32

Thoreau, Henry David, 66, 77-78, 287

Thurlow, Lester C., 246

Tillich, Paul, 18-19, 22-23

Tönnies, Ferdinand, 148, 250, 281

Toynbee, Arnold, 18-19, 60, 94, 103-

104, 271

Trotsky, Leon, 85-86, 92

Tuchman, Barbara, 169

U

Unger, Robert, 199

Urban, C. Stanley, Foreword, x-xi

Urban, Jeff, 27, 83, 112, 145, 179-180, 214, 227

Urban, Thomas, 2, 22-23, 36, 56, 83, 114, 145, 147, 171, 208, 225, 247

V

Veblen, Thorstein, Foreword, x-xi, 17, 52-56, 68, 121, 143, 170, 216-217

Vidal, Gore, 188-189

Vogel, David, 217-218, 234

Vonnegut, Kurt, 125

W

Wachtel, Paul, 245, 292

Wallenstein, Immanuel, 169

Wambaugh, Joseph, 75

Warburg, James, 168

Waters, Annette, Sister, 59

Weber, Max, 3-4, 40, 51, 151

Weinberger, Caspar W., 199

Weisskopf, Thomas E., 245

Wesson, Robert, 104

White, Lynn, Jr., 33

Wicker, Tom, 138, 153, 156, 178-179, 213, 243

Wikle, Gretel, 77

Will, George, 139, 220

Willett, Michael, 48-49

William of Occam, 23

Williams, Dianna, 162

Wilson, James G., 156,

Wilson, Woodrow, 55

Wirth, Louis, 122

Wolfe, Bertram D., 105, 108

Z

Zukerman, Seth, 289

Editors Note: Author's names must either appear as a direct citation in the text or in an explanatory footnote. The mere citation in a footnote- sans explanation- does not qualify.

SUBJECT INDEX

A

A-bomb, loss of innocence, 125

Abstract art: attack on Newtonian physics, 1; death of the human personality, 6; dehumanizes man, 6; destruction of historical space and time, 9; Platonic idealism, 3; truth through intuition, 5. See art forms.

Acheson (Dean), justification for the American Century, 168

Acid rain, threat of, 290

Advertising and the urge to consume, 206-207

Agar (Herbert), the American Century, 167

America: international dilemma, 181; messianic creed, 190. See American Dream; superpower age; United States.

American Dream: disappearance, 230, 245-246; loss and effect, 251-253. See America; poverty; progress; superpower age; United States.

Anti-communist crusade: effective in spreading capitalism, 174-177; international dangers, 192

Albanese (Catherine), community fragile, estrangement common, 65

Aquinas (Thomas), reconciliation of reason and religion, 23, 32-33

Aristotle's God, the unmoved mover, 11

Art forms: primitive as religious abstraction, 4; similarity of primitive, medieval and modern, 1-4. See Abstract Art.

Atwater (Lee), low political morality, 138, 156, 178

Auto industry, benefits from lax governmental regulation, 134-135

B

Bacon (Frances), science and early Protestantism, 41-42

Bad Neighbor Policy, Dollar Diplomacy, 119

Baptist, belief in business dominance, 71

Beard (Charles), principle, in absence of military force, property dominates, 134, 151

Belloc (Hilaire), Western offenses against individual liberty, 133-134

Benedictine Abbey, rationalization disturbs religious feeling, 11

Biblical Genesis, nature its enemy, 271

Blacks, victims of legal system, 128

Bloom (Allan),liberal arts alters life, 142-143

Boyle (Robert), science and early Protestantism, 41

Brandeis (Louis), betrayal of fiduciary trust, 215

Braque (Georges), dissolution of visible objects, 5, 8

"Broken" Christian myth: central Christian doctrine not historical fact, 17; erosion of Christ's monopoly of salvation, 21-22, 34; introduces uncertainty, 19-20

Bryan (William Jennings), bewildered witness, 44

Budget deficit, gains and losses, 238-240

Budget makers, ignore termination of world Communist threat, 200

Burawoy (Michael), principle, why bourgeois state must grant concessions to other classes, 163

Bush (George): anti-abortion stance and old Republican idea of individual sin, 139-140; stonewalls on Iran-contra scandal, 140

Business schools, lack of ethics and business scandals, 142-143

C

Calvinism, suspicious of miracle, mystery and magic, 11

Campus: defense of radicals in 60s, 145; 60s and the loss of the liberal arts spirit, 144-145; tension and the loss of tolerance, 143-144

Capital, flight abroad: facts, 213-214; not visualized by early free traders, 214-215; self-interest dictates, not patriotism, 214-215

Capitalism: anti-Communist crusade, 173-175; challenged by revival of primitive concepts of nature, Foreword, xiv; incompatibility with democracy, 218-219, 230; its ethic, profit, 203-204; profit and growth necessitates imperialism, 170-171, 193; theory of free and equal society through profit motive, 204-205

Capital shrinkage, jeopardizes welfare state, 227

Catholic theology: Church history as sacred, 23; *City of God,* influence of, 25-26; no conflict between Catholic Truth and historical truth, 22

Catholicism: conservative revolt against "reforms," 61-62; disillusionment of a theologian, 60; dissenting priests and nuns, 62-63, 76, 77; grass-roots revolution, 58-60, 75-76; liberals question thought suppression, 60-61

Cezanne's revolutionary impact, formal design, 7

Chinese civilization, lacks mythology and cosmology, 27

Christianity: cost of severance from history and science, 24; similarity with communism causes hostility, 83; solace for fall of Rome, 26; twentieth century failure, 71-73

Chrysler odometer scandal, used cars as new, 136

Civic-mindedness, Pericles and Cicero, 25

Class income division: gulf widest in 80s, 229; Iron law of oligarchy, 80; law differentiates, 152; low income and belief in miracles, 71; persistence under capitalism, 147-148, 228-229. See poverty.

Climatic changes, sudden and dramatic possible, 292

Cold War: cost, loss of economic hegemony, 185-186; four disadvantages, 185-186

Communism: attraction of early

promises, 94, 106; bourgeois state without the bourgeois, 87-88; closed society, 102, 107; comparison with primitive cultures, 97, drugs to silence intellectuals, 93; failure to compete with "free enterprise," 93-94, 109; failure to give bread and freedom, 84-85; glasnost and perestroika, impact on underground artists, 101; gulag archipelago principle, how to silence intellectuals, 93; inadequacy in Third World, 179-180; insularity hid inferiority of production, 98-99; it can't go home again, 98; menace of attempted reforms, 96-97; mistake of ignoring consumer, 99; Revolution of 1917 and early freedoms, 85-86, 104; self-deception at upper levels, 82; similarity with Christianity, 37; similarity with liberalism, 37; social salvation versus individual sinner, 90-91; suspicion of intellectual, 92, 109; undermined with Stalin's exposure, 93

Computer age: feeling of individual powerlessness, 251, 282; vulnerability of labor force, 210-212, 233, 236

Consumer Reports: critical of GM and federal regulation, 135-136; inadequacy of the Pinto, 135

Cousteau (Jacques): causes of pollution, 269-270; scientific indifference to sea pollution, 269-270; Western pollution and capitalism, 270

Cubism, revolutionary impact, static rigidity, 7-8

Cults of the True Believer: absolute redemption for absolute loyalty, 253; appeal to the psychologically deprived, 286; save materialism by magic, 254; should expand as millenium nears, 279. See also Protestant fundamentalism; TV evangelicals.

Currency depreciation: limits of, 240

D

Darrow (Clarence), Scopes trial, 44

Death of a twentieth century God, Communism, Foreword, iv

Deficit: government dances around crisis, 222-223, 267; responsible for economic plight, 220-222

Democracy: crisis of authority, 114; danger in loose use of term, 115; dilemma of poverty, 293; economic decline threatens American Dream, 123-124; education for conformity, 126-128; inability to transform Third World, 175-177, 179; peaceful is folklore, Foreword, xii; prospects not good, 148-150; ties with endangered idea of progress, 54. See American Dream; progress.

Deism, God, yes, miracles, no, 11

de Tocqueville (Alexis): democratic armies and stake in war, 172; triumph of mediocrity, 145-146. See also Democracy.

Djilas (Milovan): the death blow to communism in Russia, 92-93; latent civil war constant factor in communist state, 84-85;

Dukakis (Michael), miscues, the competent engineer approach, 138-139

E

Eisenhower (Ike), suspicion of military-industrial complex, 172. See military-industrial complex.

Election of 1988, avoidance of tough issues, 139

Electorate, why presidents avoid domestic issues, 156

El Salvador fiasco, 177, 195

Enchanted forest: modern sports heroes, 45; non-reality, 40; revival of values of medieval age, 249-250. See also Weber (Max).

Erasmus, self-serving worshipper, 40

Escape from freedom (Dostoevsky), miracle, mystery, authority, 285

Evangelical Protestantism, relation to imperialism, 180-181

Evolution, enemy of infallible Bible, 51

Extraterrestrial factor, mass popularity, 258

F

Faith: fabrication of the Resurrection?, 73; its dissolution in the 14th century, 23; relation to intolerance for faith of others, 27

Family, decline of ability to protect young, 265

Farmer (household), cause of disappearance, 217

Federal Reserve, dilemma over dollar and interest rate, 223

Ford (Henry), a museum for an age he terminated, 248

Foreign markets, necessity of in post World War II, 166, 168

Founding Fathers, no intention of democracy, 117

Four Gospels, religious treatises only, 18

Fox (Matthew), Rev., ideological clevage in the Catholic Church, 48

Frazer, James George (Sir), pre-Christian anticipates Christian doctrine, 39

Free enterprise, where art thou?, 205-206

Free inquiry, plagues both Communism and Catholic Church, 63-64

Free market system: early critics, 250-251; incapable of producing a free and equal society, 230; limits for liberated Eastern Europe, Foreword, viii; Milton Friedman's philosophy, 225; vulnerability of, Foreword, xiii-xiv; widens class divisions, 281

Freud (Sigmund), necessity of the Father lore, 3, 11

Fundamentalism (Protestant): as big

business, 71; escape from freedom, 249-250, 258; "infallible, inerrant" Bible, 72-73; religious mall, 64-65; search for past Utopia, 65. See also TV evangelicals.

G

Gadfly, go away, administrators say, 160

Galileo, science versus Catholicism, 23-24

Gatsby's green light: 150, similar to pursuit of perfectability, 231; visible, but never attained, 231

General Dynamics, rip-off, 209

German unification, outsiders helpless, 100

GM and faulty engine mounts, industry cannot police self for public safety, 135-136

Gnostics, suicide of classical reason?, 24-25

Godless Communism, why the religious loved to hate it, 260-261

Good Neighbor principle, no internal intervention in Latin America, 120

Gorbachev (Mikhail): difficulties in opening up trade and commerce, 101; early predictions by Western experts, 95-97; early reforms, 95; foes, high and low, 97, 111

Government's fear, business recession if rigid safety

standards met, 137

Graham (Billy), certainty of the Second Coming, 259

Greenhouse effect, devastating climate change, 274, 290

Grenada invasion: caused public to forget Lebanon disaster, 178; the lie to justify, 178

Gris, geometric order, 8

H

Hanford nuclear scandal, public betrayed, 133

Have gun, will travel, im-poverishes America, 217-218

Hebraic theology, servile relation of man to God, 17

Heisenburg (Werner): principle applied to life, 26-27; uncertainty principle, Foreword, iv

History: causality principle, 116-117; emancipation from theology, 32; six laws (Edward Cheyney), 54-55

Hippocrates, versus ritual man, 267, 287

Holocaust, man is alone in the universe, 253

Hyperkinesis, child victims as wards of medics, 126-127

I

Iacocca (Lee), big rewards for corporate games, 216

Illiteracy, threatens Jeffersonian democracy, 142, 158

Imperialism: Caribbean as proving ground, 173; Manifest Destiny, 190; Pax Americana, origins, 188-189, 201; poverty prevents global policeman role, 218; watch dogs for capitalism and profit economy, 179, 187-188. See Henry Luce; Herbert Agar.

Impossible Dream, social welfare of Communism and capitalist's consumer paradise, 102

Incarnation myth, primacy of to Christians, 33

Industrial age, failure of, ignored threat of pollution, 205, 232

Infotainment, instead of information, 146, 161

Intellectuals, desertion of, importance to revolutionary movements, Foreword, vii

Intolerance: communist and Christian parallels, 91-92, 107-108; predominates as America flounders, 146-147, 162

Iran-contra affair: Congressional immunity a blunder, 184; constitutional threat, 182, 196; origins, 182, 197, why no impeachment, 184-185

Iraq-Kuwait affair: origins in oil geopolitics, 187-188, 198-199; saved peace from breaking out, 187, 199

Iron Curtain's roll-back, military appeal to historic optimism, 261

Iron Triangle, top 25 corporations get half of defense contracts, 208-209

J

Jacksonian Democracy, narrow limits of, 118

Jefferson: essentials for democracy, 115-116; fear of by Federalists, 118; preference for press over government, 158; threat of illiteracy to democracy, 142

Jesus: alleged miracles embarrass Anglican hierarchy, 20-21; defies tools of historiography, 19; father figure for loveless, 262; non-historical cast, 30; transition from historical to mythological being, Foreword, ix, 17-19. See savior-hero.

Johns-Manville asbestos case, both firm and navy suppressed truth, 131, 153

Johnson (Lyndon B.), social perfectability for all, 55-56

K

Kandinsky (Vasily), unconventional and spiritual art, 8-9

Kierkegaard (Soren), inadequacy of history to support Christian faith, 17

Kennedy (Paul), possibility of race-class conflict, 147-148, 162

Kerensky's failures, postpones reforms, continues war, 81-82, 103

Keynes (John M.), better life for masses through use of state, 55

Keynesian model, full employment, welfare state, recent decline, 225

Kindergarten, first boot camp, 126-127

Kirkpatrick (Jeanne), obsession with communist menace in Latin America, 176-177

Kulturkampf, State versus Church in 19th Europe, 73-74

L

Labor movement: computer threatens both unskilled and unions, 210-212; corporations use bankruptcy to escape contracts, 212; Reagan cripples, 212; why management is hostile to unions, 212. See management.

Laissez faire, frustrates democracy, 55-56

Lenin (Vladimir Illich): "April theses", appeal to peasant conscript, 82, 103; borrows management speed-up, 87, 106; dogmatism and intolerance, 86-87; messianic qualities, 88; state slow to wither away, 87, 105

Liberal arts: classical education as basis, 142-145; decline in favor of business courses, 142, 158-159; revolutionary aspect, 142-145

Linton (Ralph), culture core erroding, 66

Lipset (Seymour), large scale management and democracy incompatible, 125

Living standard's fall, menace to domestic tranquility, 213, 236

Lotze, put self inside object, 5

Luce (Henry), the American Century, 167

Luxemburg (Rosa), sans freedom, only bureaucracy flourishes, 89

M

McConnel (James V.), why society may reshape deviants, 128

MacLaine (Shirley): attraction of Oriental values, 256-258; popularized out-of-body experiences, 256; self as God, 257, 284; spirituality is profitable, 257-258; why most followers are women, 257

Man, an irrational and religious animal, 27

Man and nature, modern man at mercy of nature, 271-272

Management: incompatibility of large scale with democracy, 125; leveraged buy-out, piracy over production, 215-216; why hostile to unions, 212. See labor.

Mannheim (Karl) principle, relation between fact and observer, 115, 122

Marsh (George P.), ambiguous on environment and tech-nology, 272

Marx (Karl): limits of social vision by society, 277-278; over-optimistic about worker internationale, 278; predicted labor's dependence and alienation, 211

Melman (Seymour) principle, U.S. counter-revolutionary reflex, 175-176

Military-industrial complex, personnel flow from government to defense industry, 207-209

Miracle, mystery and authority: what more?, 75

Miracles and faith, then and now, Foreword, ix

Miró, uninterested in visible world, 9

Mondrian, dissolution of representative content, 5, 9

Monet, 8

Money, corrupts politics, frustrates democracy, 137-138

Montefiore (Hugh), bishop: was Jesus gay?, 20-21

Morality, unconnected with religions (Lévi-Strauss), 268

N

NASA, radiation study and human guinea pigs, 130, 152

NATO, purpose to keep Germans down, 185

Nature, ecological laws, 267

New Age movement: big business, 255; escape from freedom, 249-250, 258; predictable failure, 266-267; short cut to health and happiness, 254

New Deal, immediate solutions, no long range reforms, 119; limitations, 119-120

Nicholas II, mistakes, foreign and domestic, 81

Niebuhr (Reinhold), dilemma between original sin and social reform, 50

Nisbet (Robert): history and the causality principle, 116-117; our time barren of faith in progress and meaningful religion, 115; World War I and decline of political appeal, 141. See also Revolt against reason.

Noriega fiasco, "freedom fighters" and drug traffic, 178-179

North (Ollie): threat to democratic institutions, 183, 196-197; threat to fellow soldiers, 182-183

O

O'Connor (John), Cardinal, ideological cleavage in the Catholic Church, 48

O'Keefe (Georgia), intuitive truth, 8, 9

Overpopulation: perils in Third World, 272-273; perpetual threat to environment, 274-275

Oriental religions, substitute for Christianity, 255, 283

P

Pagan antiquity, end of, imperial admission of primacy of religion, 25

Participant observers, deeply resented in a democracy, Foreword,vi, xv

Peaceful state, its mythology, 181

Pelvic theology, devastating impact on Catholicism, 62

Perfectability of man: difficult to reconcile with the facts, 149-150; highly questionable, 231

Perpetual conflict, Enlightenment versus ritual man, Foreword, vii-viii

Picasso: dissolution of human body, 7; versatility and evolution, 7, 50

Pietist: depraved man and caring God, 42-43; early ones set no limits on science and technology, 42;

Pinto scandal, public at risk, 135, 155

Poindexter, Admiral: conviction and appeal, 184; role in Iran-contra scandal, 182

Pollution: impact in America, 273-274; threatens climate, 274-275

Post-Christian era, here and now, 60

Poverty: new poor, 228-229; possible revolt against market system, 148, 213; sharp class distinctions, 228-229; threat to American Dream, 230. See also American Dream; class income divisions.

Power politics, its historical principle, 190

Powerlessness, feeling of: worker's loss supplants American Dream, 213; individual helpless in corporate world, 281

Primitive: anticipated Judeo-Christian cosmology, Foreword, ii; basic philosophy of life, 248-249, 281; hostility to individualism, 129; magic to supplement religion, 38; spared plight of separation of a real versus religious world, 27-28; values revived, 278

Prison populations, immoral manipulation of, 128-130

Privatization of religion, lack of single, satisfactory answers, 51

Progress: dissipation of idea, 253; failure to procure happiness, 276; jeopardized by over-population, 274-275; justification for obliteration of primitive, Foreword, v; man's omnipotence, 57; scientific origins, 23-24; seven crucial errors, 270-271, 289; similar miraculous appeals by prophets of democracy and communism, Foreword, iv; social reforms through state action, 55-56; worship of the machine, 247-248, 281. See American Dream.

Progressive Era, preoccupa-tion with middle class reform, 118

Protestant ethic, its demise, 206-207

Protestant fundamentalism: pentacostals, faith healing, 46; penta-costals versus fundamentalists, 258-259; restores miracle, mystery, authority, 259; simple formula for unpredictable world, 44; why appeal to middle class young, 264, 266. See Protestant-ism; TV evangelicals.

Protestantism: early denial of enchanted forest, 40-41; early dominance of experience, reason and science, 41-42; early dominance of merchant philosophy, 41; impossible to generalize about 20th century variety, 70; individualism supported by false atomic theory, 42; twentieth century decline, 43-44. See Fundamentalism; TV evangelicals.

R

Reagan (Ronald): class and tax differentials, 244; dummy or conspirator?, 183-184; Great Communicator exposed, 226, 244; hostility towards Department of Education, 243; how he killed the welfare state, 220; political philosophy, 225; welfare cuts, 227

Reagan administration: scandals due to business ethics, 184; "soft" on auto regulation, 137

Reagan doctrine, no country too small to be invaded if close by, 177

Reaganomics: bankruptcy, 219-220; purpose of federal deficit, 239

Red scares, violation of civil rights

of individuals, 116

Redfield (Robert), prerequisites for liberal arts faculties, 144

"Renegade" priests, utilize communism to aid poor, 83

Resurrection, its primacy to Christians (Karl Barth), 31. See Jesus; Saviour-hero.

Revolt against reason (Robert Nisbet), 115

Riesman (David), other and inner directed and autonomous man, 127-128

Ritual man: Catholic salvation through traditional rituals, 43; modern religious appeal to the miraculous, Foreword, vii,xiv; natural cause-effect negated, 35; prosperity in this, bliss in next world, 35; revives with decline of belief in science, 67-68; true spirit in agricultural societies, 38-39; surrender intellect to superior power, Foreword,xiv-xv

Robertson (Pat), nostalgia for past Utopia, 258-259

Roosevelt (Teddy) Corollary, be like us, or else, 119

Roosevelt, Franklin D.: compared to Gorbachev as great compromiser, 95-96; formulates Good Neighbor policy, 120; saved capitalism from the capitalists, 119

Rubaiyat, the revolving door, 247

Rugged individualists, hostile to environmental care, 275, 291

S

Savings and loan scandals: bullishness on America, 224; political fix, 141, 158

Savior-hero, demand points, 18, 29. Also see Jesus; Resurrection.

Schism within Christian churches, 47-49

Science: indifferent to man's desires, 268, 288; why slow to embrace environmentalism, 271-272

Scopes trial, agony of a voluntary witness, 70-71

Second Coming: causes early Christian indifference to history, 25-26; Hell for unbeliever, 21, 31

Secular man, substitutes for religious faith, 36

Seven sacraments, miracle, mystery, magic, 39-40

Shelley (Percy Bysshe), the folly of pride, 279-280

Social Gospel, motivation and beliefs, 49-50

Soviet Russia, House Divided, 98, 112

Spaceship earth, failure of socialism and capitalism to appreciate, 278

Stalin (Joe): erratic shifts in foreign policy, 89-90; God the Father mythology, 90; ignores warning of Nazi attack, 90; paranoia, 89; unveiled as monster, 92-93

Steffens (Lincoln): government

ethics higher than that of business, 183-184, 203-204; what struck you as corrupt appealed to businessmen, 203-204

Stock market: bad news treated as good, 222-223; crash of 1987 and international significance, 221-222, 240-241

Student concerns, from radicalism to environmentalism, 159

Superpower age, why terminated, 188

Supreme Good, offered by Christianity, democracy and communism, Foreword, xi

Surrealists, dependence on supernatural powers, 9

Syllabus of Errors, Papal intolerance, 52, 92, 108

Symbols, as true appearance of reality, 1-2

T

Technology, its inexorable limits, 272

Third World: challenges to international capitalism, 179; inability of developed countries to help, 292; poor prospects for democracy, 180

Thoreau (Henry David), religious revolution, 66, 123

Tillich (Paul), primacy of faith over history, 19

Tönnies (Ferdinand), democratic capitalism widens class gulf, 148

Toxic waste, why the public response, 289

Trotsky (Leon): enemies to "garbage-can," 85-86; intolerance, 86; right of state to conscript labor, 87; suspicion of intellectuals, 87

Truman (Harry), historical revisionism, 168-170, 193; social reform, 55

Tuskegee syphillis study, racial overtones, 130-131

TV evangelicals: appeals to losers, 262; attraction of sins of the flesh, 260; intolerance, 46-47; losing soul while attempting to conquer world?, 263; preoccupation with money, 262-263; shades of P. T. Barnum, 45-46; sexual transgressions, 46, 72 show biz, 261. See also Fundamentalism; Protestantism.

Tyranny of the minority, threat to democracy, 125-126

U

Ultimate Truth, solely a religious affirmation, Foreword, ix-x, 15-17

Uncertainty principle, predictable responses by ritual and secular man, 26-27. See Heisenburg.

Underclass (permanent), its threat to progress and democracy, 124, 140-141, 149.
See class income divisions; American Dream.

United States: post-war global power, 172-173; power decline,

Foreword, xii, 185. See superpower age, America.

V

VA, indifference to radiation and Agent Orange victims, 132-133, 153

Vandenburg (Arthur), Senator, origins of anti-Commie scare, 168-169

Vatican II, unintended revolution, 57-58

Veblen (Thorstein): business-men and warlike policies, 170; from captains of industry to business to finance, 216; ideal state Foreword, iv, v, 52-54; revolution must produce economic efficiency, Foreword, x-xi; Versailles as betrayal, 121

Villains, Middle Eastern ones in constant change, 188, 200

Voodoo economics, David Stockman, 226

Vonnegut (Kurt), revulsion at a-bomb, 125

Voter boycott: conflicting theories, 140-141; political system "brain dead?", 140, 157-158

W

Weber (Max): less magic, more rationalization in religion, 3-4; Protestantism versus causality principle, 40-41

Wedtech scandal, the Ed Meese deal, 209-210

Welfare State: error, 227; pallative for the Thirties, 171-172; public ambivalence, 227-228; successes, 243; who killed Cock Robin?, 220

Western man, severance from nature, 264

William of Occam, Christian mysticism over reason, 23

Y

Youth: anxiety, suicide, 264-266, 287; fundamentalists converts absorbed in selves, 266; predictable failure of youth for Christ, 266-267

Z

Zero growth: radical enough for social needs?, 276-277; why increasingly acceptable to science?, 275-276, 292